HARDPRESS.NET
HOME OF HARD-TO-FIND BOOKS

Specimens of American Poetry
by Samuel Kettell

Address:
HardPress
8345 NW 66TH ST #2561
MIAMI FL 33166-2626
USA
Email: info@hardpress.net

SPECIMENS

OF

AMERICAN POETRY,

WITH

CRITICAL AND BIOGRAPHICAL

NOTICES.

IN THREE VOLUMES.

BY SAMUEL KETTELL.

VOL. II.

BOSTON,—S. G. GOODRICH AND CO.

MDCCCXXIX.

BOSTON;
Press of Isaac R. Butts.

CONTENTS OF THE SECOND VOLUME.

CONTENTS.

SPECIMENS

OF

AMERICAN POETRY,

WITH

CRITICAL AND BIOGRAPHICAL NOTICES.

JOEL BARLOW.

JOEL BARLOW was born at Reading, a small village in Fairfield county, Connecticut, about the year 1755. His father was a farmer in independent, though moderate circumstances, and had ten children, of whom our poet was the youngest. He died while Joel was a lad at school, and left him little more than sufficient to give him a liberal education of such a sort as was customary at that period. He entered first at Dartmouth college in New Hampshire, but that seminary being then in its infancy, and laboring under many embarrassments, he removed after a short residence, to Yale college in New Haven. In the third year of his academic course, the revolutionary war broke out, and the Connecticut militia being called out in great numbers to strengthen Washington's army, Barlow could not resist the inclination to join the camp where four of his brothers were in arms. He shouldered his musket during the college vacations, and fought in many of the skirmishes at the beginning of the war. After completing his studies with great reputation, he received a degree in 1778, on which occasion he first came before the public as a poet, by pronouncing an original poem, which was soon after printed.   He had previously made some attempts at verse, but not it appears, of any serious character.   This earliest of his works may be found in a volume with the title of " American Poems" published at Litchfield in 1793.

On leaving college he betook himself to the study of law, but continued it only for a short time.   He was strongly urged to enter the army as a chaplain, there being a great deficiency of this kind among the troops.   Although he had never undertaken a course of theological reading, yet the high opinion entertained of his talents and character, and the influence of his friends, enabled him after a preparatory study of six weeks, to pass examination, and obtain a license to preach as a congregational minister.   He repaired immediately to the army, where in the strict and punctual discharge of his clerical duties he sustained a high reputation.   In the severe labors of his office, he did not neglect his more elegant studies, but mingled devotion to the muses with his spiritual exhortations. He composed patriotic songs and addresses to the soldiery, and made all his powers subservient to the great purpose of arousing the patriotism of the troops, and sustaining their courage under their numerous hardships and perils.   He continued with the army throughout the war, and amid these occupations was also engaged in the composition of the poem afterwards published under the title of "The Vision of Columbus."   On receiving the degree of Master of Arts at New Haven, in 1781, he recited a poem called "The Prospect of Peace."   This was published and announced as a specimen of the larger work he had in hand, in which the substance of it is still to be found.   About the same period he was married to Miss Baldwin of New Haven, a sister of the Hon. Abraham Baldwin, senator in Congress, from Georgia.

Mr Barlow had not chosen the theological profession in accordance with any decided taste for the calling, nor with any view beyond the emergency which had brought about his connexion with it.   The scenes moreover with which he had been familiarized in the discharge of his numerous labors in the ranks of the army, had induced such habits as to render it a work of difficulty for him to assume at once, and with good effect the character of a parish clergyman. He had no scruple therefore in throwing aside the clerical office, and returning to his law studies. He settled himself at New Haven, and as his profession did not bring him any great immediate profit, he undertook the management of a weekly paper. His extensive knowledge, and the ability he displayed as a writer, soon gained the work great circulation and credit, as but few of the public prints at that time were conducted with any talent, or indeed were anything more than meagre repositories for the news of the day. During this connexion he prepared for the press his Vision of Columbus, which was published in 1787. He had become so widely known in the army, and was so well aided by his friends, that a large subscription was obtained for the work. He dedicated it to Louis XVI, and had the satisfaction of seeing it meet with a very favorable acceptance from the public. A few months after its appearance, it was reprinted in London, and subsequently went through a second edition in this country, and one in Paris.

After the publication of his poem, Barlow was engaged by the general association of the clergy of Connecticut, to revise Watts's version of the Psalms which had been in general use in their churches, and were regarded by them as capable of improvement by supplying omissions and altering those parts referring to the politics and religion of Great Britain. This task he performed in a very satisfactory manner. Twelve psalms which had been omitted by Watts were added, and six nearly rewritten, besides numerous corrections, improving the grammar and poetical expression of the original, as well as adapting the national allusions to the circumstances of this country. A selection of hymns was also added from Watts, and originals by himself, in which he succeeded so well in imitating his model, that as they are interspersed in the volume without being marked with the name of the author, it is not easy to make the distinction among them. This work became the authorized version of the Connecticut churches. Some alterations were afterwards made by Dr Dwight, and it still continues in common use. Barlow upon the publication of his psalms, opened a bookstore in Hartford for the sale of the work, and as soon as this was effected, returned to the practice of law, having before abandoned his connexion with the newspaper.

As a lawyer, he did not meet with a very flattering success. His oratorical powers were by no means of a high order, and his manners wanted that engaging pliancy, which is so effectual in aiding the exertions of him who is striving for the popular favor. He does not appear to have had a sufficiently strong liking for the study, to incite him to such assiduity in the pursuit of it, as might have overcome these great hinderances. He was soon aware that he could indulge no hope of rising to eminence in the career which he had begun, or even acquire a sufficient sum for his maintenance. The property which he had acquired by his literary undertakings was rapidly disappearing, and he was under the necessity of betaking himself to some new occupation. Under these circumstances he was applied to by certain members of a land association, called the Ohio Company, and some other persons who were regarded as men of property, to go to Europe as the agent of a concern for disposing of large tracts of land in the western territory. By fraudulent manœuvres, these persons obtained the management of a large portion of the funds of the Ohio Company, and giving themselves the name of the Scioto Company, offered vast quantities of land for sale, to which they had no claim. Barlow was totally ignorant of the true character of the undertaking, and readily agreed to the proposal. He sailed for England in 1788, and from that country proceeded to France, where he succeeded in disposing of some of the lands. The agency however turned out unfortunate for Barlow.

His reputation gained him the intimacy of the public characters of the greatest note and influence in France, and the singularly novel and interesting scenes which the revolution in that country was exhibiting from day to day, caused him to enter into politics with great ardor. As an American, and one who had already lent his aid to the cause of revolution, he could not hesitate to join the republican party. He was affected with no small portion of the common enthusiasm of the day, and indulged in zealous and confident anticipations of the wonders in the political and social order of the universe, which it was judged were to be the final result of those early convulsions in the political system of Europe. He sided with that portion of the republican party, called the Girondists, and made himself distinguished as one of their most active and zealous partizans. He returned to England in 1791 and published in London the first part of a work with the title of "Advice to the privileged orders," which with subsequent additions, has been several times reprinted ; it is a performance of some ability, but abounding in the extravagances which the revolutionary effervescence had engendered. This was followed the next year by a poem called "The Conspiracy of Kings," in which, as the title manifests, he took for his subject the engrossing topic of political interest. In autumn of the same year he published a letter to the National Convention, on the defects of the first constitution, in which he suggested several improvements, such as abolishing the royal power, diminishing the public salaries, making elections more frequent and popular, and dissolving the connexion of the church with the government. Barlow in consequence of these publications, became associated with the leading characters in England, who were on the side of reform, as also with a great number of men of literature and science in London. In the latter part of 1792 the London Constitutional Society, of which he was a member, voted an address to the National Convention, and Barlow with another passed over to France to present it. The Convention, as a mark of respect, conferred on him the rights of a French citizen : rights, however, which we believe he never—exercised or claimed by any public act.

After a few weeks stay in Paris, he was about to return to England, when information of the notice which the British government had taken of his mission, led him to think he should be unsafe in England. The revolutionary spirit had

extended widely in that country, and the government became
alarmed.   Barlow's errand to Paris was suspected to have
some connexion with a secret political undertaking, and the
business was officially investigated.   In this state of things he
determined to remain in France, and sent for Mrs Barlow from
England.   In the latter part of 1792 he accompanied his friend
the Abbé Gregoire, and a deputation of the Convention to
Savoy, whither they were despatched to organise that territory, as a department of the French republic.   He spent the
winter at Chamberry, and at the request of his friends wrote
an address to the Piedmontese inciting them to throw off their
allegiance to the king of Sardinia.   It was translated into
French and Italian, and distributed throughout the country,
but failed to produce any great effect.   Another work which
has been much better received by the public, occupied the
remainder of the season.   His poem of Hasty Pudding, the
most popular of all his writings, was written at Chamberry.
From this country he returned to Paris, and engaged in commercial speculations, from which he reaped considerable profit.
    We do not find that he took any share in politics at this
period: and although many political writings of a violent and
atrocious character were given to the public under his name
about this time, we have his own assurance that he never
wrote them.   He continued to indulge hopes that the struggles
which were then convulsing France with still mightier power,
would soon work out her political regeneration ; but the scenes
of turbulence, anarchy, and blood, which recurred from day to
day, shook his faith in the cause of the revolution, and kept
him aloof from the scene of contest.   Notwithstanding he
continued to reside at Paris for about three years.   His
character as a neutral insured him a degree of safety amid
the tumults around him, which he could not otherwise have
enjoyed.
    In 1795 or near that time, he visited the north of Europe,
and on his return received information that he had been appointed by President Washington, Consul for the United
States at Algiers, and Plenipotentiary for the negotiation of a

peace with the Dey, and the redemption of all the American captives in the Barbary states. Barlow undertook the charge, and passing over to the Mediterranean through Spain, proceeded to Algiers, and began the business of negotiation. He encountered powerful obstacles from the intrigues of several of the European agents, but had the address to conclude the treaty expeditiously. The next year he negotiated a treaty with Tripoli, and ransomed all the American prisoners who could be found in Barbary. In this exertion we are assured that he was often obliged to hazard his life, to accomplish his humane purposes. Having discharged these duties, he gave up his consulship, returned to Paris, and entered again into trade, by which he acquired a handsome fortune, a great part of which he laid out in landed estates in France. One of his purchases, was the elegant hotel of Clermont Tonnere in Paris, where he lived some years in a splendid style.

Mr Barlow was not commissioned by instructions from government to set on foot any negotiation respecting the difficulties which arose at this time between the United States and France; nevertheless he made some exertions to bring about an adjustment of differences, and published some writings to the same end in the United States. About the same time he offered a memoir to the French government, on the subject of privateering, blockade, and other points in maritime warfare. In this he condemned the system of privateering, as no better than robbery, and asserted the right of neutrals to trade in articles which the international code has set down as contraband of war. The memoir was received respectfully, but the new French constitution then framing, and for which it was designed, was hurried through with all possible expedition, to answer the immediate purposes of some of the leading politicians, and Barlow's suggestions were passed by unheeded for want of time for their consideration.

He had now been absent nearly seventeen years from his native country. Paris was no longer the theatre of faction and turbulence, but had regained a sufficient degree of quiet to render it an agreeable place of abode. Its magnificent repositories of everything precious in literature and the arts, offered the strongest attractions to a man of letters, but the desire of revisiting the land of his birth, and beholding the wonderful improvements in her social and political state which the lapse of a few years had wrought, induced him to sell his property in France, and embark for America. After a short visit to England, he arrived in this country in 1805. He fixed his abode at Washington, where he purchased an elegant house, and lived in a splendid and hospitable manner, on terms of intimacy with the President, and the most noted public men.

One of his earliest undertakings after his return was the plan of a national college or academy, under the immediate patronage of the government, which had been originally suggested by Washington, and now received the approbation of Mr Jefferson. Barlow drew up a prospectus of the proposed institution, which is described as an academy to be erected at the seat of government " which should combine the two great objects of scientific investigation and of instruction, together with national views, by uniting a university to a learned society, formed on a plan resembling that of the national institute of France, and adding to both a military and naval academy, and a school of fine arts." This prospectus he published in a pamphlet at his own expense, and circulated it throughout the country. The plan met with considerable opposition from the friends of several of the literary institutions in the different states, but was so warmly received in many quarters, that it was brought before Congress. On the 4th of March 1806, a bill was introduced in the senate, to incorporate a national academy upon the plan offered by Barlow. It was passed to a second reading and referred to a committee. After some debate as to the name which the institution should bear, the bill was referred to a select committee who never reported; whether from a disapproval of the entire project, or want of time for deliberation upon the business, we are not informed. Thus the project failed, and Barlow never renewed his attempt.

He now entered upon an undertaking which he had contemplated for many years, and the preparations for which had already occupied a great portion of his life. This was the publication of his Columbiad, the title he bestowed upon the *rifacciamento* of the national poem of his early years. That production had been received by the American public with a degree of favor, highly flattering to the author. Our native literature at that period was but scanty, and a work of any pretensions though of ordinary merit, was sure to attract notice. The Vision of Columbus made its appearance in an attractive shape, and with strong claims upon the general regard. It was the most national and patriotic performance, both in frame and spirit, which any native writer had produced. The subject was familiar to every one, and the scenes of the revolution which furnished the author with so large a portion of the incidents of his story, had an interest for his readers, which disposed them to look with partiality upon the strains in which those deeds were sung. When we add, that the state of criticism was comparatively low among us in those days, and that correct taste which is formed by extensive reading, was by means an ordinary accomplishment, it will not appear surprising that such a production should be read under the influence of strong prepossessions, or that the judgment passed upon its merits, should have been regulated by no very discriminating and philosophical notion of poetical excellence. The consequence was, that the Vision of Columbus was overpraised, and Barlow, who was accustomed to be spoken of as the first in rank among the American bards, was tempted to claim a higher character in the poetical scale, by giving his work the imposing stateliness and symmetry of the epopee. For this purpose he cast the poem anew, and made such additions as he deemed requisite to give it the epic fulness and perfection. He spared no pains nor expense in the publication, and in 1808 the Columbiad was issued from the press in a style of elegance which few works, either American or European, have ever equalled. An edition in duodecimo was published the next year, and the poem was also reprinted in London.

Although the Columbiad was the performance upon which Barlow chiefly relied for his fame, yet now that it was completed and before the world, he did not seem disposed to desist in any measure from his literary enterprises. He made large collections of materials for a general history of the United States, and was busily engaged in planning the work in 1811 when he received the appointment of minister plenipotentiary to France. The objects of his mission were the negotiation of a treaty of commerce and indemnification for the French spoliations. He accepted the appointment, sailed for France, and entered immediately upon the business, which he found it difficult to accomplish, from the many delays and obstacles which the French government contrived to throw in his way. Mr Barlow spared no zeal nor perseverance to effect his purpose, and being invited in 1812 to a conference with Napoleon at Wilna, he set out in October and travelled day and night in that severe season, which annihilated the phalanxes of the French Emperor. The country through which his course lay, after leaving France, was so wasted by the ravages of war, as hardly to afford a meal to the traveller, and in a state of extreme debility from fatigue and want of food and sleep, he was exposed to sudden changes from cold to heat, in the small and crowded cottages of the Jews, which afford the only taverns to be met with in Poland. This produced a violent inflammation of the lungs, of which he died on the 22d of December, 1812, at Zarnawica, a village in Poland near Cracow.

Barlow, as a poet, can by no means be allowed the highest rank among his countrymen, even those of his own day; yet he has drawn upon himself by the publicity of his career, and the efforts he made for that purpose, a greater degree of notice, than any other of our native bards. To the European world, Barlow was the only transatlantic poet. The witlings of the British periodical press pointed their gibes at our literature in the person of this single writer, and regarded the Columbiad as the sum total of American genius in the shape of verse. A better standard of taste has now lowered the estimation of his powers among us, and it is no longer fashionable to consider the literary reputation of the country as resting upon his attempt at epic poetry. Still, the talents which he has unquestionably displayed in his writings, entitle him to no small share of our attention.

The Conspiracy of Kings is a vehement invective against the potentates of Europe, and the enemies of the French revolution. In this piece, he expatiates upon the common topics of the writers in the same cause, with great warmth and spirit. It is a good specimen of animated, vigorous declamation.

The Hasty Pudding will probably retain a greater share of popularity than any other portion of his works. This poem is executed in a lively and entertaining manner, and affords in the familiar and homely nature of the subject, and the gaiety with which it is treated, an agreeable contrast to the gravity and stateliness of the author's general style.

The Columbiad has met with small favor from the critics, and its faults, both in plan and execution, were severely commented upon at its first appearance. The absurdity of attempting to give an epic unity and interest through the medium of a vision, to a series of actions so unconnected in date and subject : and the strange and awkward neologisms by which the language of the poem is disfigured, called forth the reprehensions of the reviewers in every quarter. It had no popularity among us, and is now fallen quite into neglect,—a fate which the reader may ascribe to the improved taste and understanding in literary matters, of the present day, but which was in part occasioned by the higher character which the poem assumed over the work as it stood in its original state. The Vision of Columbus, while no one claimed for it any very exalted rank, continued to be spoken of in terms of respect. But in its new shape it came out with the high pretensions of an epic, and having been pronounced a failure, nobody reads it.

In his preface he avows the object of the Columbiad to be altogether of a moral and political nature. Most epic poems are regarded as having some similar aim. They were designed to leave some more important and durable impression than what arises from contemplating the interest of the story or the beauty of the language. We are led to conclude, however, from Barlow's explanation of his plan, that he considered more the philosophy than the poetry of his work ; that he was less solicitous for the classical regularity and interest of the fable, than for the general sentiments and moral effect of the performance, forgetting that without a proper degree of skill in arranging the narrative which was to be the vehicle of the sentiments, they must fail of accomplishing their object. It is surprising that Barlow's judgment should have allowed him to imagine that to render his poem perfectly national in character, it was necessary that it should embrace the history and topography, as it were, of the whole American continent; or that he could have hoped to excite interest by a story which extended through hundreds of years ; which treated of Manco Capac and Washington, described the conquest of Mexico, and the battle of Bunker Hill ; and contained long philosophical speculations upon almost every subject—political, moral, and scientific. How utterly he has failed in this particular we need waste no criticism in showing. His notions of what was requisite to give the epic dignity to his performance seem to have embraced the most objectionable part of the old doctrines upon the subject with ideas of his own altogether novel. The machinery which he deemed it necessary to introduce, accomplishes hardly anything of its destined purpose in controlling the main events, or bringing about the catastrophe of the story ; and the topics which he had occasion to handle offered such a temptation to speculate, descant, and moralize, that the quantity of matter in a digressory strain which he has embodied in the work, gives it the character in some parts of a philosophical instead of a narrative poem, a defect of plan which the highest graces of composition could hardly redeem.

The versification in this poem is elaborated with great care, but it is not flowing nor graceful. The language is often tumid, and extravagant, and disfigured with ornaments which denote a vitiated taste. There is throughout a want of imagination, fire, and the marks of that inbred faculty of the soul, that refined intellectual feeling which pours out its energies with a fervor that reaches the heart. Barlow was a poet by dint of study and labor; but in the creations which his fancy has bodied forth, we seek in vain for the breathings of that spirit of unearthly tone, which act like a spell upon the senses, whose visitings thrill the bosom in its deepest and most hallowed recesses, stir our sympathies with a magic potency, and stamp the memory with a deep and abiding impression.

His powers were inadequate to the accomplishment of the undertaking which he meditated in the Columbiad. The poem cannot be commended as a whole, but there are portions of it which exhibit the author's talent in a very favorable manner. It has many passages of spirited, rich, and splendid description: and in expatiating in a moral and philosophical strain, he displays a loftiness of sentiment, and an enthusiasm, which inspire noble thoughts and kindle some of our most exalted emotions. The moral scope of the work, in spite of its miscarriage as an epic, will recommend it to our regard as the earnest endeavor of a sincere philanthropist to further the progress of the human race in their advances to political and moral perfection.

THE HASTY PUDDING.

CANTO I.

Ye Alps audacious, through the heavens that rise,
To cramp the day and hide me from the skies;
Ye Gallic flags, that o'er their heights unfurled,
Bear death to kings, and freedom to the world,
I sing not you. A softer theme I choose,
A virgin theme, unconscious of the Muse,
But fruitful, rich, well suited to inspire
The purest frenzy of poetic fire.
Despise it not, ye bards to terror steel'd,
Who hurl your thunders round the epic field;
Nor ye who strain your midnight throats to sing
Joys that the vineyard and the still-house bring;
Or on some distant fair your notes employ,
And speak of raptures that you ne'er enjoy.

I sing the sweets I know, the charms I feel,
My morning incense, and my evening meal,
The sweets of Hasty Pudding. Come, dear bowl,
Glide o'er my palate, and inspire my soul.
The milk beside thee, smoking from the kine,
Its substance mingled, married in with thine,
Shall cool and temper thy superior heat,
And save the pains of blowing while I eat.
　　Oh! could the smooth, the emblematic song
Flow like thy genial juices o'er my tongue,
Could those mild morsels in my numbers chime,
And, as they roll in substance, roll in rhyme,
No more thy awkward unpoetic name
Should shun the muse, or prejudice thy fame;
But rising grateful to the accustom'd ear,
All bards should catch it, and all realms revere!
　　Assist me first with pious toil to trace
Through wrecks of time, thy lineage and thy race;
Declare what lovely squaw, in days of yore,
(Ere great Columbus sought thy native shore)
First gave thee to the world; her works of fame
Have lived indeed, but lived without a name.
Some tawny Ceres, goddess of her days,
First learn'd with stones to crack the well dried maize,
Through the rough sieve to shake the golden shower,
In boiling water stir the yellow flour:
The yellow flour, bestrew'd and stirr'd with haste,
Swells in the flood and thickens to a paste,
Then puffs and wallops, rises to the brim,
Drinks the dry knobs that on the surface swim;
The knobs at last the busy ladle breaks,
And the whole mass its true consistence takes.
　　Could but her sacred name, unknown so long,
Rise, like her labors, to the son of song,
To her, to them, I 'd consecrate my lays,
And blow her pudding with the breath of praise.
Not through the rich Peruvian realms alone
The fame of Sol's sweet daughter should be known,
But o'er the world's wide clime should live secure,
Far as his rays extend, as long as they endure.
　　Dear Hasty Pudding, what unpromised joy
Expands my heart, to meet thee in Savoy!
Doom'd o'er the world through devious paths to roam,
Each clime my country, and each house my home,
My soul is soothed, my cares have found an end,
I greet my long lost, unforgotten friend.
　　For thee through Paris, that corrupted town,

How long in vain I wandered up and down,
Where shameless Bacchus, with his drenching hoard,
Cold from his cave usurps the morning board.
London is lost in smoke and steep'd in tea;
No Yankee there can lisp the name of thee;
The uncouth word, a libel on the town,
Would call a proclamation from the crown.
For climes oblique, that fear the sun's full rays,
Chill'd in their fogs, exclude the generous maize:
A grain, whose rich, luxuriant growth requires
Short gentle showers, and bright etherial fires.
    But here, though distant from our native shore,
With mutual glee, we meet and laugh once more.
The same! I know thee by that yellow face,
That strong complexion of true Indian race,
Which time can never change, nor soil impair,
Nor Alpine snows, nor Turkey's morbid air;
For endless years, through every mild domain,
Where grows the maize, there thou art sure to reign,
    But man, more fickle, the bold license claims,
In different realms to give thee different names.
Thee the soft nations round the warm Levant
Polanta call, the French of course *Polante.*
E'en in thy native regions, how I blush
To hear the Pennsylvanians call thee *Mush !*
On Hudson's banks, while men of Belgic spawn
Insult and eat thee by the name *Suppawn.*
All spurious appellations, void of truth;
I 've better known thee from my earliest youth,
Thy name is *Hasty-Pudding !* thus our sires
Were wont to greet thee fuming from their fires;
And while they argued in thy just defence
With logic clear, they thus explain'd the sense:—
" In *haste* the boiling cauldron, o'er the blaze,
Receives and cooks the ready powder'd maize;
In *haste* 't is served, and then in equal *haste,*
With cooling milk, we make the sweet repast.
No carving to be done, no knife to grate
The tender ear, and wound the stony plate;
But the smooth spoon, just fitted to the lip,
And taught with art the yielding mass to dip,
By frequent journeys to the bowl well stored,
Performs the *hasty* honors of the board."
Such is thy name, significant and clear,
A name, a sound to every Yankee dear,
But most to me, whose heart and palate chaste
Preserve my pure hereditary taste.

There are who strive to stamp with disrepute
The luscious food, because it feeds the brute ;
In tropes of high-strain'd wit, while gaudy prigs
Compare thy nursling, man, to pamper'd pigs ;
With sovereign scorn I treat the vulgar jest,
Nor fear to share thy bounties with the beast.
What though the generous cow gives me to quaff
The milk nutritious : am I then a calf?
Or can the genius of the noisy swine,
Though nursed on pudding, thence lay claim to mine ?
Sure the sweet song, I fashion to thy praise,
Runs more melodious than the notes they raise.
　　My song resounding in its grateful glee,
No merit claims : I praise myself in thee.
My father loved thee through his length of days !
For thee his fields were shaded o'er with maize ;
From thee what health, what vigor he possess'd,
Ten sturdy freemen from his loins attest ;
Thy constellation ruled my natal morn,
And all my bones were made of Indian corn.
Delicious grain ! whatever form it take,
To roast or boil, to smother or to bake,
In every dish 't is welcome still to me,
But most, my *Hasty Pudding*, most in thee.
　　Let the green succotash with thee contend,
Let beans and corn their sweetest juices blend,
Let butter drench them in its yellow tide,
And a long slice of bacon grace their side ;
Not all the plate, how famed soe'er it be,
Can please my palate like a bowl of thee.
Some talk of *Hoe-Cake*, fair Virginia's pride,
Rich *Johnny-Cake*, this mouth has often tried ;
Both please me well, their virtues much the same
Alike their fabric, as allied their fame,
Except in dear New England, where the last
Receives a dash of pumpkin in the paste,
To give it sweetness and improve the taste.
But place them all before me, smoking hot,
The big, round dumpling, rolling from the pot,
The pudding of the bag, whose quivering breast,
With suet lined, leads on the Yankee feast ;
The *Charlotte* brown, within whose crusty sides
A belly soft the pulpy apple hides ;
The yellow bread whose face like amber glows,
And all of Indian that the bake-pan knows,—
You tempt me not—my fav'rite greets my eyes,
To that loved bowl my spoon by instinct flies.

CANTO II.

To mix the food by vicious rules of art,
To kill the stomach, and to sink the heart,
To make mankind to social virtue sour,
Cram o'er each dish, and be what they devour;
For this the kitchen muse first framed her book,
Commanding sweat to stream from every cook;
Children no more their antic gambols tried,
And friends to physic wonder'd why they died.
Not so the Yankee—his abundant feast,
With simples furnish'd and with plainness drest,
A numerous offspring gathers round the board,
And cheers alike the servant and the lord;
Whose well-bought hunger prompts the joyous taste,
And health attends them from the short repast.
While the full pail rewards the milk-maid's toil,
The mother sees the morning cauldron boil;
To stir the pudding next demands their care;
To spread the table and the bowls prepare;
To feed the children, as their portions cool,
And comb their heads, and send them off to school.
Yet may the simplest dish some rules impart,
For nature scorns not all the aids of art.
E'en *Hasty-Pudding*, purest of all food,
May still be bad, indifferent, or good,
As sage experience the short process guides,
Or want of skill, or want of care presides.
Whoe'er would form it on the surest plan,
To rear the child and long sustain the man;
To shield the morals while it mends the size,
And all the powers of every food supplies,
Attend the lesson that the muse shall bring.
Suspend your spoons, and listen while I sing.
But since, O man! thy life and health demand
Not food alone, but labor from thy hand,
First in the field, beneath the sun's strong rays,
Ask of thy mother earth the needful maize;
She loves the race that courts her yielding soil,
And gives her bounties to the sons of toil.
When now the ox, obedient to thy call,
Repays the loan that fill'd the winter stall,
Pursue his traces o'er the furrow'd plain,
And plant in measured hills the golden grain.
But when the tender germ begins to shoot,
And the green spire declares the sprouting root,
Then guard your nursling from each greedy foe,

The insidious worm, the all-devouring crow.
A little ashes, sprinkled round the spire,
Soon steep'd in rain, will bid the worm retire ;
The feather'd robber with his hungry maw
Swift flies the field before your man of straw,
A frightful image, such as schoolboys bring,
When met to burn the pope, or hang the king.
    Thrice in the season, through each verdant row
Wield the strong ploughshare and the faithful hoe ;
The faithful hoe, a double task that takes,
To till the summer corn, and roast the winter cakes.
    Slow springs the blade, while check'd by chilling rains,
Ere yet the sun the seat of Cancer gains ;
But when his fiercest fires emblaze the land,
Then start the juices, then the roots expand ;
Then, like a column of Corinthian mould,
The stalk struts upward and the leaves unfold ;
The busy branches all the ridges fill,
Entwine their arms, and kiss from hill to hill.
Here cease to vex them, all your cares are done :
Leave the last labors to the parent sun ;
Beneath his genial smiles, the well-drest field,
When autumn calls, a plenteous crop shall yield.
    Now the strong foliage bears the standards high,
And shoots the tall top-gallants to the sky ;
The suckling ears the silky fringes bend,
And pregnant grown, their swelling coats distend ;
The loaded stalk, while still the burthen grows,
O'erhangs the space that runs between the rows ;
High as a hop-field waves the silent grove,
A safe retreat for little thefts of love,
When the pledged roasting-ears invite the maid,
To meet her swain beneath the new-form'd shade ;
His generous hand unloads the cumbrous hill,
And the green spoils her ready basket fill ;
Small compensation for the two-fold bliss,
The promised wedding, and the present kiss.
    Slight depredations these ; but now the moon
Calls from his hollow trees the sly raccoon ;
And while by night he bears his prize away,
The bolder squirrel labors through the day.
Both thieves alike, but provident of time,
A virtue rare, that almost hides their crime.
Then let them steal the little stores they can,
And fill their gran'ries from the toils of man ;
We 've one advantage, where they take no part,—
With all their wiles they ne'er have found the art

To boil the *Hasty-Pudding*; here we shine
Superior far to tenants of the pine ;
This envied boon to man shall still belong,
Unshared by them, in substance or in song.
  At last the closing season browns the plain,
And ripe October gathers in the grain ;
Deep loaded carts the spacious corn-house fill,
The sack distended marches to the mill ;
The lab'ring mill beneath the burthen groans,
And showers the future pudding from the stones ;
Till the glad housewife greets the powder'd gold,
And the new crop exterminates the old.

CANTO III.

  THE days grow short ; but though the falling sun
To the glad swain proclaims his day's work done,
Night's pleasing shades his various tasks prolong,
And yield new subject to my various song.
For now, the corn-house fill'd, the harvest home,
The invited neighbors to the *husking* come ;
A frolic scene, where work, and mirth, and play,
Unite their charms, to chase the hours away.
  Where the huge heap lies centred in the hall,
The lamp suspended from the cheerful wall,
Brown corn-fed nymphs, and strong hard-handed beaus,
Alternate ranged, extend in circling rows,
Assume their seats, the solid mass attack ;
The dry husks rustle, and the corn-cobs crack ;
The song, the laugh, alternate notes resound,
And the sweet cider trips in silence round.
  The laws of husking every wight can tell ;
And sure no laws he ever keeps so well :
For each red ear a general kiss he gains,
With each smut ear he smuts the luckless swains ;
But when to some sweet maid a prize is cast,
Red as her lips, and taper as her waist,
She walks the round, and culls one favored beau,
Who leaps, the luscious tribute to bestow.
Various the sport, as are the wits and brains
Of well pleased lasses and contending swains ;
Till the vast mound of corn is swept away,
And he that gets the last ear wins the day.
  Meanwhile the housewife urges all her care,
The well-earn'd feast to hasten and prepare.
The sifted meal already waits her hand,
The milk is strain'd, the bowls in order stand,

The fire flames high; and, as a pool (that takes
The headlong stream that o'er the mill-dam breaks)
Foams, roars, and rages, with incessant toils,
So the vex'd cauldron rages, roars and boils.
   First with clean salt, she seasons well the food,
Then strews the flour, and thickens all the flood.
Long o'er the simmering fire she lets it stand;
To stir it well demands a stronger hand;
The husband takes his turn: and round and round
The ladle flies; at last the toil is crown'd;
When to the board the thronging huskers pour,
And take their seats as at the corn before.
   I leave them to their feast.   There still belong
More copious matters to my faithful song.
For rules there are, though ne'er unfolded yet,
Nice rules and wise, how pudding should be ate.
   Some with molasses line the luscious treat,
And mix, like bards, the useful with the sweet.
A wholesome dish, and well deserving praise,
A great resource in those bleak wintry days,
When the chill'd earth lies buried deep in snow,
And raging Boreas dries the shivering cow.
   Blest cow! thy praise shall still my notes employ,
Great source of health, the only source of joy;
Mother of Egypt's god,—but sure, for me,
Were I to leave my God, I'd worship thee.
How oft thy teats these precious hands have press'd
How oft thy bounties prove my only feast!
How oft I've fed thee with my favorite grain!
And roar'd, like thee, to find thy children slain!
   Yes, swains who know her various worth to prize,
Ah! house her well from winter's angry skies.
Potatoes, pumpkins, should her sadness cheer,
Corn from your crib, and mashes from your beer;
When spring returns, she'll well acquit the loan,
And nurse at once your infants and her own.
   Milk then with pudding I would always choose;
To this in future I confine my muse,
Till she in haste some further hints unfold,
Well for the young, nor useless to the old.
First in your bowl the milk abundant take,
Then drop with care along the silver lake
Your flakes of pudding; these at first will hide
Their little bulk beneath the swelling tide;
But when their growing mass no more can sink,
When the soft island looms above the brink,

Then check your hand ; you 've got the portion due,
So taught our sires, and what they taught is true.
    There is a choice in spoons.   Though small appear
The nice distinction, yet to me 't is clear.
The deep bowl'd Gallic spoon, contrived to scoop
In ample draughts the thin diluted soup,
Performs not well in those substantial things,
Whose mass adhesive to the metal clings ;
Where the strong labial muscles must embrace,
The gentle curve, and sweep the hollow space.
With ease to enter and discharge the freight,
A bowl less concave but still more dilate,
Becomes the pudding best.   The shape, the size,
A secret rests, unknown to vulgar eyes.
Experienced feeders can alone impart
A rule so much above the lore of art.
These tuneful lips, that thousand spoons have tried,
With just precision could the point decide,
Though not in song ; the muse but poorly shines
In cones, and cubes, and geometric lines :
Yet the true form, as near as she can tell,
Is that small section of a goose egg shell,
Which in two equal portions shall divide
The distance from the centre to the side.
    Fear not to slaver ; 'tis no deadly sin :——
Like the free Frenchman, from your joyous chin
Suspend the ready napkin ; or like me,
Poise with one hand your bowl upon your knee ;
Just in the zenith your wise head project,
Your full spoon, rising in a line direct,
Bold as a bucket, heeds no drops that fall,
The wide mouth'd bowl will surely catch them all !

———

FROM THE VISION OF COLUMBUS.

WHERE Spring's coy steps, in cold Canadia stray,
And joyless seasons hold unequal sway ;
He saw the pine its daring mantle rear,
Break the rude blast, and mock the inclement year,
Secure the limits of the angry skies,
And bid all southern vegetation rise.
Wild o'er the vast impenetrable round,
The untrod bowers of shadowy nature frown'd ;
The neighboring cedar waved its honors wide,
The fir's tall boughs, the oak's resistless pride,

The branching beech, the aspin's trembling shade,
Veil'd the dim heavens and brown'd the dusky glade.
Here in huge crowds those sturdy sons of earth,
In frosty regions, claim a nobler birth ;
Where heavy trunks the sheltering dome requires,
And copious fuel feeds the wintry fires.
While warmer suns, that southern climes emblaze,
A cool deep umbrage o'er the woodland raise ;
Floridia's blooming shores around him spread,
And Georgian hills erect their shady head ;
Beneath tall trees, in livelier verdure gay,
Long level walks a humble garb display ;
The infant corn, unconscious of its worth,
Points the green spire and bends the foliage forth ;
Sweeten'd on flowery banks, the passing air
Breathes all the untasted fragrance of the year ;
Unbidden harvests o'er the regions rise,
And blooming life repays the genial skies.
Where circling shores around the gulf extend,
The bounteous groves with richer burdens bend ;
Spontaneous fruits the uplifted palms unfold,
The beauteous orange waves a load of gold,
The untaught vine, the wildly-wanton cane
Bloom on the waste, and clothe the enarbor'd plain,
The rich pimento scents the neighboring skies,
And woolly clusters o'er the cotton rise.
Here, in one view, the same glad branches bring
The fruits of autumn and the flowers of spring ;
No wintry blasts the unchanging year deform,
Nor beasts unshelter'd fear the pinching storm :
But vernal breezes o'er the blossoms rove,
And breathe the ripen'd juices through the grove.
Beneath the crystal wave's inconstant light,
Pearls undistinguish'd sparkle on the sight ;
From opening earth, in living lustre, shine
The various treasures of the blazing mine ;
Hills, cleft before him, all their stores unfold,
The quick mercurius and the burning gold ;
Gems of unnumber'd hues, in bright array,
Illume the changing rocks and shed the beams of day.

EMBASSY OF ROCHA.

FROM THE COLUMBIAD.

Soon the glad prince, in robes of white array'd,
Call'd his attendants, and the sire obey'd ;
A diamond broad, in burning gold imprest,
Display'd the sun's bright image on his breast ;
A pearl-dropt girdle bound his waist below,
And the white lautu graced his lofty brow.
They journey'd forth, o'ermarching far the mound
That flank'd the kingdom on its Andean bound ;
Ridge after ridge through vagrant hordes they pass'd,
Where each new tribe seem'd wilder than the last ;
To all they preach and prove the solar sway
And climb fresh mountains on their tedious way.
At length, as through disparting clouds they rise,
And hills above them still obstruct the skies,
While a dead calm o'er all the region stood
And not a leaf could fan its parent wood,
Sudden a strange portentous noise began ;
The birds fled wild, the beasts for shelter ran ;
Slow, sullen, loud, with deep astounding blare,
Swell the strong tones of subterranean war ;
Behind, before, beneath them groans the ground,
Earth heaves and labors with the shuddering sound ;
Columns of smoke, that cap the rumbling height,
Roll reddening far through heaven and choke the light ;
From tottering steeps descend their cliffs of snow,
The mountains reel, the valleys rend below ;
The headlong streams forget their usual round
And shrink and vanish in the gaping ground.
The sun descends ; but night recalls in vain
Her silent shades, to recommence her reign ;
The bursting mount gapes high, a sudden glare
Corruscates wide, till all the purpling air
Breaks into flame ; it wheels and roars and raves
And wraps the welkin in its folding waves.
Light sailing cinders, through its vortex driven,
Stream high and brighten to the midst of heaven ;
And, following slow, full floods of boiling ore
Swell, swoop aloft, and through the concave roar.
Torrents of molten rocks, on every side,
Lead o'er the shelves of ice their fiery tide ;
Hills slide before them, skies around them burn,
Towns sink beneath and heaving plains upturn ;

O'er many a league the flaming deluge hurl'd,
Sweeps total nations from the staggering world.
 Meanwhile, at distance through the livid light,
A busy concourse met their wondering sight ;
The prince drew near ; where lo! an altar stood,
Rude in its form and fill'd with burning wood ;
Wrapt in the flames a child expiring lay
And the fond father thus was heard to pray :
" Receive, O dreadful power, from feeble age
This last pure offering to thy sateless rage ;
Thrice has thy vengeance on this hated land
Claim'd a dear infant from my yielding hand,
Thrice have those lovely lips the victim press'd,
And all the mother torn that tender breast,
When the dread duty stifled every sigh
And not a tear escaped her beauteous eye.
Our fourth and last now meets the fatal doom ;
Groan not, my child, thy god remands thee home ;
Attend once more, thou dark infernal name,
From yon far streaming pyramid of flame ;
Snatch from his heaving flesh the blasted breath,
Sacred to thee and all the fiends of death ;
Then in thy hall, with spoils of nations crown'd,
Confine thy walks beneath the rending ground ;
No more on earth the embowell'd flames to pour,
And scourge my people and my race no more."
 Thus Rocha heard ; and to the trembling crowd
Turn'd the bright image of his beaming god.
The afflicted chief, with fear and grief oppress'd,
Beheld the sign, and thus the prince address'd :
" From what far land, O royal stranger, say,
Ascend thy wandering steps this nightly way ?
From plains like ours, by holy demons fired ?
Have thy brave people in the flames expired ?
And hast thou now, to stay the whelming flood,
No son to offer to the furious god ? "
 " From happier lands I came," the prince returns,
"Where no red flaming flood the concave burns,
No furious god bestorms our soil and skies,
Nor yield our hands the bloody sacrifice ;
But life and joy the Power delights to give,
And bids his children but rejoice and live.
Thou seest through heaven the day-dispensing Sun
In living radiance wheel his golden throne,
O'er earth's gay surface send his genial beams,
Force from yon cliffs of ice the vernal streams ;
While fruits and flowers adorn the cultured field,

And seas and lakes their copious treasures yield:
He reigns our only god.   In him we trace
The friend, the father of our happy race.
Late the lone tribes, on those unlabor'd shores,
Ran wild, and served imaginary powers ;
Till he in pity taught their feuds to cease,
Devised their laws and fashion'd all for peace.
My sacred parents first the reign began,
Sent from his courts to guide the paths of man,
To plant his fruits, to manifest his sway,
And give their blessings where he gives the day."

*　　　*　　　*　　　*　　　*　　　*

The legates now their further course descried,
A young cazique attending as a guide,
O'er craggy cliffs pursued their eastern way,
Trod loftier champaigns, meeting high the day :
Saw timorous tribes in these sublime abodes
Adore the blasts and turn the storms to gods ;
While every cloud that thunders through the skies
Claims from their hands a human sacrifice.
Awhile the youth, their better faith to gain,
Strives with his usual art, but strives in vain ;
In vain he pleads the mildness of the sun ;
A gale refutes him ere his speech be done ;
Continual tempests from their orient blow,
And load the mountains with eternal snow.
The sun's own beam, the timid clans declare,
Drives all their evils on the tortured air ;
He draws the vapors up their eastern sky,
That sail and centre round his dazzling eye ;
Leads the loud storms along his mid-day course
And bids the Andes meet their sweeping force,
Builds their bleak summits with an icy throne,
To shine through heaven, a semblance of his own ;
Hence the sharp sleet, these lifted lawns that wait,
And all the scourges that attend their state.
　Two toilsome days the virtuous Inca strove
To social life their savage minds to move ;
When the third morning glow'd serenely bright,
He led their elders to an eastern height ;
The world unlimited beneath them lay,
And not a cloud obscured the rising day.
Vast Amazonia, starr'd with twinkling streams,
In azure drest, a heaven inverted seems ;
Dim Paraguay extends the aching sight,
Xaraya glimmers like the moon of night,

Land, water, sky, in blending borders play
And smile and brighten to the lamp of day.
When thus the prince : What majesty divine !
What robes of gold ! what flames about him shine !
There walks the god ; his starry sons on high
Draw their dim veil and shrink behind the sky ;
Earth with surrounding nature 's born anew,
And men by millions greet the glorious view.
Who can behold his all delighting soul
Give life and joy, and heaven and earth control,
Bid death and darkness from his presence move,
Who can behold and not adore and love ?
Those plains, immensely circling, feel his beams,
He greens the groves, he silvers gay the streams,
Swells the wild fruitage, gives the beast his food,
And mute creation hails the genial god.
But richer boons his righteous laws impart,
To aid the life and mould the social heart,
His arts of peace through happy realms to spread,
And altars grace with sacrificial bread ;
Such our distinguish'd lot, who own his sway,
Mild as his morning stars and liberal as the day.
    His unknown laws, the mountain chief replied,
May serve perchance your boasted race to guide ;
And yon low plains, that drink his partial ray,
At his glad shrine their just devotions pay.
But we nor fear his frown nor trust his smile ;
Vain as our prayers is every anxious toil ;
Our beasts are buried in his whirls of snow,
Our cabins drifted to his slaves below.
Even now his placid looks thy hopes beguile,
He lures thy raptures with a morning smile ;
But soon (for so those saffron robes proclaim)
His own black tempest shall obstruct his flame,
Storm, thunder, fire against the mountains driven,
Rake deep their sulphur'd sides, disgorging here his
        heaven.
    He spoke ; they waited, till the fervid ray
High from the noontide shot the faithless day ;
When lo, far gathering under eastern skies,
Solemn and slow, the dark red vapors rise ;
Full clouds, convolving on the turbid air,
Move like an ocean to the watry war.
The host, securely raised, no dangers harm,
They sit unclouded and o'erlook the storm ;
While far beneath, the sky-borne waters ride,
Veil the dark deep and sheet the mountain's side ;

The lightning's glancing fires in fury curl'd
Bend their long forky foldings o'er the world;
Torrents and broken crags and floods of rain
From steep to steep roll down their force amain
In dreadful cataracts; the bolts confound
The tumbling clouds, and rock the solid ground.
   The blasts unburden'd take their upward course,
And o'er the mountain top resume their force.
Swift through the long white ridges from the north,
The rapid whirlwinds lead their terrors forth;
High walks the storm, the circling surges rise,
And wild gyrations wheel the hovering skies;
Vast hills of snow, in sweeping columns driven,
Deluge the air and choke the void of heaven;
Floods burst their bounds, the rocks forget their place,
And the firm Andes tremble to their base.
   Long gazed the host; when thus the stubborn chief,
With eyes on fire, and fill'd with sullen grief:
Behold thy careless god, secure on high,
Laughs at our woes and peaceful walks the sky,
Drives all his evils on these seats sublime,
And wafts his favors to a happier clime;
Sire of the dastard race, thy words disclose,
There glads his children, here afflicts his foes.
Hence! speed thy flight! pursue him where he leads,
Lest vengeance seize thee for thy father's deeds,
Thy immolated limbs assuage the fire
Of those curst powers, who now a gift require.
   The youth in haste collects his scanty train
And with the sun flies o'er the western plain;
The fading orb with plaintive voice he plies,
To guide his steps and light him down the skies.
So when the moon and all the host of even
Hang pale and trembling on the verge of heaven,
While storms ascending threat their nightly reign,
They seek their absent sire and sink below the main.

GEORGE RICHARDS,

WAS born in Rhode Island. He lived for some time in
Boston, where he became a preacher of the Universalist
persuasion. He afterwards removed to Portsmouth, New
Hampshire, and thence to Philadelphia. He has been de-
ceased we believe, twenty years or more. He wrote much

poetry in the Massachusetts Magazine, among other pieces, a
long poem called the Zenith of Glory, which was published
from time to time in that journal.   He printed in 1793, a poem
called The Declaration of Independence; in this production
he has contrived to introduce the name of every individual
who signed the Declaration.   We shall extract the first part.

THE DECLARATION OF INDEPENDENCE.

THE daring muse with retrospective eye,
    Throws back her glance, to that immortal day,
When millions sworn to conquer or to die,
    Roused as a lion panting for the prey,
And rushing headlong to the field of war,
Rode, vengeful rode, on slaughter's gore-besprinkled car.

Why burnt thus fierce within the frenzied soul,
    Undying freedom's life-enkindled flame?
Who led the lightning? bade the thunder roll?
    What godlike power? what deathless son of fame,
Rent the dark veil of ancient days in twain,
And gave to independence, liberty's loosed rein?

Say, can'st thou count the sum of untold wrong,
    Which fired to rage this last discover'd world,
To high wrought valor drove the impassion'd throng,
    And the hot bolt of tricene vengeance hurl'd,
At the proud puppets of a venal throne,
Whom eastern lust of haughtiest rule had blush'd to own?

As well, might gaze intense on yon gemm'd spheres,
    Bring to one point of view the stars of heaven;—
As soon, the dew drops, nature's pearly tears,
    Or autumn's leaves by rapid whirlwinds driven,
Shall be wrote down on registers of time,
As art numeric, number more than countless crime.

Heard ye that sigh? it is the sigh of law,
    The grand palladium of terrestrial right;

Lies crush'd by despotism's Typhœan paw,
   And justice sinks to realms of brooding night:
Juries are driven before the rising storm,
And king-paid judges, judgment's gold-ruled bench deform.

Are there no Hampdens, Pyms who dare to rise
   No Marvels who abhor the Danaen shower?
Yes! Roman patriots crowd these western skies,
   Nor heed the scorpion lash of Nimrod power:
Temperate, yet firm, they poise the dubious scales—
But private vice, awhile, o'er public good prevails.

The mild petition, bold remonstrance fail;
   Infuriate demons, lust of power and gold,
(Whose cheeks ne'er turn'd at human misery pale)
   The reins of government triumphant hold:
New deeds of wrong, and acts first penn'd in blood,
Howl, as wild furies, o'er the Atlantic flood.

Spirit of Wolfe! and ghost of gallant Howe:
   Was it for this, Columbia's yeomen bled,
When 'mid the vale, or on the mountain's brow,
   Your arms to death, or crest-plumed victory led,
A bold, intrepid, hardy, rustic train,
Whose life, with elder Albion's, dyed the reeking plain.

Lo, 'mid the bowers of sweet, domestic peace,
   Intrusive treads the son of hated war:
Whilst harpies sworn, a bleeding land to fleece,
   The merchant trap in iron nets of law:
Trade dies away—and commerce quits the shore,
Where right to hard earn'd property, is known no more.

     *   *   *   *

See, ravage mark a desolated coast.——
   Old ocean groans beneath the sharks of power.——
In panoply of steel, a Gorgon host,
   Snuff blood afar—and wait the opening hour,
Which hurl'd on Lexington the volleyed storm,
And onward pour'd, in vengeance, life-demanding form.

Behold! that curling flame which mounts in air,
   'T is Charlestown, rolling flagrant to the skies:
How deep those groans of agony, despair!

What piercing screams in wild discordance rise!
These run, those fly, t' avoid encircling fire,
Give one fond look at home, fall down, convulse, expire.
    *   *   *   *

Cry not the ghosts of gallant freemen slain,
  How long! how long! ere vengeance strikes the blow?
The dust of Charlestown flitting o'er the plain,
  All eloquent, accuses loud the foe.
Heavens! shall their union'd voice a boon demand,
And rouse not into agonies a madd'ning land?
    *   *   *   *

Black in the south, grim Afria's soot-steep'd race,
  Lift at a master's throat the sharp edged knife.
Red in the north, the biped of the chase,
  Quaffs from embowell'd captives streaming life;
Whilst fierce Areskoui, frantic, fires his soul,
And raging, stamps to atoms, mercy's wine fill'd bowl.

All ages, sexes, ranks are doom'd the prey,
  Of loosen'd havock's cannibalian hounds:
Cities and villas melt in flame away:
  And foul dishonor tramples virgin mounds:
The son, the sire, the husband, wife are kill'd:
And Abel's righteous blood, by Cain's rude hand, is spill'd.

Eternal Judge of everlasting right!
  Shall thine own image bend beneath the stroke?
Forbid it earth! forbid it worlds of light!
  Oh nerve the arm, as nature nerves the oak,
Which, whilst the sounding axe repeats the blow,
Acquires new strength, and scorns the idly threatening foe.

'T is done! the councils of the sky decree,
  That ancient compacts shall for ever cease:
The trump of heaven, it hails Columbia, free:
  As enemies, in war; as friends, in peace,
America, henceforth, Britannia eyes:
The last appeal is lodged; it thunders to the skies.

Strong, in reliance on the power divine,
  United Delegates impress the seal:—
Heroes and statesmen, hail! Your names shall shine
  On glory's page, when heaven, earth, ocean, feel,
Those chymic fires which purge the dross away,
And leave creation's gold impassive of decay.

Shall not the muse, record each patriot name,
   On the rich tablet of harmonic sound?
Glows not the goddess of immortal fame,
   To waft their praises, wide, the world around?
Yes! poesy and fame enraptured join,
Inspire the beating heart, and swell the emphatic line.

MERCY WARREN.

MRS WARREN was the wife of General James Warren, of Plymouth, and the daughter of James Otis of Barnstable, celebrated in the political history of Massachusetts. She had an extensive acquaintance with the public men of the revolutionary period, and the chief persons of literary distinction in the country. These advantages enabled her to compose a History of the American Revolution, and this work has made her favorably known. She also wrote before the Revolution, two political works called The Adulator, and The Group. In 1790, she published a volume containing two tragedies, and some miscellaneous poems. She died in 1814. Her writings are very creditable to her for learning, good judgment, and a cultivated mind. Her versification is distinguishable for correctness and ease.

SIMPLICITY.

DEEP in the bosom of old Time there stood,
Just on the margin of the sea-green flood,
A virgin form, in lucid robes array'd,
Whose ebon tresses negligently play'd
In flowing ringlets, as the wavy main
Felt the soft breeze that fann'd the verdant plain;
While the young blush of innocence bespoke
Her innate worth in every graceful look;
Her meek-eyed aspect, modest and benign,
Evinced the fair one's origin divine;
Virtue, at once her ornament and shield,
And truth the trident that the goddess held.
Beneath her reign, behold a happy race,

Who ne'er contested titles, gold, or place.
Ere commerce's whiten'd sails were wafted wide,
And every bosom caught the swelling pride
Of boundless wealth, surcharged with endless snares,
Exotic follies, and destructive cares;
Ere arts, or elegance, or taste refined,
And tempting luxury assail'd mankind;
There oaks and evergreens, and poplar shades,
In native beauty, rear'd their conic heads;
The purple tinge with golden hues inwrought,
In dappled forms, as sportive nature taught;
The silken foliage open'd through the mead,
And the clear fount in wild meanders play'd;
Beside whose gentle murmuring stream there stood
The humble hamlet, by the peasant trod,
Whose heart, unblacken'd by so mean a vice,
As lust of gold, or carking avarice;
No guilty bribes his whiten'd palm possess'd,
No dark suspicion lurk'd within his breast:
Love, concord, peace, and piety and truth,
Adorn'd grey hairs and dignified the youth;
There stingless pleasures crown'd the temperate feast,
And ruddy health, a constant welcome guest,
Fill'd up the cup, and smiled at every board,
The friend and handmaid of her generous lord.
    The rosy finger'd morn, and noontide ray,
The streaked twilight or the evening gray,
Were pass'd alike in innocence and mirth,
No riot gendering slow but certain death;
Unclouded reason guided all their way,
And virtue's self sat innocently gay.
The winged hours serenely glided by,
Till golden Phœbus deck'd the western sky; .
And when enwrapp'd in evening's sable vest,
And midnight shadows hush'd the world to rest,
On the famed ladder, whose extended bars,
From earth's low surface reach'd beyond the stars,
From orb to orb, thought reach'd the airy void,
Through widen'd space the busy mind employ'd,
While angel guards to watch his fate were given
Prelusive dreams anticipated heaven.
    But ere the bird of dawn had hail'd the day,
Or warbling songsters chirp'd their early lay,
The grateful heart its joyful matins raised,
And nature's God in morning anthems praised.
    Thus happy that ideal golden age,
That lives descriptive in the poet's page;

But now, alas ! in dark oblivion lost,
The sons of Adam know it to their cost ;
Since God forbade the mother of mankind
To taste the fruit to which she most inclined :
Her taste so delicate, refined and nice,
That the exuberance even of Paradise,
The grassy banks beside the blue cascade,
The winding streams from Pison's golden head,
The spicy groves on Gihon's lengthen'd side,
Hiddekel's fount, Assyria's blooming pride,
The fruits luxuriant on Euphrates' shores,
The rich profusion that all Eden pours,
The shady dome, the rosy vaulted bower,
And nature deck'd with every fruit and flower
Were insufficient, rude, and incomplete.
For taste ran wanton, and the fair must eat.
   Since which the garden's closely lock'd by fate,
And flaming cherubs guard the eastern gate ;
This globe is traversed round from pole to pole,
And earth research'd to find so rich a dole
As happiness unmix'd :—the phantom flies,
No son of Eve has ever won the prize.
   But nearest those, who nearest nature live,
Despising all that wealth or power can give,
Or glittering grandeur, whose false optics place,
The *summum bonum* on the frailest base ;
And if too near the threshold of their door,
Pride blazes high, and clamors loud for more—
More shining pomp, more elegance and zest,
In all the wild variety of taste ;
Peace and contentment are refined away,
And worth, unblemish'd, is the villain's prey.
   Easy the toil, and simple is the task,
That yields to man all nature bids him ask ;
And each improvement on the author's plan,
Adds new inquietudes to restless man.
As from simplicity he deviates,
Fancy, prolific, endless wants creates ;
Creates new wishes, foreign to the soul,
Ten thousand passions all the mind control,
So fast they tread behind each other's heels,
That some new image on the fancy steals ;
Ere the young embryo half its form completes,
Some new vagary the old plan defeats ;
Down comes the Gothic or Corinthian pile,
And the new vista wears the Doric style.
The finer arts depopulate and waste,

And nations sink by elegance and taste :
Empires are from their lofty summits rent,
And kingdoms down to swift perdition sent,
By soft, corrupt refinements of the heart,
Wrought up to vice by each deceptive art.
    Rome, the proud mistress of the world, displays
A lasting proof of what my pen essays ;
High-wrought refinement—usher'd in replete,
With all the ills that sink a virtuous state ;
Their sumptuary laws grown obsolete,
They, undismay'd, the patriot's frown could meet ;
Their simple manners lost—their censors dead,
Spruce *petit maitres* o'er the forum tread.
    I weep those days when gentle Maro sung,
And sweetest strains bedeck'd the flatterer's tongue ;
When so corrupt and so refined the times,
The muse could stoop to gild a tyrant's crimes.
    Then paint and sculpture, elegance and song,
Were the pursuits of all the busy throng ;
When silken commerce held the golden scales,
Empire was purchased at the public sales :
No longer lived the ancient Roman pride,
Her virtue sicken'd, and her glory died.
    What blotted out the Carthaginian fame,
And left no traces but an empty name ?—
Commerce ! the source of every narrow vice,
And honor, barter'd at a trivial price.
By court intrigues, the Commonwealth 's disgraced,
Both suffetes, and senators debased :
By soft refinement, and the love of gold,
Faction and strife grew emulous and bold,
Till restless Hanno urged his purpose on,
And Scipio's rival by his arts undone.
    From age to age since Hannibal's hard fate,
From Cæsar's annals to the modern date,
When Brunswick's race sits on the British throne,
And George's folly stains his grandsire's crown ;
When taste improved by luxury high wrought,
And fancy craves what nature never taught ;
Affronted virtue mounts her native skies,
And freedom's genius lifts her bloated eyes ;
As late I saw, in sable vestments stand,
The weeping fair, on Britain's naked strand.
    The cloud-capt hills, the echoing woods and dales,
(Where pious Druids dress'd the hallow'd vales ;
And wrote their missals on the birchen rind,
And chanted dirges with the hollow wind,)

Breathe murmuring sighs o'er that ill fated isle,
Wrapt in refinements both absurd and vile.
    Proud Thames deserted—her commercial ports
Seized and possess'd by hated foreign courts;
No more the lofty ships her marts supply,
The Neriads flap their watery wings and die:
Gray Neptune rises from his oozy bed,
And shakes the sea-weed from his shaggy head;
He bids adieu to fair Britannia's shore,
The surge rebounds, and all the woodlands roar;
His course he bends toward the western main,
The frowning Titans join the swelling train,
Measure the deep, and lash the foaming sea,
In haste to hail the brave Columbia free:
Ocean rebounds, and earth reverberates,
And heaven confirms the independent states;
While time rolls on, and mighty kingdoms fail,
They, peace and freedom on their heirs entail,
Till virtue sinks, and in far distant times,
Dies in the vortex of European crimes.

THOMAS DAWES

WAS born in Boston in 1757, and was educated for the law. He was appointed a Judge of the Supreme Court in 1792. This station he resigned in 1802, and was then made Judge of Probate for the county of Suffolk, and Judge of the Municipal Court in Boston. The former office he retained till his death in July 1825. He wrote some pieces of occasional poetry in the early part of his life.

THE LAW GIVEN AT SINAI.

THROUGH heaven's high courts the trump eternal roars—
Lift up your heads ye everlasting doors;
And wait the God of gods!—Lo, at the sound,
Wide fly the portals, blazing all around.
And see he comes! adown the rending skies,

Borne on the whirlwind's rapid wing he flies,
Cherub and seraphim prepare his way,
Black thunder rolls and livid lightnings play.
Heaven's radiant bow his awful head arrays,
His face the sun's refulgent beam displays;
Beneath his feet the avenging bolts are hurl'd,
The avenging bolts that shake a guilty world.—
Sounds but his dread command, when down they fly,
The deep-mouth'd thunder rends the vaulted sky;
All nature trembles as they issue down,
Deep groans the earth, her utmost regions groan.
  And lo, on Sinai's top descends the God,
That wrapt in tempest, trembled as he trod.
Flame, smoke, and whirlwind clothe its awful brow,
While earthquake heaves the groaning base below.
Tremendous scene, oh how shall men withstand,
When God in thunder gives the world command!
And hark! the trumpet's intermitted sound
Roars from the mount and shakes all nature round.
"I am the King of Kings, the Lord of all,
At whose dread shrine even Gods in honor fall:
By whom creation rose, divinely fair,
Who form'd the stars, and launch'd them in the air:
Whose mighty nod the rough tumultuous sea,
The whirlwind's sweep, and rending bolt obey.
I speak—and lo ten thousand thunders roll—
I breathe—and lightning gleams from pole to pole.
The Almighty is my name—at my command
Thick darkness rose that veil'd the Memphian land.
Empower'd by me, your leader smote the main,
And call'd up plagues that poison'd all their plain;
That e'en the earth and air, which gave them birth,
Conspired and smote them with enormous death.—
I spake the word, asunder Jordan rode,
That Israel o'er its dry foundations trod.—
Egypt pursued, I bade the same dread wave
Roll back, and whelm their millions in a grave.
'Twas said—the raging elements combined,
The rushing tempest and the warring wind;
Till own'd too late a God's superior power,
They sunk in depths, and sunk to rise no more!
  Still would ye have the assistance of that God
Continued through a life's perplexing road;
That when at last the heavens and earth expire,
And nature rolls in one devouring fire,
Ye might in transport view the advancing hour,

In transport hear the last dread thunders roar;
Then like the day emerging from the gloom,
Arise to flourish in eternal bloom——
With due respect, with holy awe receive
Those institutions which your God will give!——
For this he trod the unhallow'd realms below,
In all the pomp the powers of heaven could show.

*   *   *   *   *   *

Thus spake the Legislator of the sky——
And earth's long shores return the loud reply.
Peal push'd on peal, the doubling thunders roar,
Bellow the winds—the flamy lightnings glare.——

*   *   *   *   *   *

   Such shall the scene be at that dreadful time,
When the last trump shall sound his wrath sublime:
That potent trump which every head shall call
From each dark chamber of the bursting ball.
Then at the flames which in his nostrils glow,
The everlasting hills in streams shall flow——
The affrighted sun shall from yon arch retire,
Shook from his sphere, and help the general fire.——
Yon moon in blood! then every star shall fall,
In rude combustion o'er a flaming ball:
Creation sunk, and all God's thunder hurl'd
Down on the wrecks of each expiring world.
   But where 's the muse?—behold the Almighty rise:
The whirlwind bears him up the flaming skies.
Follow harmonious all the tuneful choir,
Sweet concert sweeping from the swelling lyre.
Such notes as at creation's birth they sung,
When heaven's broad arch with hallelujahs rung.
Hark—at the strain the enraptured spheres rebound;
And laboring echo lengthens out the sound.
"Lift up your heads, celestial gates!" they sing:
And see—they open to receive the king.
The expecting host their loudest accents raise——
"Eternal God, how glorious are thy ways!
O for some great, some more than angel song,
To speak the praises which to thee belong!
Imagination faints on this great scene;
Thought is too low, and majesty too mean:
So great thy condescension thus to own
Vile man, the meanest prostrate at thy throne
May from his grateful altar ever rise
A glad perfume of incense to the skies."

RICHARD DEVENS

WAS born at Charlestown, Massachusetts, October 23d, 1749. He displayed in early life such a passion for letters as to induce his father to give him a collegiate education.   He was sent to Princeton college in 1764, and received a degree in 1768.   The three following years he spent in teaching schools in New Jersey and New York ; after which he was appointed tutor and professor of mathematics at Princeton college.   He exercised the duties of these offices till 1774, when in consequence of too intense application to his studies, he fell into a state of mental derangement, in which he has continued from his 24th year to the present day.

He wrote a Paraphrase of a part of the Book of Job, published in 1773, and subsequently in 1795 with alterations.

———

WHOSE art, where human foot ne'er access found,
Adorns, in wild diversity, the ground ?
Makes lonely walks to bloom confusedly gay,
And with rich fragrance to perfume the day ?
Through all her lately flourishing increase,
When vegetation droops, canst thou release
From wasting drought the summer ?   Will the rain
Rush at thy bidding, down in floods amain ?
When the black clouds th' impetuous torrent pour,
Canst thou in middle-deluge stop the shower ?
Whose thunder, when fierce flames the welkin wrap,
Stuns nature's ear with the tremendous clap ?
Didst thou the rainbow fix ? its hues impart—
Those hues that distance the exploits of art?
Who generates the hoary frost ? and who
Bespangles morning with his orient dew ?
Hath mist a sire ? canst thou congeal the main ?
From whom descend the pearly streams of rain ?
Dost thou ordain the seasons of the year ?
And govern all the changes of the air ?
Who gives the live-green earth its vernal hue ?
Dost thou the odor of the fields renew ?
Ripen the harvest ? drive the eastern blast?
And lay the opulence of autumn waste ?

Give meads with yellow pomp to cheer the sight?
Or deck in majesty of winter's white?
By whom instructed do the planets know,
Where orient or meridian beams must glow?
Who taught Arcturus, round the northern pole,
His destined circuit with his suns to roll?
Or Mazaroth to wind athwart the night,
In his appointed hours, his length of light?
When th' early Pleiades benignly gleam,
Canst thou in bands of crystal bind the stream?
The beauties of th' enamell'd spring withhold,
And blast the foliage with autumnal cold?
Oppress'd by Sirius, when the fields complain,
His unpropitious influence restrain?
With vernal showers the parching wind allay,
And chase the fervor of th' inclement day?
Or when Orion glares upon thy view,
Make earth to bloom and vegetate anew?

*   *   *   *   *

Breathes the minutest rover of the air,
Held by thy power, or nourish'd by thy care?
Who feeds the ravens, when the croaking brood
Raise hoarsely querulous their plaint to God?
Didst thou the ostrich clothe with plumes so neat,
Who leaves her eggs exposed to heedless feet?
Hatch'd by the genial influence of the sun,
Alone, the unfledged brood are left to run.
In flight she scorns the rider and his steed;
Through eddies of the sand upspurn'd, her speed
Impetuously she skims; than winds more fleet;
She triumphs in th' alertness of her feet.
The peacock view, still exquisitely fair,
When clouds forsake, and when invest the air:
His gems now brightened by a noontide ray;
He proudly waves his feathers to the day.
A strut, majestically slow, assumes,
And glories in the beauty of his plumes.
The hawk, before autumnal tempests rise,
Pursues the summer through the southern skies:
Knows she from bleak inclement months to flee,
And find perpetual August, taught by thee?
Who lifts the eagle on her lofty way,
To rove exulting in a cloudless day?
On high and craggy cliffs she dwells alone;
Their strength remains impregnably her own:

With darting haste, behold her ample size,
Full to th' enjoy'd, though distant victim hies :
Couch'd horrid now she nimbly hovers o'er
Her untorn prey, in raptures of its gore.
Back to her nest she shapes her upward flight,
Her young suck up the blood, with dire delight.

SAMUEL DEXTER,

Born 1761.   Died 1816.

Mr. Dexter's biography belongs to a department distinct
from that of poetry.   As a statesman and lawyer, a man of
profound intellect, and splendid powers of eloquence, he claims
no ordinary notice, yet as he never aimed at distinction in the
character of a poet, we think it unnecessary to introduce any
details of his life here.   The lines which follow are from a
piece written in his youth, and delivered at a public exhibition
at Harvard College.

THE PROGRESS OF SCIENCE.

Let martial souls, whom wild ambition warms,
The trumpet's clangor, and rude din of arms,
Point out the path victorious heroes trod,
The pest of nations, and the scourge of God :
Mine be the task, in humbler verse to trace
The real greatness of the human race.
Though rude and savage Afric's sons we find,
Yet there first science dawn'd upon mankind,
There curb'd the passions in perpetual strife,
And there begat the softer arts of life.
Blest by kind nature with a generous soil,
That yielded herbage, though not dress'd with toil,
In philosophic ease they pass'd their years,
And watch'd the motions of the rolling spheres.
Their modest wants plain nature could redress,
And science gave them rural happiness.
Egypt beheld her twilight's fainter ray,

And form'd fond hopes of her meridian day ;
When, lo ! tyrannic rage usurp'd the whole,
And cramp'd with fetters each high swelling soul.
Disorder'd fancy superstition bred ;
She clapp'd her wings, and thought her foe was dead ;
Yet she but fled, to gain in happy Greece,
What Egypt had denied her—rural peace.
The Grecian souls, form'd of the subtlest kind,
In freedom nurtured, strengthen'd and refined,
Quick catch'd the flame ; it ran from soul to soul,
And like electric fire, inspired the whole.
Here poets sang, and rhetoricians plead,
Here statesmen sat, and patriot worthies bled.
Ah blindness to the future ! headlong toss'd,
They grasp'd the shadow, but the substance lost.
Greece led her armies Troy's high walls to raze ;
The city shook and tottered to its base,
At length it fell—but from its ruins rose
A vagrant band to subjugate their foes.
Imperial Rome, the mistress of the world,
Towns, cities, kingdoms into ruin hurl'd,
And reign'd supreme alone.   Greece felt her force,
Nor stemm'd the torrent in its rapid course ;
All victims fell to its resistless rage,
The rough Barbarian, and the Grecian sage.
Ardent the Romans Grecian science view'd,
Nor scorn'd to learn of those they had subdued ;
They reach'd the same sublimity of thought,
And those, who learned, equall'd those, who taught.
There godlike Homer rear'd his awful head,
Here Virgil sang, and here great Tully plead.
As when some mighty torrent, swoln with rain,
Falls rushing, dashing, till it meets the plain,
O'er craggy rocks bends its resistless force,
From clift to clift loud thundering in its course ;
So did the Athenian patriotic rave,
And taught his country to be nobly brave.
Not so the Roman.   As the ancient Nile
Glides smoothly on within its banks a while :
Slow, gradual, rising, then o'erspreads the plain,
And adds all Egypt to the swelling main ;
So syren Tully onward gently rolls,
Enchants, enraptures, and subdues our souls.
  Behold far north the gathering tempest rise,
Rushing impetuous, as the whirlwind flies ;

Towns, cities, kingdoms from their basis fall,
And one wide ruin overwhelms them all.
Eternal Rome sinks to the common grave,
Bursts, like a bubble dancing on the wave,
Flies off in smoke, and rules the world no more—
Oh! blush then, earthly grandeur! pageant power!
Age after age in one sad tenor ran,
A blank—a chasm in the page of man.
Men drudged their labor'd dulness to rehearse,
To form an anagram, or egg in verse;
They stifled genius with pedantic rules,
And labor'd hard to prove that——they were fools.
No mighty task, though labor'd in so long,
Each line was proof, was demonstration strong;
And men, Oh dulness to perfection brought!
Blush'd to be guilty of a noble thought.
Yet in this gloom did Roger Bacon rise,
Like lightning flashing through the clouded skies,
He burst the barrier of pedantic rules,
And all the labor'd jargon of the schools.
As forked lightnings, with their hasty light,
Serve but to show the horrors of the night;
So he but show'd the dulness of the age,
A stain—a blot upon th' historic page.
As when cold Zembla, wrapt in darkest shade,
First sees the sun erect his radiant head,
In gratitude to the benignant power,
They gather round and Persian-like adore;
He gives them light, not only light, but heat;
Warms with new life, and makes that life complete.
The expanding blossoms smile on every clod,
And laughing valleys own the present God;
Loud hymns of praise the feather'd tribes employ,
And savage beasts howl their tremendous joy.

ST JOHN HONEYWOOD

Wᴀs born at Leicester, in Massachusetts, in 1765. His parents died in his youth, and left him without resources ; but through the generosity of some individuals, he was placed in a Latin school at Lebanon in Connecticut, and from thence transferred to Yale College, where he became a favorite of Dr Stiles, the president, and received much assistance from him. He was distinguished at college for his superior classical attainments. After completing his studies, he went to reside at Schenectady, in New York, where he continued about two years as Preceptor to an Academy. He then removed to Albany and studied law. After being admitted to the bar he fixed his residence at Salem, in the county of Washington, and there passed the remainder of his life. He was made a Master in Chancery, but resigned the office on being appointed Clerk of the county. He was one of the Electors of the President when Adams succeeded Washington. He died September 1st, 1798, in his 34th year.

ON THE PRESIDENT'S FAREWELL ADDRESS.

As the rude Zemblian views with anxious eyes
The sun fast rolling from his wintry skies,
While gathering clouds the shaded vaults deform,
And hollow winds announce the impending storm,
His anguish'd soul recoils with wild affright,
From the dread horrors of the tedious night ;
Such fears alarm'd—such gloom o'ercast each mind,
When Washington his sacred trust resign'd,
And open'd to his much loved country's view,
The instructive page which bid the long adieu.
So erst *Nunnides*, of prophetic tongue,
Chief victor seer, to Judah's listening throng,
Gave his last blessings : So long ages since,
Mild Solon and the stern Laconian prince,
Those boasts of fame, their parting counsels gave,
When worn with toil they sought the peaceful grave.

Columbians! long preserve that peerless page,
Stamp'd with the precepts of your warrior sage ;
In all your archives be the gift enroll'd,
Suspend it to your walls encased with gold ;
Bid schools recite it, let the priestly train
Chant it on festal days, nor deem the task profane :
When round your knees your infant offspring throng,
To join the matin prayer or evening song,
Those rites perform'd, invite them to attend
The farewell counsels of their good *old friend*,
And say, he left you, as his last bequest,
These golden rules to make a nation blest.
O land, thrice blest, if to thy interest wise,
Thy senates learn this precious boon to prize :
While guilty Europe's blood-stain'd empires fall,
While heaven incensed lets loose the infuriate Gaul,
Thy states in phalanx firm, a sacred band,
Safe from the mighty wreck unmoved shall stand.

  * * * * *

Behold the man ! ye crown'd and ermined train,
And learn from him the royal art to reign ;
No guards surround him, or his walks infest,
No cuirass meanly shields his noble breast ;
His the defence which despots ne'er can find,
The love, the prayers, the interest of mankind.
Ask ye what spoils his far famed arms have won,
What cities sack'd, what hapless realms undone ?
Though Monmouth's field supports no vulgar fame,
Though captured York shall long preserve his name,
I quote not these—a nobler scene behold,
Wide cultured fields fast ripening into gold !
There, as his toil the cheerful peasant plies,
New marts are opening, and new spires arise ;
Here commerce smiles, and there *en groupe* are seen,
The useful arts and those of sprightlier mien :
To cheer the whole, the Muses tune their lyre,
And Independence leads the white robed choir.
Trophies like these, to vulgar minds unknown,
Were sought and prized by Washington alone,
From these, with all his country's honors crown'd,
As sage in councils as in arms renown'd ;
All of a piece, and faithful to the last,
Great in this action as in all the past,
He turns—and urges as his last request,
Remote from power his weary head to rest.
 Illustrious man, adieu ! yet ere we part,

Forgive our factions which have wrung thy heart;
Still with indulgent eyes thy country see,
Whose ceaseless prayers ascend the heavens for thee:
Go, 'midst the shades of tranquil Vernon stray,
In vain attempt to shun the piercing ray
Of circumambient glory, till refined
All that could clog to earth the heaven-lent mind,
Then soar triumphant to the blest abodes,
And join those chiefs whom virtue raised to gods.

ON THE CAPTURE OF ROME BY THE FRENCH.

On Rome's devoted head the bolt descends;
The proud oppressor's long dominion ends:
Spirits of martyrs pure! if aught ye know,
In the bright realms of bliss, of things below,
Join the glad hymn of triumph, ye who stood
Firm for the faith, and seal'd it with your blood.
No more shall Rome disturb the world's repose,
Quench'd is her torch, and blood no longer flows;
Crush'd is the fell destroyer in *her* turn,
And the freed world insults her hated urn.
O Truth divine! thou choicest gift of God!
Man's guide and solace in this drear abode!
Plain was thy garb, and lovely was thy mien,
When usher'd by the spotless Nazarene:
From shouting crowds and pageantry he fled,
To the lone desert or the pauper's shed;
There taught his humble followers to despise
All that the proud affect, or worldlings prize;
Truly he gave to man's repentant race,
The peerless treasures of his sovereign grace;
Yet bade no fires descend, no thunders roll,
To force his bounty on the wayward soul.
Join then, celestial Truth, the glad acclaim;
Crush'd is the proud usurper of thy name;
Who first with blood thy snow-white robes distain'd,
And with vain pomp thy holy rites profaned.

MODERN ARGUMENTATION.*

'T WAS at *Commencement* tide, so goes the tale,
At Harvard, Dartmouth, Princeton, King's, or Yale,
A candidate for learning's prime degree
Proposed this question to the faculty :
" This horse will always from a tan-yard fly,
While that, unmoved, a tan-yard passes by ;
Which is the wiser horse, say, learned sirs,
The one that starts, or he that never stirs ? "
The question thus proposed and understood,
Pro more solito, debate ensued.

     *   *   *   *   *   *

The starting advocates this truth premise :
" That of all excellence below the skies,
Man is the standard ; hence, whene'er we find
In beasts or birds strong semblance to mankind,
We count it worth, and are well pleased to see
In instinct aught that apes humanity.
Exempli gratia, who, since time began,
E'er hurt the bird that builds her nest with man ?
If Mrs *Airy,* though involved in debt,
Paid ten bright dollars for a paroquet,
And for a monkey six, the cause we know ;
This talk'd, that flutter'd, like her favorite beau—
Yet the same lady loathed the serpent's form,
And call'd for hartshorn if she saw a worm :
Now to apply this reasoning to our case,
We deem him worthiest of the human race
Who, at the mention of atrocious deeds,
Starts back with horror, and with pity bleeds.
But the vile miscreant, whose supreme delight
Is placed in havoc and in scenes of fight,
Who rudely revels in the house of wo,
We hate, and blush that man can sink so low.
Why starts the steed whene'er a tan-yard's spied,
But that he sees a *brother's* reeking hide ?
Here then, they say, a strong resemblance lies,
Ergo, the horse that starts is *quasi* wise."

     *   *   *   *   *   *

" Ay, but to man and horse this rule extends,
The means must be subservient to the ends.
What 's the chief end of horse ?—his lord to please,
To bear his weight with *safety, speed,* and *ease* ;

---

* Written *extempore,* with a pencil, while the author was riding with a friend,
whose horse started on passing a tan-yard.

'T is not to start, to heave, to weep, to whine,
In notes distracted, *Methodist*, like thine.
Can he be said with *safety* to convey
His lord, who starts and stumbles by the way?
Doth he with *speed* transport his master's weight,
Who stops to start at every tanner's gate?
And, lastly, where 's the ease?—at every breath
The rider fears the horse will prove his death;
'T is plain, the starter deviates from all rule
Of right, and when he deviates, is a fool."
   Thus, sophists, have your arguments been plied,
What now remains but that we should decide?
On *due consideration*, then, we say,
" He is the *wiser* horse who fearless speeds his way."

ROYALL TYLER

WAS born in Boston, and educated at Harvard College.
He received a degree in 1776. When the rebellion of Shays
broke out, he was *aide de camp* to General Lincoln who com-
manded the troops that marched against him. On this occasion he was charged with a special mission to the government
of Vermont. About 1790 he removed his residence to that
state, and soon distinguished himself in his profession of law.
He was an assistant Judge to the Supreme Court for six years
and chief Judge of the same six years more. He died at
Brattleboro', Vermont, August 16th, 1825.

Judge Tyler was a dramatic writer of respectable talent.
The first piece which he composed for the stage, was "The
Contrast"—this was produced soon after the revolution, and
played at New York and Philadelphia, with considerable applause. It was also represented in Boston at the Board Al-
ley Theatre. In 1796, he wrote a farce called "The Georgia
Spec, or Land in the Moon," in which he turned to ridicule
the rage then prevalent in New England for speculating in
Georgia lands of the Yazoo purchase. This was performed
repeatedly at the Haymarket Theatre. He wrote besides,
other dramatic pieces which have not been made public. His
writings of a light and sportive character in prose and verse

are very numerous. The greater part of them first appeared in the Farmer's Museum, a paper of high celebrity published at Walpole in New Hampshire. Tyler was the associate of Dennie, its editor, and contributed many of the best articles in that journal. He was also the author of the Algerine Captive, a novel of great merit and interest, which passed with some readers in England for a story of real life. A critic of that country, as we are informed, undertook to show that it contained some errors in point of fact. In addition to these works he published a collection of legal cases in two volumes 8vo, entitled Vermont Reports.

His poems are lively and entertaining, but we are not acquainted with any one among, them of magnitude. They are short unstudied sallies of a sprightly fancy.

COUNTRY ODE FOR THE FOURTH OF JULY.

SQUEAK the fife, and beat the drum,
Independence day is come!!
Let the roasting pig be bled,
Quick twist off the cockerel's head,
Quickly rub the pewter platter,
Heap the nutcakes, fried in butter.
Set the cups, and beaker glass,
The pumpkin and the apple sauce,
Send the keg to shop for brandy;
Maple sugar we have handy.
Independent, staggering Dick,
A noggin mix of swingeing thick,
Sal, put on your russet skirt,
Jotham, get your *boughten* shirt,
Today we dance to tiddle diddle.
—Here comes Sambo with his fiddle;
Sambo, take a dram of whiskey,
And play up Yankee doodle frisky.
Moll, come leave your witched tricks,
And let us have a reel of six.
Father and mother shall make two;
Sal, Moll and I stand all a-row,
Sambo, play and dance with quality;
This is the day of blest equality.

Father and *mother* are but *men*,
And Sambo—is a citizen.
Come foot it, Sal—Moll, figure in,
And, mother you dance up to him;
Now saw as fast as e'er you can do,
And father, you cross o'er to Sambo.
—Thus we dance, and thus we play,
On glorious Independent day.—
Rub more rosin on your bow,
And let us have another go.
Zounds! as sure as eggs and bacon,
Here 's ensign Sneak, and uncle Deacon,
Aunt Thiah, and their Bets behind her,
On blundering mare, than beetle blinder.
And there 's the 'Squire too, with his lady—
Sal, hold the beast, I 'll take the baby.
Moll, bring the 'Squire our great arm chair,
Good folks, we 're glad to see you here.
Jotham, get the great case bottle,
Your teeth can pull its corn-cob stopple.
Ensign,—Deacon, never mind;
'Squire, drink until you 're blind.
Thus we drink and dance away,
This glorious Independent day!

MY MISTRESSES.

LET Cowley soft in amorous verse
The rovings of his love rehearse,
   With passion most unruly,
Boast how he woo'd sweet Amoret,
The sobbing Jane, and sprightly Bet,
The lily fair and smart brunette,
   In sweet succession truly.

But list, ye lovers, and you 'll swear,
I roved with him beyond compare,
   And was far more unlucky.
For never yet in Yankee coast
Were found such girls, who so could boast,
An honest lover's heart to roast,
   From Casco to Kentucky.

When first the girls nicknamed me beau,
And I was all for dress and show,

I set me out a courting.
A romping miss, with heedless art,
First caught, then almost broke, my heart.
Miss Conduct named ; we soon did part,
    I did not like such sporting.

The next coquette, who raised a flame,
Was far more grave, and somewhat lame,
    She in my heart did rankle.
She conquer'd, with a sudden glance :
The spiteful slut was call'd Miss Chance ;
I took the gipsy out to dance ;
    She almost broke my ankle.

A thoughtless girl, just in her teens,
Was the next fair, whom love it seems
    Had made me prize most highly.
I thought to court a lovely mate,
But, how it made my heart to ache ;
It was that jade, the vile Miss Take ;
    In troth, love did it slyly.

And last Miss Fortune, whimpering came,
Cured me of love's tormenting flame,
    And all my beau pretences.
In widow's weeds, the prude appears ;
See now—she drowns me with her tears,
With bony fist, now slaps my ears,
    And brings me to my senses.

ADDRESS TO DELLA CRUSCA.

O Thou, who, with thy blue cerulean blaze,
Hast circled Europe's brow with love-lorn praise ;
Whose magic pen its gelid lightning throws,
Is now a sunbeam, now a fragrant rose.
Child of the dappled spring, whose green delight,
Drinks, with her snow-drop lips, the dewy light.
Son of the summer's bland, prolific rays,
Who sheds her loftiest treasures in thy lays ;
Who swells her golden lips to trump thy name,
Which sinks to whispers, at thy azure fame.
Brown autumn nursed thee with her dulcet dews,
And lurid winter rock'd thy cradled muse.
Seasons and suns, and spangled systems roll,
Like atoms vast, beneath thy cloud-capt soul.

Time wings its panting flight in hurried chase,
But sinks in dew-dropt languor in the immortal race.
O thou, whose soul the nooky Britain scorns;
Whose white cliffs tremble, when thy genius storms.
The sallow Afric, with her curled domains,
And purpled Asia with her muslin plains,
And surgy Europe—vain—thy soul confined,
Which fills all space—and e'en Matilda's mind !
Anna's capacious mind, which all agree,
Contain'd a wilderness of words in thee.
More happy thou than Macedonia's lord,
Who wept for worlds to feed his famish'd sword,
Fatigued by attic conquest of the old,
Fortune to thee a novel world unfolds.
Come, mighty conqueror, thy foes disperse;
Let loose thy epithets, those dogs of verse;
Draw forth thy gorgeous sword of damask'd rhyme,
And ride triumphant through Columbia's clime,
Till sober letter'd sense shall dying smile,
Before the mighty magic of thy style.
What tawny tribes in dusky forest wait,
To grace th' ovation of thy victor state.
What ochred chiefs, vermilion'd by thy sword,
Mark'd by thy epithets, shall own thee lord.
The punic Creek, and nigrified Choctaw,
The high boned Wabash, and bland hanging Maw;
Great little Billy, Piamingo brave,
With pity's dew-drops wet M'Gilvery's grave.
What sonorous streams meander through thy lays,
What lakes shall bless thy rich bequest of praise,
Rough Hockhocking, and gentle Chicago,
The twin Miamis—placid Scioto.
How will Ohio roll his lordly stream,
What blue mists dance upon the liquid scene,
Gods! how sublime shall Della Crusca rage,
When all Niagara cataracts thy page.
What arts, what arms, unknown to thee belong?
What ruddy scalps shall deck thy sanguined song?
What fumy cal'mets scent the ambient air,
What love-lorn war-whoops capitals declare.
Cerulean tomahawks shall grace each line,
And blue-eyed wampum glisten through thy rhyme.
Rise, Della Crusca, prince of bards sublime,
And pour on us whole cataracts of rhyme.
Son of the sun, arise, whose brightest rays,
All merge to tapers in thy ignite blaze.

Like some colossus, stride the Atlantic o'er,
A leg of genius place on either shore,
Extend thy red right arm to either world ;
Be the proud standard of thy style unfurl'd ;
Proclaim thy sounding page, from shore to shore,
And swear that sense in verse, shall be no more.

CHOICE OF A WIFE.

FLUTTERING lovers, giddy boys,
Sighing soft for Hymen's joys,
Would you shun the tricking arts,
Beauty's traps for youthful hearts,
Would you treasure in a wife,
Riches, which shall last through life ;
Would you in your choice be nice,
Hear Minerva's sage advice.
Be not caught with shape, nor air,
Coral lips, nor flowing hair ;
Shape and jaunty air may cheat,
Coral lips may speak deceit.
Girls unmask'd would you descry,
Fix your fancy on the *eye* ;
Nature there has truth design'd,
'T is the eye, that speaks the mind.
Shun the proud, disdainful eye,
Frowning fancied dignity,
Shun the eye with vacant glare ;
Cold indifference winters there.
Shun the eager orb of fire,
Gloating with impure desire ;
Shun the wily eye of prude,
Looking coy to be pursued.
From the jilting eye refrain,
Glancing love, and now disdain.
Fly the fierce, satiric eye,
Shooting keen severity ;
For nature thus, her truth design'd
And made the eye proclaim the mind.

ON A RUINED HOUSE IN A ROMANTIC COUNTRY.

AND this reft house is that the which he built,
Lamented Jack ! and here his malt he piled,

Cautious in vain! these rats that squeak so wild,
Squeak, not unconscious of their father's guilt.
Did ye not see her gleaming through the glade!
Belike, 't was she, the maiden all forlorn.
What though she milk no cow with crumpled horn,
Yet, aye, she haunts the dale where erst she stray'd ;
And, aye, beside her stalks her amorous knight!
Still on his thighs their wonted brogues are worn,
And through those brogues, still tatter'd and betorn,
His hindward charms gleam an unearthly white ;
As when through broken clouds at night's high noon
Peeps in fair fragments forth the full orb'd harvest moon!

––––

THE TOWN ECLOGUE.

SEE, see, bluff winter quits the town,
And congees with her surly frown :
In her train the beldame carries
All sweet fashion's gay vagaries ;
Her cork-soled shoes, and bonnet rough,
Her camel shawl, and bearskin muff,
Her beaver gloves and fleecy dress,
Red comforter and silk pelisse ;
And what is worse, the beldame 's stole
Of all our bliss the very soul,
Has stole the concert, play, and ball ;
And what is still the worst of all,
Has Cooper stole, and with him fled,
And left us ****** in his stead.
See the town-bred Spring advancing,
Friend to grass, and foe to dancing!
See adorn her lovely tresses
Cabbage sprouts and water cresses!
While for plume, the hoyden lass
Sports a bunch of sparrow-grass.
See, beneath her market wreath,
She smiles her dandelion teeth ;
Whilst with voice as sweet, or sweeter,
Than Billings' strains or Sternhold's metre,
With voice which music cannot ape her,
Like nightingale or Mrs Draper,
She cheers her pannier'd mare and screams
Her strawberries and fresh string-beans :
Or, whilst her one wheel'd chariot rattles,
She bawls her epicurean chattels ;

Her shelly stores from old Cape Cod,
Her mackerel, lobsters, and tom-cod :
Or, in her awning stalls displays,
Her tempting lures to hungry gaze ;
Her luscious stores of fish, fowl, flesh,
Her salmon smoked and salmon fresh ;
Cod's tongues and sounds, and smelt, and eel,
Calves' feet and head, and pluck, and veal—
Far richer flowers than rural spring
From all her scented hoards can bring.
For can the rose's gayest dye
With salmon soused in beauty vie ?
Or can the rose's sweetest smell
Vie with a fresh caught mackerel ?
Her rustic coz let others sing,
But let me taste the town-bred Spring.
Close by her side see ****** smile,
That critic in dumb fish and oil,
Who thinks there 's heaven in good dinners,
And hell is fill'd with hungry sinners.
Close by her side the glutton stands,
And takes his snuff, and rubs his hands,
With critic nose assays her trash,
And licks his lips and pays the cash.

RICHARD ALSOP.

Richard Alsop was born at Middletown, in Connecticut,
in 1759, and resided in that place during the most of his life.
He was bred to the mercantile profession, but devoted himself
occasionally to letters, from a native taste for the pursuit. His
object in writing appears to have been amusement rather than
distinction, as few of his productions were given to the world
under his name. His works are numerous, and embrace a
great variety of subjects. He published various translations
from the French and Italian ; among others, a portion of Ber-
ni's Orlando Inamorato, which was printed in 1808, under the
title of The Fairy of the Enchanted Lake. He left a large
number of unpublished works behind him, one of them a poem

of considerable length, called The Charms of Fancy. He died at Flatbush, on Long Island, August 20th, 1815.

Mr Alsop made too little effort for literary distinction to acquire much credit or notoriety as a writer beyond the circle of his own acquaintance. His talents have not been displayed to the world at large, nor perhaps sufficiently appreciated by the few who were admitted to his intimacy. His powers were certainly above the ordinary level of our native authors, and had they been prompted to exercise by a strong endeavor to establish a name, rather than an occasional desire for recreation with the pen, would have placed him in a conspicuous rank among his countrymen. Many of his pieces show him to have been possessed of a luxuriant fancy and a happy facility of poetical thought and expression. Others exhibit a talent at light raillery and the treatment of humorous subjects, which we do not often see equalled. We are disposed to believe that the publication, at the present day, of his best performances would be alike honorable to his memory and creditable to the country.

He was one of the contributors to the Echo, a work, which on several accounts is deserving of particular notice. This is a medley of burlesque and satirical pieces, designed originally to expose the pedantry and affectation of newspaper writers; and is executed by turning into rhyme such paragraphs in the public journals as presented a proper scope for ridicule, and setting their extravagance of style or sentiment in a ludicrous view, by arraying them in a mock-heroical dress. The plan of the work owed its origin to an accidental and momentary freak of literary sportiveness, in this manner.—In the year 1791, some young gentlemen, consisting of Alsop, Theodore Dwight, Dr Cogswell, and a few others, were casually met one evening, at the office of William Brown, in Hartford. The editor of the Connecticut Courant had just taken his papers from the post office, and as he passed by, threw a number of them in for the amusement of the party. An inflated description of a thunder-storm at Boston caught the eye of one of the gentlemen, who read it aloud for the diversion of his compan-

ions. This turned the conversation upon the absurd and con-
ceited productions with which most of the newspapers of that
day were filled ; and the notion was suggested of ridiculing
this bad taste by versifying some extravagant piece of that
sort. The Boston thunder-storm was fixed upon ; each contributed a few lines, and a considerable part of the work was
soon executed. Alsop took the writing home, gave it a few
finishing strokes, and sent it to the editor of the Hartford paper.
The performance was happily executed. The solemn bombast
and bathos of the gazetteer's eloquence were dressed out in a
figure of the most ludicrous cut, and the public were so much
entertained as to induce the authors to execute other pieces in
the same strain. Hopkins, Trumbull, and others, soon united
in the business, the work gained an extensive notice, and the
appellation of the " Hartford wits " became a widely known
and honorable designation.

The novelty of the plan, and the high degree of talent which
the writers of the work brought to the undertaking, were singularly effectual in accomplishing the designed object. The
Echo obtained great influence. No scheme could have been
devised better fitted for casting derision upon the wordy and
bombastic nonsense so common in the newspaper effusions of
that period. The plan of the work was soon extended. From
ridiculing affectations of style, the writers passed to a wider
field for the exercise of their satiric weapons, and levelled their
shafts against the political doctrines of which they were oppo-
nents, for party dissensions had begun to wax warm. The
Echo soon became principally occupied in responding traves-
ties of public speeches, and writings of a political cast. It
took sides with the Federal party, and inveighed zealously
against the principles of the French revolution, and Mr Jefferson's administration. The satire which it dealt in, is not
without severity, but is in general free from that coarse, illib-
eral abuse, and bitterness of animosity, which characterize
most of the party writings of the same stamp. The humorous part is very happy in its way, and the general execution of
the work spirited and easy. Its defects are a want of harmo-

ny and correctness occasionally in the versification ; faults however, which the critic will be less disposed to quarrel with, upon the reflection that the main object of the work left out of sight and significance these minor perfections. The wit and sarcasm adapted for popular effect, were relied upon by the writers, rather than the grace and euphony of the numbers, if indeed the harsh and rugged style of versification in which the Echo is written, were not purposely selected as the most appropriate to its character and purpose.

The politics of the Echo, we do not feel called upon to criticise. We speak of it in its literary character alone, without the intention of having our remarks construed into approbation or disapprobation of the doctrines which it was the principal design of that performance to uphold. The originality of plan which it exhibits, and the reputation and ability of its authors, call it into notice as the most remarkable production of the poetical kind which our country has seen. The several pieces of which it consists were collected into a volume, and illustrated with some excellent designs by Tisdale. The volume was published in connexion with some other poems by the same authors, in 1807.

Alsop wrote a greater portion of the Echo than any other contributor, though it is impossible to assign the separate authorship of more than one or two pieces. Dr Hopkins, who excelled his associates in bold and inventive genius, furnished many original thoughts to Alsop, and devolved upon him, on account of his readiness at versification, the task of clothing them in numbers. The poem of Guillotina and the first of the new year's verses, which accompany the Echo, were principally the work of Hopkins. The Political Green-House in the same volume, was written for the most part by Alsop. These display much of the characteristic talent of their authors, but are too deeply involved in matters which have lost their interest, to be read with satisfaction at the present day.　.

ECHO NO. I. *

On Tuesday last great Sol, with piercing eye,
Pursued his journey through the vaulted sky,
And in his car effulgent roll'd his way
Four hours beyond the burning zone of day ;
When lo ! a cloud, o'ershadowing all the plain,
From countless pores perspired a *liquid* rain,
While from its cracks the lightnings made a peep,
And chit-chat thunders rock'd our fears asleep.
But soon the vapory fog dispersed in air,
And left the azure blue-eyed concave bare :
Even the last drop of hope, which dripping skies
Gave for a moment to our straining eyes,

* In order that this piece may be understood, the newspaper paragraph which furnished the occasion for it is here subjoined.

" On Tuesday last, about four o'clock, P. M. came on a smart shower of rain, attended with lightning and thunder, no ways remarkable. The clouds soon dissipated, and the appearance of the azure vault, left trivial hopes of further needful supplies from the *uncorked bottles of heaven.* In a few moments the horizon was again overshadowed, and an almost impenetrable gloom mantled the face of the skies. The wind frequently shifting from one point to another, wafted the clouds in various directions, until at last they united in one common centre and shrouded the visible globe in thick darkness. The attendant lightning, with the accompanying thunder, brought forth from the treasures that embattled elements to awful conflict, were extremely vivid, and amazing loud. Those buildings that were defended by electric rods, appeared to be wrapped in sheets of livid flame, and a flood of the pure fire rolled its burning torrents down them with alarming violence. The majestic roar of disploding thunders, now bursting with a sudden crash, and now wasting the rumbling Echo of their sounds in other lands, added indescribable grandeur to the sublime scene. The windows of the upper regions appeared as thrown wide open, and the trembling cataract poured impetuous down. More salutary showers, and more needed, have not been experienced this summer. Several previous weeks had exhibited a melancholy sight : the verdure of fields was nearly destroyed ; and the patient husbandman almost experienced despair. Two beautiful rainbows, the one existing in its native glories, and the other a splendid reflection of primitive colors, closed the magnificent picture, and presented to the contemplative mind, the angel of mercy, clothed with the brilliance of this irradiated arch, and dispensing felicity to assembled worlds. It is not unnatural to expect that the thunder storm would be attended with some damage. We hear a barn belonging to Mr Wythe of Cambridge caught fire from the lightning, which entirely consumed the same, together with several tons of hay, &c. "

Like *Boston rum*, from heaven's *junk bottles* broke,
Lost all the corks, and vanish'd into smoke.
    But swift from worlds unknown, a fresh supply
Of vapor dimm'd the great horizon's eye ;
The crazy clouds, by shifting zephyrs driven,
Wafted their courses through the high-arch'd heaven,
Till piled aloft in one stupendous heap,
The seen and unseen worlds grew dark, and nature 'gan to
      weep:
Attendant lightnings stream'd their tails afar,
And social thunders waked ethereal war,
From dark deep pockets brought their treasured store,
Embattled elements increased the roar—
Red crinkling fires expended all their force,
And tumbling rumblings steer'd their headlong course.
Those guarded frames by thunder poles secured,
Though wrapp'd in sheets of flame, those sheets endured ;
O'er their broad roofs the fiery torrents roll'd,
And every shingle seem'd of burning gold.
Majestic thunders, with disploding roar,
And sudden crashing, bounced along the shore,
Till, lost in other lands, the whispering sound
Fled from our ears and fainted on the ground.
Rain's house on high its window sashes oped,
And out the cataract impetuous hopp'd,
While the grand scene by far more grand appear'd,
With lightnings never seen and thunders never heard.
    More salutary showers have not been known,
To wash dame Nature's dirty homespun gown—
For several weeks the good old Joan's been seen,
With filth bespatter'd like a lazy quean.
The husbandman fast travelling to despair,
Laid down his hoe and took his rocking chair:
While his fat wife, the well and cistern dried,
Her mop grown useless, hung it up and cried.
    Two rainbows fair that Iris brought along,
Pick'd from the choicest of her color'd throng ;
The first born deck'd in pristine hues of light,
In all its native glories glowing bright,
The next adorn'd with less refulgent rays,
But borrowing lustre from its brother's blaze ;
Shone a bright reflex of those colors gay
That deck'd with light creation's primal day,
When infant Nature lisp'd her earliest notes,
And *younker Adam* crept in petticoats :
And to the people to reflection given,

" The sons of Boston, the elect of heaven,"
Presented Mercy's angel smiling fair,
Irradiate splendors frizzled in his hair,
Uncorking demi-johns, and pouring down
Heaven's liquid blessings on the gaping town.

     N. B. At Cambridge town, the selfsame day,
A barn was burnt well fill'd with hay.
Some say the lightning turn'd it red,
Some say the thunder struck it dead,
Some say it made the cattle stare,
And some it kill'd an aged mare;
But we expect the truth to learn,
From Mr Wythe, who own'd the barn.

VERSES TO THE SHEARWATER—ON THE MORNING AFTER
A STORM AT SEA. *

     WHENCE with morn's first blush of light
       Com'st thou thus to greet mine eye,
     Whilst the furious storm of night
       Hovers yet around the sky ?

     On the fiery tossing wave,
       Calmly cradled dost thou sleep,
     When the midnight tempests rave,
       Lonely wanderer of the deep ?

     Or from some rude isle afar,
       Castled 'mid the roaring waste,
     With the beams of morning's star,
       On lightning pinion dost thou haste ?

     In thy mottled plumage drest,
       Light thou skimm'st the ocean o'er,
     Sporting round the breaker's crest
       Exulting in the tempest's roar.

     O'er the vast-rolling watry way
       While our trembling bark is borne,
     And joyful peers the lamp of day,
       Lighting up the brow of morn;

     * This piece, we believe, has never before been printed.

As through yon cloud its struggling beams
   Around a partial lustre shed,
And mark at fits with golden gleams
   The mountain billow's surging head ;

Whilst the long lines of foamy white,
   At distance o'er the expanse so blue,
As domes and castles spiring bright,
   Commingling, rise on fancy's view——

From wave to wave swift skimming light,
   Now near, and now at distance found,
Thy airy form, in ceaseless flight,
   Cheers the lone dreariness around.

Through the vessel's storm-rent sides,
   When the rushing billows rave ;
And with fierce gigantic strides,
   Death terrific walks the wave,

Still on hovering pinion near,
   Thou pursuest thy sportive way ;
Still uncheck'd by aught of fear,
   Calmly seek'st thy finny prey.

Far from earth's remotest trace,
   What impels thee thus to roam ?
What hast thou to mark the place
   When thou seek'st thy distant home ?

Without star or magnet's aid,
   Thou thy faithful course dost keep ;
Sportive still, still undismay'd,
   Lonely wanderer of the deep !

THE INCANTATION OF ULFO.

FROM THE CONQUEST OF SCANDINAVIA.

FORTH from his camp the dire enchanter stray'd,
'Mid the weird horrors of the midnight shade,
Till a lone dell his wandering footsteps found,
Fenced with rough cliffs, with mournful cypress crown'd ;

There stayed his course : with stern, terrific look,
Thrice waved on high, his magic wand he shook ;
And thrice he raised the wild funereal yell,
That calls the spirits from th' abyss of hell.
When, shrilly answering to the yell afar,
Borne on the winds, three female forms appear ;
Dire as the hag who, 'mid the dreams of night,
Pursues the fever'd hectic's trembling flight.
With gestures strange, approach the haggard band,
And nigh the wizard take their silent stand.
Near, in a rock, adown whose rugged side
The lonely waters of the desert glide,
O'ergrown with brambles, oped an ample cave,
-Drear as the gloomy mansions of the grave.
Within, the screech-owl made her mournful home,
And birds obscene that hover round the tomb ;
Dark, from the moss-grown top, together clung,
Ill-omen'd bats, in torpid clusters, hung ;
And o'er the bottom, with dank leaves bestrow'd,
Crept the black adder, and the bloated toad.
Thither the magic throng repair'd, to form
Their spells obscure, and weave the unhallow'd charm.
Muttering dire words, thrice strode the wizard round ;
Thrice, with his potent wand, he smote the ground ;
Deep groans ensued ; on wings of circling flame,
Slow-rising from beneath, a cauldron came ;
Blue gleam'd the fires amid the shades of night,
And o'er the cavern shot a livid light.
  Now oped a horrid scene : all black with blood,
Th' infernal band, prepared for slaughter, stood.
Two beauteous babes, by griffons borne away,
While lock'd in sleep the hapless mothers lay,
Whose smiles the frozen breast to love might warm,
And e'en the unsparing wolf to pity charm,
The hags unveil'd ; and sportive as they play'd,
Deep in their hearts embrued the murderous blade ;
Their dying pangs with smile malignant view'd,
And life's last ebbings in the sanguine flood.
Now, mix'd with various herbs of magic power,
In the dark cauldron glows the purple gore :
The night-shade dire, whose baleful branches wave,
In glooms of horror o'er the murderer's grave ;
The manchineel, alluring to the eye,
Where, veil'd in beauty, deadliest poisons lie ;
The far-famed Indian herb, of power to move
The foes of nature to unite in love,

The serpent race to infant mildness charm,
And the fierce tiger of his rage disarm,—
Known to the tribes that range the trackless wood
Where mad Antonio heaves the headlong flood;—
The monster plant that blasts Tartaria's heath;
And Upas fatal as the stroke of death:
Boil'd the black mass, the associate fiends advance,
And round the cauldron form the magic dance.
Three times around, in mystic maze they trod,
With hideous gesture, and terrific nod;
While Runic rhymes, and words that freeze the soul,
From their blue lips, in tones of horror, roll.
The wizard raised his voice, the cavern round,
Wild shuddering, trembled at the fearful sound;
In mute attention stood the haggard throng,
As thus he woke th' incantatory song.

> From the dreary realms below,
>   From the dark domains of fear,
> From the ghastly seats of wo,
>   Hear! tremendous Hela, hear!

> Dreadful Power! whose awful form
> Blackens in the midnight storm;
> Glares athwart the lurid skies,
> While the sheeted lightning flies;
> When the thunder awful roars;
> When the earthquake rocks the shores;
> Mounted on the wings of air,
> Thou rulest the elemental war.
> When famine brings her sickly train;
> When battle strews the carnaged plain;
> When pestilence her venom'd wand
> Waves o'er the desolated land;
> Rush the ocean's whelming tides
> O'er the foundering vessel's sides;
> Then ascends thy voice on high;
> Then is heard thy funeral cry;
> Then, in horror, dost thou rise
> On th' expiring wretch's eyes.

> From the dreary realms below,
>   From the dark domains of fear,
> From the ghastly seats of wo,
>   Hear! tremendous Hela, hear!

Goddess! whose terrific sway
Nastrond's realms of guilt obey;
Where, amid impervious gloom,
Sullen frowns the serpent dome;
Roll'd beneath th' envenom'd tide,
Where the sons of sorrow 'bide;
Thee, the mighty demon host;
Thee, the giants of the frost;
Thee, the genii tribes adore;
Fenris owns thy sovereign power:
And th' imperial prince of fire,
Surtur, trembles at thine ire.
Thine, the victor's pride to mar;
Thine, to turn the scale of war;
Chiefs and princes at thy call,
From their spheres of glory fall;
Empires are in ruin hurl'd;
Desolation blasts the world.

From the dreary realms below,
    From the dark domains of fear,
From the ghastly seats of wo,
    Hear! tremendous Hela, hear!

Queen of terror, queen of death!
Thee, we summon from beneath.
From the deep infernal shade;
From the mansion of the dead;
Niflheim's black, funereal dome;
Hither rise, and hither come!
By the potent Runic rhyme,
Awful, mystic, and sublime;
By the streams that roar below;
By the sable fount of wo;
By the burning gulf of pain,
Muspel's home, and Surtur's reign;
By the day when, o'er the world,
Wild confusion shall be hurl'd,
Rymer mount his fiery car,
Giants, genii, rush to war,
To vengeance move the prince of fire,
And heaven, and earth, in flames expire

From the dreary realms below,
　　From the dark domains of fear,
From the ghastly seats of wo,
　　Hear! tremendous Hela! hear.

He ceased—the flames withdrew their magic light,
And, clothed in deeper horrors, frown'd the night.
At once, an awful stillness paused around,
Hush'd were the winds, and mute the tempest's sound,
One deep, portentous calm o'er nature spread,
Nor e'en the aspen's restless foliage play'd;—
Such the dire calm that glooms Caribean shores,
Ere, roused to rage, the fell tornado roars:—
Not long, for lo! from central earth released,
Shrill through the cavern sigh'd a hollow blast;
Wild wails of wo, with shrieks of terror join'd,
In deathful murmurs groan along the wind;
Peal following peal, hoarse bursts the thunder round,
Redoubling echoes swell the dreadful sound;
Flash the blue lightnings in continual blaze;
One sheet of fire the kindling gloom displays;
And o'er the vault, with pale, sulphureous ray,
Pour all the horrors of infernal day.
Now heaved the vale around, the cavern'd rock,
The earth, deep trembling, to its centre shook,
Wide yawn'd the rending floor, and gave to sight
A chasm tremendous as the gates of night.
Slow from the gulf, 'mid lightnings faintly seen,
Rose the dread form of death's terrific queen;
Of wolfish aspect, and with eyes of flame,
Black Jarnvid's witch, her fell attendant, came;
Than whom, no monster roams the dark abodes,
More fear'd by friends, more hated by the gods.
　More frightful, more deform'd, than fancy's power
Pourtrays the demon of the midnight hour,
In hideous majesty, of various hue,
Part sallow pale, and part a livid blue,
A form gigantic, awful Hela frown'd:
Her towering head with sable serpents crown'd;
Around her waist, in many a volume roll'd,
A crimson adder wreathed his poisonous fold;
And o'er her face, beyond description dread,
A sulphury mist its shrouding mantle spread.
Her voice, the groan of war, the shriek of wo,
When sinks the city whelm'd in gulfs below,

In tones of thunder, o'er the cavern broke,
And nature shudder'd as the demon spoke.
   "Presumptuous mortal! that, with mystic strain,
Dost summon Hela from the realms of pain,
What cause thus prompts thee rashly to invade
The deep repose of death's eternal shade?
What, from the abodes of never-ending night,
Calls me, reluctant, to the climes of light?"
   "Empress supreme! whose wide-extended sway
All nature owns, and earth and hell obey;
The solemn call no trivial wish inspires;
No common cause thy potent aid requires;
The dooms of empires on the issue wait,
And doubtful tremble in the scale of fate.
The glow of morn, on yon extended heath,
Will light the nations to the strife of death.
There Saracinia's sons their force unite
With Scandia's monarch, Woldomir, in fight;
By strength combined, proud Odin to o'erwhelm,
The fierce invader of the Scandian realm;
By Woden favor'd with peculiar grace;
Friend of the gods, and odious to thy race.
Then, in th' impending fight, thy succor lend,
And o'er our host thy arm of strength extend;
The hostile bands, protected by thy foes,
With dangers circle, and with ruin close;
With wild dismay their shrinking ranks pervade;
Whelm their pale numbers in th' eternal shade;
And wing, with certain aim, the missive dart,
Or point the falchion, to the leader's heart."
   Thus Ulfo spoke—and Hela thus return'd.
"Know, while in primal night creation mourn'd,
The eternal cause, the great, all-ruling mind,
The various term of human life assign'd;
Irrevocably firm, the fix'd intent
No power can vary, and no chance prevent.
Mark'd by the fates, for years of bloody strife,
Rolls the long flood of Odin's varied life;
Nor is it ours the stern decree to thwart
By open violence, or by covert art.
Yet still the power is left us to annoy,
Whom rigid heaven denies us to destroy;
And, though of life secure, the hostile chief,
The wretched victim of severest grief,
Shall mourn his arms disgraced, on yonder plain,
His laurels blasted, and his heroes slain."

She ceased ;—in thunder vanishing from view,
The fiends, the cauldron, and the hags withdrew.
Back to the camp the enchanter sped his way,
Ere, o'er the east, arose the first faint glimpse of day.

THEODORE DWIGHT.

Mr Dwight is a native of Northampton in Massachusetts, and brother of the late President Dwight. He received a degree at Yale College in 1798, and followed the profession of law in the early part of his life at Hartford, Connecticut. He was appointed to several public offices, among others, that of Representative in Congress from Connecticut. About the year 1810, he established the Connecticut Mirror at Hartford, and sometime afterward removed to Albany, where he had the editorial charge of the Daily Advertiser of that place. He has since established a new paper under the same title, in New York. These journals he has conducted with distinguished ability. Mr Dwight is now principally known as a statesman and political writer, but in early life he gave himself occasionally to poetry, and was one of the most noted among the "Hartford wits." His New Year's rhymes, written under the strong excitement of party feeling both before and during the late war, must be well recollected. In a species of dignified Hudibrastic verse he has had few equals, although from the transient interest of the topics which the most of his writings embrace, his poetical talents have not been exerted in a way to obtain a lasting reputation in this department of literature. He has the credit of having furnished some of the best pieces in the Echo.

AFRICAN DISTRESS.

"Help! oh, help! thou God of Christians!
    Save a mother from despair!
Cruel white men steal my children!
    God of Christians, hear my prayer!

"From my arms by force they're rended,
  Sailors drag them to the sea;
Yonder ship, at anchor riding,
  Swift will carry them away.

"There my son lies, stripp'd, and bleeding;
  Fast, with thongs, his hands are bound.
See, the tyrants, how they scourge him!
  See his sides a reeking wound

"See his little sister by him;
  Quaking, trembling, how she lies!
Drops of blood her face besprinkle;
  Tears of anguish fill her eyes.

"Now they tear her brother from her;
  Down, below the deck, he's thrown;
Stiff with beating, through fear silent,
  Save a single, death-like, groan."

Hear the little creature begging'—
  "Take me, white men, for your own!
Spare, oh, spare my darling brother!
  He's my mother's only son.

"See, upon the shore she's raving:
  Down she falls upon the sands:
Now, she tears her flesh with madness;
  Now, she prays with lifted hands.

"I am young, and strong, and hardy;
  He's a sick, and feeble boy;
Take me, whip me, chain me, starve me,
  All my life I'll toil with joy.

"Christians! who's the God you worship?
  Is he cruel, fierce, or good?
Does he take delight in mercy?
  Or in spilling human blood?

"Ah, my poor distracted mother!
  Hear her scream upon the shore."—
Down the savage captain struck her,
  Lifeless on the vessel's floor.

Up his sails he quickly hoisted,
  To the ocean bent his way;
Headlong plunged the raving mother,
  From a high rock, in the sea.

———

ECHO NO. 14.*

" Our song resounds a thunder storm once more—
" But Norwich' far transcends Bostonia's roar."

On Monday last, the sun with scorching ray,
Pour'd down on Norwich rocks a red hot day,
Along the streets no verdant weeds appear'd,
No blades of grass the geese and goslings cheer'd,
No brook, nor pond, mud-puddle, slough, nor pool,
Where ducks might paddle, and where pigs might cool :
But all was so completely burnt and bare,
That had old Babel's king been pastured there,
On such short feed, (I do not mean to joke)
He never wo: ld have staid without a poke.
At length, slo rising up north-western skies,
Some little clouds about Elijah's size,
Told us in hints and indications plain,
That they were sensible we wanted rain.
At first the teazing showers our patience tried,
By sailing northerly at distance wide,
Till three o'clock—when lo! a wondrous cloud,

*From the *Norwich Packet,* of June* 20, 1793.

" Monday the 27th inst. being very warm, there appeared in the N. W. several
small clouds, which indicated what the earth greatly stood in need of, viz. showers
of rain, which afterwards collected and directed their course to the northward of
this place, till about three o'clock, when a cloud clothed in sable black gathered in
the west, arose and passed in a direct line over this city : wafted with uncommon
violence by the wind fluctuating in various directions, presented to the human
mind a spectacle alarming to behold : it was highly charged with electric fluid,
and almost incessantly burst in streams of crimson fire, which streaked the heavens
with astonishing lustre ; several of which, from the near connexion between the
blaze and report, must have reached the earth not far distant, though we do not
learn of any consequential damages sustained. It continued to disburden itself of
its contents with unremitted ardor and violence until the shades of evening had
spread around us the curtains of the night, when it gradually disappeared ; and
the horizon shone again clear and bright. Gay *Luna* who in majestic sway was
now travelling the downward skies shone with unusual splendor, and the star be-
spangled canopy of heaven furnished a scene at once beautiful to the eye of the
beholder. The feathered tribe who during the storm were hushed in silence, now
erected their plumy wings, as one, attuned to the God of nature their feeble songs
of praise, and the neighboring groves amidst creation's smiles, harmonized music
echoed through the skies ! the earth has received a goodly supply of rain, and the
works of nature, undisturbed, laugh and rejoice ; let audible gratitude awake the
voice of man on this occasion for one of the choicest of heaven's blossings.

" We hear that three cows were killed at Bolton last Monday evening, by the
lightning."

Full dress'd in *sable black* like funeral shroud,
Rose in the west, and climb'd its awful way,
In proud defiance of the god of day,
Who soon perceived his rays were vainly shed,
And therefore rashly stripp'd, and went to bed.
But not much used to blankets in the heat
Of June, his godship soon began to sweat,
And snore, and puff, and piteously complain,
Which we mistook for thunder, wind and rain.
This reverend cloud came on with dreadful rumpus,
Wafted by winds which blew all round the compass,
And to the mind (the medium of sight)
A scene presented pregnant with affright.
For overcharged with true electric shot,
(Which all who 've felt, well know are rather hot)
As musket loaded deep on training day,
When Captain Flip commands to " *bouze away*,"
From breech to muzzle splits in splinters dire—
The cloud incessant burst in streams of fire ;
While o'er the inky vault the lustre spread,
And streak'd the concave with surprising red.
Some of these streaks were follow'd by a roar,
Which came so near the streak that went before,
That if the first the earth did ever find,
The latter surely was not far behind.
And though we have not heard which way they went,
What place they stopp'd at, where their fury spent,
Whene'er they 're found, like birds of equal feather,
I 'll lay my ears you 'll find them both together.
The ardent cloud continued to unlade,
Like sea-sick man in violent cascade,
Till evening shades, afraid to see the light,
Took care to spread the curtains of the night,
But all in vain—old Sol, his sweating o'er,
Kick'd off the clothes, and still'd his tuneful snore,
Just raised his head and oped his drowsy eyes,
And gave one flash of lightning through the skies,
When lo ! the stars who thought the night begun,
In wild amazement started back and run ;
While nodding Phœbus, trimm'd in slumbering cap,
Yawn'd out a smile and took his evening nap.
But Luna, somewhat wiser than the rest,
Stepp'd softly out, in pink and silver dress'd,
And trode with cautious step the western way,
To see if all were safe where Phœbus lay :
For well she knew if Sol again should rise,

And catch her idly flaunting round the skies,
He 'd make her strip to gratify his ire,
And dress herself in every day's attire.
But when she found he certainly reposed,
His lamp in truth burnt out, his eye-lids closed,
Round heaven's high arch her car celestial roll'd,
O'er starry pavements gemm'd with living gold,
From orb to orb her fiery coursers flew,
And new born splendors clothed the etherial blue.
The feather'd tribe o'erjoy'd to lose the storm,
Now ventured forth in many a cackling swarm.
And fill'd with noise upraised the plumy wing,
And stretch'd on tiptoe oped their throats to sing,
And all around, from every stump and tree,
Proceeded songs of praise, and songs of glee;
While men and beasts stood staring all the while,
To see creation ope her mouth and smile.
The earth has got of rain a good supply,
And everything is wet that late was dry—
Now nature's self with mighty legs and voice,
May skip in earthquakes and in songs rejoice,
While man, the master of the tuneful throng,
Shall sound the pitch, and lead the choral song.

    P. S.   As such a storm does rarely fly
    For nought across the azure sky,
    'T is said that on the self-same night
    Three cows were kill'd at Bolton by 't!
    Poor Mr Wythe two years ago,
    Had his barn burnt exactly so.

LINES ON THE DEATH OF WASHINGTON.

Far, far from hence be satire's aspect rude,
No more let laughter's frolic-face intrude,
But every heart be fill'd with deepest gloom,
Each form be clad with vestments of the tomb.
From Vernon's sacred hill dark sorrows flow,
Spread o'er the land, and shroud the world in wo.
From Mississippi's proud, majestic flood,
To where St. Croix meanders through the wood,
Let business cease, let vain amusements fly,
Let parties mingle, and let faction die,
The realm perform, by warm affection led,
Funereal honors to the mighty dead.

Where shall the heart for consolation turn,
Where end its grief, or how forget to mourn?
Beyond these clouds appears no cheering ray,
No morning star proclaims th' approach of day.
Ask hoary Age from whence his sorrows come,
His voice is silent, and his sorrow dumb;
Enquire of Infancy why droops his head,
The prattler lisps—"great Washington is dead."
Why bend yon statesmen o'er their task severe?
Why drops yon chief the unavailing tear?
What sullen grief hangs o'er yon martial band?
What deep distress pervades the extended land?
In sad responses sounds from shore to shore—
"Our Friend, our Guide, our Father is no more."
Let fond remembrance turn his aching sight,
Survey the past, dispel oblivion's night,
By Glory led, pursue the mazy road,
Which leads the traveller to her high abode,
Then view that great, that venerated name,
Inscribed in sunbeams on the roll of Fame.
No lapse of years shall soil the sacred spot,
No future age its memory shall blot;
Millions unborn shall mark its sacred fire,
And latest Time behold it and admire.
A widow'd country! what protecting form
Shall ope thy pathway through the gathering storm
What mighty hand thy trembling bark shall guide,
Through Faction's rough and overwhelming tide!
The hour is past—thy Washington no more
Descries, with angel-ken, the peaceful shore.
Freed from the terrors of his awful eye,
No more fell Treason seeks a midnight sky,
But crawling forth, on deadliest mischief bent,
Rears her black front, and toils with cursed intent.
Behold! arranged in long, and black array,
Prepared for conflict, thirsting for their prey,
Our foes advance,—nor force nor danger dread,
Their fears all vanish'd when his spirit fled.
Oft, when our bosoms, fill'd with dire dismay,
Saw mischief gather round our country's way;
When furious Discord seized her flaming brand,
And threatened ruin to our infant land;
When faction's imps sow'd thick the seeds of strife,
And aim'd destruction at the bliss of life;
When war with bloody hand her flag unfurl'd,

And her loud trump alarm'd the western world ;
His awful voice bade all contention cease,
At his commands the storms were hush'd to peace.
   But who can speak, what accents can relate,
The solemn scenes which marked the great man's fate !
Ye ancient sages, who so loudly claim
The brightest station on the list of Fame,
At his approach with diffidence retire,
His higher worth acknowledge, and admire.
When keenest anguish rack'd his mighty mind,
And the fond heart the joys of life resign'd,
No guilt, nor terror stretch'd its hard control,
No doubt obscured the sunshine of the soul.
Prepared for death, his calm and steady eye,
Look'd fearless upward to a peaceful sky ;
While wondering angels point the airy road,
Which leads the Christian to the house of God.

LINES ADDRESSED TO A MOTHER, WHO HAD BEEN ABSENT
FROM HOME SEVERAL WEEKS, ON HER SEEING HER
INFANT CHILD ASLEEP.

WRAPP'D in innocent repose,
Lost to all its little woes,
See that lovely infant rest,
On the pillow's downy breast.
Wearied with the toils of day,
Little frolics, childish play,
Frequent joy, and frequent grief,
Nature yields a short relief.
Say, my sleeping cherub, say,
Whither doth thy spirit stray ?
Art thou flown to realms above,
On some angel's wings of love,
Where, array'd in purest white,
Dwell the sainted sons of light,
Hymning round the eternal throne,
Praise to God's Almighty Son ?
Or dost thou now at random roam ;
Through creation's nightly tomb,
Borne by Death's insidious power,
To his temporary bower ?

Hush the thought!—I see thee smile!
Dreams thy little heart beguile;
O'er thy sweet, enchanting face,
Steals inimitable grace.
Say, my little cherub, say,
Whither doth thy spirit stray?
Hark!—his answering smile replies—
"Far from hence my spirit flies;
Borne on Fancy's wing, I move
To a mother's arms of love,
And clasp'd in sweet embraces, rest
On her balmy angel-breast.
Here the tides of pleasure roll,
Rapture charms the licensed soul,
Here divinest transports play,
Here affection loves to stray,
Here I share the envied kiss,
Sink in pleasure, drown in bliss.
Spotless as the beams of light,
Crowding on the ravish'd sight,
Ever new its beauties rise,
Charming unforbidden eyes.
Hark!—My mother's voice benign,
Speaks in harmony divine"—
Peaceful here, my infant rest,
On your raptured parent's breast.
Here no hand shall enter rude,
No unhallow'd eye intrude;
In this paradise of joy,
Dwells no spirit to destroy;
But, on Virtue's spotless throne,
Thy happy Father reigns alone,
Licensed here alone to move,
Bathing in voluptuous love,
Pleasure here without alloy,
Pours an endless stream of joy,
While its blissful currents roll,
Through the mazes of his soul.

SARAH WENTWORTH MORTON,

WIFE of the Hon. Perez Morton, Attorney General of Massachusetts, is a native of Boston, and occupied the first rank among the female writers of America in the early part of her life. Her verses published under the name of Philenia, enjoyed about thirty years since a wide popularity. Of late years she has not devoted herself much to poetry; but in 1823 she published a volume of prose and verse, entitled "My Mind and its Thoughts."

THE AFRICAN CHIEF.

SEE how the black ship cleaves the main,
  High bounding o'er the dark blue wave,
Remurmuring with the groans of pain,
  Deep freighted with the princely slave!

Did all the gods of Afric sleep,
  Forgetful of their guardian love,
When the white tyrants of the deep,
  Betrayed him in the palmy grove.

A chief of Gambia's golden shore,
  Whose arm the band of warriors led,
Or more—the lord of generous power,
  By whom the foodless poor were fed.

Does not the voice of reason cry,
  "Claim the first right that nature gave,
From the red scourge of bondage fly,
  Nor deign to live a burden'd slave."

Has not his suffering offspring clung,
  Desponding round his fetter'd knee;
On his worn shoulder, weeping hung,
  And urged one effort to be free?

His wife by nameless wrongs subdued,
  His bosom's friend to death resign'd;
The flinty path-way drench'd in blood;
  He saw with cold and frenzied mind.

Strong in despair, then sought the plain,
   To heaven was raised his steadfast eye,
Resolved to burst the crushing chain,
   Or 'mid the battle's blast to die.

First of his race, he led the band,
   Guardless of danger, hurling round,
Till by his red avenging hand,
   Full many a despot stain'd the ground.

When erst Messenia's sons oppress'd,
   Flew desperate to the sanguine field,
With iron clothed each injured breast,
   And saw the cruel Spartan yield,

Did not the soul to heaven allied,
   With the proud heart as greatly swell,
As when the Roman Decius died,
   Or when the Grecian victim fell?

Do later deeds quick rapture raise,
   The boon Batavia's William won,
Paoli's time-enduring praise,
   Or the yet greater Washington!

If these exalt thy sacred zeal,
   To hate oppression's mad control,
For bleeding Afric learn to feel,
   Whose chieftain claim'd a kindred soul.

Ah, mourn the last disastrous hour,
   Lift the full eye of bootless grief,
While victory treads the sultry shore,
   And tears from hope the captive chief;

While the hard race of pallid hue,
   Unpractised in the power to feel,
Resign him to the murderous crew,
   The horrors of the quivering wheel.

Let sorrow bathe each blushing cheek,
   Bend piteous o'er the tortured slave,
Whose wrongs compassion cannot speak,
   Whose only refuge was the grave.

JOSIAS LYNDON ARNOLD

Was born at Providence, Rhode Island, about the year 1768, and was the son of one of the first settlers and proprietors of St Johnsbury in Vermont. He studied at Dartmouth College, and afterwards officiated for a short time as rector of the Academy at Plainfield in Connecticut. He then removed to Providence and began the study of law. He was admitted to the bar, but did not pursue this profession, as we presently find him exercising the office of a tutor in the college at Providence. On the death of his father he settled in St Johnsbury, where he died June 7th, 1796, in his 29th year. His performances, consisting of a few light and hasty effusions in verse, were published after his death.*

A MODERN ECLOGUE.

Caryl the barber, and his wife, of late
Had, journeying homeward, words of high debate;
He long had lived suspicious of the fair;
("To jealous bosoms, trifles light as air
Are confirmations strong") yet ne'er had been
So prompt before to charge her with the sin.
The Muse was by, and, pleased with such rare sport,
Has told the dialogue in *this here* sort.

CARYL.

At three new Boston shopsters have I tried,
And bought a chintz would ornament a bride;
This bosom-pin, this locket tied with blue,
I bought for Susan, thinking she was true:
But, ah! for all my love what sad return,
Since you for swains beside your Caryl burn.
'T is well I saw you not—these eyes had flow'd
Away in tears, and I had lifeless stood.
How times have alter'd since I first thee knew!
How am I left the wedding day to rue!
Ah, luckless Caryl! Susan, faithless fair,
Has soil'd her fame, and sunk thee to despair!

*The piece entitled "The Last Words of Shalum," which the editor has included in Arnold's volume, is by Freneau.

SUSAN.

'Tis true, O Caryl, times have alter'd quite,
Since first you kiss'd me on the nuptial night;
Indeed they 've alter'd in four seasons gone;
But charge not me—the fault is all thy own.
While stood our cot on Bagley's fertile plain,
I was thy nymph, and thou my only swain.
Then in thy presence brighten'd every scene,
More red the rose grew, and the grass more green
Soon as the sun from eastern skies arose,
We left our leafy couch and sweet repose;
Then did I first beneath the ashes hide
Twice twenty *rough-skins*, and our meal provide;
Then swept—and to my spinning-wheel sat down,
Nor envied her who wears a golden crown;
And when at noon, with labor spent and heat,
Thou didst, O Caryl, to thy cot retreat,
I cheer'd thee fainting with a cup of whey,
From Comstock's brought, and fann'd the heat away.
How often then, attest ye stars above,
Did Susan, breadless, make a meal on love.
How oft did she refrain from every crust,
Though pinch'd with hunger, and, to quench thy thirst,
To thee, O Caryl, all the whey resign'd,
Contented always while her swain was kind.
How oft, O sun, within yon pine-tree grove,
Hast thou heard Caryl tell me tales of love;
And when thou, hastening down the western sky,
Didst seek at eve in Thetis' lap to lie,
Then did we to our humble cot repair,
And seek for rest and satisfaction there.
But now, alas! the happy glass is run,
Caryl is faithless—Susan is undone.

CARYL.

Stay, Susan, stay; from all reproach refrain,
And prove me faithless, ere thou dost complain.
Here Caryl stands, a pure and spotless youth,
(So heaven preserve me as I speak the truth)
Here stands he—pure as thou, my lovely bride,
Six months before the nuptial knot was tied;
But say'st thou this thy own disgrace to cure?
Ha! that's a trick I never will endure.
I'll beat thee, Susan, for thou art my wife;
I'll beat thee, though I love thee as my life.

SUSAN.

Stay, Caryl, stay; thy beating love restrain,
And I'll unfold the reasons why I 'plain.
When first, on fame and worldly riches bent,
Thee to Pawtucket thy base genius sent,
Then fled the sunshine of my former life,
And fortune frown'd on Caryl's faultless wife;
When at thy shop three customers a day
Were shaved, and each his coppers three did pay;
How didst thou strut, and talk, and look as big
As old M'Laughlin in his horse-tail wig.
E'en then I saw some symptoms of disdain,
And thought thee colder than my country swain.
But when to every house in town you run,
And shaved and dress'd them every mother's son,
Then money rattled in your once lank purse,
And all was prinking, pranking, mince and fuss
Now Caryl drinks with gentry, and carouses
At gaming tables and at brothel houses.
Now oft at midnight Susan opes the door,
And lets him in, a traveller on all four.

CARYL.

Take that—you hussy, for your lie.——

SUSAN.

                  Have done.

CARYL.

I have, you baggage; now you may go on.

SUSAN.

Then your affection to decay began,
And first I knew th' inconstancy of man.
But still your love I did not cease to prize,
And tried to make me pleasing in your eyes.
When you came home and call'd me *swarthy brown*,
And said such colors would not do in town,
Did I not try, at morning, noon and night,
And wash and scour and labor to be white?
Did I not eat of pipe-stems near a gross,
And take of herb-drinks many a bitter dose?
Devour raw rice and paper—Indian meal,
And chalk—as much as ever I could steal?
And when, in scorn, "d—n such a shape," you cried,
Did I not lace me till I almost died?

Yet still I fail'd—you sought another fair,
And Dermot saw you, Caryl, you know where.
You loathed my love, your Susan's arms you fled,
And cruel left me in a lonely bed;
A female weakness then usurp'd my breast;
I sought revenge—my tears must tell the rest.

CARYL.

Dermot was false, and all he told thee lies;
But I forgive thee, Susan; wipe thine eyes.

SUSAN.

This is the only reason I can give
For my past conduct; but with thee I 'll live
In future, Caryl, spotless as the dove,
And faithful as the redbreast to her love.
But now let 's leave this vile Pawtucket town,
And in the country once more settle down:
Let 's move our hut to Bagley's fertile plain,
And dwell in love and happiness again.

———

THE WARRIOR'S DEATH SONG.

DEEP in the west the sun is gone,
And darkness rapidly comes on;
But soon his beams again shall rise,
And radiant light o'erspread the skies.

Thus, though the raging flame destroy
This mortal flame, to scenes of joy
The soul shall fly, where Podar reigns
O'er pleasant woods and fertile plains.

There nations shall no more be foes,
Nor warriors tribe to tribe oppose;
No hideous war-song shall be heard,
But peace inspire the ravish'd bard.

No arrows tipt with polish'd bone,
Nor tomahawk shall there be known;
But all, till time itself shall cease,
Shall live in harmony and peace.

Urge then the torments, haughty foes;
Thus death the sooner shall disclose

The land where every torment flies,
Where endless joys and pleasures rise.

Bid fiercer flames around him roll,
And try to bend his stubborn soul;
Yet vain the hope, the trial vain,
To make great Ellac's son complain.

No sting of wo, nor pain severe,
Shall from his eyelids draw a tear;
But e'en his foes themselves shall say,
A noble chief has fall'n today.

Tell then your sons, ye warriors, tell
Without complaint how Kallack fell;
How his firm breast no fear appall'd,
To die whene'er his nation call'd.

Thus shall their manly bosoms glow,
With souls invincible by wo,
Exult like Ellac's son to die,
And to the realms of Podar fly.

Thus spake the hero of the shore,
Where broad Kanhawa's waters roar;
Then closed his eyes, untaught to weep,
And sunk in glory's arms to sleep.

FRAGMENT, DESCRIPTIVE OF THOSE EXTRAORDINARY ANIMALS WHOSE BONES HAVE BEEN FOUND IN THE WESTERN COUNTRY.

THE monsters rage, and round the earth
  Spread ruin and destruction fell,
Sent by the great *Pehoogthsi's wrath,
  Fierce from the angry gates of hell.
    Haste, my Shootai, haste away,
    Destruction waits upon delay!

Above the highest pines they raise
  In horrid majesty their head;
Their eyes in vengeful anger blaze,
  Their jaws grind nations of the dead.

*Evil Spirit.

Haste, my Shootai, haste away,
Destruction waits upon delay!

Save us, †Oroonoh! at a leap
O'er Allegany's height they bound,
O'er Huron's darkly rolling deep,
And with convulsions rend the ground.
Haste, my Shootai, haste away,
Destruction waits upon delay!

They breathe, the woods are prostrate laid,
The rocks are moved; they roar,
Old Erie on his fall is stay'd,
Kanhawa trembles on his shore.
Haste, my Shootai, haste away,
Destruction waits upon delay!

SONG.

WHILE zephyrs fan the verdant groves,
And flowerets grace the plain,
While shepherds tell the nymphs their loves,
And flaunt in pleasure's train;
To yonder cottage of my fair
My anxious footsteps tend;
What joy so great as viewing there
A lover and a friend?

To her I fear not to disclose
The feelings of my heart;
She bears a part in all my woes,
In all my joys—a part.
If e'er she weeps, I kiss the tear,
And bid her sorrows end;
If she is pleased, joy shows me near
A lover and a friend.

She 's youthful, innocent and gay,
Of perfect mind and mien;
She quickly steals all hearts away,
Wherever she is seen.
But though each shepherd's heart she charms,
And they before her bend,
Round me alone she throws her arms,
A lover and a friend.

* Good Spirit.

WILLIAM BOYD

WAS born in 1777. He was graduated at Harvard College in 1796, and had nearly completed a course of medical studies, when he was seized with a consumption, of which he died January 13th, 1800, in his 24th year. He published at the age of nineteen, a poem, entitled "Woman," delivered by him at a public exhibition at college.

WOMAN.

WHEN time was young, and nature first began
To form this odd, fantastic being, man,
She rack'd her fancy to invent a joy
Unknown before, to please the smiling boy.
Her choicest viands from the field she brought,
Cherish'd each herb, and all their uses taught;
Press'd the cold earth, and bade the fountain pour
Its stream meandering to the distant shore.
To cheer the day and banish every pain,
She spread luxuriance o'er the festive plain,
Smiled on the scene, and call'd the choirist's song
To sweeten pleasure, and the joy prolong.
　　Though far around was pour'd the plenteous tide,
No charm forgotten, and no bliss denied;
Though rich profusion lavish'd all its store,
Man saw the tasteless sweets, and pined for more.
Still anxious care his feeling heart oppress'd,
And pensive languor rankled on his breast.
The plague ennui his dearest joys had stole,
And solitude's cold pleasure chill'd his soul.
Parental care again the task renew'd,
Again each art, with fondest zeal pursued;
From opening roses cull'd the blushing dye,
And the mild lustre of the new-born sky;
From every sweet expanding to the view
The magic power a soft perfection drew;
Bestow'd each grace, that nicest skill could give,
And call'd the lovely composition, Eve.
　　The winning fair, from nature's wardrobe dress'd,
By heaven applauded, and by man caress'd,

Each melting charm with artless pride display'd,
In form an angel, and in heart a maid.
Now pleasure, chaste as virtue's self could feign,
Refined the heart and warm'd the lingering vein;
Each joy complete; and man exulting wove
The silken fetters of connubial love.
   Had heaven's behest in providence denied
Nature's best gift, and man's too charming pride,
No gentle tie the savage breast could bind,
And instinct only rule the vacant mind.
Enchanting woman bade an Eden smile,
Where the rough glebe defied the laborer's toil;
On the bare rock a pleasing banquet spread,
And taught the flint to yield a downy bed.
   The happy peasant climbs the mountain's brow,
Builds on the cliff, nor asks the plain below;
Content and peace beneath the tempest dwell,
And lovely woman cheers the humble cell.
   In softer climes, where beams a milder ray,
Where laughing fields enjoy eternal May,
Enlighten'd man, to female merit true,
Has paid the homage to perfection due.
The hardy veteran quits the fatal plain,
Where laurell'd honor strode amid the slain;
To gentler passions yields the willing heart,
Bows to the fair, and owns the pleasing smart.
   The sceptred despot, now no longer proud,
Deserts the throne, and leaves the fawning crowd,
Himself a suppliant, to the fair he flies,
Lives in her smile, and in her frown he dies.
   Empires and states in maddening discord rage,
Forget affection, and the combat wage
For some fair she, whom artful man beguiled,
And Troy expires, because a Helen smiled.
   Cornelia's worth shall grace th' historic page,
And all her virtues live to latest age;
A shining portrait e'er held up to life,
An ancient model for a modern wife.
The modest matron, far from public show,
Bent the young mind, and taught the heart to grow;
Deep in the nursery's shade unenvied shone,
Nor wish'd the gewgaws of the world her own.
No diamond there its blazing lustre shed,
No toilet splendor to the eye was spread;
The infant's prattle, and the winning play,

With dearer joys beguiled the tedious day,
Than tinsell'd show and fading wealth impart,
These charm the head, but those delight the heart.
  Far to the north, where Lapland deserts lie,
A waste unpitied by the inclement sky,
The savage boor, to sympathy unknown,
Aud mutual pleasures, which decrease his own,
Stretch'd at his ease, neglects the husband's care.
While menial labors grind the hapless fair.
  From Afric sands, where Siroc's poisonous breath
Blasts the young herb, and teems with wasting death,
To the mild clime where Ganges laves the plain,
Where smiling spring and whispering zephyrs reign,
Still lives this truth, by savage man confess'd,
Woman beloved, yet woman the oppress'd.
  The Turk, a tyrant to the captive maid,
Confines her beauties to the haram's shade ;
There, on its wall each dastard act engraved,
He counts his glories by the fair enslaved.
The jealous knave would tame a female's hate
With splendid trifles and the charms of state ;
With regal pride the lover's warmth would give,
And in a prison bid affection live.
Preposterous thought! where slavery's galling chain
Chills the young wish, and turns each joy to pain,
Love, free as air, from cursed oppression flies,
Pines at the fetter, and imprison'd dies.
  In milder Europe, when the infant ray
Of pure refinement beam'd uncertain day,
The hapless fair each humble labor plied,
And cold neglect attended at her side.
Now genial science, on the mind has shone,
Its rigor soften'd, and its passions won ;
Now female worth shall honest praise assume,
Nor fade neglected in the cloister's gloom.
  Columbia hail! along thy favor'd shore,
The fiend oppression shall be heard no more :
No tyrant lord, with jealous fear, shall bind
The soft affections of the female mind ;
No groveling wretch with impious zeal shall dare,
Assault the rights of heaven-protected fair.
  Soon shall the world receive the generous fire,
Blush at its follies, and the fair admire ;
Soon shall the time, by ancient bards foretold,
A joyful era to the heart unfold ;

When female worth with purest beam shall shine,
Nor rival man with sordid envy pine;
When mutual pleasures undisturb'd shall roll,
And the rude Arab own a woman's soul.

WILLIAM CLIFFTON.

WILLIAM CLIFFTON was the son of a quaker of Philadephia, and was born in 1772. He is said to have manifested in his early years an uncommon vivacity and quickness of mind, and soon distinguished himself for his attachment to elegant literature, and strong thirst for every kind of liberal knowledge. His health, which was precarious from infancy, received so severe a shock by the rupture of a blood vessel at the age of nineteen, as to disqualify him for all kinds of active business. His feeble condition having from the beginning held out nothing favorable for his future prospects in life as regards the common occupations of the world, he was not educated with a view to any particular profession. The circumstances of his father, who was a wealthy man, enabled him to devote the intervals of his time, which debility and disease allowed, to study. He mingled little in society, and was led by no control or advice in the course of his literary pursuits, trusting to his own sound judgment and correct taste. Under this guidance the great masters of poetry and eloquence were studied and imitated, with all the zeal and assiduity which his physical infirmities gave opportunity for exerting.

By his parents, who were among the straitest of their sect, he was brought up in a rigid adherence to the quaker manners and principles. These, however, although not altogether incompatible with a taste for polite letters, as recent examples have shown, yet were found quite unsuitable to the character and partialities of the young devotee of the muses. In the latter part of his life, therefore, he threw off the quaker dress and manners, and applied himself to those elegant pursuits which are excluded by the society of friends from their severe and simple system of education. He died in December 1799, at the age of twentyseven. His earliest performances were various satirical effusions in prose and verse, upon the subjects of political debate at the period of Jay's treaty with Great Britain. Upon the publication in this country of Gifford's Baviad and Mæviad, he wrote a poetical epistle to the author, which was prefixed to the work as an introduction. This performance, although of no great length, is executed throughout with much taste and poetical feeling.

The greater part, however, of Cliffton's poetry is of a description that will find little acceptance with readers of the present time. The politics of the hour afforded the principal theme for his satirical talent, and most of his pages are filled with vituperations of the French revolutionists, and the party enemies of the writer. These outpourings of spleen and sarcasm were relished in their day, but we prefer recommending to our readers the few compositions which he left behind him of a different character.

MARY WILL SMILE.

THE morn was fresh, and pure the gale,
  When Mary, from her cot a rover,
Pluck'd many a wild rose of the vale
  To bind the temples of her lover.
As near his little farm she stray'd,
  Where birds of love were ever pairing,
She saw her William in the shade,
  The arms of ruthless war preparing.
"Though now," he cried, "I seek the hostile plain,
Mary shall smile, and all be fair again."

She seized his hand, and " Ah ! " she cried,
  " Wilt thou to camps and war a stranger
Desert thy Mary's faithful side,
  And bare thy life to every danger ?
Yet go, brave youth ! to arms away !

WILLIAM CLIFFTON.

My maiden hands for fight shall dress thee,
And when the drum beats far away,
    I'll drop a silent tear and bless thee.
Return'd with honor, from the hostile plain,
Mary will smile, and all be fair again.

The bugles through the forest wind,
    The woodland soldiers call to battle,
Be some protecting angel kind,
    And guard thy life when cannons rattle!"
She sung, and as the rose appears
    In sunshine, when the storm is over,
A smile beam'd sweetly through her tears,
    The blush of promise to her lover.
Return'd in triumph from the hostile plain,
All shall be fair, and Mary smile again.

TO A ROBIN.

From winter so dreary and long,
    Escaped, ah! how welcome the day,
Sweet Bob with his innocent song,
    Is return'd to his favorite spray.

When the voice of the tempest was heard,
    As o'er the bleak mountain it pass'd,
He hied to the thicket, poor bird!
    And shrunk from the pitiless blast.

By the maid of the valley survey'd,
    Did she melt at thy comfortless lot?
Her hand, was it stretch'd to thy aid,
    As thou pick'dst at the door of her cot?

She did; and the wintery wind,
    May it howl not around her green grove;
Be a bosom so gentle and kind,
    Only fann'd by the breathings of love.

She did; and the kiss of her swain,
    With rapture, the deed shall requite,
That gave to my window again
    Poor Bob and his song of delight.

WILLIAM CLIFFTON.

TO FANCY.

Airy traveller, queen of song,
Sweetest fancy, ever young,
I to thee my soul resign;
All my future life be thine:
Rich or beggar'd, chain'd or free,
Let me live and laugh with thee.

Pride perhaps may knock, and say,
"Rise thou sluggard, come away:"
But can he thy joy impart,
Will he crown my leaping heart?
If I banish hence thy smile
Will he make it worth my while?

Is my lonely pittance past,
Fleeting good too light to last,
Lifts my friend the latch no more,
Fancy, thou canst all restore;
Thou canst, with thy airy shell,
To a palace raise my cell.

At night, while stretch'd on lowly bed,
When tyrant tempest shakes my shed,
And pipes aloud; how bless'd am I,
All cheering nymph, if thou art by,
If thou art by to snatch my soul
Where billows rage and thunders roll.

From cloud, o'er peering mountain's brow
We'll mark the mighty coil below,
While round us innocently play
The lightning's flash, and meteor's ray:
And, all so sad, some spectre form
Is heard to moan amid the storm.

With thee to guide my steps I'll creep
In some old haunted nook to sleep,
Lull'd by the dreary night-bird's scream,
That flits along the wizard stream,
And there, till morning 'gins appear,
The tales of troubled spirits hear.

Sweet's the dawn's ambiguous light,
Quiet pause 'tween day and night,
When, afar, the mellow horn
Chides the tardy-gaited morn,
And asleep is yet the gale
On sea-beat mount, and river'd vale.

But the morn, though sweet and fair,
Sweeter is when thou art there ;
Hymning stars successive fade,
Fairies hurtle through the shade,
Love-lorn flowers I weeping see,
If the scene is touch'd by thee.

When unclouded shines the day,
When my spirits dance and play,
To some sunny bank we 'll go
Where the fairest roses blow,
And in gamesome vein prepare
Chaplets for thy spangled hair.

Thus through life with thee I 'll glide,
Happy still whate'er betide,
And while plodding sots complain
Of ceaseless toil and slender gain,
Every passing hour shall be
Worth a golden age to me.

Then lead on, delightful power,
Lead, Oh ! lead me to thy bower ;
I to thee my soul resign,
All my future life be thine.
Rich or beggar'd, chain'd or free,
Let me live and laugh with thee.

A FLIGHT OF FANCY.

For lonely shades, and rustic bed,
  Let philosophic spirits sigh ;
 ask no melancholy shed,
  No hermit's dreary cave, not I.

But where, to skirt some pleasant vale,
   Ascends the rude uncultured hill,
Where 'midst its cliffs to every gale,
   Young Echo mocks the passing rill :

Where spring to every merry year,
   Delighted trips her earliest round ;
Sees all her varied tints appear,
   And all her fragrant soul abound ;

There let my little villa rise,
   In beauty's simple plumage drest :
And greet with songs the morning skies,
   Sweet bird of art, in nature's nest !

Descending there, on golden wing,
   Shall fancy, with her bounties roam ;
And every laurell'd art shall bring
   An offering fair to deck my home.

Green beds of moss, in dusky cells,
   When twilight sleeps from year to year,
And fringed plats, where Flora dwells,
   With the wild wood shall neighbor near.

The fairies through my walks shall roam,
   And sylphs inhabit every tree ;
Come Ariel, subtlest spirit, come,
   I'll find a blossom there for thee ;

Extended wide, the diverse scene,
   My happy casement shall command,
The busy farm, the pasture green,
   And tufts where shelter'd hamlets stand.

Some dingle oft shall court my eye
   To dance among the flow'rets there,
And here a lucid lake shall lie,
   Emboss'd with many an islet fair.

From crag to crag, with devious sweep,
   Some frantic flood shall headlong go,
And, bursting o'er the dizzy steep,
   Shall slumber in the lake below.

In breezy isles and forests near,
  The sylvans oft their haunts shall leave ;
And oft the torrent pause to hear
  The lake-nymph's song, at silent eve.

There shall the moon with half shut eye,
  Delirious, hear her vocal beam,
To fingering sounds responsive sigh,
  And bless the hermit's midnight dream.

No magic weed nor poison fell
  Shall tremble there ; nor drug uncouth,
To round the muttering wizard's spell,
  Or bathe with death the serpent's tooth.

No crusted ditch nor festering fen
  With plagues shall teem, a deadly brood.
No monster leave his nightly den
  To lap the 'wilder'd pilgrim's blood.

But on the rose's dewy brink,
  Each prismy tear shall catch the gleam ;
And give the infant buds to drink,
  The colors of the morning beam.

The waters sweet, from whispering wells,
  Shall loiter 'neath the flowery brake ;
Shall visit oft the Naiad's cells,
  And hie them to the silver lake.

The muse shall hail, at peep of dawn,
  Melodiously the coming day ;
At eve her song shall soothe the lawn,
  And with the mountain echoes play.

There spring shall laugh at winter's frown,
  There summer blush for gamesome spring,
And autumn, prank'd in wheaten crown,
  His stores to hungry winter bring.

'T is mine ! 't is mine ! this sacred grove,
  Where truth and beauty may recline,
The sweet resort of many a love ;
  Monimia, come and make it thine.

For thee the bursting buds are ripe,
   The whistling robin calls thee here,
To thee complains the woodland pipe ;
   Will not my loved Monimia hear ?

A fawn I 'll bring thee, gentle maid,
   To gambol round thy pleasant door ;
I 'll curl thee wreaths that ne'er shall fade,
   What shall I say to tempt thee more ?

The blush that warms thy maiden cheek,
   The morning eye's sequester'd tear,
For me, thy kindling passion speak
   And chain this subtle vision here.

Spots of delight, and many a day
   Of summer love for me shall shine ;
In truth my beating heart is gay,
   At sight of that fond smile of thine.

Come, come, my love, away with me,
   The morn of life is hastening by,
To this gay scene we 'll gaily flee,
   And sport us 'neath the peaceful sky.

And when that awful day shall rise,
   That sees thy cheek with age grow pale,
And the soul fading in thine eyes,
   We 'll sigh and quit the weeping vale.

ROBERT TREAT PAINE.

ROBERT TREAT PAINE* was born at Taunton in Massachusetts, December 9th, 1773.   His father was the Hon. Robert Treat Paine, one of the signers of the Declaration of Independence.   In his eighth year his father removed to Boston,
and he entered Harvard University in 1788, where he began

* His name was originally Thomas Paine, and altered by an act of the legislature in 1801.

to write verses on the occasion of having been the subject of some satirical lines scrawled upon the walls of the college. His success prompted him to further endeavors, and he soon acquired a high reputation for poetry among his associates. After a temporary suspension in consequence of refractory behaviour in certain matters connected with the discipline of the seminary, he was graduated in 1792. On leaving college, he was placed in the counting room of a merchant in Boston, most probably rather in accordance with the wishes of his parents, than his own inclination, as he does not appear to have applied himself to business with any degree of industry or good will. He continued for a year or two penning stanzas when he should have engrossed, till his minority was expired, when he bade adieu to the leger, and began his career as a man of letters, by setting up a weekly newspaper in Boston, with the title of "The Federal Orrery." His ambition for excelling in poetry had before this received a new stimulus by the reception of a gold medal for a prize poem, at the opening of the Boston Theatre in 1793. This was the foundation of an attachment to the pleasures of the stage which exerted a powerful influence upon his fortunes. In 1795 he married Miss Baker, a beautiful and accomplished actress, who belonged to the first company of comedians that occupied the Federal street boards. The match produced a separation between him and his father, whose prejudices against the character of a public performer could not be overcome, although Mrs Paine never appeared upon the stage after her marriage.

The Federal Orrery was not successful in his hands. A large subscription was first obtained for it in consequence of the high opinion entertained of the talents of the editor, but the public expectation was disappointed. Paine gave hardly any attention to the concerns of the paper. Amusements and indolent habits consumed his time, and he suffered a work with which he had connected his name and reputation, to sink into disregard. During this period, he wrote the Invention of Letters, a poem which he delivered at Cambridge on receiving a Master's degree. This was printed, and obtained such a popularity as to pass through two editions, and bring the author a profit of fifteen hundred dollars. In April 1769, he gave up his paper, and devoted himself to the business of the theatre, where he had been appointed Master of Ceremonies, an office to which was attached a salary sufficient for his maintenance. He was selected in 1797 by the society of Phi Beta Kappa to pronounce a poem before them; on which occasion he produced The Ruling Passion, which has been the most highly esteemed of his larger poems, and was nearly as profitable to him as The Invention of Letters. The song of Adams and Liberty written shortly after this, was still more so, considering the comparative quantity of matter. The sale of it yielded him the sum of seven hundred and fifty dollars, more than eleven dollars for each line of the piece, a munificence of reward for literary labor, which has rarely been equalled in any age or country. And considering the real merit of the performance, certainly no rhymes were ever more generously paid for. His friends at this time prevailed upon him to abandon his connexion with the theatre, and devote himself to the law, a career in which it was judged his splendid talents and wide reputation, would secure him an undoubted success. He removed to Newburyport, and began as a student under the direction of Theophilus Parsons, afterwards chief justice of the Supreme Court of Massachusetts. The next year Mr Parsons removed his office to Boston, whither Paine accompanied him, and in July 1802, he was admitted to the bar. He had a good flow of business in the outset, but his interest and resolution in the pursuit soon languished, and after neglecting his occupation for a few years, he gave up his office. A course of dissipated habits, which we have no inclination to dwell upon, but which the kind officiousness of his biographer has detailed to the world in a pretty ample catalogue, broke his health and reduced him to the lowest state of penury. He died November 13th, 1811, in his thirtyeighth year.

No writer of our country has enjoyed a higher flow of popularity during his lifetime than Paine, and no one has more rapidly sunk into neglect. His poems gained him enormous sums of money, and the most extravagant praise, but a volume of his works could not now be sold. His prose writings in the shape of orations, occasional addresses, and the like, which received no less applause than his effusions in verse, are among the most remarkable specimens of bad taste which that species of writing can exhibit. Some of his most elaborate pieces rise above mediocrity, but the bulk of his poetry has about the same degree of merit, as the common run of magazine rhymes. His stage prologues and epilogues, are next to one or two of his smaller pieces, perhaps the best of his works. His national song of Adams and Liberty is the most widely known. The patriotic spirit of the piece gave it a currency which its merits as a literary production alone, would have failed to secure. There is an approach towards a poetical idea in a single stanza, but the general strain of thought and expression, is quite commonplace.

Paine was immoderately overrated in the heyday of his popularity, yet his talents were respectable. His fancy was rich and lively, but not reined in by a proper taste. We are told he endeavored to form his style of composition after the manner of Dryden; it is surprising that the study of such a model should not have rendered him more attentive to the correctness and polish of his diction.

ADAMS AND LIBERTY.

Ye sons of Columbia, who bravely have fought
  For those rights, which unstained from your sires had de-
    scended,
May you long taste the blessings your valor has bought,
  And your sons reap the soil which their fathers defended.
      'Mid the reign of mild peace,
      May your nation increase,
With the glory of Rome, and the wisdom of Greece;
  And ne'er shall the sons of Columbia be slaves,
  While the earth bears a plant, or the sea rolls its waves.

In a clime, whose rich vales feed the marts of the world,
  Whose shores are unshaken by Europe's commotion,

The trident of commerce should never be hurl'd,
  To incense the legitimate powers of the ocean.
      But should pirates invade,
      Though in thunder array'd,
Let your cannon declare the free charter of trade.
      For ne'er shall the sons, &c.

The fame of our arms, of our laws the mild sway,
  Had justly ennobled our nation in story,
Till the dark clouds of faction obscured our young day,
  And enveloped the sun of American glory.
      But let traitors be told,
      Who their country have sold,
And barter'd their God for his image in gold,
      That ne'er will the sons, &c.

While France her huge limbs bathes recumbent in blood,
  And society's base threats with wide dissolution ;
May peace, like the dove who returned from the flood,
  Find an ark of abode in our mild constitution.
      But though peace is our aim,
      Yet the boon we disdain,
If bought by our sovereignty, justice, or fame.
      For ne'er shall the sons, &c.

'T is the fire of the flint, each American warms
  Let Rome's haughty victors beware of collision,
Let them bring all the vassals of Europe in arms,
  We 're a world by ourselves, and disdain a division.
      While with patriot pride,
      To our laws we 're allied,
No foe can subdue us, no faction divide.
      For ne'er shall the sons, &c.

Our mountains are crown'd with imperial oak ;
  Whose roots, like our liberties, ages have nourish'd ;
But long e'er our nation submits to the yoke,
  Not a tree shall be left on the field where it flourished.
      Should invasion impend,
      Every grove would descend.
From the hill-tops, they shaded, our shores to defend.
      For ne'er shall the sons, &c.

Let our patriots destroy Anarch's pestilent worm ;
  Lest our liberty's growth should be check'd by corrosion ;

Then let clouds thicken round us ; we heed not the storm ;
  Our realms fear no shock, but the earth's own explosion.
      Foes assail us in vain,
      Though their fleets bridge the main,
For our altars and laws with our lives we 'll maintain.
      For ne'er shall the sons, &c.

Should the tempest of war overshadow our land,
  Its bolts could ne'er rend freedom's temple asunder ;
For, unmoved, at its portal, would Washington stand,
    And repulse, with his breast, the assaults of the thunder !
      His sword from the sleep
      Of its scabbard would leap,
And conduct, with its point, every flash to the deep !
      For ne'er shall the sons, &c.

Let fame to the world sound America's voice ;
  No intrigues can her sons from their governments sever .
Her pride is her Adams ; her laws are his choice,
  And shall flourish, till liberty slumbers for ever.
      Then unite heart and hand,
      Like Leonidas' band,
And swear to the God of the ocean and land,
  That ne'er shall the sons of Columbia be slaves,
  While the earth bears a plant, or the sea rolls its waves.

THE STREET WAS A RUIN.

THE street was a ruin, and night's horrid glare
Illumined with terror the face of despair ;
    While houseless, bewailing,
    Mute pity assailing,
A mother's wild shrieks pierced the merciless air.
Beside her stood Edward, imploring each wind,
To wake his loved sister, who linger'd behind ;
    Awake, my poor Mary,
    Oh ! fly to me, Mary ;
In the arms of your Edward, a pillow you 'll find.

In vain he call'd, for now the volumed smoke,
Crackling, between the parting rafters broke ;
Through the rent seams the forked flames aspire,
All, all, is lost ; the roof, the roof 's on fire !

A flash from the window brought Mary to view,
She scream'd as around her the flames fiercely blew;
 Where art thou, mother?
 Oh! fly to me, brother!
Ah! save your poor Mary, who lives but for you!
 Leave not poor Mary,
 Ah! save your poor Mary!
Her vision'd form descrying,
On wings of horror flying,
The youth erects his frantic gaze,
Then plunges in the maddening blaze!
 Aloft he dauntless soars,
 The flaming room explores;
 The roof in cinders crushes,
 Through tumbling walls he rushes!
 She's safe from fear's alarms;
 She faints in Edward's arms!

Oh! nature, such thy triumphs are,
Thy simplest child can bravely dare.

ODE SUNG AT THE ANNIVERSARY OF THE FAUSTUS ASSOCIATION.

On the tent-plains of Shinah, truth's mystical clime,
 When the impious turret of Babel was shatter'd,
Lest the tracks of our race, in the sand-rift of time,
 Should be buried, when Shem, Ham and Japheth were scat
  tered,
  Rose the genius of art,
  Man to man to impart,
By a language, that speaks, through the eye, to the heart.
   CHORUS.
Yet rude was invention, when art she reveal'd,
For a block stamp'd the page, and a tree plough'd the field.

As time swept his pennons, art sigh'd, as she view'd
 How dim was the image, her emblem reflected;
When, inspired, father Faust broke her table of wood,
 Wrought its parts into shape, and the whole reconnected,
  Art with mind now could rove,
  For her symbols could move,
Ever casting new shades, like the leaves of a grove.

CHORUS.

And the colors of thought in their elements run,
As the prismatic glass shows the hues of the sun.

In the morn of the west, as the light roll'd away
From the grey eve of regions, by bigotry clouded,
With the dawn woke our Franklin, and, glancing the day,
Turn'd its beams through the mist, with which art was en
shrouded;
To kindle her shrine,
His Promethean line
Drew a spark from the clouds, and made printing divine!

CHORUS.

When the fire by his rod was attracted from heaven,
Its flash by the type, his conductor, was given.

Ancient wisdom may boast of the spice and the weed,
Which embalm'd the cold form of its heroes and sages;
But their fame lives alone on the leaf of the reed,
Which has grown through the clefts in the ruins of ages;
Could they rise, they would shed,
Like Cicero's head,
Tears of blood on the spot, where the world they had led.

CHORUS.

Of Pompey and Cæsar unknown is the tomb,
But the type is their forum, the page is their Rome.

Blest genius of type! down the vista of time
As thy flight leaves behind thee this vex'd generation,
Oh! transmit on thy scroll, this bequest from our clime,
The press can cement, or dismember a nation.
Be thy temple the mind!
There, like Vesta, enshrined,
Watch and foster the flame, which inspires human kind!

CHORUS.

Preserving all arts, may all arts cherish thee;
And thy science and virtue teach man to be free!

JOHN LATHROP.

JOHN LATHROP was born in Boston, in January, 1772, and was the son of the Rev. John Lathrop of the same place. He studied at Harvard University, and commenced business in Boston as a lawyer. He afterwards removed to Dedham, where he was appointed clerk of the court for that county. He held the office only for a short time, and returned to Boston. He met with so little success in his profession, that he determined to leave his country, and seek his fortune in India. It does not appear that he had any very distinct views or expectations in that quarter, but we are told that he met with disappointments, and after some time, opened a school in Calcutta, in which, however, he was not allowed to pursue so extensive a system of education as he contemplated. He presented to the Marquis Wellesley, Governor General of India, a plan of a literary institution in which the youth of India might be educated without going to England to prosecute their studies. The proposal was rejected from the apprehension that such an establishment would tend to weaken the dependence of British India upon the mother country, and lay the foundation for a revolt.

He passed ten years in India, employed in the cares of his school, and in writing for the public journals, but without realizing any of those golden prospects of success, the anticipation of which had enticed him from his home. The government was jealous of foreigners, the public press was under severe restrictions, and the paths to wealth and distinction were occupied by more adventurous and fortunate competitors. He returned to this country in 1809, and at first meditated the establishment of a literary journal, but the period was most unfavorable to such an enterprise. The violence of party disputes which occupied the public attention, had nearly banished all taste and inclination for literary pursuits, and hardly anything was relished which did not relate in some shape or other to the local politics of the day. Lathrop had little partiality for such avocations, besides that his absence from home had estranged him from all interest and familiarity with most of the prominent topics of political debate. The design of the journal was dropped, and as he was prevented by the long interval which he had passed out of practice, from resuming his profession of the law, he betook himself to his later employment of teaching. He superintended a school in Boston for several years, besides delivering scientific lectures, addresses and orations. He was enabled to gain a support in this manner, but after a while the prospect of better success induced him to remove to the south. He pursued the business of instruction, delivered lectures, and exercised his pen in that quarter, and finally obtained a situation in the post office. He died January 30th, 1820.

Lathrop possessed talents which might have secured him wealth, and distinction, but his facility of disposition, his want of foresight, and his improvidence, hindered them from being exerted much to the emolument or renown of the possessor. His benevolent feelings prompted him to acts of kindness which threw him into embarrassments, and materially hindered the accomplishment of many of his plans.

His poems consist mostly of occasional pieces, on miscellaneous topics, published in the newspapers in this country and India. We believe no collection has ever been made of them. His longest piece is the Speech of Canonicus, written on the voyage to India, and first published at Calcutta. It was reprinted in Boston, in 1803, but has been so little known among us, that a biographer of the poet was ignorant that it had ever passed through the American press. This poem is a sort of Indian Theogony, made up of the aboriginal traditions.

_____

SPEECH OF CANONICUS.

Our God commands. To fertile realms I haste,
Compared with which, your gardens are a waste ;
There, in full bloom, eternal spring abides,
And swarming fishes glide through azure tides ;
Continual sunshine gilds the cloudless skies,

No mist conceals Keesuckquand* from our eyes,
Herds of red deer before the hunter bound,
And fragrance floats along th' enamell'd ground.
There, your forefathers, dexterous with the bow,
Urge the fleet chase, and o'er the greensward glow ;
Or, in a grove recount their deeds of war,
Number their scalps, and glory in each scar,
Or, contemplate—their most exalted theme—
The power and goodness of their chief supreme !
    Yet ere he goes, your Sachem will relate,
Your primal origin and future fate,
Nor think th' important history too long,
An idle story, or a foolish song ;
For him, when young, his parent king inform'd,
And while the impressive tale his bosom warm'd,
Deep in his memory sunk the truths sublime,
And still their prints are unimpaired by time.
    Observe ye then ; when summer's heats are gone,
The north wind rushes from the frozen zone,
Borne by the blasts, the shivering seabirds fly
To milder regions and a warmer sky,
Through the keen air they skim their lofty way,
To where the sun beams ever genial day,
And far beyond Potomac's swelling tides,
They seek the pleasant fields where God resides :
There, coeternal with the earth he reign'd,
And a long solitary rule maintain'd ;
For then, these plains no verdant herbage bore,
No cheerful wigwam show'd its matted door,
No forests waved their foliage in the wind,
Nor round the chestnut clung the sheltering rind ;
This ample range no living creature trod,
And in the universe, alone, was God !
    First, in his image, Manitoos he made,
Inferior spirits, his designs to aid,
He bade Keesuckquand live in yon bright blaze,
And o'er creation shed enlivening rays :—
Placed Paumpagussit† in the heaving seas,
Subjecting winds and waves to his decrees.
Next in mild radiance shone the silent moon,
Queen of the sprites that gleam in night's pale noon,
Whose strong enchantment and mysterious spell,
Can e'en the dead from their repose compel ;
With heat accursed dissolve our flesh away,

---

* The deity who resides in the sun.   † The sea-god.

And torture, as they mould the magic clay.
Yotaanit,* too, he form'd, who, when 't is dark,
Elicits from a stone, the precious spark,
That, the poor Indian, cold and weary, warms,
And cheers the tedious hours when winter storms
Bid the chill'd blood through all life's channels flow,
And draws a beverage pure and sweet from snow,
When, bridged with ice, the stagnant rivers sleep,
And cease to pour their tributes to the deep.
Tempt not his rage, for dreadful is his ire,
Then harvests, trees and towns ascend in fire ;
If his consuming wrath our crimes provoke,
He scatters to the winds our wealth in smoke ;
From him our comfort or distress proceeds,
Evil or good proportioned to our deeds.
   Then burst our mother Earth's prolific womb ;
Then, groves aspired and meads began to bloom,
The living streams, each mountain source to shun,
Roll sparkling down, and in their courses run ;
The Seipmanitog,† confluent waters wed,
And o'er the teeming soil a green luxuriance spread.
   Next, beasts were formed, the tenants of the wood,
Birds for the air, and fishes for the flood.
First in the briny depth, the cumbrous whale ;
The eagle, yon blue eminence to scale ;
The wily fox, whose sense eludes our arts,
And venomed snake, that on the unwary darts ;
The reasoning beaver ; and the moose we prize,
Whose flesh our meat—whose skin our garb supplies ;
Innumerous animals of various brood,
That prey with ravenous teeth, or browsing, gain their food.
   Creation groan'd when with laborious birth,
Mammoth was born to rule his parent earth,—
Mammoth ! I tremble while my voice recounts,
His size that tower'd o'er all our misty mounts,—
His weight a balance for yon pine-crowned hills,
On whose broad front half heaven in dew distils ;—
His motions forced the starry spheres to shake,
The sea to roar—the solid land to quake.
His breath a whirlwind. From his angry eye,
Flash'd flames like fires that light the northern sky ;
The noblest river scarce supplied him drink,—
Nor food, the herds that grazed along its brink ;—

---

* The god of fire.   † River gods.

Trampling through forests would the monster pass,
Breasting the stoutest oaks like blades of grass!
 Creation finished, God a sabbath-kept,
And twice two hundred moons profoundly slept;
At length, from calm and undisturbed repose,
With kind intent the sire of nature rose;—
Northward he bent his course, with parent care,
To view his creatures and his love declare,
To bless the works his wisdom erst had plann'd,
And with fresh bounties fill the grateful land.
Hoar Paumpagussit swell'd with conscious pride,
And bore the Almighty o'er each looming tide;
Sweet flowering bushes sprang where'er he trod,
And groves, and vales, and mountains, hail'd their God;
With more effulgent beams Keesuckquand shone,
And lent to night a splendor like his own.
Thus moved the deity. But vengeful wrath,
Soon gather'd awful glooms around his path,
Approaching near to Mammoth's wide domain,
He view'd the ravage of the tyrant's reign.
Not the gaunt wolf, nor cougar fierce and wild,
Escaped the tusks that all the fields despoil'd;
No beast that ranged the valley, plain or wood,
Was spared by earth's fell chief and his insatiate brood.
 Nor did just anger rest. Behold, a storm
Of sable horrors clothe the eternal's form.
Loud thunders burst while forked lightnings dart,
And each red bolt transfix'd a Mammoth's heart,
Tall cedars crash'd beneath them falling prone,
And heaven rebellow'd with their dying groan.
So, undermined by inward fires, or time,
Some craggy mount that long has tower'd sublime,
Tumbles in ruins with tremendous sound,
And spreads a horrible destruction round;
The trembling land through all its caverns roars,
And ocean hoarsely draws his billows from the shores.
 Mammoth, meanwhile, opposed his maily hide,
And shagged front, that thunderbolts defied;
Celestial arms from his rough dead he shook,
And trampling with his hoofs, the blunted weapons broke.
 At length, one shaft discharged with happier aim,
Pierced his huge side and wrapp'd his bulk in flame.
Mad with the anguish of the burning wound,
With furious speed he raged along the ground,
And pass'd Ohio's billows with a bound,—
Thence, o'er Wabash and Illinois he flew,—

Deep to their beds the river gods withdrew,
Affrighted nature trembled as he fled,
And God alone, continued free from dread.
Mammoth in terrors—awfully sublime,
Like some vast comet, blazing from our clime,
Impetuous rush'd.   O'er Allegany's brow
He leap'd, and howling plung'd to wilds below;
There, in immortal anguish he remains,
No peace he knows ;—no balm can ease his pains ;
And oft his voice appals the chieftain's breast,
Like hollow thunders murmuring from the west,—
To every Sachem dreadful truths reveals,
And monarchs shudder at its solemn peals.
Such is the punishment, by righteous fate,
The dread avenger of each injured state,
Reserved for tyrant chiefs, who madly dare
Oppress the tribes committed to their care.
Almighty wrath pursues them for their deeds,—
They stab their souls in every wretch that bleeds,
The hideous wound eternal shall endure,—
Remorse, despair,—alas, what skill can cure !

    *   *   *   *   *   *

  Onega then, the forest's fairest child,
Sweet as the violet, as the turtle mild,
Bloom'd in her sixteenth summer's perfect charms,
And fill'd each bosom with love's soft alarms.
One favor'd youth her gentle breast inspired,
One youth her heart with mutual passion fired :
Yet chastely tender was the virgin flame,
That warm'd life's genial current through her frame ;
The beauteous novice gave it friendship's name ;—
Alas ! too soon the maid was forced to prove,
What sad misfortunes owe their birth to love.
  Oswego, pride of Narraghanset's plains,
Tower'd as the cedar, o'er his fellow swains ;
His air was noble,—every motion grace,—
His soul's high valor lighten'd from his face ;—
Fearless of death he ranged the dangerous field,
And scorn'd the raging boar—or foe conceal'd,
The insidious serpent in the tangled brake,
Or herds of moose, whose hoofs the champaign shake
  Each night,—how welcome every night return'd !
While his true heart with fond impatience burn'd,
He flew, Onega in the grove to meet,
And lay his choicest trophies at her feet,

To pass mild evening's happy hours away,
And rest in love's embrace from all the toils of day.
    Ah mortals! reckless of approaching doom,
How soon the sun of pleasure sets in gloom,
The fairy fields of juvenile delight,
Are veiled in shades of unexpected night!
    One summer eve, as by a limpid stream,
In pleasing converse on their darling theme,
Lost to the world—no truant thought had flown,
To other pleasures than were their's alone;
In sweet idea rose their calm retreat,
Their russet cabin—mild contentment's seat,
Where every joy concentered should create,
A state of bliss to mock the frowns of fate,
And as the raptured mind uncheck'd could trace,
Each other's beauties in their infant race,
A modest glow suffused Onega's face.
Sudden she shriek'd! Aghast the Indian swain,
Beheld her life-blood!—Speech and sense are vain—
What words can utter what no breast can know—
Murder's first pang—and nature's primal throe!
Death instant seized his prey!—A fatal dart
Pierced to the inmost fountain of her heart.
    Oswego!—what avail'd thy speed or skill,
Thy love, thy faith, to avert the blow of ill.
Happy for thee had he that skill possess'd,
Who aim'd the erring arrow at thy breast!—
    God's mission'd Wakon * when her spirit fled,
To his abode th' angelic stranger led,
The Sire divine a gracious welcome smiled,
And view'd well pleased his pure and fairest child;
Companion now of him and first restored,
She shines in heaven—by grateful man adored.
Next to the moon, she sheds her genial light,
The brightest star that decks the breast of night.
But when Keesuckquand rolls his orb on high,
She shuns the intenser ardor of the sky,
With Cawtontowwit's love supremely blest,
In paradise she finds the balm of rest.
    O'er sad Oswego's heart-afflicting tale,
Sweet Indian girls shall many an eve bewail!—
Ere yet his mind was from delirium free,
The ruthless murderers bound him to a tree;
With cruel taunts, exulting in his wo,

* The wakon-bird.

And savage yells they broke his useless bow,—
Thus break thy heart, they cried, that love repaid,
With the fond passion of the matchless maid,
Now gone to heaven! Ah hadst thou fallen alone,
Our ears had feasted on her piteous moan—
Her life protracted through long years of wo,
Had caused our hearts with ecstasies to glow.
No joy remains for us. Peace ne'er shall come,
With scented breath to cheer our dreary home,
No parent's welcome meet us at the door,—
For us no feasts shall load the verdant floor,
No wives or children soothe our toil or care,
Ours is the deepest hell of black despair.
We fly from this ensanguined scene, and leave
Our fathers, mothers, sisters, friends to grieve;
Die then, before we go! and taste a joy
We cannot covet, witness or destroy—
A friendly tomax then like lightning driven,
Released Oswego's soul—it flew to love and heaven!
  This deed of death perform'd, the vagrant band,
Sojourn'd in exile to a distant land,
And near Ontario's hoarsely murmuring wave
They form'd a tribe,—blood-thirsty, bold and brave:
At length, in justice to Oswego's fame,
They gave their council town his deathless name—
And long as Onondaga's waters flow,
Shall live th' effects of murder—war and wo;—
Deep in our woods and round our rock-bound coasts,
Shall rage, alas! their mad infuriate hosts,
And transient peace, but deadlier vigor yield
To rush with wilder vengeance to the field.
Hence, train'd to arms our strong and dauntless bands
Yell the loud war-whoop through offending lands;
Snuff the red smoke that mantles o'er the plain,
Crimson'd with gore and reeking with the slain,
Till full revenge hath satisfied our wrongs,
And the clouds echo with triumphant songs.

JOSEPH STORY.

JUDGE STORY is the author of a volume of poems published in 1804, since which time we believe he has altogether abandoned the muses, and devoted himself to the severer labors of the profession in which he has become so eminent. His principal work is of the descriptive kind, and entitled The Power of Solitude. The volume does not appear to have been widely known, but we think its merits should preserve it from neglect.

FROM THE POWER OF SOLITUDE.

FAR from the world, its pleasures and its strife,
The good St. Aubin passed his tranquil life;
Deep in a glen the rural mansion rose,
And half an acre spann'd its modest close;
Just by the door a living streamlet roll'd,
Whose pebbly bottom gleam'd with sandy gold,
There first the woodlark hail'd propitious spring,
The humming insect dipp'd his glossy wing,
The branching elms in ancient grandeur spread,
Inweaved with myrtles near its babbling head.
Behind, vast mountains closed the wondrous vi   c
Hung o'er the horizon veil'd in hazy blue,
Save when the shutting eve mid vapors hoar
Roll'd its last gleams their woody summits o'er;
And, seen at distance, through some opening brake
Transparent brightness lit the neighboring lake.
—Scenes, where Salvator's soul had joy'd to climb
Mid wilds abrupt, and images sublime,
Or caught with kindling glance the bold designs,
Where horror's form on beauty's lap reclines.
Meek was St. Aubin's soul, his gentle air,
Spoke to the searching glance the man of care;
Unlike the giant oak, which propp'd on high,
Looks o'er the storm, and dares its bolts defy,
But as the humbler reed, whose pliant train
Bend to the breeze, and rise to bloom again.
His ready smile relieved the welcome poor,
Who throng'd with daily joy his opening door;
Unskill'd by worldly arts the soul to scan,

His social nature loved the race of man ;
Nor sought by godly rites religious praise,
More pleased to pay obeisance, than to raise ;
Nor wish'd the book-taught lore, whose schemes confined
To one small spot the charities of mind.
Let the vain Levite pass the other side
In courtly pomp, in dull, official pride,
His proffer'd alms the wandering stranger found,
Wine for his heart, and ointment for his wound ;
The cheer reply, the scholar's modest jest,
In want a shelter, and a home for rest.
　One darling daughter claim'd the good man's care,
Gay, as the lark, but scarce more gay than fair ;
Light were the sportive locks, whose curls profuse
Hung o'er her neck in native wildness loose ;
Blue were the speaking eyes, whose bended lash
Half hid and half betray'd a fluttering flash ;
Health's glowing rose, in shadow'd lustre sleek,
Diffused its virgin blush o'er either cheek ;
Love in her form the bright perfection traced,
Yet dress'd the model, still to nature chaste ;
No sober tricks, no mawkish whims confined
Her lively ease, her innocence of mind ;
A parent's taste, each pure refinement taught,
And fix'd the polish, when it form'd the thought,
To fancy's lustre lent the touch of art,
And gave the judgment force to guide the heart.
　Up with the morn the hermit skimm'd the dew,
And through the echoing woods his shrill horn blew ;
At noon well pleased beside some rippling stream
Wove blameless fiction's legendary dream,
Or, lull'd to peace, with curious love pursued
The courteous muse through every changing mood,
Wept at her woes, of many a tear beguiled,
And felt her joys, and acted o'er the child.
But when the curfew toll'd the hour of rest,
And eve's fine blush imbued the glowing west,
Beneath a shadowy bower, with myrtles crown'd,
His moral lectures constant audience found.
Charm'd to his knees his cheerful infant came
To lisp with trembling voice a father's name,
Rehearsed her early task, and pleased awhile
With earnest sweetness drew his anxious smile.
There too in riper age the artless Jane
Pour'd in wild tones her melancholy strain,
Or touch'd the lute with many a pensive air,
Or breath'd her grateful soul in thanks and prayer ;

Such holy rites the good man loved to keep,
Till praise and blessing brought the hour of sleep.
Well may remembrance love the favor'd day
My truant footsteps chance to pass that way,
When on his door-stone sat the sage and told,
How mind and sense their gradual powers unfold;
Then higher raised the moral pleasures traced,
Whose touch harmonious charms the nascent taste,
With love and rapture warms the poet's page,
Or moulds to deeds divine a slothful age;
And thence, as holier purpose fired his soul,
Sung the First Cause, whose wisdom form'd the whole.
The while he spoke, methought his spirit shed
Some heavenly dew of mingled hope and dread;
Mysterious influence seem'd to haunt the shade,
And round his face transfiguring brightness play'd.
But all is past, and scarce the eye can trace
One ruin'd monument of former grace.
Short is the tale, nor power, nor harsh disdain,
With lordly triumph grasp'd his small domain,
Nor base seduction lured by syren charms
His rifled treasure from a father's arms:
Heaven frown'd severe, its awful mandate sent,
And claim'd the darling hope its bounty lent.
Beside the couch, where Jane expiring lay,
The hermit knelt, and prayed, or seem'd to pray.
Dim were his eyes, with anxious vigils worn,
Yet spoke a soul with no harsh tumults torn;
E'en in the agonies of dumb despair,
Devotion's smile was seen and cherish'd there:
And, as the lingering powers of life decayed,
Faith beam'd her radiance through the deepening shade,
With firm reliance drank the parting breath,
Kiss'd the pale lips, and closed the eyes in death.
Through brighter realms the unbodied cherub sought,
Realms pure in bliss beyond the soar of thought.
Slow through the narrow path, by misery worn,
Pass'd the veil'd corpse, in shrouded silence borne;
No vain parade, no courtly pageant spread
Their sickly honors round the virgin dead;
Strew'd o'er the bier some vernal flowers were seen,
And here and there a sweet briar fell between.
The father came in sorrow's holiest gloom,
His raised eye fix'd on hopes beyond the tomb,
Still, as the tempest, hush'd in dread suspense,
Yet mild, as twilight greets the wakening sense;
No mutter'd groans, no stifled anguish shook

His meek repose, his calm, unalter'd look,
Save, when the ritual closed its sainted strain,
And o'er the coffin roll'd the earth again,
One lingering tear, that seem'd the man to speak.
With briny lustre trickled down his cheek,
One lingering tear was all his spirit gave,
Then bow'd a last farewell, and left the grave!
Yet had not memory lost her soothing art,
Nor fancy closed her empire in the heart:
When up the groves unclouded moonlight stream'd.
At the lone hour, to goblins sacred deem'd,
When sober day, mid vapory glooms descried,
Shot its faint crimson round at eventide,
Oft would he rove some mountain's brow along,
And pour in shatter'd tones his plaintive song;
Kiss the stray flowers, which dress'd the streamlet's marge,
Or row athwart the lake his aged barge;
And when some spot, where Jane was wont to roam
Some favorite pastime call'd his spirit home,
If once a sigh his heaving bosom press'd,
His trust in heaven was all that sigh express'd.
Oft would he trim his wintry hearth, and court
Remember'd scenes of pleasantry and sport,
Mark, where the lute secured its dusty place,
The needled landscape on the wainscot trace,
The quaint remark, the evening task review,
And chase the fleeting shades, and dream anew.
Nor smile, ye proud, if thoughts, like these, engage
The friendless soul in melancholy age,
More sweet, than all the hymns of active joy,
One moment sacred to this chaste employ,
One pious hour, to moral musing given,
Its relish truth, its harmonies from heaven!
And, as the hapless wretch, by storms o'ercast,
Clings, shuddering clings him, to the fatal mast,
So hope and love, yet buoyant on the wave,
Shall snatch their relics from the ravenous grave,
And most, as life recedes, with fond alarms
Fold the dear types immortal in their arms.
Near where a cypress shades the lonely heath,
Long has St. Aubin slept the sleep of death;
O'er the rude hillock waves the rank grass high,
And moans the wild blast, as it hurtles by:
One simple stone, with village rhymes bedight,
Just tells the tale to every passing wight,
And bids his drooping soul aspire to raise
Such love in life, in death such honest praise.

DAVID EVERETT

WAS born at Princeton, in Massachusetts, and educated at Dartmouth College, where he was graduated about the year 1795. He was the editor of a newspaper in some part of the state of New Hampshire, in the early part of his life, and also contributed to the Farmer's Museum. He was afterwards one of the editors and proprietors of the Boston Patriot. He died a few years since in the state of Ohio.

He wrote a volume of essays in prose, entitled "Common Sense in Dishabille:" and a work upon the Prophecies. His poetry consists of a few short pieces, and a tragedy called Daranzel, or the Persian Patriot, which was acted and published at Boston in 1800. The play is deficient in accurate and striking representations of individual character, but has many eloquent passages, and scenes of high dramatic interest.

A BRANCH OF THE MAPLE.

LET the tall oak the bolts of heaven deride,
Or deal his mimic thunder on the tide;
Be this the theme for Albion's lofty muse,
An humbler task, my fameless pen pursues.
Shall roses bloom in verse from age to age,
Shrubs spread their foliage on the poet's page;
The willow, poplar, fir and cedar throng
Alike the rustic and the classic song;
Pines wave in Milton, and no bard be found,
To plant the maple on poetic ground?
Columbia's muse forbids, in simple strain,
She sings the maple and the hardy swain,
Who draws the nectar from her silver pores,
Nor envies India all its pamper'd stores.
What though the cane, our colder clime denies;
The cultured plant a native tree supplies;
A tree, the fairest of the forest kind,
Alike for use and ornament design'd.
For use to those, who first essay the wood,
To form the table and supply its food;

To warm the laborer by its bounty fed ;
And rear the lowly cottage o'er his head :
For ornament, to grace the winding rill,
Shade the green vale or wave upon the hill :
Or leave the forest, where it useless grows,
Rise in the cultured field in stately rows,
Spread o'er the rocky waste a shady grove,
The haunt for sportive mirth and pensive love.
   Ere jarring seasons rest in equal scales ;
While winter now, and now the spring prevails ;
Sol's milder beams around the maple play,
Frost chills by night, a thrilling warmth by day,
Dilates each tube ; the tube, by mystic laws,
The sap nutritious from earth's bosom draws ;
As higher still the swelling tube distends,
The circling sap to every branch ascends ;
Now each young bud the rich donation shares,
For laurel'd spring his earliest wreath prepares.
   Great universal cause, mysterious power !
That clothes the forest, and that paints the flower :
Bids the fell poison in the Upas grow,
And sweet nutrition in the maple flow ;
Let Berkeley's pupil dream in endless trance ;
The wilder'd athiest form his world by chance,
By this, his reason, that his sense belied,
A world discarded, and a God denied ;
In spite of these, the impartial eye must see
Each leaf a volume—its great author, thee ;
Nor less in every twig than Aaron's rod,
Behold the agency of nature's God !

THOMAS GREEN FESSENDEN.

Mr Fessenden is the son of a clergyman of Walpole, in
New Hampshire. His father having a numerous family, he
was indebted to his own exertions for the means of his education, and by teaching schools during the terms of vacation,
was enabled to accomplish a collegiate course at Dartmouth,
where he was graduated in 1796, after which he applied him-

self to the study and practice of law. In 1801, he left this country on an errand to Europe, as agent for a company formed in Vermont, for the purpose of securing a patent in London of a newly invented hydraulic machine. On his arrival at London, he had the mortification of finding that the machine was a deception. Mr Fessenden, who was a member of the company as well as agent, and therefore a sufferer in the failure of the undertaking, made attempts to retrieve the loss by an invention of his own; he succeeded in constructing a hydraulic apparatus, which was pronounced by several gentleman of high mechanical skill and reputation, to be new, ingenious and useful; but the great expense of obtaining a patent, and the difficulty which always accompanies the attempt to procure efficient patronage to a new scheme, were such as to deter him from prosecuting his enterprise.

Under these discouragements, and further loss in consequence of having been induced to become a partner in another patent concern, which turned out to be the scheme of a swindler, Mr Fessenden was forced to resort to his pen for the means of support. He had before made trial of his powers in sundry poetical essays, which had been published with approbation in some of the American newspapers. In the great metropolis of England he was at no loss in the search of objects for the exercise of his satirical talent, the faculty in which he was best adapted to shine. At this period, the metallic tractors of Perkins were a great object of attention in England, and Fessenden fully believing in their efficacy, undertook to promote the cause of his countryman's invention, by attacking with the weapons of ridicule such of the medical profession and other distinguished persons, as had opposed the new discovery. With this view he wrote his burlesque poem of the Modern Philosopher, or Terrible Tractoration, a work which was highly popular while the matter which afforded the theme of it continued to occupy the public mind. About the same time he also published a volume of miscellaneous poems, which were very favorably noticed in England and in this country. After his return to America, he gave to the world his Democracy Unveiled, another satire in Hudibrastic verse, which enjoyed high favor so long as the public appetite was in a state to relish whatever came hotly seasoned with the red pepper of party vituperation.

Mr Fessenden has succeeded best in his light and burlesque compositions. For many years past he has nearly abandoned his rhymes. He has conducted a paper at Bellows Falls in Vermont, and is now the editor of the New England Farmer in Boston.

ELEGY ON THE DEATH OF WASHINGTON.

WHY moves to mournful measures slow
Yon sable retinue of wo,
   With tearful eye and visage pale?
And why this universal gloom?
Sure Nature trembles o'er her tomb,
   And bids her wilder'd children wail!

Do plagues infest, do wars alarm,
Has God in wrath made bare his arm,
   To hurl his bolts of vengeance round?
Have towns been sack'd by hostile ire,
Have cities sunk in floods of fire,
   While earthquakes shook the shuddering ground?

Ah! no, thy sons, Columbia, mourn,
A hero past that fatal "bourne
   From whence no traveller returns;"
Before him none more good, more great,
E'er felt th' unerring shafts of fate,
   Though glory's lamp illume their urns.

Behold yon pallid war-worn chief,
A marble monument of grief,
   Who once our troops to victory led;—
The burst of sorrow now control,
But now the tears of anguish roll,
   A tribute to th' immortal dead!

Fain would the muse those virtues scan,
Which dignified the godlike man,

And launch in seas without a shore;
But sure his name alone conveys
More than a thousand hymns of praise,
The matchless Washington's no more!

AN ODE.

ALMIGHTY Power! the One Supreme!
Our souls inspire, attune our lays
With hearts as solemn as our theme,
To sing hosannas to thy praise!

Then, while we swell the sacred song,
And bid the pealing anthem rise,
May seraphim the strain prolong,
And hymns of glory fill the skies.

Thy word omnific form'd this earth,
Ere time began revolving years—
Thy fiat gave to nature birth
And tuned to harmony the spheres.

When stern oppression's iron hand
Our pious fathers forced to roam,
And o'er the wild wave seek the land
Where freedom rears her hallow'd dome—

When tempests howl'd, and o'er the main,
Pale horror rear'd his haggard form;
Thou didst the fragile bark sustain
To stem the fury of the storm!

When savage hordes, from wilds immense,
Raised the shrill war-whoops frantic yell,
Thine arm made bare in our defence,
Dispersed the gloomy hosts of hell!

Thou bad'st the wilderness disclose
The varied sweets of vernal bloom—
The desert blossom'd like the rose,
And breathed Arabia's rich perfume!

Look down from heaven's empyreal height,
  And gild with smiles this happy day.
Send us some chosen son of light
  Our feet to guide in wisdom's way.

The sons of Faction strike with awe,
  And hush the din of party rage,
That liberty, secured by law,
  May realize a golden age.

On those thy choicest blessings shower
  To whom the cares of state are given;
May justice wield the sword of power,
  Till earth's the miniature of heaven!

TABITHA TOWZER.

Miss Tabitha Towzer is fair,
  No guinea pig ever was neater,
Like a hakmatak slender and spare,
  And sweet as a mush-squash, or sweeter.

Miss Tabitha Towzer is sleek,
  When dress'd in her pretty new tucker,
Like an otter that paddles the creek,
  In quest of a mud-pout, or sucker.

Her forehead is smooth as a tray,
  Ah! smoother than that, on my soul,
And turn'd, as a body may say,
  Like a delicate neat wooden-bowl.

To what shall I liken her hair,
  As straight as a carpenter's line,
For similes sure must be rare,
  When we speak of a nymph so divine.

Not the head of a Nazarite seer,
  That never was shaven or shorn.
Nought equals the locks of my dear,
  But the silk of an ear of green corn.

My dear has a beautiful nose,
   With a sled-runner crook in the middle,
Which one would be led to suppose
   Was meant for the head of a fiddle.

Miss Tabby has two pretty eyes,
   Glass buttons shone never so bright,
Their love-lighted lustre outvies
   The lightning-bug's twinkle by night.

And oft with a magical glance,
   She makes in my bosom a pother,
When leering politely askance,
   She shuts one, and winks with the other.

The lips of my charmer are sweet,
   As a hogshead of maple molasses,
And the ruby-red tint of her cheek,
   The gill of a salmon surpasses.

No teeth like her's ever were seen,
   Nor ever described in a novel,
Of a beautiful kind of pea-green,
   And shaped like a wooden-shod-shovel.

Her fine little ears, you would judge,
   Were wings of a bat in perfection;
A dollar I never should grudge
   To put them in Peale's grand collection.

Description must fail in her chin,
   At least till our language is richer;
Much fairer than ladle of tin,
   Or beautiful brown earthern pitcher.

So pretty a neck, I'll be bound,
   Never join'd head and body together,
Like nice crook'd-neck'd squash on the ground,
   Long whiten'd by winter-like weather.

Should I set forth the rest of her charms,
   I might by some phrase that's improper,
Give modesty's bosom alarms,
   Which I would n't do for a copper.

Should I mention her gait or her air,
   You might think I intended to banter;
She moves with more grace you would swear,
   Than a founder'd horse forced to a canter.

She sang with a beautiful voice,
   Which ravish'd you out of your senses;
A pig will make just such a noise
   When his hind leg stuck fast in the fence is.

SIGNIOR SQUEAK'S DANCING ADVERTISEMENT.

A GENTLEMAN of vast agility,
Who teaches capers and civility,
And whose whole life consists of play days,
Informs the gentlemen and ladies
Of Bellows Falls, and other places,
That he 's grand master of the graces—
Professor of the violin,
And hopes to suit them to a pin
In teaching arts, and fascinations,
Dancing and other recreations.
   Amphion, Orpheus, or Apollo,
In fiddling he can beat all hollow;
And all those wonder-working elves,
Who made huge houses build themselves,
And rocks responsive to their ditties,
Rise into palaces and cities,
Compared with him, are every one
Like fire-bugs liken'd to the sun.
   He steps a hornpipe so genteel,
You 'd think him dealing with the de'il.
   Can teach young ladies nineteen millions
Of spick and span new French cotillions,
With flourishes, and turns, and twists,
Of arms and elbows, toes and wrists,
And attitudes of fascination,
Enough to ravish all creation.
   He whirls, and bounds, and sinks and rises,
Makes figures of all sorts and sizes,
Flies nine times round the hall, before
He condescends to touch the floor,
And now and then like lightning springs
And borne aloft on pigeons' wings,·

Cuts capers wonderful and rare
Like fairy frolicking in the air.
  He waltzes in a style so smart
A lady's adamantine heart
Will be inevitably melted,
Like ore that's in a furnace smelted.
  All these and fifty other capers
Not fit to print in public papers,
Which put the genteel polish on,
And fit a tippy for the ton,
Said Signior Squeak will teach his scholars;—
Terms, per quarter, twenty dollars.

☞ *Nota Bene*—ladies grown,
Said Signior waits upon alone,
Teaching graces, arts, and airs,
And other delicate affairs;
How to look and act as prettily
As belles of England, France, or Italy.

JOHN BLAIR LINN

Was born at Shippensburg in Pennsylvania, March 14th, 1777. His father removed with him to New York about nine years after his birth. Having passed two or theo years at school in Flatbush on Long Island, he entered Columbia college in New York, where he completed his education. He studied law under the direction of Alexander Hamilton, but at the end of a year discovered that he had no inclination for the pursuit. He had imbibed a strong partiality for the stage, and before quitting his legal studies, produced a play called Bourville Castle, which was represented with success, but the plans which this might have led him to form, were quickly laid aside for an undertaking of a totally different cast. The religious impressions which from his earliest life had at intervals occupied his mind, now took such powerful hold of him, that he determined to embrace the ministry. As he had a repugnance to exercise his new profession at New York, amid the scenes of his juvenile gaieties, and in an intimacy with the companions who had been familiar with the light amusements of his former life, he removed to Schenectady, where he completed a course of theological study, and was settled as a preacher in the First Presbyterian Church in Philadelphia, in 1799.

The vacillation of purpose which he had displayed in changing his pursuits from the law to the stage, and from the stage to the desk, seems not to have left him at any period of his life. He had assumed the character of a clergyman in obedience to one of those strong impulses of feeling which lead a man of ardent and sanguine temperament to the hasty adoption of any novel object of pursuit. His disposition was warm and enthusiastic, and his fervid imagination gilded the prospect which opened upon him with the splendor which a youthful fancy will confer upon the scenes of its own creating. But in his new profession he was still doomed to disappointment. The recurrence of his wavering inclination disturbed his repose, clouded his fond anticipations. It is easy to perceive that while prosecuting his studies of divinity, he was dissatisfied and gloomy ; but in adopting his last profession he had taken a step which he felt scrupulous in retracing without a more specious and solid reason, than an abatement of zeal in the undertaking. He evidently struggled hard to reconcile himself to his situation, the strong sense of duty prevailing over the transient inclinations of which his mind was susceptible. He exerted himself with unwearied assiduity in the discharge of his clerical functions, mingling the elegant avocation of a poet with the grave and severe duties of a minister, paying court to the muses, and dealing in the subtilties of polemical argumentation. Dr Priestley had published a religious tract which called forth the animadversions of the theologians, and Linn was among the foremost who strove for the distinction of breaking a lance with the great champion of Unitarianism. He received the degree of Doctor of Divinity from the university of Pennsylvania at an earlier age than the same honor had ever been bestowed upon another.

He was married to the object of his early attachment, but the endearments of his domestic circle, could not charm away the effect of those melancholy broodings, in which he was accustomed to indulge. His temperament had a strong hypocondriacal cast, which under the pressure of ill health, at last settled down into an incurable melancholy. A violent fever, occasioned by an exposure to the sun during a journey, seized him in 1802, from which he experienced a temporary amendment, but its effects were too deep to be removed. The constitutional bias to consumption, which had long been the object of his dread, received a potent aid by this accident, and he soon began to sink rapidly under his disease. The exertions of medicine, relaxation from his employment, and travelling, were of no avail. Neither his bodily ailment, nor the tone of his spirits, showed any symptoms of improvement, and he formed the resolution of abandoning his ministerial pursuits, for some occupation better suited to the feeble state of his powers. What particular design he contemplated, he did not live long enough to show. His disease continued to advance, and his mind to droop, presenting a scene of melancholy suffering to the last, which is mournful to contemplate. He died on the 30th of October, 1805.

Linn is best known as a writer, by his Powers of Genius, a poem which has gone through repeated editions in this country and England. It is of the didactic order, and the design in the words of the writer, is " to draw the general outlines of genius, to describe its progress, to ascertain the marks by which it may be known, and to give the prominent features of those writers who have excelled in its different departments ; " a subject sufficiently copious and extensive, but which the author has not treated with any philosophical regularity of plan, or any very accurate conception of the matter which he attempts to illustrate. In the proper execution of such a work as his description gives us an idea of, it should be the writer's aim to distinguish the higher intellectual powers from those of a common order, to mark the nicer shades of variety in the human faculties, and to illustrate the superiority of those rare and lofty mental endowments, which are the gift of nature, over those of a factitious and conventional stamp, such as are acquired by study and imitation.   Linn makes some endeavor in his preface, at a regular analysis of that great power of the human mind which forms the subject of his work, but in the poem he is totally deficient in metaphysical accuracy.   His ideas are vague and indistinct, and his attempts to illustrate them, embarrassed by a great incorrectness of style and confusion of imagery.   His poem is not as it purports to be, a philosophical view of the development and operation of the highest power of the soul, but a string of desultory sketches made up by glancing indiscriminately at the various phenomena which the works of human intellect, of whatever degree or nature, exhibit.

In the argumentative part of the poem, he has certainly failed, but in some of his descriptive passages he gives evidence of considerable imaginative power.   His posthumous poem of Valerian, which his friends considered it due to his memory to publish, has little to recommend it to our notice.

THE POWERS OF GENIUS.

THE human fabric early from its birth
Feels some fond influence from its parent earth :
In different regions different forms we trace,
Here dwells a feeble, there an iron race ;
Here genius lives and wakeful fancies play,
Here noiseless stupor sleeps its life away.
A rugged race the cliffs and mountains bear,
They leap the precipice and breast the air,
Follow the chamois on the pointed rock,
And clamber heights to seek their bearded flock.
Loud from the Baltic sounds the dreadful storm,
And gathering hosts the face of day deform :
Beneath their rage the soft Italian yields
His boasted laurels and his blooming fields.
The wandering Tartars by their rigorous land,
Were led to war, to victory and command.

While southern climes were sunk in deep repose,
(An easy conquest to invading foes.)
—Where spreads the quiet and luxuriant vale,
For ever fann'd by spring's ambrosial gale;
Where over pebbles runs the limpid rill,
And woods o'ershade the wildly sloping hill:
There roves the swain, all gentle and serene,
And guards his sheep while browsing on the green.
He leads the dance by Cynthia's silver light,
And lulls with sport the dusky ear of night;
Breathes from his pipe the dulcet strain of love,
And warbles Ellen through the mead and grove.
—In those drear climes where scorching suns prevail,
And fever rides the tainted burning gale;
Where draws the giant snake his loathsome train,
And poisons with his breath the yellow plain;
There languid pleasure waves his gilded wings,
And slothful ease the mental power unstrings.
Where Iceland spreads her dark and frozen wild
On whose fell snows no cheering sunbeam smiled,
There in their stormy, cold, and midnight cell,
The cheerless fishermen with stupor dwell:
Wrapt in their furs they slumber life away,
And mimic with their lamps the light of day.—
Chill through his trackless pines the hunter pass'd,
His yell arose upon the howling blast:
Before him fled, with all the speed of fear,
His wealth and victim, yonder helpless deer.
Saw you the savage man, how fell and wild,
With what grim pleasure as he pass'd he smiled?
Unhappy man! a wretched wigwam's shed
Is his poor shelter, some dry skins his bed;
Sometimes alone upon the woodless height
He strikes his fire and spends his watchful night;
His dog with howling bays the moon's red beam,
And starts the wild-deer in his nightly dream—
Poor savage-man, for him no yellow grain
Waves its bright billows o'er the fruitful plain;
For him no harvest yields its full supply
When winter hurls his tempest through the sky.
No joys he knows but those which spring from strife,
Unknown to him the charms of social life.
Rage, malice, envy, all his thoughts control,
And every dreadful passion burns his soul.—

Should culture meliorate his darksome home,
And cheer those wilds where he is wont to roam.;
Beneath the hatchet should his forests fall
And the mild tabor warble through his hall,
Should fields of tillage yield their rich increase,
And through his wastes walk forth the arts of peace;
His sullen soul would feel a genial glow,
Joy would break in upon the night of wo;
Knowledge would spread her mild, reviving ray,.
And on his wigwam rise the dawn of day.

JOHN SHAW.

DR JOHN SHAW was born at Annapolis in Maryland, May
4th, 1778. He was educated at St John's college in that place,
where he received a degree in 1795. He began the study of
medicine in Annapolis, and in 1798 removed to Philadelphia to
attend the medical lectures there. At this time a fleet was
fitting out at Philadelphia for the Mediterranean, and Shaw
who had a natural desire for rambling, was tempted by a va-
cancy in the office of surgeon of the fleet, to join the expedition. This resolution was hastily adopted, without consulting
his father, and against the remonstrances of his friends, and
caused him no little regret afterwards. The fleet arrived at
Algiers in February 1800, and afterwards visited Tunis, where
Shaw remained as secretary to the American consul, General
Eaton. He was induced to accept this station, by the hope of
profit in the practice of physic, but the negotiations between
our consul and the Bey, were thrown into such difficulties that
Shaw was soon despatched to London, to consult the American minister there. During his stay at Tunis he appears to have
made pretty diligent observation of the state of the country and
manners of the people, the result of which he has given in
his journal. "In my inquiries respecting poetry and litera-

ture," he remarks, "I was surprised to find that they have in Tunis a translation of the well known song of Marlborough. This simple, melancholy air is said to please all nations that are in a state of nature. An instance of it is given in Cook's voyages, and Captain Geddes assured me that he had seen it have the effect of engaging the earnest attention of the natives of Madagascar, when all other tunes failed in exciting any emotion."

The vessel in which he sailed from Tunis, met with bad weather, and after being driven about the Mediterranean, put into Gibraltar, from which place Shaw returned to America. In 1801 he embarked for Europe, and completed his medical studies at Edinburg. In 1803 he accompanied Lord Selkirk upon his expedition for forming a settlement on St John's island in Upper Canada. Selkirk's account of this colony speaks in high terms of the conduct of Dr Shaw in his labors to restore health to the settlement, which at the time of his arrival was languishing under the attacks of an infectious fever. In 1805 he returned to Annapolis and began the practice of physic, in connexion with Dr Shaaf his former preceptor. In 1807 he married a lady to whom he had been long attached, and shortly after removed to Baltimore, not meeting with a sufficiency of business at Annapolis for his maintenance. At Baltimore he soon grew into credit, and was appointed one of the physicians to the dispensary, and Professor of chemistry in the new college. In 1808 while making some chemical experiments, he took a violent cold which brought on a consumption. With the hope of improving his health he sailed for South Carolina in the autumn of 1808. From Charleston he embarked for the Bahama islands, and died on the passage, January 10th, 1809. His poems were published after his death.

THE AUTUMNAL FLOWER.

WRITTEN AT MALTA.

Ah why, when all the scene around
  Has told approaching Winter nigh,
When dark November's gloom has frown'd
  And sadden'd all the sickly sky ;

Ah why, soft flow'ret, dost thou dare
  Upon this bleak ascent to bloom ?
Thou com'st amid the dying year
  To waste, untimely, thy perfume.

Thou shouldst have hail'd the vernal tide,
  When first the green bud clothed the plain,
Or sought the breezy valley's side
  When Summer held his golden reign.

Then many a morning's sunny sheen
  Had waked thee with soft magic spells,
And many a dewy eve had seen
  Thee close, unhurt, thy tender bells.

Soft fostering gales had made their care
  To chase each nipping frost away,
And murmuring wild bees linger'd near
  Thy odors, all the joyful day.

But Summer's golden reign is o'er,
  And genial Spring, long since, has flown ;
The wild bees murmur here no more,
  And every tepid gale is gone.

Already, o'er the sea-girt hill,
  The blasts that lead the tempest blow ;
And lo ! the frighten'd billows swell,
  And whiten all the shore below.

Soft flower, thy fate the wanderer mourns,
  Who o'er these rocky summits strays,
While eve with chilling damps returns
  And dims the sun's departing rays.

Poor flower ! before those rays once more
  Shall kindle up the tardy day,

Thy life, thy fragrance shall be o'er,
Thy simple beauties die away.

No sunny morn shall call thee forth,
Nor evening smile on thy repose ;
For dark and cold the coming North
Bids all thy shrinking flow'rets close.

    *   *   *   *   *

In vain the radiant step of Spring
Awakes the year e'er Autumn close ;
No vernal joys now spread the wing :—
No—give me to my native snows !

To these I go.—Farewell, sweet flower !
Thou rocky, sea-girt isle, farewell !
Where hostile strangers strive for power,
And fear and superstition dwell.

Yon vessel in the bay below
Tomorrow bears me o'er the foam ;
And some returning morn shall show
A land of freedom and a home.

He said, and from the lonely height
He turn'd, and downward bent his way ;
And sought, while darker grew the night,
The ship at anchor in the bay.

But many a sun shall seek the sea,
And many a long, long night be o'er,
Ere morn, returning, smile to see
The wanderer on his native shore.

———

SONG.

Who has robb'd the ocean cave,
To tinge thy lips with coral hue ?
Who from India's distant wave,
For thee, those pearly treasures drew ?
Who, from yonder orient sky,
Stole the morning of thine eye ?

Thousand charms, thy form to deck,
  From sea, and earth, and air are torn ;
Roses bloom upon thy cheek,
  On thy breath their fragrance borne.
  Guard thy bosom from the day,
  Lest thy snows should melt away.

But one charm remains behind,
  Which mute earth can ne'er impart ;
Nor in ocean wilt thou find,
  Nor in the circling air a heart.
    Fairest ! wouldst thou perfect be,
    Take, oh take that heart from me.

WILLIAM LEIGH PIERCE,

A NATIVE, we believe, of the western part of the state of
New York, where he died several years since, published at
the age of 22 a poem called "The Year." It is a review of
the political occurrences of the year 1812 relating to this
country, and displays considerable talent, for one of his age
The object of the poem, as the writer informs us, was "peculiarly confined to circulating more generally in society such
political tenets as he conceived were correct." Party prejudices and antipathics, in which he seems to have participated
deeply, will account for the harshness of his invectives, and
the gloomy and distorted picture which in many cases he has
drawn of the state of affairs.

THE YEAR.

In all the varied change and state of life,
The calm of solitude, or noisy strife,
Man still is man, and read him as you will,
Unstript, he stands the child of interest still ;
The wandering Tartar, and the swarthy Moor ;
The Parthian archer, and Norwegian boor ;

The booted Pole, whose birthright is his sword;
The bearded Saxon, barter'd by his lord;
The stubborn Russ, devoted to his czar;
The crafty Frenchman, clamorous for war;
The whisker'd Spaniard, solemn, grave, and sad;
The Highland soldier, in his tartan plaid;
The soft Italian, studious of wile;
The generous Briton, faithful to his isle;
The brave Columbian, freedom's favor'd son;
All, all alike, the race of interest run.
Seldom the wise man may expect to find
That rich, rare diamond, an unbiass'd mind;
Few, few are those whose pure, exalted hearts
Are proof against corruption's cunning arts,
Who act for others, not themselves alone,
No pliant courtiers bending round a throne.
In this drear age, when misery's cup o'erflows,
When fate has loosed the train of human woes;
In this drear age, which rouses virtue's fears,
When intrigue triumphs o'er a world in tears;
Thine too, my country, has high heaven decreed,
Be the hard lot to suffer and to bleed.
Alas! what crime has stern, unyielding fate,
Doom'd all thy woes, dear land, to expiate?

 * * * * * *

 Columbia spurn'd at heaven's just decree,
To idols bow'd, and bent her votive knee;
In days of prosperous peace she swell'd with pride,
And madly vain, eternal right defied;
Behold her punishment, deception's art
Has planted rankling sorrow in her heart;
Outcasts and wretches, foster'd on her soil,
Her riches plunder, load themselves with spoil,
While virtue wandering through her ruin'd shore,
Is left to batten on a meagre moor.
Yet deeper grief her land is doom'd to bear;
Her harvests smile, with each revolving year;
Her wealth still grows beneath her careful hand,
But grows, to glut intrigue's rapacious band;
Prometheus thus, in fabled days of old,
Crown'd with success, grew arrogant and bold;
Braved heaven's high lord, with blest immortals strove,
And raised his arm against the throne of Jove;
The god enraged, with mighty vengeance hurl'd

The daring miscreant to the nether world ;
In durance stretch'd, and bound with massy chains,
Condemn'd to torment and eternal pains ;
On his torn breast a greedy vulture fares,
Sucks the warm blood, the tender liver tears ;
In vain devours, in vain the torrent flows,
Still, still, the bloody feast immortal grows.
    May heaven, all bounteous, with benignant hand,
Shower choicest blessings o'er thee, dearest land !
But, ah ! be faithful to thyself the while,
And guard against the arts of crafty wile ;
With harvest's sheaf her ruddy temples bound,
Does not blithe Ceres cheerful smile around ?
Are not thy hills with verdant honors spread ?
Does not the oak thus warn thee from its shade ?
" Behold, Columbia, yon extended plain ;
Do all its luscious fruits thus blush in vain ?
Where is the hand that harvest to collect,
Or where the force, such plenty to protect ?
Shall idle waste permit those fruits to die,
Or fall to earth and there neglected lie ?
Cerulean waves old ocean stretches wide,
Thy girting strands yet eager kiss his tide ;
Freight the blue billows of the roaring deep,
Thy commerce loiters—lo ! kind zephyrs sweep ;
Let me descend from every hill and plain
And bear your produce o'er the briny main,
To save your commerce from dark plunder's stroke
Bid freedom's thunders clothe her native oak."
Alas, my country ! why in darkness lay ?
Why close thine eyes and shun the dawning day ?
The gaunt wolf prowls, the tiger is abroad ;
The shepherds see their havoc, and applaud ;
Remember, oh, remember who have bled !
Thy youth's defenders, stern oppression's dread.
Dear was the treasure which your ransom bought,
For many, and gallant, were the brave who fought ;
O, then respect thyself, thy rights preserve,
Stand forth in vigor, swell each generous nerve ;
With high-soul'd honor raise the arm of force,
Nor longer wayward tread a devious course ;
Arrest corruption, strip delusion bare,
And drive the artful leopard from his lair ;
Behold thy sons in meanest bondage lie,
Forge their own chains, for stripes and slavery sigh

What magic charm, what incantation fell,
Has mix'd the potion, wove the fatal spell?
Is he less slave, who yields to wear the chain,
While one, or while one thousand tyrants reign?
Trust me, the difference is not vastly great
If demagogues or despots rule a state;
Self is the shrine where either basely bend;
Self all the object, self the dearest friend.
    And are you free? behold your barter'd polls!
Wisdom is silent—while intrigue cajoles.
Hear yon unletter'd upstart coarsely bawl,
He seeks your suffrage for the congress hall;
What virtues brings he to that lofty seat?
Deception's scholar, skill'd to cringe and cheat.
He pours the whiskey in a copious flood,
While reeling drunkards call him wise and good;
Nay more, perhaps from distant lands he came,
And sports the tinsel of a foreign name;
Perhaps in France, with eager eyes, he saw
Disorder triumph over prostrate law:
Perhaps he heard around a bleeding queen,
A nation shout, "God save the guillotine!"
Perhaps he tells you with exulting smile,
The rebel story of his dear green isle;
Besides, Columbia's native sons are weak,
Smite them on one, they turn the other cheek.
Their recreant arms are quite unskill'd to wield
The warrior's blade, and rule the battle field;
Much prone to fear, the coward souls aspire
No further than the cravings of desire;
Illiterate they, in science dull and slow,
So Europe says, and sure it must be so.

LUCIUS M. SARGENT,

OF Boston, gave to the world in 1813, the poem of Hubert
and Ellen, with other pieces. He is also the author of a
translation of the Culex of Virgil, which was published with
the text in 1807. We believe he has not on any recent
occasion come before the public as a poet.

THE PLUNDERER'S GRAVE.

SNOW hides the green mountain,
Beneath its white billow ;
And chill'd is the fountain,
And leafless the willow :
The tempest, loud swelling,
Now drives along, dreary ;
Before the storm, yelling,
The sea-mew flies, weary,
And, cowering, seeks shelter, from ocean's wild roar.
While billows are bounding,
O'er rude rocks, surrounding
The long sandy beach, and the craggy lee-shore.
Where now does the bark ride,
The wild water braving ?
Where now, o'er the dark tide,
The gay streamer waving ?
And where now, so fearless,
The mariner, helming,
'Mid clouds, dark and cheerless,
And ocean o'erwhelming ?
Where now is the heart of that mariner brave ?
That bark is dismasted !
That mariner blasted !
That streamer has drunken the wild water-wave

O'er breakers, loud crashing,
The waves fiercely bound her ;
While rude billows, dashing,
In riot, roll round her.
Go, helmsman, mid ocean,
Thine arm now must save thee !
Oh ! kiss with devotion,

The pledge, that she gave thee,
Who ne'er may behold thee, her sailor, again !
Think of her, who is dearest,
When danger is nearest,
Then plunge thy bold form, in the rough, rolling main '

Now tall waves dash o'er him,
Ah ! vainly contending ;
Hope sinks fast, before him ;
His struggles are ending.
Now, waves, gently growing,
Seem rising to save him ;
Now, o'er the beach, flowing,
More softly they lave him :
His motionless corse, on the lone shore, they lay.
Rude waves, loudly roaring,
Along the strand, pouring,
Now bear him again, o'er the watery way !
Again rise the surges ;
Again they restore him :
Again the wave urges
Its refluence o'er him !
Who, reckless of danger,
Now braves, 'mid the ocean ?
How wild looks the stranger !
How frantic his motion !
He rescues the corse, from the rough rolling wave !
The strand, for its pillow,
From out the salt billow,
He rescues the corse—but it is not to save !

There stands, dark and lonely,
The plunderer's dwelling ;
He seeks the strand only
When sea-mews are yelling.
When, 'mid the storm howling,
No star is seen beaming,
The wretch then is prowling ;
The false fire is gleaming,
To lead the poor mariner, on to his doom !
When waves bear him, senseless,
He robs the defenceless,
And plunges the corse, in the billowy tomb !
The foul hearted demon,
The sailor despoiling,
Now rends, from the seaman,
The fruit of his toiling !

O'er wild ocean, braving,
Hard earn'd was the treasure,
Through tempest, loud raving ;
Though toiling was pleasure,
For her, who was dear, to the mariner bold.
The fierce hand, unsparing,
Now rudely is tearing
The poor humble garb from the corse that is cold!
The pledge of devotion
Thine arm still is wearing!
That pledge, 'mid the ocean,
Gave heart to thy daring.
When eyes, brightly beaming,
Have ever beset thee ;
When false fears were dreaming,
Thy girl would forget thee ;
It brighten'd thy love, and it solaced thy fears :
For, the girl, who was dearest,
When danger was nearest,
There bound the fair pledge, and bedew'd it with tears.

The eye of the demon
Glares, horrid, in pleasure ;
Poor, heart-sunken seaman!
He grasps at thy treasure!
And shall he bereave thee ?
Thy darling pledge sever ?
And cruelly leave thee ?
No, mariner, never!
The tall wave indignantly rolls to the shore!
The arm of the Thunderer
Seizes the plunderer !
Floods overwhelm him! he rises no more!

The refluent billow
Now leaves the beach, waveless ;
The flood is the pillow
Of mariner, graveless.
But, mark the wave, stranding,
More boldly aspiring ;
The mariner landing,
Then slowly retiring !
The plunderer comes not along with the tide !
The shark is heard, dashing,
Amid the wave, splashing !
The froth of the billow with crimson is dyed !
While chill blasts are blowing,

Who, o'er the corse, gazes?
His garb, round it, throwing,
The sailor he raises.
From winds, cold and storming,
The stranger has borne him;
The blaze, kindly warming,
To life, shall return him:
The stranger shall aid him, the stranger defend.
His pulse now is flowing,
His bosom is glowing;
He ne'er shall forget the poor mariner's friend.

The white winter billow
Has left the green mountain;
Now leaves dress the willow;
Now ripples the fountain.
Where tempests were swelling,
Soft breezes are sweeping,
The sea-mew, late yelling,
Is, 'neath the rock, sleeping;
The sailor is far from the rough rolling main.
The girl, that was dearest,
When danger was nearest,
Now holds to her bosom, her sailor again!

WILLIAM RAY.

WILLIAM RAY was born at Salisbury, in the county of
Litchfield, Connecticut, December 9th, 1771. He wrote
verses at about ten years of age, which the minister of his parish pronounced wonderful, and flattered the young author
with the hopes of becoming as great a poet as Dr Watts.
His father removed to the state of New York, and in the remote and solitary spot which he occupied, the youth had little
chance to pursue his inclination for letters. At the age of
nineteen, he went to reside in Dover, in Dutchess county,
where he taught a school. This occupation he soon abandoned, and betook himself to trade, which he pursued for a few

years, when he became bankrupt, and finding it impossible to obtain a release from his creditors, or support himself at home in any manner, he was forced to leave his wife, and set off for another quarter. He reached Philadelphia, with the prospect of finding a situation as an editor, but meeting with disappointment in this and every other attempt he made to provide for himself, and destitute of resources, he entered in a low capacity on board the frigate Philadelphia, according to his own statement, "without either inquiring or caring where she was bound." She sailed in July, 1803, for the Mediterranean.

The Philadelphia was destined to join our squadron against Tripoli. After cruising in several ports of the Mediterranean, she fell in with an enemy's ship off the harbor of Tripoli, on the 31st of October, and while giving her chase four or five miles from the town, the frigate struck on a rock, and in spite of all the efforts made to save her, was obliged to surrender to the Tripolitan gunboats. The crew were stripped, marched on shore, and set to hard labor. In their captivity, which endured more than a year and a half, they suffered great miseries, of which Ray has given us a very striking picture in his narrative. "One hundred and fifty of our men, myself among the rest, were sent to raise an old wreck of a vessel, deeply barred in the sand under water, eastward from the town. It was now the coldest season of the year,—we were almost naked, and were driven into the water up to our armpits. We had to shovel the sand from the bottom, and carry it in baskets to the banks. The chilling waves almost arrested the flow of life for ever, and the Turks seemed more barbarous than usual, beating us with their bamboos, and exulting in our sufferings. They kept us in the water from about sunrise, until two o'clock P. M., before we were permitted to come out, or to taste a mouthful of food for that day. When we had 'snatched a short repast,' we were driven again into the water, and kept there until sunset. We had no clothes to change, but were obliged to sleep in our wet ones, on the damp earth the following night. With such usage, life became almost insupportable, and every night, when I laid my head on the 'lap of earth,' I most sincerely prayed that I might never experience the horrors of another morning." * * * "February, 17th, early in the morning, and much earlier than usual, our prison doors were unbolted, which had been doubly guarded the night before, and the keepers rushed in amongst us, like so many fiends, and fell to beating and cursing every one they could see, spitting in our faces, gnashing their teeth, and hissing like dragons. Word was soon brought, that the wreck of the frigate Philadelphia lay smoking in the rocks, at a point where she had drifted, burned down to the water. We could not disguise our joy at this event, which exasperated the Turks still more, so that every boy we met in the streets, took the liberty to spit on us as we passed, not forgetting to pelt us severely with stones. Our tasks were also redoubled, our bread withheld for three days, and every driver exercised cruelties over us tenfold more rigid than before. We were so hungry, that for my part, I was glad to pick up the peels of oranges in the dirty streets and eat them, filth and all. * * * Many of us had to drag a heavy wagon, (left by Bonaparte, in his expedition to Egypt) five or six miles into the country, over the burning sands, barefoot and shirtless, and back again, loaded with timber, before they had anything to eat, except perhaps, a few raw carrots." * * * "The Tripolitans began to be frightened, *(during the bombardment of the city by the American fleet,)* and some of their principal officers treated us with more respect than before the attacks, but the low wretches continued to abuse and insult us, and some of the keepers, who had lost friends in the engagements, were more savage than ever. The management of the prisoners was in a great manner confided to these inhuman villains, and they almost starved us to death. December 10th—starving again. Our keepers opened the prison doors in the morning, and ordered us *tota fora* (all out.) Not a man moved, and we unanimously resolved, that if death should be the consequence, not to turn out another day without food, and this brought the Turks to terms for that time."

In June, 1805, a peace was concluded with the Tripolitan government, and Ray, on regaining his liberty, entered as captain's clerk on board the frigate Essex, and the next year returned home.   In 1809, he settled in Essex county, New York, and resumed his occupation of trading, but with no better success than before.   On the declaration of war in 1812, he was made a major in the detached militia, which was stationed at Plattsburgh.   After a short term of service in that quarter, he resided in several parts of the state of New York, and finally settled in Onondaga, holding the office of a Justice of the Peace, and commissioner in courts of record.   He died at Auburn, in 1827.

His volume of poems was published in 1821.   They cannot be allowed any very high praise, but a claim upon our attention is put forth in their favor, after a manner not to be resisted, in the closing couplet of the writer's " Exordium."

> " When you 're captured by a Turk
> Sit down and write a better work."

TRIPOLI.

Ye lurid domes! whose tottering columns stand,
Marks of the despot's desolating hand:
Whose weed-grown roofs and mouldering arches show
The curse of tyranny, a nation's wo;
In every ruin—every pile I find
A warning lesson to a thoughtful mind.
Your gloomy cells expressive silence break,
Echo to groans, and eloquently speak;
" The Christian's blood cements the stones he rears;
This clay was moisten'd with a Christian's tears;
Pale as these walls, a prisoner oft has lain,
Felt the keen scourge and worn the ruthless chain;
While scoffing foes increasing tortures pour,

Till the poor victim feels, alas! no more!"
Here thy brave tars, America, are found
Lock'd in foul prisons and in fetters bound.
Heavens! what sad times! must free Columbians bow
Before yon tinsel tyrant's murky brow?
Cringe to a power which death and rapine crown?
Smile at a smile, and tremble at a frown?
Kneel at a throne, its clemency implore,
Enrich'd by spoils, and stain'd with human gore?
Bear the sharp lash, the ponderous load sustain,
Suppress their anger, and revenge restrain?
Leave a free clime, explore the treacherous waves,
The sport of miscreants and the slave of slaves?
Heavens! at the sight each patriot bosom glows
With virtuous hatred on its country's foes;
At every blow indignant passions rise,
And vengeance flashes from resentful eyes.
But heaven is just, though man's bewilder'd mind
To the dark ways of providence is blind;
Else why are some ordain'd above the rest,
Or villains treated better than the best?
Why, martyr'd virtue, hang thy injured head?
Why lived an Arnold, while a Warren bled?
Earth's murderers triumph, proud oppressors reign,
While patriots bleed, and captives sigh in vain?
Yet slumbering justice soon shall wake and show
Her sword, unsheath'd, and vengeance wing the blow:
Columbia's genius, glorious as the sun,
With thy blest shade, immortal Washington!
Unite to guard us from nefarious foes,
And heaven defend, and angels interpose,
Devoted tyrants cause just wrath to feel,
Make Beys and Bashaws in submission kneel;
Man's equal right, sweet liberty, restore,
And despotism crush, to rise no more.

THE WAY TO BE HAPPY.

Do troubles overwhelm thy soul,
    Like billows of the ocean,
That o'er the shipwreck'd victim roll,
    In terrible commotion;
Seize bold Imagination's wing,

And soar to heaven, so seeming,
Or reign a potentate and king—
'T is all obtain'd by—dreaming.

Do pain and poverty unite
   To rob thee of all pleasure—
Like thieves break in at dead of night,
   And steal away thy treasure,
The treasure of a tranquil mind
   With joy and rapture teeming,
Seek—seek, my friend, and thou shalt find
   More solid joy in—dreaming.

For let the world still darker frown
   Than night-clouds on creation,
And shower its tenfold vengeance down,
   Its wrath and indignation,
On this devoted head of mine,
   One star is still left gleaming,
One light that will for ever shine—
   The hope—the bliss of dreaming.

The world can neither give nor take
   Away these mental riches ;
They 're mine—and sleeping or awake,
   I love the little witches ;
They charm my senses to repose,
   While cares and wants are screaming
My eyes and ears, to misery close,
   And give me peace in—dreaming.

Whene'er I lay me down to rest,
   With toils and sorrows weary—
A heart most feelingly distress'd,
   And all on earth looks dreary ;
Aerial powers around me throng,
   With light and glory beaming,
And waft my raptured soul along
   The paradise of—dreaming.

And oft as pensively I walk
   In solitary places,
I hear celestial spirits talk,
   And think I see their faces ;

They bid me leave all earthly things,
  While tears of grief are streaming—
I mount Imagination's wings,
  And find my heaven in—dreaming.

VILLAGE GREATNESS.

In every country village, where
Ten chimney smokes perfume the air,
  Contiguous to a steeple,
Great gentlefolks are found, a score,
Who can't associate, any more,
  With common " country people."

Jack Fallow, born amongst the woods,
From rolling logs, now rolls in goods,
  Enough awhile to dash on—
Tells negro stories—smokes segars—
Talks politics—decides on wars—
  And lives in stylish fashion.

Tim Ox-goad, lately from the plough,
A polish'd gentleman is now,
  And talks of " country fellows;"
But ask the fop what books he's read—
You'll find the brain-pan of his head
  As empty as a bellows.

Miss Faddle, lately from the wheel,
Begins quite lady-like to feel,
And talks affectedly genteel,
  And sings some tasty songs, too;
But my veracity impeach,
If she can tell what part of speech
  Gentility belongs to.

Without one spark of wit refined,
Without one beauty of the mind—
  Genius or education,
Or family, or fame, to boast,
To see such gentry rule the roast,
  Turns patience to vexation.

To clear such rubbish from the earth,
Though real genius—mental worth,
  And science to attend you,
You might as well the sty refine,
Or cast your pearls before the swine,
  They'd only turn and rend you.

WILLIAM CRAFTS

Was born at Charleston, South Carolina, January 24th, 1787.
He received his education at Harvard University, and studied
law and spent the remainder of his life in his native city,
where he became noted as a lawyer of great ability and eloquence.   He was a member of the legislature of South Carolina, and was for some time editor of the Charleston Courier.
He died at Lebanon Springs, New York, September 23d
1826, at the age of 39.   A collection of his works, comprising
poems, essays in prose, and orations, with a biographical memoir, was published at Charleston during the last year.

RAPIDS IN LOVE.

There are rapids in love, but they fall as they flow,
Thus pleasure inhabits the bodies of wo,
And the tears of their union though sunbeams illume,
They meet in the rainbow, and part in the gloom.

There are rapids in love, but they must be past o'er
By those who will not be confined to the shore;
Even danger has charms when it points to delight,
And morning is lovelier for following night.

Let us risk the descent—our barks shall combine,
Our hopes and our hearts shall together incline:
Love beckons us on to the perilous wave,
One moment shall ruin us both, or shall save.

Protect us, ye stars of the fond and the true,
The dangers of lovers are sacred to you;

The rapids are over,—surviving, secure,
In the sea of delight our barks we will moor.

SERENADE SONG.

BEWARE the soft seducer;
  Elude his silken snare,
And guard thy tender bosom
  From anguish and despair.

Believe him not, young lady!
  Though by the stars he swear;
The night is past! already
  The stars do disappear.

But there is one remaining,
  The morning star alone,
Just like a maid complaining
  When all her hopes are gone.

SELLECK OSBORN.

SELLECK OSBORN was born, we believe, in Litchfield, Connecticut, and brought up to the trade of a printer. He conducted a newspaper in Litchfield, about 1806 or 1808, and was imprisoned in that place for a publication which, under the influence of party excitement, was declared libellous. The sympathy of his political friends was powerfully excited by this event, and a public procession was made to the place of his confinement.

This circumstance, leads to the mention of another anecdote respecting him, which illustrates the influence of political attachments and prejudices, while it offers a conjuncture of incidents, which might afford the ground work of a good comedy. Osborn had been engaged to deliver an oration at

Ridgefield, in Fairfield county, on the 4th of July. The day came, the audience had assembled, and the orator mounted the desk, when he discovered that he had lost his manuscript in his way to the meeting-house. He had ridden a long distance, to search for it was hopeless, and the confusion and perplexity into which the loss had thrown him, rendered it impossible to prepare any off-hand succedaneum for his written performance. A situation more awkward can hardly be imagined. A thronging auditory collected on the great national holiday, animated with the excitement of politics, at the most busy and over-heated time of party turbulence, and the orator with nothing to say! Meanwhile a post rider on his course from Ridgefield, had spied the manuscript upon the road and picked it up; on examining it, the first glance discovered to him that it was a production designed for public recital on that day, and perhaps at that moment. Here the catastrophe of the affair stood upon a sharp edge. The post rider was a warm partizan, (every man was a politician then) and it depended upon the political character of the oration whether it should be returned seasonably to the owner. Fortunately for Osborn, the finder of his manuscript was one of his own party, and he was placed in the dilemma of either hastening back with the writing to the owner, and thereby incurring a forfeiture for delay in transporting the mail, or subjecting his friends to the mortification and disappointment of losing their oration. He hesitated but for a moment, and turned his horse back. He arrived at Ridgefield in time to hand the manuscript to the orator just as he had abandoned himself to despair and was descending from the rostrum.

Osborne once edited a paper at Windsor, Vermont, and in the latter part of his life he was the editor of a paper in the state of Delaware. He published a collection of his poems at Boston, in 1823, and died in Philadelphia in 1826.

THE RUINS.

I 've seen, in twilight's pensive hour,
The moss-clad dome, the mouldering tower,
   In awful ruin stand;
That dome, where grateful voices sung,
That tower, whose chiming music rung,
   Majestically grand!

I 've seen, 'mid sculptured pride, the tomb
Where heroes slept, in silent gloom,
   Unconscious of their fame;
Those who, with laurel'd honors crown'd,
Among their foes spread terror round,
   And gain'd—an empty name!

I 've seen, in death's dark palace laid,
The ruins of a beauteous maid,
   Cadaverous and pale!
That maiden who, while life remain'd,
O'er rival charms in triumph reign'd,
   The mistress of the vale.

I 've seen, where dungeon damps abide,
A youth, admired in manhood's pride,
   In morbid fancy rave;
He who, in reason's happier day,
Was virtuous, witty, nobly gay,
   Learn'd, generous and brave.

Nor dome, nor tower, in twilight shade,
Nor hero fallen, nor beauteous maid,
   To ruin all consign'd—
Can with such pathos touch my breast
As (on the maniac's form impress'd)
   The ruins of the mind!

THE QUARRELS OF LOVE.

MARK ye that cloud, whose sudden shade
   Succeeds the recent smile of morn;
Such was the frown of my dear maid
   Whose early love was turn'd to scorn!

Oh, how that frown did chill my heart,
 And quench my too presumptuous flame!
Of my regret how keen the smart!
 How glow'd my burning cheek with shame!

How could I, with unhallow'd lip,
 That bosom's purity profane?
Or dare ambrosial sweets to sip,
 For which e'en love had sued in vain?

Mark how that cloud, in drops of pearl,
 Dissolves, as sunshine breaks the while;
So wept my kind, relenting girl,
 When penitence regain'd her smile.

Mark, how that mild, cerulean hue,
 Expands, amidst retiring shade;
'T was thus her eye, of heavenly blue,
 All her returning love betray'd.

Mark too, that bow, of splendid light,
 That bends o'er earth its graceful form,
That shines so cheering to the sight,
 When bursting sunbeams chase the storm:

As glows that signal, from above,
 Of promised peace 'tween man and heaven,
So glow'd the blush of yielding love,
 While gently murm'ring, "thou 'rt forgiven

THE SAILOR.

"The wary sea-bird screams afar—
 Along the wave dire omens sweep—
From the veil'd sky no friendly star
 Beams on the undulating deep.

Hark! from the cliffs of distant shores,
 The Loru emits his dismal cry—
The wave portentous warning roars,
 And speaks the threatening tempest nigh.

What guardian angel's watchful power
   Shall snatch me from the angry deep,
Or bid, in that tremendous hour,
   The demon of the waters sleep?

Or who, if on some desert wild
   I drift, weak, famished and distrest,
Shall hush the sorrows of my child,
   Or soothe Lavinia's wounded breast?

Sweet objects of my early love,
   For you with aching heart I mourn;
Far from your peaceful vale I rove,
   Ah! hopeless ever to return!

Yet, should it be my happy lot
   To hail again my native shore,
Secure within my humble cot,
   I'll brave the restless deep no more."

His prayer was heard—the rolling bark
   Rode through the storm with stubborn pride;
And William, blithe as morning lark,
   Flew to his sweet enraptured bride.

Yet Will, with love and liquor warm,
   Ere yet a month had pass'd in glee,
Forgot the terrors of the storm,
   And, singing, squared away for sea!

WASHINGTON ALLSTON

WAS born in South Carolina, and received his education in New England. He was graduated at Harvard University in 1800. He has since made himself well known to the world as a painter, in which capacity he has given evidence of a genius of the first order. He has resided in the course of his labors in Italy and England, but is at present in Boston, em-

ploying his pencil upon an historical subject of a highly interesting character. His poems, consisting of The Sylphs of the
Seasons, and a few short pieces, were published in 1813.

THE PAINT KING.

FAIR Ellen was long the delight of the young,
    No damsel could with her compare ;
Her charms were the theme of the heart and the tongue,
And bards without number in ecstasies sung,
    The beauties of Ellen the fair.

Yet cold was the maid ; and though legions advanced,
    All drill'd by Ovidean art,
And languish'd, and ogled, protested and danced,
Like shadows they came, and like shadows they glanced
    From the hard polish'd ice of her heart.

Yet still did the heart of fair Ellen implore
    A something that could not be found ;
Like a sailor she seem'd on a desolate shore,
With nor house, nor a tree, nor a sound but the roar
    Of breakers high dashing around.

From object to object still, still would she veer,
    Though nothing, alas, could she find ;
Like the moon, without atmosphere, brilliant and clear,
Yet doom'd like the moon, with no being to cheer
    The bright barren waste of her mind.

But rather than sit like a statue so still
    When the rain made her mansion a pound,
Up and down would she go, like the sails of a mill,
And pat every stair, like a woodpecker's bill,
    From the tiles of the roof to the ground.

One morn, as the maid from her casement inclined,
    Pass'd the youth with a frame in his hand.
The casement she closed—not the eye of her mind
For, do all she could, no, she could not be blind ;
    Still before her she saw the youth stand.

" Ah, what can he do," said the languishing maid,
    " Ah, what with that frame can he do?"
And she knelt to the goddess of secrets and pray'd,
When the youth pass'd again, and again he display'd
        The frame and a picture to view.

"Oh, beautiful picture!" the fair Ellen cried,
    " I must see thee again or I die."
Then under her white chin, her bonnet she tied,
And after the youth and the picture she hied,
    When the youth, looking back, met her eye.

" Fair damsel," said he, (and he chuckled the while
    " This picture I see you admire:
Then take it, I pray you, perhaps 't will beguile
Some moments of sorrow ; (nay, pardon my smile)
    Or, at least, keep you home by the fire."

Then Ellen the gift with delight and surprise
    From the cunning young stripling received.
But she knew not the poison that enter'd her eyes,
When sparkling with rapture they gazed on her prize—
    Thus, alas, are fair maidens deceived!

'T was a youth o'er the form of a statue inclined,
    And the sculptor he seem'd of the stone ;
Yet he languish'd as though for its beauty he pined,
And gazed as the eyes of the statue so blind
    Reflected the beams of his own.

'T was the tale of the sculptor Pygmalion of old ;
    Fair Ellen remember'd and sigh'd ;
" Ah, couldst thou but lift from that marble so cold,
Thine eyes too imploring, thy arms should enfold,
    And press me this day as thy bride."

She said : when behold, from the canvas arose
    The youth, and he stepp'd from the frame :
With a furious transport his arms did enclose
The love-plighted Ellen : and, clasping, he froze
    The blood of the maid with his flame!

She turn'd and beheld on each shoulder a wing.
    " Oh, heaven! cried she, who art thou?"
From the roof to the ground did his fierce answer ring,

As frowning, he thunder'd "I am the Paint-King!
 And mine, lovely maid, thou art now!"

Then high from the ground did the grim monster lift
 The loud-screaming maid like a blast;
And he sped though the air like a meteor swift,
While the clouds, wand'ring by him, did fearfully drift
 To the right and the left as he pass'd.

Now suddenly sloping his hurricane flight,
 With an eddying whirl he descends;
The air all below him becomes black as night,
And the ground where he treads, as if moved with affright,
 Like the surge of the Caspian bends.

"I am here!" said the fiend, and he thundering knock'd
 At the gates of a mountainous cave;
The gates open flew, as by magic unlock'd,
While the peaks of the mount, reeling to and fro, rock'd
 Like an island of ice on the wave.

'Oh, mercy!" cried Ellen, and swoon'd in his arms,
 But the Paint-King, he scoff'd at her pain.
"Prithee, love," said the monster, "what mean these alarms?"
She hears not, she sees not the terrible charms,
 That work her to horror again.

She opens her lids, but no longer her eyes
 Behold the fair youth she would woo;
Now appears the Paint-King in his natural guise;
His face, like a palette of villainous dies,
 Black and white, red, and yellow, and blue.

On the skull of a Titan, that Heaven defied,
 Sat the fiend, like the grim giant Gog,
While aloft to his mouth a huge pipe he applied,
Twice as big as the Eddystone Lighthouse, descried
 As it looms through an easterly fog.

And anon, as he puff'd the vast volumes, were seen,
 In horrid festoons on the wall,
Legs and arms, heads and bodies emerging between,
Like the drawing-room grim of the Scotch Sawney Beane,
 By the Devil dress'd out for a ball.

"Ah me!" cried the damsel, and fell at his feet.
"Must I hang on these walls to be dried?"
"Oh, no!" said the fiend, while he sprung from his seat,
"A far nobler fortune thy person shall meet;
Into paint will I grind thee, my bride!"

Then, seizing the maid by her dark auburn hair,
An oil jug, he plung'd her within.
Seven days, seven nights, with the shrieks of despair,
Did Ellen in torment convulse the dun air,
All cover'd with oil to the chin.

On the morn of the eight, on a huge sable stone
Then Ellen, all reeking, he laid;
With a rock for his muller, he crush'd every bone,
But, though ground to jelly, still, still did she groan;
For life had forsook not the maid.

Now reaching his palette, with masterly care
Each tint on its surface he spread;
The blue of her eyes, and the brown of her hair,
And the pearl and the white of her forehead so fair,
And her lips' and her cheeks' rosy red.

Then, stamping his foot, did the monster exclaim,
"Now I brave, cruel fairy, thy scorn!"
When lo! from a chasm wide-yawning there came
A light tiny chariot of rose color'd flame,
By a team of ten glow-worms upborne.

Enthroned in the midst on an emerald bright,
Fair Geraldine sat without peer;
Her robe was a gleam of the first blush of light,
And her mantle the fleece of a noon-cloud white,
And a beam of the moon was her spear.

In an accent that stole on the still charmed air
Like the first gentle language of Eve,
Thus spake from her chariot the fairy so fair:
"I come at thy call, but, oh Paint-King, beware,
Beware if again you deceive."

"'T is true," said the monster, "thou queen of my heart,
Thy portrait I oft have essay'd;
Yet ne'er to the canvas could I with my art

The least of thy wonderful beauties impart;
    And my failure with scorn you repaid.

" Now I swear by the light of the Comet-King's tail ! "
    And he tower'd with pride as he spoke,
" If again with these magical colors I fail,
The crater of Etna shall hence be my jail,
    And my food shall be sulphur and smoke.

" But if I succeed, then, oh, fair Geraldine !
    Thy promise with justice I claim,
And thou, queen of fairies, shalt ever be mine,
The bride of my bed ; and thy portrait divine
    Shall fill all the earth with my fame."

He spake ; when, behold, the fair Geraldine's form
    On the canvas enchantingly glow'd ;
His touches—they flew like the leaves in a storm ;
And the pure pearly white and the carnation warm
    Contending in harmony flow'd.

And now did the portrait a twin-sister seem
    To the figure of Geraldine fair :
With the same sweet expression did faithfully teem
Each muscle, each feature ; in short, not a gleam
    Was lost of her beautiful hair.

'T was the fairy herself ! but, alas, her blue eyes
    Still a pupil did ruefully lack ;
And who shall describe the terrific surprise
That seized the Paint-King when, behold, he descries
    Not a speck of his palette of black !

" I am lost," said the fiend, and he shook like a leaf;
    When, casting his eyes to the ground,
He saw the lost pupils of Ellen with grief
In the jaws of a mouse, and the sly little thief
    Whisk away from his sight with a bound.

" I am lost ! " said the fiend, and he fell like a stone ;
    Then rising the fairy in ire
With a touch of her finger she loosen'd her zone,
(While the limbs on the wall gave a terrible groan,)
    And she swell'd to a column of fire.

Her spear now a thunder-bolt flash'd in the air,
    And sulphur the vault fill'd around ;
She smote the grim monster ; and now by the hair
High-lifting, she hurl'd him in speechless despair
    Down the depths of the chasm profound.

Then over the picture thrice waving her spear,
    "Come forth !" said the good Geraldine ;
When, behold, from the canvass descending, appear
Fair Ellen, in person more lovely than e'er,
    With grace more than ever divine !

WILLIAM MAXWELL,

A NATIVE of Virginia, received his education at Yale College, and was for some time editor of the New York Journal of Commerce. We believe he has since resided in Norfolk as a lawyer. He published a volume of poems at Philadelphia in 1816.

THE REVERY.

I AM come to this sycamore tree,
    And lay myself down in its shade :
The world has no pleasure for me ;
    The hopes of my youth are betray'd.
Flow on, thou sweet musical stream,
    My murmurs shall mingle with thine ;
My spirit is wrapt in a dream,
    The sadness I feel is divine.

Hope took me, a gay little child,
    And soothed me to sleep on her breast
And, like my own mother, she smiled
    O'er the dreams of my innocent rest.
Then beauty came whispering sweet,
    Every word had a magical power ;
And pleasure, with eyes of deceit,
    Enticed me to enter her bower.

There love show'd his glittering dart,
    Just bathed in the nectar of bees;
While fancy persuaded my heart,
    That his only design was to please.
And fame held her wreath of renown,
    All blooming with laurels divine;
And promised the flourishing crown,
    To circle these temples of mine.

Then I said to myself in my sleep,
    How lovely is all that I see!
I shall never have reason to weep,
    For the world is a garden to me.
But an angel came down from the skies,
    And claim'd me at once as her own;
Fair truth shed her light on my eyes,
    And the shades of delusion are flown.

I sigh for the dreams of my youth,
    All melted away into air;
Yet say, that the sweet light of truth
    Betray my poor heart to despair?
Ah no! I may mourn for awhile,
    Till my bosom is freed from its leaven;
Then peace shall return with a smile,
    And faith waft my spirit to heaven.

THE PRIZE.

CLODPOLE, a simple rustic clown,
Lived just a few miles out of town—
The city's name? I wont be sure,
I think though, it was Baltimore—
An honest countryman by trade,
Extremely clever with his spade,
Could drive his plough off in a race,
And plant potatoes with a grace.
His wife too was a tidy soul,
A thriving pair upon the whole.
But times grew hard; Embargo came;
Poor things! they did 'nt know who to blame.
Some said, "the English are the cause:"
Some said, "Red-Breeches—burn his laws!"

But now a lottery appear'd !
Poor Clodpole read the scheme and stared.
For certainly the plan was great,
And was n't it sanction'd by the state ?
He goes at once to buy a ticket,
And begs the clerk to let him pick it ;
('T was at the office kept by Waite,
That is so truly fortunate ;)
Then looks and looks with all his eyes,
And wisely thinks to choose the prize,
And now all day he reads the scheme,
And ev'ry night he dreams—a dream.
He thought the money in his pocket,
And bought a chest and key to lock it.
    At length the lottery is drawn.
Clod hears the news, and he is gone.
"My wife," says he, " I 'm off for town,
To see if I am still a clown.
So if you see me coming, Harriot,
A sure 'nough great man in my chariot,
Mind, see it well with both your eyes,
You may be sure I 've got the prize.
Then seize your longest-handled broom,
And fly like lightning round the room ;
Break ev'rything you 've got—more too—
And we 'll buy everything that 's new.
Yes ! and I 'll give you such a gown !
Like Mrs Dashaway 's in town."
    He goes to town, or rather flies :
" My ticket, Sir, is it a prize ? "
The clerk soon read the fellow through,
And felt a little waggish too.
So with a strange, mysterious look,
He turns, and turns, and turns his book.
" Your ticket, friend"——Clod stretch'd his eyes—
" Has drawn—has drawn—" " what ? what ?"—" no
      prize
But a dead blank ! " Clod heard no more,
But down he fell upon the floor.
" A doctor ! run ! the man will die."
A doctor was just riding by ;
(These doctors are as thick as crows ;)
He smelt the carrion I suppose.
He feels Clod's pulse, and shakes his head
" It is a fit : he must be bled.

His constitution though 's good stuff.
I 'll give him medicine enough.
They 'll cure him—if they should n't kill—
At any rate they 'll help the bill."
Out lancet, and he stuck a vein.
The clown comes to himself again,
And rolls around his wondering eyes,
Like a wise owl, in great surprise.
The doctor bears him off in haste
To his own chariot, sees him placed,
And bids the coachman drive him home.
Dame Harriot sees the carriage come,
"O! he has got the prize! we 're made!
Good by t' ye to the hoe and spade!"
Away she ran, and seized the broom,
And flew like lightning round the room,
Breaking up all she could get at—
Except the jug—she could n't break that—
A present from her mother Gray,
And given her on her wedding day:
There was none like it to be sold,
And such fine beer as it would hold!
But all the rest demolished quite,
You never saw now such a sight.
    Just then poor Clodpole enters in:
"Stop! stop!" he cries; "it is a sin.
For mercy quit this foolish prank,
He says my prize has drawn a blank."
See! there they stand as stiff as posts;
And white as two meal-powder'd ghosts!
At last Clod cries, "Give me a hug.
I 'm glad to find you 've saved the jug.
Confound all lotteries, I say!
Stick to the plough, and work away!
Bad luck has made me monstrous wise,
So, spite of chance, I 've got the prize."

TEA.

Give me, give me here my tea;
Ladies' nectar! give it me;
Sweet as what the Hummer sips,
Or the dew on Beauty's lips.
Tea 't is makes the spirits flow,

Tickles up the heart of wo,
Sets the tongue, enlivens wit,
Gives the sweet poetic fit.
Tea 't is makes the charming fair
Sprightly, pleasing, as they are.
What is more than all, 't was Tea,
Tea, that set Columbia free.

———

TO A FAIR LADY.

FAIREST, mourn not for thy charms,
Circled by no lover's arms ;
While inferior belles, you see,
Pick up husbands merrily.
Sparrows when they choose to pair,
Meet their matches anywhere ;
But the Phœnix, sadly great,
Cannot find an equal mate.
Earth, though dark, enjoys the honor
Of a moon to wait upon her ;
Venus, though divinely bright,
Cannot boast a satellite.

———

ROBERT S. COFFIN,

WAS born in the state of Maine, and spent the early portion of his life in Newburyport, where he served an apprenticeship as a printer, an occupation which he afterwards pursued in Boston, New York, and Philadelphia. He dreamed that the gods had made him poetical, and put forth quantities of metre at an early age. In the latter part of his life, his rhymes, under the name of "The Boston Bard," obtained him some notice as an inditer for the poet's corner of the newspapers, and his various pieces were collected and published in a volume, in 1826. It contains but a small amount of tolerable matter. We remember while a schoolboy, to have read some local satires of his

in manuscript, which showed respectable powers of sarcasm
and ridicule.   He died at Rowley, near Newburyport, in May,
1827, at the age of about thirty.   His life was chequered by
considerable variety, he having been at one time a sailor; the
public sympathy was much excited for him toward the close of
his career, and Mr Bryan wrote a poem, the profits of which
were given to relieve his necessities.

SONG.

Love, the leaves are falling round thee ;
   All the forest trees are bare ;
Winter's snow will soon surround thee,
   Soon will frost thy raven hair :
      Then say, with me,
      Love, wilt thou flee,
   Nor wait to hear sad autumn's prayer ?
      For winter rude
      Will soon intrude,
   Nor aught of summer's blushing beauties spare.

Love, the rose lies withering by thee,
   And the lily blooms no more ;
Nature's charms will quickly fly thee,
   Chilling rains around thee pour :
      Oh, then with me,
      Love, wilt thou flee,
   Ere whirling tempests round thee roar,
      And winter dread
      Shall frost thy head,
   And all thy raven ringlets silver o'er ?

Love, the moon is shining for thee ;
   All the lamps of heaven are bright ;
Holy spirits glide before thee,
   Urging on thy tardy flight ;
      Then say, with me,
      Love, wilt thou flee,
   Nor wait the sun's returning light ?
      Time's finger rude,
      Will soon intrude
Relentless, all thy blushing beauties blight.

Love, the flowers no longer greet thee,
   All their lovely hues are fled !

No more the violet springs to meet thee,
  Lifting slow its modest head:
    Then say, with me,
    Love, wilt thou flee,
And leave this darkling desert dread?
    And seek a clime
    Of joy sublime,
Where fadeless flowers a lasting fragrance shed?

WILLIAM B. WALTER,

Was born in Boston, and educated at Bowdoin College, in Maine. He afterwards studied divinity at Cambridge, but never entered the pulpit. He died at Charleston, S. C., in 1822, aged about twentysix or seven. He wrote "Sukey," and a volume of poems, published in 1821.

ROMANCE.

'T is the last hour! far o'er the beetling steep,
The glorious sun descends into the deep,
And flings around a fiery flood of light,
In farewell beams magnificently bright!—
The shadowing clouds in mingled clusters driven,
In lingering splendor float along the heaven:
On roseate wings all softly now are stealing,
Veil his bright beams then suddenly revealing;
Tinging the towering cliffs and glowing skies,
With radiant streaks of blue and purple dyes;
While the long gleam that sweeps the crimson west,
Traces the mighty limits of his rest.
So sink the powerful, and the good of earth,
From this fair world, that gloried in their birth!
Their fame beams bright o'er death's dispersing gloom,
And crowns with living light their hallow'd tomb!
  'T is the last hour! and all around is still!—
No murmur breaks on Calvary's lone hill!—

Gihon's green banks and waves of heavenly blue,
And vales and woods touch'd with a soften'd hue,
Shine gladly forth, and greet the raptured view!—
Hush'd is the fall of waters! evening's purple dew
Is all around—the sweet flowers blossoming
Droop their bright heads over the sacred spring!
The high blue depths of air are silent now!—
And spirits crowd along that mountain's brow!—
Their rushing plumes are waving in the light,
Spangled with stars, their waving tresses bright,
Circled with diadems enwreath'd with flowers!
They come in glory from immortal bowers;
Hark!—'t is the music of a golden string,
Swept by the sweet winds softly quivering!
That trembles on the air with thrilling wing,
And soothes the soul with its wild wandering!
Like the loved hymn of early joys departed,
That leaves the pilgrim almost broken-hearted;
Too richly dear, its deep enchanting swell
That has no name—but only breathes farewell!—
'T is gone!—and silent now the broad blue skies,
Rolling in splendor as they gently rise!
Soaring on radiant wings, far, far away!
How solemnly beautiful departing day!
And oh! how changed from that when Jesus died
On that lone mountain's solitary side!—
Thick clouds of darkness veil'd its hallow'd crest,
And hovering lower'd upon its awful breast;
Heavy and still the gathering volumes form;
Hark! 't is the hollow muttering of the storm!—
It comes at last, in gloom and wildering terror;
The skies hang heavy like a mighty mirror,
Despoil'd of all its splendor and its light!
Dim crowding shapes are thronging down the night!-
Redoubling peal on peal the thunder rolls,
And rends the reddening vapor's bloody folds!

*   *   *   *   *   *   *

Sudden and quick the lurid flashes driven
In angry quiverings shot along the heaven,
Shivering the foldings of that darksome shroud!
Rent are the mountain rocks! earth shrieks aloud!
The tempest winds are struggling fierce—and far
Down the deep vale rolls on the fearful war!
The volumed mass, all trembling, now receding,

In wandering fires, high o'er the proud crest spreading
In billowy flames! high on their flashing wings,
Wrecks of old clouds and awful thunderings!
And meteors stricken from the firmament
Shower round their sulphurous rains!—in wild lament,
Phantoms of light burst from the yawning earth
On burning wings, the earthquake's wondrous birth!—
The sun goes down in blood, and day is gone!
Nature convulsive shakes, groans deep, 't is done!
The whirlwinds rage, the graves give up their dead!
Thousands of thunders roll! Where is that spirit fled ?
   The godhead's power was there! and all was night!
The godhead's power was there! and all was light!—

    *   *   *   *   *   *

   Lo! rising from the shade of years,
Visions of light are beaming!
They pass away!—a host appears!
How bright the visionary shapes are gleaming!—
Hark!—'t is the trumpet clang!—the warrior band
Sweep the dark waters for the holy land;—
Knights, chieftains, paladins and kings!
Amid ten thousand banner'd things!
Bright gleam the far off spears—and golden armor ringing,
Proud plumage waving, and red crosses flinging,
Are all around, where upward they are winging,
   In pomp and pride of chivalry,
Their streaming terrors to the sky!—
And see, where burns the crescent high,
Melting in clouds of purple dye!
And gay pavilions proudly shine,—
Gilded throne and gorgeous shrine
Are stretched on Syria's strand!
And there the Moslem banner throws,
Its threatening folds to coming foes!—
See the Saracen lines are unveil'd, and display,
The burning crests of their long array,
And glance in fearful light,—the sun's last trembling ray!
   Hear ye no cry on Gaza's shore ?—
   No victor shout, no battle roar ?—
   The ringing trump come piercingly—
   On the startled ear, and the hoarse war cry!
   The peal of drum rolling deeply on!
   The war horn's din, and gonfalon;
Saw ye no flash of the scimetar's wave.

As it fell on the crests of the warrior brave?—
The crimson plume mingling with crescent of light;
The struggles of death in the heat of the fight!
Where the wild war horse trampled over the dead,
And crush'd out the souls of the living,—and fled?
His fetlocks all gory, and ghastly his eye!—
And the groan and the curse, and the horrible yell
Of the victor and vanquish'd, like spirits of hell
From their chains unbound and warring high,
Shrieking out the long curse of their agony!—
　Banners are spread on the mountain rock!
Dark shadows are melting! and lo! there's a shock,
And the battle is ending!—a loud stirring cry
Swells on the cloud wind exultingly!—
The dark volumed smoke rolls awfully there!
Livid flashes of light through its canopy glare!
Like meteor flame in the stormy air—
Million of shafts giving dreadful token!
Spears kindling along! all bloody and broken!—
Like the angry clouds of the lowering morn!
Wildly they rush through the smoke and flame,
Fighting to win a glorious name,
　Or lonely there to die!
Whence is that form that comes terribly on?
With a helmet of light—in the dark battle won.
　In the splendor of youth! it is vanish'd and gone!
O, gone for aye in the whirlwind breath
Of the spirit that rides on the clouds of death!
His white courser plunging with terrible wrath
And leaping along the encumber'd path!—
His rider he drags o'er the carnage ground;
Still muttering out an encouraging sound,
And waving in vain—his broken sabre round;
His bosom gore stained with a sabre wound!
In vain! the scimetars are nearer clashing!—
And arms of blood—like death stars flashing!
Rolling of drums, and shrieks for life!
The earthquake motion of the strife!—
And hark! a fearful pause in that din profound!
The dark fight deepens, and gathers round!
The red cross banners are up on the gale!
And their floating is like the shattered sail
Of the proud ship wreck'd by the ocean storm!
Some frigate of air, of the bravest form,
Flashing in blood, by the thunder torn!—

How they hurry along ; by their flight upborne !
The crescents are down ! there are suns in the sky !
And hark ! the glad shout of victory !——
Dark as the wave when spectres lower
And shroud the deep at midnight hour !——
Thick as the leaves when autumn tide,
Has reft the forest of its pride !
Swift as the clouds by whirlwinds driven
Far—far along the troubled heaven !
   The glorious vision pass'd !
Red ruin grasped his scythe, and strode along the waste !——

  *   *   *   *   *   *   *

The moon rides high in heaven ; the stars are bright
Along the azure depths, shedding a timid light !
Who has not felt the mysteries of night ?
Yea ! there is something hallow'd in this hour,
When the mind wanders in its newborn power,
Far from the things of earth to things above,
And worships in the world of holiness and love !——
In regions pure, where veil'd archangels dwell,
Circling the eternal front of life ineffable !——
   Sometimes we wander to the fairy land,
Where the soul dances and her wings expand !
Fair land !—all brighten'd o'er with turf and flowers,
And dewy shrubbery, and moonlight bowers,
Retreat of fancy's glittering vagrant powers.
Fair heaven !—where many color'd clouds enfold,
Bright islets floating in the sea of gold !
Proud domes and palaces are shining there,
With ivory columns, gemm'd with fire-stain'd spar !
There wanton zephyrs dance on budding flowers,
And waft the fragrant leaves in snowy showers ;——
By sunny banks the silver waters whirl
A wildering music o'er their sands of pearl !——
And birds are singing from their star-lit bowers,
To lull the sleeping of the blue eyed hours !
Light things are flitting in this world of air !
Gay creatures born of thought, are dwelling there !——
The elfin race, who bathe in dews of morn !
And climb the rainbow of the summer storm !——
Floating about, in thinnest robes of light,
From meteors caught, that shoot along the night.
Crowns, studded o'er with gems, their brows adorn,
Stole from the eyelids of the waking morn !——

They wave bright sceptres, wrought of moonlight beams,
And spears of crystal, tinged with lightning gleams!—
Young naked Loves are sporting on the main,
Or glide on clouds along the ethereal plain!
Their snowy breasts floating the waves among,
Are kiss'd by shapes of light, and swim along
In liquid sapphire—with their humid locks
Dropping thick diamonds o'er their mossy rocks!—
The sea-green realm is all with emeralds shining,
With rainbow arches o'er the depths reclining!—
And other skies are deeply rolling under,
With clouds of trembling flame and slumbering thunder!
And minstrels blow their horns of tulip flowers!
In echoes softly from their air-borne towers,
Floats back the music, with a dreamy sound!
A dove-wing'd presence, hovering round and round!—
Visions of joy! in sun-robe garments sporting,
Dear Loves! with gay looks in green pathways courting!
Who speak with eyes, and move with steps of sadness,
And now, we list a cheerful song of gladness!

RICHARD DABNEY,

A NATIVE of Virginia; he resided for a time in Philadelphia, where he was engaged in some literary occupations. Further than this, we have obtained no information respecting him. He is the author of a small volume of poems published in 1814 at Philadelphia, several of which were included in Roscoe's specimens of American poetry, and received a good deal of commendation from the editor in his critical remarks.

THE SPRING OF LIFE.

'T is not enough that virtue sways
Our present hours and passing days;
'T is not enough, our purpose be
From every base intention free;

All that polluted life's first source
Will float along its downward course,
And dark shall be each future year,
Unless the spring of life is clear.

Though words of truth eternal say,
Repentance washes guilt away ;
If former times display a stain,
The future shall the blot retain ;
The hue and color of the past
Upon the coming hour is cast ;
And dark shall be each future year,
Unless the spring of life be clear.

O then, upon those future years,
Bestow not agony and tears !
Though all thy sins shall be forgiven,
And blotted from the book of heaven ;
Their shades shall flit around, and fling
Dark horror from their raven wing ;
And bitter be each future year,
Unless the spring of life is clear.

* * * * *

In early life when trusting youth
Thinks all is goodness, worth, and truth,
A holy inmate charms man's breast,
And lulls its many woes to rest.
It watches o'er his pillow'd head,
And lures sweet slumbers to his bed ;
It adds fresh charms to morning's ray,
And guards him through the eventful day—
No might, but his, can bid depart,
That holy inmate from his heart—
'T is stainless conscience—boon of heaven,
To man, for heavenly purpose, given.

But when amidst the world he roves,
And that he ought to hate, he loves,
Unheeded pass its frequent cries,
The holy inmate quickly dies ;
But oft within the varying scene,
When thought his follies wakes between ;
But oft within the gloom of night,

Its shade, avenging, meets his sight—
Comes, deck'd with all the warmth of youth,
When life was love, and peace, and truth,
Comes, deck'd with all the charms that blest,
In early life, his guiltless breast.
It smiles—in fancied view, appears,
The virtuous bliss of youthful years ;
It frowns—before his blasted eyes,
His present vices hideous rise.

A WESTERN WAR SONG.

To the north-western wilds, has our gallant youth gone—
Though his breast, with a tempest of feeling, was torn,
Yet he scorn'd a weak tear, and disdained a weak sigh—
He is wedded to vengeance, or bounden to die,
For the horror-fraught fate of the victim so dear
To the heart of the hero, the brave volunteer.

On his dauntless steed borne, he hastens to ride,
On his shoulder his rifle, his sword by his side—
O'er rivers, through forests, like the swift wind he flies
To the sounds, that he pants for, the battle-field's cries.
For wedded to vengeance, and stranger to fear,
Is the heart of the hero, the brave volunteer.

Hurra, at Moravia, that battle-cry wakes,
From the ranks the dire peal of the musketry breaks.
The brave volunteer, 'midst the death-flashing cloud,
Invokes the dear name of the murdered, aloud ;
Then quick to the charge, with his death-dealing blow,
Pours his wrath on the friends of the hatchet and bow.
For wedded to vengeance, a stranger to fear,
Is the soul of the hero, the brave volunteer.

At that dread hour of night, when his cherish'd love bled,
And her mangled form slept with the massacred dead,
He had sworn a dread oath, that his rifle and steel,
On the merciless demons, deep vengeance should deal,
For the horror-fraught fate of the victim so dear
To the heart of the hero, the brave volunteer.

Then joy to the brave volunteer, who has sp
To the wilds of the north-west, where thousands have bled,
Who, wedded to vengeance, a dread oath has sworn,
On the arms of his comrades, a corse to be borne;
Or the deep debt of vengeance in tenfold to deal
On the merciless fiends, with his rifle and steel,
For the soul-harrowing scathe of the victim so dear
To the heart of the hero, the brave volunteer.

THE HEROES OF THE WEST.

How sweet is the song of the festal rite,
  When the bosom with rapture swells high;
When the heart, at the soft touch of pleasure, beats light,
  And bright is the beam of the eye.
In the dirge, that is pour'd o'er affection's bier,
  How holy an interest dwells,
When the frequent drop of the frequent tear,
  The heart-rending anguish tells;
But sweeter the song that the minstrel should raise
  To the patriot victor's fame,
And livelier the tones of the heart-gender'd praise,
  That should wake from the harp at his name:
But holier the dirge that the minstrel should pour
  O'er the fallen hero's grave,
Whose arm wields the sword for his country no more,
  Who has died the death of the brave.

There lives in the bosom a feeling sublime;
  Of all, 't is the strongest tie;
Unvarying through every change of time,
  And only with life does it die.
'T is the love that is borne for that lovely land,
  That smiled on the hour of our birth;
'T is the love, that is planted by nature's hand,
  For our sacred native earth.
'T was this that the patriot victor inspired,
  Was strong in the strength of his arm,
With the holiest zeal his brave bosom fired,
  And to danger and death gave a charm.
'T was this that the dying hero blest,
  And hallow'd the hour when he fell,

That throbb'd in the final throb of his breast,
  And heaved in his bosom's last swell:

When a thousand swords, in a thousand hands,
  To the sunbeams of heaven shone bright;
When the willing hearts of Columbia's bands,
  Were firm for Columbia's right;
When the blood of the west, in the battle was pour'd,
  In defence of the rights of the west;
When the blood of the east stain'd the point of the sword,
  At the Eastern king's behest:
Till the angel form of returning peace,
  O'er the plain and the mountain smiled—
Bade the rude blast of war from its ravage to cease,
  And the sweet gale of plenty breathe mild.
She smiled—and the nation's mighty woes
  Ceased to stream from the nation's eyes;
She smiled—and a fabric of wisdom arose,
  And exalted its fame to the skies.

Then firm be its base, as the giant rock
  'Midst the ocean waves alone,
That the beating rain and the tempest shock,
  For numberless years has borne.
And blasted the parricide arm, that shall plan
  That glorious structure's fall;
But still may it sanction the rights of man,
  And liberty guardian to all.
Then sweet be the song that the minstrel should raise,
  To the patriot victor's fame,
And lively the tones of the heart-gender'd praise,
  That should wake from the harp at his name.
Then holy the dirge that the minstrel should pour,
  O'er the fallen hero's grave,
Whose hand wields the sword for his country no more,
  Who has died the death of the brave.

TURN NOT TO THE EAST.

Can the heart, which first glow'd in a far foreign seat,
For a different land feel its warm pulses beat?
Can the eye, oped not here, prop the heart-gender'd tear
On the blood that was spilt for the blessings we bear?

Turn not to the East with the eye of desire
Turn not to the East like the sect'ry of fire;
For the wind of the East in its poison'd gale brings
The fell breath of despots, and curses of kings.

See the star of the West in its mild glories rise,
See the star of the West tread its path in the skies:
How sweet is the sight, while its soft radiance beams
On my native land's hills, and my native land's streams.

That star, when the proud boasting sons of the East
Have danced through their day, and have finish'd their feast—
That star then shall shine over millions more blest,
In the realms doom'd to rise in the wilds of the West.

Then look to the Eastern horizon's blue bound,
As if past its precincts no mortal is found ;
Then look to the Eastern horizon's red light,
As if past its rays brood oblivion and night.

Can the heart, which first glow'd in a far foreign seat,
For a different land feel its warm pulses beat?
Can the eye, oped not here, drop the heart-gender'd tear,
On the blood that was spilt for the blessings we bear?

TO A LADY.

Lady, that form so slight and fair
Was, surely, never framed to bear
The season's change, the hand of pain,
And fell disease's racking train,
That must, from year to year, attend
Life's course, till life itself shall end.

That heart, so pure, so soft, so good,
That scarce has yet a pang withstood,
Was, surely, never meant to bear
Grief, sorrow, wo, deceit, despair,
And all the mental ills, that rend
The human heart, till life shall end.

Some happy island far removed,
Whose groves of bliss an angel loved,

Wh▮▮ winter's gloom was never known,
Nor fell disease's hollow groan ;
Where grief, deceit, despair and wo
Dare not their forms of horror show,

Lady, was placed thy destined lot—
But fate, that destiny forgot ;
Or, envious of thy blissful state,
Some fiend of earth, and earthly hate,
Gave thee to pain and sorrow here—
Betray'd thee to this world of care.

WASHINGTON IRVING

Was born in the city of New York, and educated at Columbia College. His earliest productions were written at about the seventeenth year of his age, and appeared first in the New York Morning Chronicle, under the title of The Letters of Jonathan Oldstyle. These light and hasty performances of his youth were a few years since collected and republished in a volume. He began the study of law, but in 1805, the declining state of his health induced him to undertake a voyage to Europe. He travelled over most of the South of Europe, and England, and returned to this country in 1807. He completed his law studies, but feeling more attachment to literary occupations he did not pursue the profession. In 1807 he began in connexion with Mr Paulding and Mr Verplanck, the publication of Salmagundi, which appeared in numbers at irregular periods, and attained to such a popularity, that in a year it ran through six editions. In 1810 he gave to the world Knickerbocker's History of New York, a work which gave him a wide reputation. He furnished a great amount of matter for the Analectic Magazine, among other articles, the biographies of our most distinguished naval commanders. During the war, Mr Irving was military secretary, and aide-de-camp to the Governor of the state of New York. In 1815 he went to Europe, where he has since resided. The Sketch Book, Bracebridge Hall, Tales of a Traveller, The Life of Columbus, and biographies of the principal writers of Great Britain, works which he has executed since he left this country have extended his fame wherever English literature is known.

The subjoined extract is the only poetry to our knowledge, that has been published with his name.

THE FALLS OF THE PASSAIC.

In a wild, tranquil vale, fringed with forests of green,
Where nature had fashion'd a soft, sylvan scene,
The retreat of the ring-dove, the haunt of the deer,
Passaic in silence roll'd gentle and clear.

No grandeur of prospect astonish'd the sight,
No abruptness sublime mingled awe with delight;
Here the wild flow'ret blossom'd, the elm proudly waved,
And pure was the current the green bank that laved.

But the spirit that ruled o'er the thick tangled wood,
And deep in its gloom fix'd his murky abode,
Who loved the wild scene that the whirlwinds deform,
And gloried in thunder, and lightning, and storm;

All flush'd from the tumult of battle he came,
Where the red men encounter'd the children of flame,
While the noise of the war-whoop still rang in his ears,
And the fresh bleeding scalp as a trophy he bears:

With a glance of disgust, he the landscape survey'd,
With its fragrant wild flowers, its wide waving shade;—
Where Passaic meanders through margins of green,
So transparent its waters, its surface serene.

He rived the green hills, the wild woods he laid low;
He taught the pure stream in rough channels to flow;
He rent the rude rock, the steep precipice gave,
And hurl'd down the chasm the thundering wave

Countless moons have since roll'd in the long lapse of time—
Cultivation has softened those features sublime ;
The axe of the white man has lighten'd the shade,
And dispell'd the deep gloom of the thicketed glade.

But the stranger still gazes, with wondering eye,
On the rocks rudely 'orn, and groves mounted on high ;
Still loves on the cliff's dizzy borders to roam,
Where the torrent leaps headlong embosom'd in foam.

HENRY T. FARMER,

A NATIVE of Charleston S. C., where he now resides as a
physician, is the author of a volume of poems published in
1819.

THE BATTLE OF THE ISLE.

A COMICO-TRAGICAL TALE.

PART I.—THE ISLE.

On the verge of the deep, where the dark sea-bird hovers,
Where the wave, in loud fury, bursts wild on the shore ;
Near the light-house, whose flame to the wanderer discovers
A beam, like the glance of those long-sever'd lovers,
Who meet in blest rapture, to sever no more ;
An isle of white sand, like a desert is seen,
Where no wild flower blushes in meadow of green ;
But, where long tangled sea-weed is cast on the strand,
Like the gray locks of age, pluck'd by merciless hand ;
For the storm tore it up from its deep oozy bed,
As the ruffian tears locks from the wanderer's head :
Oh ! ye who would view "this famed desert" aright,
Go visit the strand by the "pale starry light ;"
When the bleak wind is high, and the breakers are gleaming,
And the owl is abroad, and the sea-gull is screaming ;
Then, sit near yon circummured castle awhile,
And behold the fell grandeur of Sullivan's isle.
The moonbeam just gleams on yon ruin so bare,

One moment the moonbeam has fled ;
Like the quick frantic smile on the face of despair,
When she bends o'er the couch of the dead.
Oft to visit this spot a blest seraph is seen,
With an eye ever bright, and a robe ever green,
And a cheek, where the red rose for ever must bloom :
And she covers with daisies the path to the tomb ;
The youth that she smiles on is certainly blest,
He has strength for the chase, and fair visions for rest ;
I have wiped the big drops from a brow cold as stone,
But I have seldom seen health on her diamond throne.

Far famed was the castle, now lost in decay,
That frown'd o'er the high surging sea ;
Though pale is the blood-stain, and long past the day,
Still, who has not heard of that noble affray,
And its banner, the green island tree ?

PART II.—THE NIGHT.

In bugle bed-gown frown'd the night,
Like angry witch with baneful spite ;
She scarce allow'd the stars to light
    The sandy hills around.
The moon, 't is thought, was fast asleep,
In distant cavern dark and deep,
Where silence doth her vigils keep,
    In mystery profound.
The stricken drum announced the hour,
The sentry paced round fosse and tower,
And fearing much a drenching shower,
    Around his watch-coat drew :
A sudden sorrow fill'd his mind,
His memory, with hint unkind,
Spoke of past times, and he repined
    His coat was now not new.
Ah ! little did that watchman dream
Of battle field e'er morning beam,
Of noisy shout and piercing scream,
    From virgin beauty fair ;
Or he had bow'd his lofty crest,
And wiped his eyes, and smote his breast,
And 'gainst his brow steel gauntlet press'd,
    In token of despair.
Now arm in arm, or hand in hand,
Two knights pass'd slowly o'er the strand,

Unarm'd with battle-axe or brand,
  Or faulchion broad, or spear :
Anon they stopp'd before the tower,
Where fair Floressa* slept in bower,
Far from enchanter's baneful power,
  Or haggard wizard drear.
"I know this beauteous virgin rare,
And by yon vaulted arch I swear,
A foot more light, a face more fair,
  And 'sooth an eye more bright,
On earth before has never been,
And she yclept the fairy queen
By wilder'd knight or damsel seen,
  Would wither in her sight.
Let poet Spenser deftly tell,
Of Britomart and Florimel,
And loudly wild his numbers swell,
  In either damsel's praise :
Or e'en let Ariosto rear
A trophy to Marphisa's spear,
Or Tasso crown his virgin dear
  With never-fading bays :
For these must bow before her shrine,
And e'en the Amazon divine,
Who tasted Alexander's wine,
  And Joan of Arc beside."
Thus spoke the foremost knight, and strode
In silence o'er the sandy road,
That led toward her blest abode ;
  The gate flew open wide.

PART III.—THE VISIT.

  Slow o'er the platform paced a knight,†
In glittering vest and armor dight ;
High on his helm, like passing cloud,
With awful nod, a horsetail bow'd.
'Twas said by Douglas, in his pride,
"Right fairly" doth Lord Marmion ride ;
To give this mailed chief his due,
He rode as well and fairly too.
The steed Bucephalus of yore,

<hr>

  * A rich widow.
    † The hero of the piece, who kept livery stables.

Triumphant through the battle bore
Great Philip's son, in warlike pride ;
'T is said, when that famed stallion died,
The monarch many a tear-drop shed,
And built a city o'er his head :
Our chief, for love of faithful steed,
Had done almost as good a deed ;
To build a city, though not able,
He built, 't was all he could—a stable.
The knights* who to the gateway came,
Call'd on Floressa's honor'd name,
Saying, within that lady's bower,
They came to spend a short half hour.
The mailed chieftain, turning, said,
"That lady bright has gone to bed : "
The knight his manly port admired,
And bowing—would have soon retired ;
When quick they heard a mighty jar,
A tumult wild, a din of war :
High on the castle's slanting stair,
Appear'd the form of female fair ;
Wild was her look with haggard fright,
Her hair was loose, her dress was white :
Down—down she swept, like fell Simoom,
Left all her armor in her room,
Toss'd from her eyes the flowing hair,
Brandish'd her stalwart arm in air ;
And thus 'midst thunders, fire, and smoke,
That tender, lovely virgin spoke.

PART IV.—THE BATTLE.

"Hold ! thieves and murderers, on your lives,
Bring pistols, scissors, carving knives,
    And shed their impious gore : "
She caught the foremost by his coat,
Grasp'd with her sinewy hand his throat,
    To dash him on the floor ;
"A knife, a knife, fly quickly, fly,
Attack the villains or I die.
What, pistols, ho ! is no one nigh ?
    Quick, minion, on thy life ;
My castle for a gleaming steel,

* Two officers belonging to the United States army.

To make those damned robbers feel
The deadly blow this arm can deal;
    My kingdom for a knife!!—
Fire quick"—a flash beam'd ruddy bright,
A bullet took its erring flight
    From smoking petronel.
Death now appear'd to call his court,
For soon, as if in playful sport,
    A seeming victim fell.
" Off, from my hall, you scoundrels base,
Let no one longer show his face,
This is my own domain and place,
    Let no damn'd slave deride it;
Who dares among you all to frown?
I paid in yonder distant town,
Each farthing of the money down,
    The very hour *I buy'd it.*
Down with the huge portcullis straight,
Go, quick as lightning shut the gate,
    The lowly villains bind;"
With that, she gave a hearty damn
To either knight, the gate goes slam,
    And one remains behind:
Gleam'd in her hand the pointed knife,
'T is aim'd at that lone captive's life,
    With many a deadly thrust;
The servants shudder with affright,
For never was a mortal wight
    So handled, and so cursed.
Against such gentleness, such charms,
What knight could wield his missile arms?
    Sure all must be subdued!
And he who tarried in her hold,
And saw her meek demeanor bold,
    In cool amazement stood!!—
The chieftain with the waving crest
Felt some compunction in his breast,
    And oped the gate again;
From whence the captive soon withdrew,
And oaths like hailstones after flew
    In Eleusinian strain.
Thus ended, without blood or spoil,
The battle's rage and loud turmoil,
    And imprecations vile;
From hence ye warriors all beware,

Still ponder on that lady fair,
And ever in your memories bear,
The battle of the isle.

JAMES K. PAULDING

Is a native of the state of New York, and resides at present in the city of New York in the capacity of Navy Agent of the United States. Mr Paulding is well known to the public as one of the writers of Salmagundi, and the author of many other popular prose compositions. He wrote during the late war with Great Britain, The Lay of the Scottish Fiddle, a sprightly and entertaining parody of one of Scott's poems. His poem of "The Backwoodsman," published in 1818, was written with the view of pointing out to our native writers the rich materials for poetry with which our country abounds. The most striking characteristic of this work is its distinct and decided nationality. The author has aimed at giving a patriotic and vernacular cast to the train of sentiment which prevails throughout the poem, as well as at preserving the truth and identity of his local descriptions. The design of the work is carried into effect with a proper attention to all the circumstances necessary to give it success so far as the plan can be pronounced suitable; but the writer has not succeeded in giving sufficient interest to his performance to obtain for it any considerable popularity. There is in the story too little attempt to chain our attention by variety and novelty of incident, or striking delineation of individual character. Had more care been bestowed upon the narrative, The Backwoodsman might have been a favorite work. The descriptive parts are the best, and are entitled to much commendation for spirit and fidelity.

THE BACKWOODSMAN.

'Twas sunset's hallow'd time—and such an eve
Might almost tempt an angel heaven to leave.
Never did brighter glories greet the eye,
Low in the warm and ruddy western sky :
Nor the light clouds at summer eve unfold
More varied tints of purple, red, and gold.
Some in the pure, translucent, liquid breast
Of crystal lake, fast anchor'd seem'd to rest,
Like golden islets scatter'd far and wide,
By elfin skill in fancy's fabled tide,
Where, as wild eastern legends idly feign,
Fairy, or genii, hold despotic reign.
Others, like vessels gilt with burnish'd gold,
Their flitting airy way are seen to hold,
All gallantly equipp'd with streamers gay,
While hands unseen, or chance directs their way ;
Around, athwart, the pure ethereal tide,
With swelling purple sail, they rapid glide,
Gay as the bark, where Egypt's wanton queen
Reclining on the shaded deck was seen,
At which as gazed the uxorious Roman fool,
The subject world slipt from his dotard rule.
Anon, the gorgeous scene begins to fade,
And deeper hues the ruddy skies invade ;
The haze of gathering twilight nature shrouds,
And pale, and paler, wax the changeful clouds.
Then sunk the breeze into a breathless calm,
The silent dews of evening dropt like balm ;
The hungry nighthawk from his lone haunt hies,
To chase the viewless insect through the skies ;
The bat began his lantern-loving flight,
The lonely whip-poor-will, our bird of night,
Ever unseen, yet ever seeming near,
His shrill note quaver'd in the startled ear ;
The buzzing beetle forth did gaily hie,
With idle hum, and careless blundering eye ;
The little trusty watchman of pale night,
The fire-fly trimm'd anew his lamp so bright,
And took his merry airy circuit round
The sparkling meadow's green and fragrant bound,
Where blossom'd clover, bathed in balmy dew,
In fair luxuriance, sweetly blushing grew.

*   *   *   *   *   *   *

Now all through Pennsylvania's pleasant land,
Unheeded pass'd our little roving band,
—For every soul had something here to do,
Nor turn'd aside our cavalcade to view—
By Bethlehem, where Moravian exiles 'bide,
In rural paradise, on Lehigh's side,
And York and Lancaster—whose rival rose
In this good land, no bloody discord knows.
Not such their fate !—the ever grateful soil
Rewards the blue-eyed German's patient toil ;
Richer and rounder every year he grows,
Nor other ills his stagnant bosom knows
Than caitiff grub, or cursed Hessian fly,
Mildews, and smuts, a dry or humid sky ;
Before he sells, the market's sudden fall,
Or sudden rise, when sold—still worse than all !
Calmly he lives—the tempest of the mind,
That marks its course by many a wreck behind :
The purpose high that great ambition feels,
Sometimes perchance upon his vision steals,
But never in his sober waking thought
One stirring, active impulse ever wrought.
Calmly he lives—as free from good as blame,
His home, his dress, his equipage the same,
And when he dies, in sooth, 'tis soon forgot
What once he was, or what he once was not—
An honest man, perhaps,—'tis somewhat odd,
That such should be the noblest work of God !
So have I seen in garden rich and gay,
A stately cabbage waxing fat each day ;
Unlike the lively foliage of the trees,
Its stubborn leaves ne'er wave in summer breeze,
Nor flower, like those that prank the walks around.
Upon its clumsy stem is ever found ;
It heeds not noontide heats, or evening's balm,
And stands unmoved in one eternal calm.
At last, when all the garden's pride is lost,
It ripens in drear autumn's killing frost,
And in a savory sourkrout finds its end,
From which detested dish, me heaven defend !

*   *   *   *   *   *

Our Basil beat the lazy sun next day,
And bright and early had been on his way,

But that the world he saw e'en yesternight,
Seem'd faded like a vision from his sight.
One endless chaos spread before his eyes,
No vestige left of earth or azure skies,
A boundless nothingness reign'd everywhere,
Hid the green fields, and silent all the air.
As look'd the traveller for the world below,
The lively morning breeze began to blow,
The magic curtain roll'd in mists away,
And a gay landscape laugh'd upon the day.
As light the fleeting vapors upward glide,
Like sheeted spectres on the mountain side,
New objects open to his wondering view
Of various form, and combinations new.
A rocky precipice, a waving wood,
Deep winding dell, and foaming mountain flood,
Each after each, with coy and sweet delay,
Broke on his sight, as at young dawn of day,
Bounded afar by peak aspiring bold,
Like giant capt with helm of burnish'd gold.
So when the wandering grandsire of our race
On Ararat had found a resting place,
At first a shoreless ocean met his eye,
Mingling on every side with one blue sky;
But as the waters, every passing day,
Sunk in the earth, or roll'd in mists away,
Gradual, the lofty hills, like islands, peep
From the rough bosom of the boundless deep,
Then the round hillocks, and the meadows green.
Each after each, in freshen'd bloom are seen,
Till, at the last, a fair and finish'd whole
Combined to win the gazing patriarch's soul.
Yet oft he look'd, I ween, with anxious eye,
In lingering hope somewhere, perchance, to spy,
Within the silent world, some living thing,
Crawling on earth, or moving on the wing,
Or man, or beast—alas! was neither there,
Nothing that breathed of life in earth or air;
'T was a vast silent mansion rich and gay,
Whose occupant was drown'd the other day:
A church-yard, where the gayest flowers oft bloom
Amid the melancholy of the tomb;
A charnel house, where all the human race
Had piled their bones in one wide resting place;

Sadly he turn'd from such a sight of wo,
And sadly sought the lifeless world below.
   Now down the mountain's rugged western side,
Descending slow, our lonely travellers hied,
Deep in a narrow glen, within whose breast
The rolling fragments of the mountain rest;
Rocks tumbled on each other, by rude chance,
Crown'd with grey fern, and mosses, met the glance,
Through which a brawling river braved its way,
Dashing among the rocks in foamy spray.
Here, 'mid the fragments of a broken world,
In wild and rough confusion, idly hurl'd,
Where ne'er was heard the woodman's echoing stroke,
Rose a huge forest of gigantic oak;
With heads that tower'd half up the mountain's side.
And arms extending round them far and wide,
They look'd coeval with old mother earth,
And seem'd to claim with her an equal birth.
There, by a lofty rock's moss-mantled base,
Our tired adventurers found a resting place;
Beneath its dark, o'erhanging, sullen brow,
The little bevy nestled snug below,
And with right sturdy appetite, and strong,
Devour'd the rustic meal they brought along.
   The squirrel eyed them from his lofty tree,
And chirp'd as wont, with merry morning glee;
The woodcock crow'd as if alone he were,
Or heeded not the strange intruders there,
Sure sign they little knew of man's proud race
In that sequester'd mountain 'biding place;
For wheresoe'er his wandering footsteps tend,
Man never makes the rural train his friend;
Acquaintance that brings other beings near,
Produces nothing but distrust or fear:
Beasts flee from man the more his heart they know,
And fears, at last, to fix'd aversion grow,
As thus in blithe serenity they sat,
Beguiling resting time with lively chat,
A distant, half heard murmur caught the ear,
Each moment waxing louder, and more near,
A dark obscurity spread all around,
And more than twilight seem'd to veil the ground,
While not a leaf e'en of the aspin stirr'd,
And not a sound but that low moan was heard.
There is a moment when the boldest heart

That would not stoop an inch to 'scape death's dart,
That never shrunk from certain danger here,
Will quail and shiver with an aguish fear;
'T is when some unknown mischief hovers nigh,
And heaven itself seems threatening from on high.
  Brave was our Basil, as became a man,
Yet still his blood a little cooler ran,
'Twixt fear and wonder, at that murmur drear,
That every moment wax'd more loud and near.
The riddle soon was read—at last it came,
And nature trembled to her inmost frame;
The forest roar'd, the everlasting oak,
In writhing agonies the storm bespoke,
The live leaves scatter'd wildly everywhere,
Whirl'd round in maddening circles in the air,
The stoutest limbs were scatter'd all around,
The stoutest trees a stouter master found,
Crackling, and crashing, down they thundering go,
And seem to crush the shrinking rocks below :
Then the thick rain in gathering torrents pour'd,
Higher the river rose, and louder roar'd,
And on its dark, quick eddying surface bore
The gather'd spoils of earth along its shore,
While trees that not an hour before had stood
The lofty monarchs of the stately wood,
Now whirling round and round with furious force,
Dash 'gainst the rocks that breast the torrent's force,
And shiver like a reed by urchin broke,
Through idle mischief, or with heedless stroke ;
A hundred cataracts, unknown before,
Rush down the mountain's side with fearful roar,
And as with foaming fury down they go,
Loose the firm rocks and thunder them below ;
Blue lightnings from the dark cloud's bosom sprung,
Like serpents, menacing with forked tongue,
While many a sturdy oak that stiffly braved
The threatening hurricane that round it raved,
Shiver'd beneath its bright resistless flash,
Came tumbling down amain with fearful crash.
Air, earth, and skies, seem'd now to try their power,
And struggle for the mastery of the hour;
Higher the waters rose, and blacker still,
And threaten'd soon the narrow vale to fill.

PAUL ALLEN.

PAUL ALLEN was born at Providence, Rhode Island, February 15th, 1775. His father, Paul Allen, was a representative from that town in the General A sembly, toward the close of the Revolutionary war. Mr Allen was educated at Rhode Island College, and received his degree in 1703. He was educated for the bar, but never practised. After residing some time in Providence, he went to Philadelphia, and was engaged as a writer in the Port Folio and the United States Gazette in that place. About the same time, he was employed to prepare the travels of Lewis and Clark for the press, a piece of work which gave him credit and notoriety as a writer, although the performance was certainly not calculated to call any high degree of talent into exercise. He was directly after this, engaged as one of the editors of the Federal Republican, and assisted in conducting that paper for some time, but not being able to obtain a support from the business, and disagreeing with his partner in the editorship, he abandoned it, and fell into a nervous affection, under which he was impressed with a fixed belief that he was to be waylaid and murdered. In addition to this mental disorder, he was in a condition of extreme indigence, with a widowed mother to support, who had left her home in her old age, and journeyed to Baltimore to reside with her favorite son.

Some years before this, he had proposed to write a History of the American Revolution, and for a long time it was announced every few months as nearly ready for publication. Meantime he had not written a line of the work, nor as it appears from the relation of those who were intimate with him at that period, so much as made the preparation of reading a single book upon the subject. His poverty was such at this time, that he was thrown into jail for a debt of thirty dollars, and the bad state of his health so increased his nervous malady, that he would leave his bed at midnight, under the impression that there were persons in his room or under his window, conspiring to take his life. In the midst of his troubles, however, he had friends, and an undertaking was set on foot in his behalf, by the establishment of the Journal of the Times, the direction of which was entrusted to him. The paper went on for a short time, but was discontinued for want of capital. He was about this period a writer in the Portico, a magazine published at Baltimore, in which enterprise he was associated with Pierpont and Neal, names since highly distinguished in American literature.

At last, his friends succeeded in establishing the Baltimore Morning Chronicle, a paper which under his care, soon obtained a wide, and apparently a profitable circulation. While Allen's reputation was at the height, it was determined to bring out the History of the Revolution, which the public had been so long expecting, and for which a subscription unequalled it is believed, in this country, had been obtained. Allen had done nothing, and could do nothing toward the work, and after a deal of negotiation, the whole work was actually written by Neal and Watkins,* although it appeared, in order to correspond with the proposals, under the name of Allen, who wrote only a page or two of the preface. His poem of Noah was also submitted to Neal, and by him cut down to about one fifth of its original size, and revised and altered throughout before publication. It made its appearance in 1821.

He continued, we believe, editor of the Morning Chronicle till his death, which took place in 1826.

Allen was a member of the Delphian Club of Baltimore, and by an incident occasioned by his connexion with that body, got considerable reputation as a humorist, nevertheless, we are assured by one who knew him well, that he had little humor of any sort in him. "As a man," the same authority proceeds, "he was one of the best I ever knew; as child-like

* Neal began with the Declaration of Independence, and finished the first volume. It was very badly printed : he informs us that he never saw a proof.

and credulous with most, and as full of suspicion towards others, as anybody that ever breathed."

Besides his Noah, he published a volume of miscellaneous poems in 1801. Allen's poetry is not characterized by those qualities, which distinguish his prose,—brilliancy and show. His muse does not attempt any lofty flights. His earlier verses have the common marks of juvenility, but Noah has feeling and simplicity, and is, we think, deserving of more attention than it has yet received.

NOAH.
CANTO. II.

THE sun had sunk behind the watery waste,
When night's pale regent, beautiful and chaste,
With silent footsteps stole upon the sight,
As fearful to awake the dreams of night;
Calmly she mounted up the azure plain,
With all her twinkling vassals in her train ;
Cloud after cloud, in long fantastic chase,
Sweep in succession o'er her pallid face ;
But she still travelling up the blue serene,
Holds her calm course, and lifts her light between,
Till, by no intervening shade o'ercast,
She gives a steady settled ray at last :
The treacherous deep, so late by tempests worn,
And storms, as if by human passions torn,
Now like a blessed spirit, once forgiven,
Reflects the pure and sacred light of heaven.
  The ark, now gliding under easy sail,
Urged by the pressure of a gentle gale,
While no rude breath of wind the prospect mars,
Moves o'er a liquid firmament of stars.
At length she rests—but with a shock so light,
That not a single slumberer of the night
Wakes from his dream. At morn's returning ray
Shem oped the window to behold the day ;
He gazed around, and o'er his head was seen
The smiling olive, with its leaf of green.
" Father, come forth ! " he cries, with heart elate,
" For now the waters do indeed abate."
  Strange to relate, in these unthinking times,
The traveller, while exploring distant climes,

Leaves thee, O Ararat! and feels no shame,
And scarcely do his lips inquire thy name.
Had not thy towering summit long before
Redeem'd the burden, that the deluge bore,
Thou hadst not worn memorials so unjust,
The prints of thoughtless footsteps in thy dust:
And earth until this very hour had run
A silent planet round the golden sun.
'T was Ararat alone preserved from death
The little portion of almighty breath.
    When the fierce warfare of the heaven is o'er;
And thunders, answering thunders cease to roar,
How beautiful to see the sun's bright helm
Shining serene in his recover'd realm!
The victor in his robes of triumph drest,
Looks gay and smiling from the rosy west!
The dew drops catch the triumphs of the sky,
And flash a little sun on every eye!
Such joy did in the patriarch's bosom reign,
When first the arch reposed on earth again.
    He cries, " in reverence to this holy place.
Put off your sandals, all of Noah's race!
It is the hour of mercy, and invites
The bleeding sacrifice and solemn rites."
    The few survivors of the flood draw near;
An altar form'd with pious haste they rear,
And fain would female pity intercede,
The favorite lamb is now condemn'd to bleed;
He, unsuspecting injury, draws nigh,
Nor thinking he is ever doom'd to die,
Bounds by the altar, with his merry feet;
The mountain echoes still return his bleat;
When Japheth grasps him by his snowy fleece,
Upward he looks, his eyes betoken peace,
So pure is innocence, so undismay'd!
He sees no terror in the lifted blade:
Then faint and dying at the altar's base,
One look he casts upon the female face,
And while the ruddy drops his vesture stain
He wonders why he feels the sudden pain.
The flame ascends, and while the suppliants kneel,
And offer up their prayers with pious zeal,
They start, they listen, for a sudden sound
Disturbs the sacred quiet reigning round;
It calls thee! Noah, and the accent flows,
Soft as a zephyr's whisper to a rose.

He turn'd, and saw a face that seem'd to wear
A mingled character of joy and care:
It was not joy; for though upon the cheek
A smile appear'd, it was a smile so meek,
So coy, so placid, every eye might know
'T was touch'd with memory of former wo;
And though the foreheads yielding ivory wore
The marks that Care's rude hand had sculptured o'er,
The traces now were fugitive and faint,
Smoothed to the resignation of a saint.
He saw an eye, that when it cast a look
Down on the deluge, instantly partook
Of deep anxiety; when on the face
Of Noah, it had found a resting place,
Sorrow was banish'd from its orbit quite,
It sparkled with a tender mild delight.
The patriarch gazed, and felt, he knew not why,
Uncommon reverence for that pensive eye;
But when he saw the bow that rose and spread
Its mellow'd radiance round the stranger's head;
When he beheld upon her panting breast
The dove alight, and close his wings to rest;
Doubt was removed, he cried with welcome brow,
Angel of mercy, I behold thee now!
  "Thee, Patriarch, I have known," the vision said;
"From earliest infancy I've watched thy head.
I knew thee in that season, when the toy
Of merry childhood could afford thee joy:
Saw thee, when truant from a parent's care
With spirits high, and heart as light as air,
Thy infant eye had caught in summer hour
The insect plunderer of the fragrant flower,
Loading his little thighs with waxen spoil
And humming like a laborer o'er his toil.
Beheld thy hand that could not then forbear
To seize the poor mechanic seated there,
The little captive look'd, and saw with dread
The infant blossom closing o'er his head;
Disconsolate, he roam'd his narrow cell,
The petty prisoner of a floweret bell.
Be it my present office to display
Some great events that time's unfolding ray
In long futurity shall bring to light,
Though now deep buried in the shades of night.
  No more the thorns and thistles in thy ground,
Shall raise their martial points to fence thee round;

That sad and mournful family, that shun
All vegetation and the cheering sun,
And seem in some secluded spot to tell,
In whispers to the wind, that Adam fell.
Thy spot of ground no ruffian weed shall taunt,
But in its stead, thy hand the vine shall plant,
The fruitful vine, and, while thou joy'st to know
How full and dark its clustering honors grow,
More shalt thou joy to hear what God enjoins :—
Thy progeny shall far exceed the vine's.
    But ah! thou little know'st what depth of sin,
What idiot frenzy dwells the grape within;
Reason no longer holds her balance true,
With eyes once bathed in this bewildering dew;
He tastes ;—the victim knows not when to stop,
Though frantic demons poison every drop.
Down, down, he sinks in ruin and despair ;
In vain may sacred friendship, weeping there,
In vain may fathers, brothers intercede,
In vain may honor execrate the deed.
Still does the charm, the infernal spell allure,
The demon laughs, his prey is now secure.
    The solid earth presents too small a space
To bound the enterprise of Adam's race ;
A hardy race of men shall spring from thee
Whose only residence an ark shall be.
For lo! astonish'd ocean shall survey,
In future times, though distant now the day,
Such wonders as have never reach'd his ken.
His empire humbled by the sons of men.
Arks beyond number, borne by heavenly breath,
Shall dare the surface of the roaring death.
Vain does he fret and climb the heights of air,
Like some proud steed that scorns his lord to bear.
In vain he foams and rears, for human skill
Has conquer'd, and he feels the bridle still.
    Ocean's proud giant sees the roaring main
Usurp'd by man, and flies, but flies in vain,
O'er liquid mountains, horrible to name,
Intent on death, man seeks the timorous game—
In vain the monster trembles, and retreats
To his dark caverns, and his coral seats.
The persecutor, anxious for his prey,
Waits his return unto the beams of day ;
There struck—he flies and flounders with the pain,

And seeks the dark recesses of the main;
Vain is his flight opposed to human skill,
For there, the barb of death pursues him still;
Again he rises to the upper air,
In vain, for hostile vengeance follows there;
Now see! the monster spouts away his breath,
Lashes the foaming surge, then sinks to death,
His native element is no retreat,
He pours his life-blood at his conquerer's feet.
    Would that his life alone might ocean stain!
Ah no, the spirit of departed Cain
Henceforth shall rise and walk the earth again.
In vain may suppliant mercy intercede,
How many Abels shall be doom'd to bleed!
More wonders still!—thy race, by vengeance driven,
Shall seize and hurl the thunderbolt of heaven!
Yea, the dread lightning by divine command,
Shall flash hereafter in a human hand.
O while ye grasp the bolts of heaven—forbear!
The life of brother! man, in pity spare!
O cherish still the transitory breath,
Nor call these agents to the aid of death!
    Vain is the wish, the man in future days
Shall claim the high reward, his country's praise:
For all the varied misery that appears
In father's, brother's, widow's, orphan's tears;
For lives so dear—thus butcher'd day by day,
A leaf of paltry laurel shall repay;
Detested plant! see all its verdant veins
Are running now with deep and scarlet stains!
Fann'd by, O innocence! thy sacred sighs,
The floweret smells and blossoms to the skies!
How horrible to tell! and yet how true!
The plant is nourish'd by a bloody dew.
    I hear the thunder roar,—the dying shriek—
The raven flap—the terrors of his beak!
He sees the tumult in his airy way,
He scents the carnage, and he stoops for prey.
O righteous heaven! why is Almighty love
So long delay'd, why lingers yet my dove?
The earth shall mourn, and desolate with grief,
And rue the absence of the olive leaf—
Refrain, my sons—this dreadful deed refrain
Let not the tears of mercy plead in vain!
    The eagle towering in his pride of place,

Shall see some venturous son of Adam's race,
Mounted on wings, with balance just and true,
Scouring with him the firmament of blue ;
Such wonders shall be known in future times ;
Unterrified from cloud to cloud, he climbs,
Till from the height of his celestial seat,
Rivers shall vanish underneath his feet.
And even Ararat that towers so grand,
Shall seem diminish'd to a grain of sand.
Behold him where the ærial tribes are seen
Supported by a bubble, sail serene,
And though the sport of all the winds that blow,
He sees a subjugated world below.
Now, in a cloud the glittering wonder hides,
Anon, it skims along the clear blue tides,
While shouting thousands with admiring gaze,
Pursue this sailor of the solar blaze.
    The time shall come, so speaks Almighty doom,
When human art shall triumph o'er the tomb ;
The body form'd with such transcendant art,
Such nicety of skill in every part,
Shall, though the seat of an immortal mind,
Vanish from earth, and leave its shade behind.
Thy tame, obsequious shadow in thy way,
That humble offspring of the solar ray,
Lives to proclaim this truth to all thy line,
A sunbeam boasts a longer date than thine.
Go worship at ambition's bloody fane,
Till even rapine would its rage restrain ;
Go climb the fields of air, the heights explore,
Beyond where even eagles dare to soar ;
Go set thy footstep on the roaring wave,
Defy the ocean's depth, his coral cave ;
Go snatch the lightning from the azure field,
And teach thy hand the bolt of heaven to wield ;
Then, son of Adam, count thy mighty gains,
Of all thy glory, but the corpse remains ;
Poor heir of sickness, sorrow, and decay,
Thou wretched tenant of a little day,
One moment moving, like a god august,
The next—a mass of silent mouldering dust ;
Though death with such remorseless vengeance drives,
Thy cold insensate shadow still survives.
It lives to tell how small the human span
What frail materials constitute a man ;

It lives a satire on the very name
Of human grandeur, and thy hopes of fame.
  Still art shall triumph with the conqueror's wreath,
And teach the rugged marble how to breathe ;
The human form beneath her magic shock
Breaks from the rude recesses of the rock ;
The frowning quarry that no tempest fears,
That bears the brunt of heaven for endless years,
When touch'd by art, and fashion'd by her skill,
Dissolves in female beauty at her will.
Behold, enrapturing every heart and hand,
Cold and serene the marble virgin stand !
What harmony, what symmetry, what grace,
Move o'er each limb and languish on the face !
How loose, how lovely all the tresses flow
Upon that bosom's pure and lustrous snow ;
She frowns, each bold intruder to reprove,
Ah ! why does not the lovely vision move ?
Wherefore this silence, why this steadfast air ?
Rouse from thy slumber, speak, thou lovely fair !
Alas ! how vain is all this blaze of skill,
The breath, the Almighty breath is wanting still ;
Stay, and this lovely prodigy behold,
How beautiful to view, and yet how cold.
What idle industry, what fruitless pain—
The virgin steps into the block again.
Monarchs shall strive amidst an empire's shock
To gain possession of this beauteous block :
Poets shall sing its praise in strains so sweet,
That even listening angels might repeat ;
From distant nations, pilgrims still shall come,
And gaze till admiration's self be dumb ;
'T is still bereft of an Almighty breath,
And stands a steadfast monument of death.
  Unconquer'd man, by science guided far,
Shall boldly measure every brilliant star,
Till all these orbs in glory so replete
Shall roll in silent homage at his feet.
Here is a triumph for thy honor'd brow :
Is man encircled with the laurel now ?
  This conquest, purchased by no bloody stains,
Among thy kindred no distinction gains,
In vain the lights of yonder heaven may plead
If carnage does not consecrate the deed ! '

The angel paused ; her face so fair to view
Look'd lovelier in the drops of sorrowing dew ;
The patriarch gazed, the vision sunk in air,
But Mercy's tears were still remaining there.

CRYSTALINA.

"CRYSTALINA, a Fairy Tale, by an American," was published at New York in 1816.   We have not been able to learn
the name of the author, but the high merit of the poem will
not allow us to pass it without notice.   It is a tale of wild and
wondrous adventure, replete with all the marvels of Fairy
Land, and the potent and wonder-working machinery of magic
and incantation.   The execution is very unequal, but a great
portion of the work shows extraordinary power of imagination, and command of poetical language.   It would be difficult
to produce from the whole body of English literature, anything of the same kind superior to the passages of bold and
magnificent description with which this anonymous production
abounds.

*   *   *   *

THEN down the vale, the hermit led the way;
The Knight pursued, impatient of delay :
Dark was that vale, of tall gigantic wood,
The grim abode of elves and beasts of blood ;
The couchant tiger scream'd as they pass'd by,
And on them wildly roll'd his meteor-eye !
The wolf sprang frighted from the crackling brake,
And in their pathway coil'd the hissing snake.
High o'er their heads, umbrageous oaks outspread
Their giant arms, and awful murmurs made.
Scarce had they reach'd the centre of the vale,
When lo ! black clouds, before a northern gale,
Came sweeping on, and with a dusky veil

Shrouded the moon—the mountain tops, oak crown'd,
Toss'd in the storm, and echoed to the sound
Of trees uptorn, and thunders rolling round.
They sat them down beneath an aged oak,
Which, though late riven by a thunder-stroke,
Seem'd tempest-proof, and there the fearless Knight
Waited impatient for returning light.

      *   *   *   *

  Tremendous scene! the prowlers of the wood
Stopp'd in mid-chase and spared their victim's blood,
Fled to their caves, or crouching with alarm,
Howl'd at the passing spirits of the storm!
Eye-blasting spectres and bleach'd skeletons,
With snow-white raiment, and disjointed bones,
Before them strode; and meteors, flickering dire,
Around them trail'd their scintillating fire,
Livid and pale as light of funeral pyre.
  Serenely grand, the venerable Sage
Beheld the scene and heard the tempest rage,
Then rose abruptly, and with accents dire,
Bade the fierce demons of the storm retire!
The clouds dispersed; again the tranquil moon
Sat in mid sky upon her silver throne,
And heaven's blue vault with stars unnumber'd shone.
No sound was heard, save where the torrent hoar
Down the steep mountain fell with sullen roar,
Or far away, exploding long and loud,
The deep-toned thunder rent the fiery cloud.
Then thus, beneath the thunder-riven oak,
The hoary wizard to Rinaldo spoke—
"See'st thou yon glade, where quivering moon-beams play,
Like dancing spectres on a tomb-stone gray?
In that still glade, a fairy-circle lies—
When Cynthia, Night's torch-bearer, lights the skies
There sportive Fairies dance till Phœbus rise;
If so thou dar'st, approach that circle dread,
And thrice three times around it boldly tread.
Then shall the earth beneath thy feet expand,
And a dark road disclose to Fairy land."
The Hermit ceased, and by the dim moon-light,
Rinaldo spied the circle, glistening bright.
Back to his cave the old magician went,
Whilst bold Rinaldo towards the circle bent
His desperate course—his temper'd steel he drew,
And thrice around the mystic circle flew.

Then rose from earth deep groans and fearful cries,
And lurid meteors shot along the skies.
When round the ring he hurried thrice again,
The earth sent up a blue sulphureous flame,
That burnt and quiver'd like a dying lamp—
But on he press'd with firm and fearless tramp.
Now when nine times the Knight had hasted round,
The hollow earth sent forth a rumbling sound,
And, wide and sudden, yawn'd the rocking ground.
Down the dark chasm the desp'rate warrior strode,
With random steps along a viewless road ;
Till massy rocks his onward march opposed,
And o'er his head the earth in thunder closed ;
But soon a passage in the cloven stone
With joy he found, and boldly hurried on.
But slow and cautious, with his pond'rous spear,
Poised his bold march along the labyrinth drear.
Through rayless glooms ; through silence deep and dread,
Down, downward far the dismal cavern led.
At length beneath him shone a silver light,
Like glow-worm twinkling through the gloom of night,
And tuneful sounds, celestial, high, and clear,
Rose from beneath and charm'd his wondering ear.
Thither he sped, and from the narrow way
Sprang with delight into a realm of day,
And upright stood upon the radiant plain
Of Fairy land, a heavenly domain.
O ! 't was a valley of enchanting view,
Where all things lovely and delightful grew ;
Where groves of orange, cinnamon, and myrrh,
Trees that bled frankincense and balsams rare,
With grateful odors fill'd the breezy air—
Elysian groves of harmony and flowers,
Leafy pavilions and ambrosial bowers ;
With many a mead, and many a winding stream,
Glade flowering fair, and glittering lake between.
Not the spiced breeze, from Ceylon's groves that springs,
Or shakes Arabian odors from its wings ;
Not shining gardens of Hesperides,
Whose golden rivers and auriferous trees,
The setting sun from his prone chariot sees,
Nor aught on earth for fragrance could compare,
Nor yet for beauty with this valley fair.
This gay, celestial valley to enclose,
Mountains sublime in even circle rose,

And towering high, on tip-toe seem'd to stand,
To gaze enchanted on the radiant land.
Glowing aloft a golden cloud was spread,
Whose splendid vault a rich effulgence shed
On all below—for sun, nor moon, nor star
Was ever seen, or ever needed there.
Like a vast amphitheatre it seem'd,
With mountain-walls; from storm and sunshine screen'd
By costly canopy of sheeted gold—
But greater far and fairer to behold.
In sweet amaze and exultation high,
O'er all the scene the youth directs his eye—
His wilder'd thoughts in floods of rapture float,
And time, and place, and being are forgot—
"Celestial visions!" cried th' astonish'd Knight—
"Ye golden prospects that enchant my sight!
Are ye indeed substantial? or but vain,
And wild illusions of a love-sick brain?
Methinks I dream!" When thus Rinaldo said,
His well-known self, he doubtfully survey'd,
And waved his arm and shook his plumed head.
But soon the memory of his captive love
The sweet amazement from his senses drove.
"Fair land!" he cried—"and dangerous as fair,
A foe to thy prosperity is near;
Darkness shall soon thy saffron skies o'erwhelm—
I come to spoil thee of thy richest gem—
But where, where fly to find my captive fair?
No cities, fields, or cottages appear.
'Tis desert all—th' unnumber'd flow'rets sweet
Lift their gay heads unbruised by living feet;
Even at my hand the fearless songsters sing,
And round me flutter with familiar wing;
Or 'mid the flowers, like sunbeams, glance about,
Sipping with slender tongues the dainty nectar out.
* * * *
He ceased, and now a glittering palace sees,
Deep in the vale amid embowering trees!
A splendid pile of precious gems it seems,
Wrapt in a blaze of variegated beams—
With cautious steps he thither bent his way,
Whilst all around, irradiations gay
Full on his pathway beam'd celestial day.
He trode on carpets, gorgeously display'd,
Of woven flowers and grassy verdure made.

From all the waving trees, the plumy throngs,
Welcomed the warlike stranger with their songs
And lo! from bowers of myrtle, fair and green,
A choir of damsels dance with smiling mien!
Their silken robes the playful zephyrs throw
From side to side, and wantonly bestow
Delightful glimpses of their limbs of snow.
With lily-hands they strike the trembling strings
Of golden lyres—the grove responsive rings,
Soothing his soul with endless echoings.

      *   *   *   *

   Towards the palace, silent and alone
The hero moved—afar the fabric shone
Like gorgeous clouds that throng the setting sun:
But ere he reach'd that palace, huge and bright,
A glorious scene detain'd the wondering Knight—
A pearly river! whose melodious tide
Laved golden shores! whose banks were beautified
With trees wide-waving, paridisian bowers
And all the gaudy multitude of flowers
That on spring's lap the liberal Flora showers.
This stream, dividing, roll'd its branches twain,
In circling sweep around a flowery plain,
Through vocal groves, then fondly met again.
The Islet fair, so form'd, arose between,
With dome-like swell, array'd in richest green.
So fair it was, so smooth, so heavenly sweet,
It seem'd made only for angelic feet.
   On this green isle the splendid palace stood,
And rainbow bridges arch'd the pearly flood—
A fairer bow fair Juno ne'er display'd
In vernal skies, though not, like Juno's, made
Of subtle sun-beams, but of solid gems,
Such as adorn imperial diadems.
Its blue was solid sapphire. Its gay green
Was massy emerald. The ruby sheen
Form'd its bright curve of rich and rosy red;
Its yellow hue the golden topaz shed.
Seem'd either end on snow-white clouds to lie—
They were not clouds, but sculptured ivory!
And now a bugle breathed a silver sound,
Whose notes with soft reverberations, round
Rang sweet and long; now silently unfold
The diamond gates on hinge of polish'd gold;

And now rode out a fairy cavalcade
In order'd march ; with banners bright display'd,
With diamond lances and with golden helms,
And shields of gold emboss'd with sparkling gems,
Advanced the pageant ; proud beneath each knight,
O'er grassy levels pranced their steeds milk-white,
Whose ivory hoofs in glittering silver shod,
With nimble grace on blushing flow'rets trod.
Prancing they came, and as the trumpets blew,
They neigh'd for pride, and arch'd their necks of snow ;
Toss'd their proud heads indignant of the rein,
Champ'd their foam'd bits and paw'd the trembling plain.
Warrior and steed array'd for battle shone,
Whose burnish'd mail and bright caparison
Illumed, far round, the flower-enwoven field,
And restless splendors flash'd from shield to shield.
Loud in the van the wreathed bugle spoke,
Till woods and floods with martial clamors shook.

    *   *   *   *

   Now sad, amid a shady solitude,
On the green margin of a prattling flood,
Rinaldo paused—as there forlorn he stood,
The swell of distant melody he heard ;
Anon, a golden chariot appear'd,
Proudly advancing, drawn by peacocks fair,
With gorgeous plumery, dancing in the air.
On that bright chariot, in imperial state,
The queen of Oberon, fair Titania, sate :
On downy cushion, rich with gold and green,
Aloft she sat, like Jove's celestial queen,
When, through the skies, she drives her glowing car,
And gazing gods adore her from afar.
   Around Titania, youths and damsels throng,
Warbling, with dulcet breath, a magic song,
Whose mazy tide intoxicates the soul—
From neighboring rocks a thousand echoes roll
The refluent sounds, and fondly multiply,
With busy tongues, th' angelic harmony.
   In robes of green, fresh youths the concert led,
Measuring, the while, with nice, emphatic tread
Of tinkling sandals, the melodious sound
Of smitten timbrels ; some, with myrtles crown'd,
Pour the smooth current of sweet melody,
Through ivory tubes ; some blow the bugle free,

And some, at happy intervals, around,
With trumps sonorous swell the tide of sound;
Some, bending raptured o'er their golden lyres,
With cunning fingers fret the tuneful wires;
With rosy lips, some press the syren shell,
And through its crimson labyrinths, impel
Mellifluous breath, with artful sink and swell.
Some blow the mellow, melancholy horn,
Which, save the Knight, no man of woman born,
E'er heard and fell not senseless to the ground,
With viewless fetters of enchantment bound.
The nodding trees its magic influence own,
And, spell-struck, drop their golden clusters down;
The forests quaver, and elysian bowers,
With pleasing tremors shed their fragrant flowers.
An awful silence, winds and waters keep;
And spell-chain'd brooks, that bound from steep to steep,
On jutting rocks, delay their headlong leap.
The cross alone, the holy cross disarms
The Fairy fiends, and baffles all their charms.

SONG OF THE SEER.

On sweet May-eve, when groves were green,
And wild birds chanted merrily,
When the air was calm, the sky serene,
It was a lady of high degree,
And she sat under a green-wood tree,

O! she waited there for her dear knight,
But the sun had set, the birds were mute,
The dark wolf howl'd on the mountain height;
The raven croak'd, the owl did hoot,
And pale-red meteors round her shoot.

O! oft she gazed, and oft she sigh'd;
Oft listened for Alonzo's tread—
"Why tarries thus my love?" she cried—
"The hour, the appointed hour has fled,
The night-dew chills my houseless head.

"Ah! why did I believe his tale,
And leave my father's castle gay,
To meet him in this secret vale?
Or why, ah! why does Alonzo stay?
'T is night, and the castle is far away!

"But hark! a distant voice I hear!—
'T is not my love, but the night owl's cry "—
Thus wails Syrenna, wild with fear;
Her raven-locks on the night-winds fly,
Her breath is quick and her heart beats high.

Now the sky grew black, the winds blew loud,
The lightning gleam'd on the dusky vale
And thunder spoke from his deep-blue cloud—
Up rose Syrenna, wild and pale,
And shriek'd and fled through the stormy gale—

But when she reach'd a lonely glade,
Where wild-briars rude and thistles stood,
A ghastly fiend her eyes survey'd!
It beckon'd her to a gloomy wood—
"'T is my love!" she cried—and swift pursued.

It led the maid to a cavern deep!
But on the gulf the lightning glared,
Before she took the fatal leap!
The spectre laugh'd and disappear'd—
But the Benshie's fatal scream she heard.

And she heard, in her ear, a death-bell toll,
And the raven croak on a blasted tree—
The Lord have mercy on her soul!
It was a piteous sight to see
The sorrows of that sweet lady.

And now a-down that dusky glen
She saw, she chased the fell rush-light—
It led her to a watery fen,
Then shriek'd, and quench'd its taper bright—
And all was horror, all was night.

And now strange voices fill the air,
And yells, and shouts both loud and long—
Ah fly! ah fly! distracted fair,
For fierce and fast the fiends come on,
And see! grim phantoms round thee throng.

Syrenna fled, in vain fled she;
For the ghastly crew met her blasted view,
And a black fiend spoke, and fierce spoke he,

As his arms round her snow-white neck he threw,
"We, lady fair! are the Elfin crew!

"Thrice welcome to our merry glen!
And thou shalt be our mistress bright,
And dance with us on the quaking fen,
To the rush-light's red and glimmering light,
When tempests howl at dead of night."

They grasp'd her hard by her tender hand,
They dragg'd her away by her raven hair;
Her shrieks were loud, but the ghastly band
To a stormy heath led the lady fair,
And bared her breast to the driving air.

On the stormy heath a ring they form;
They place therein the fearful maid,
And round her dance in the howling storm—
The winds beat hard on her lovely head;
But she clasp'd her hands and nothing said.

O! 'twas, I ween, a ghastly sight,
To see their uncouth revelry;
The lightning was the taper bright,
The thunder was the melody,
To which they danced with horrid glee!

The fierce-eyed owl did on them scowl;
The bat play'd round on leathern wing;
The coal-black wolf did at them howl,
The coal-black raven did croak and sing
And o'er them flap his dusky wing.

An earthquake heaved beneath their feet;
Pale meteors revel'd in the sky;
The clouds sail'd by like a routed fleet,
The night-winds shriek'd as they pass'd by,
The dark-red moon was eclipsed on high—

But hark! what voice, as thunder loud,
Now shakes the wilderness profound?
Whose form appears so tall and proud?
Beneath whose foot-step quakes the ground,
And whose bright armor gleams around?

O! 'tis Alonzo true and brave,
And loud he calls on his true-love's name—
He comes! he comes the maid to save,
Through thunder, lightning, wind and rain,
With buckler broad and sword of flame.

Alonzo spied his lady fair,
He spied her amid that ghastly crew,
And he spurr'd his steed and couch'd his spear—
But the holy cross on his breast they knew,
And shriek'd, and away like lightning flew.

"And hast thou come?" cried the lady bright—
"Alonzo comes!"—the knight replied,
"To keep his promise with thee to-night;
For spite of thy father's cruel pride,
Sweet lady! thou shalt be my bride."

He spoke, and mounted his foamy steed,
He took his lady fair, behind,
And away he rode to their bridal bed,
More swiftly than the mountain-hind
When the hunter's cry is on the wind.

But all that night raved the tempest dire;
A thunder shaft on the castle fell,
Of dark Almanzor, the lady's sire,
And the winds all night rung his castle-bell—
They rung it loud for Almanzor's knell!

LYDIA HUNTLEY SIGOURNEY.

MRS SIGOURNEY is a native of Norwich, Connecticut. During the first twenty years of her life she resided in her native town; she has since lived at Hartford, and is now the wife of Charles Sigourney, Esq. of that city.

It is an omen of favorable import to our national literature, that the claims of female talent have been ably advanced, and readily acknowledged. The value of such an accession to its interests, cannot fail of being duly estimated in an age, which is enjoying the pure and delightful breathings of Mrs Heman's poetry and the strong practical sense of Miss Edgeworth. To these cherished names we do no discredit, when we associate with them that of the accomplished lady, of whom we now speak.

It was in the year 1815 that Mrs Sigourney, (then Miss Huntley,) first gave her name to the world, as the authoress of "Moral pieces in prose and verse." "This volume, which," to adopt her own unpretending account of it, " was written solely for the sake of improvement, and to gratify a love of composition, owed its publication to a benevolent gentleman, whose pleasure it was to encourage industry, and to raise intellect from obscurity." No ordinary acknowledgments are due to the penetration which thus discovered the latent gem, and to the kindness and liberality with which "its purest ray serene" was developed to the world. The work itself does not indeed afford any very decided earnest of the present most deserved reputation of its authoress ; but every page of it is instinct with that purity of purpose, and fruitful in those sentiments of virtue, which distinguish all her writings ; while several of the pieces which it contains, as the "Excuse for not fulfilling an engagement," "The Dove," "The Solitary Star," "Morning Prayer," and the "First Morning in May," are, in no small degree, honorable to her talents. From the first named of these, the reader will learn, that, like Mrs Barbauld, and

Mrs More, Mrs Sigourney has devoted some of her earlier years to the instruction of youth. A more complete refutation of the current slander against this most useful and ennobling employment, as tending to produce morosity and querulousness, need not be desired, than that which is furnished by the playful, contented, and affectionate spirit which animates the "Excuse."

In 1816 appeared the "Writings of Nancy Maria Hyde, with a sketch of her Life." The motives which induced Miss Huntley to undertake this performance, are alike honorable to her as a friend and as a Christian; and the pious office was discharged with affection and fidelity.

In 1822, "Traits of the Aborigines of America, a poem," was offered to the public—the avails of the work being devoted exclusively to religious charities. Had the author given to this work more of the narrative, and less of the didactic character, better justice might have been done to her subject, and the expectation excited by the title, would have been more completely answered. She also erred, at least in our judgment, in preferring blank verse to rhyme, as the vehicle of her sentiments. Notwithstanding these objections, it evinces much talent and information, and is written in an engaging spirit of Christian philanthropy.

The "Sketch of Connecticut, Forty Years Since," is written in prose, and appeared in 1824. It was designed to pourtray, with an allowable degree of embellishment from fiction, the character of the author's earliest benefactress, and the manners of the period in which she lived. Judged by the elevated standard of fictitious composition which has been established in our day, faults and deficiencies will be discovered. Such a judgment of its merits, however, would be unfair. It professes to be no more than a "Sketch"—and though the parts may not always be in perfect keeping, nor the details touched with the exquisite delicacy of a miniature, there is spirit and boldness in the outline, and fidelity in the coloring. A biographical notice of Hannah More, written for the new American edition of her works, in two volumes 8vo. of which it is sufficient to say, that it is worthy of its subject, and of its author, and a volume entitled " Poems by the Author ' Moral Pieces,' " complete the catalogue of Mrs Sigourney's publications.

Upon none of the volumes, however, which have been the subject of our remarks, does the literary reputation of our author depend. Our specimens, the first excepted, have all been written since 1824. Within that period, she has exhibited a rapid improvement, and we rejoice to say, that this improvement is yet in full career. It is in the department of fugitive poetry—an appellation, certainly, most inappropriate, when applied to much which has been written under that name in this, its golden age, that Mrs Sigourney has reaped her most enduring laurels. It is no disparagement to her talents, to say, that this is the field for which they are best adapted. The highest living talent has been exerted in it, and found its recompense. To be classed with Watts, and Hervey, and Bryant, and Halleck, and Mrs Hemans, is an association, of which the most successful votary of the muse, in any age, might justly boast. Only less popular than the last of these gifted minds, the productions of our author have been widely wafted with hers, on the wings of the periodical press. There is indeed, no other shape, in which the widest popularity may so well be combined with the most permanent endurance. We trust, therefore, that Mrs Sigourney will not suffer this rich vein of her genius to lie unworked. The circulation which, in this refined age, its treasures have enjoyed, is the best evidence of their sterling value. And so far from being exhausted, we venture to predict, that as she digs more deeply, the golden ore will be found more rich, and more abundant.

The prevailing attributes of Mrs Sigourney's poetry are

tenderness and religious feeling. She is an ardent lover, an accurate observer, and an eloquent revealer of the charms of nature. A most captivating tone of plaintiveness mingles with every breathing of her harp—but it is a plaintiveness which we may safely admire and cherish, for it never sinks into sadness. She loves to sing of "decay and death"—but it is that she may mingle with the mournful strains which they awaken, the cheering promise of renovated life and beauty.

We confidently refer the reader, for ample confirmation of all that we have said, to her last volume of poems. Had Mrs Sigourney written no more than our "Specimens" exhibit, she would still possess undoubted claims to the proud title of the American HEMANS.

EXCUSE FOR NOT FULFILLING AN ENGAGEMENT.

WRITTEN IN SCHOOL, AUGUST, 1814.

My friend, I gave a glad assent
　To your request at noon,
But now I find I cannot leave
　My little ones so soon.—
Early I came, and as my feet
　First enter'd at the door,
"Remember!"—to myself I said,
　"You must dismiss at four."
But slates, and books, and maps appear,
　And many a dear one cries,
"O tell us where that river runs,
　And where these mountains rise,
And where that blind old monarch reign'd,
　And who was king before,
And stay a little after five,
　And tell us something more."—
And then my little Alice * comes,
　And who unmoved can view,
The glance of that imploring eye,
　"Pray, teach *me* something too."

*A child deprived of the powers of speech and hearing.

Yet who would think amid the toil,
   (Though scarce a toil it be,)
That through the door the *muses* coy
   Should deign to peep at me.——
Their brow is somewhat cold and stern,
   As if it fain would say,
" We did not know you kept a school,
   We must have lost our way."
Their visit was but short indeed,
   As these slight numbers show,
But ah ! they bade me write with speed,
   My friend,—I cannot go.

THE CORAL INSECT.

Toil on ! toil on ! ye ephemeral train,
Who build in the tossing and treacherous main ;
Toil on,—for the wisdom of man ye mock,
With your sand-based structures and domes of rock
Your columns the fathomless fountains lave,
And your arches spring up to the crested wave ;
Ye 're a puny race, thus to boldly rear
A fabric so vast, in a realm so drear.

Ye bind the deep with your secret zone,
The ocean is seal'd, and the surge a stone ;
Fresh wreaths from the coral pavement spring,
Like the terraced pride of Assyria's king ;
The turf looks green where the breakers roll'd ;
O'er the whirlpool ripens the rind of gold ;
The sea-snatch'd isle is the home of men,
And mountains exult where the wave hath been.

But why do ye plant 'neath the billows dark
The wrecking reef for the gallant bark ?
There are snares enough on the tented field,
'Mid the blossom'd sweets that the valleys yield ;
There are serpents to coil, ere the flowers are up :
There 's a poison-drop in man's purest cup,
There are foes that watch for his cradle breath,
And why need ye sow the floods with death ?

With mouldering bones the deeps are white,
From the ice-clad pole to the tropics bright :——
The mermaid hath twisted her fingers cold
With the mesh of the sea-boy's curls of gold,
And the gods of ocean have frown'd to see
The mariner's bed in their halls of glee ;——
Hath earth no graves, that ye thus must spread
The boundless sea for the thronging dead ?

Ye build,——ye build,——but ye enter not in,
Like the tribes whom the desert devour'd in their sin :
From the land of promise ye fade and die,
Ere its verdure gleams forth on your weary eye ;——
As the kings of the cloud-crown'd pyramid,
Their noteless bones in oblivion hid ;
Ye slumber unmark'd 'mid the desolate main,
While the wonder and pride of your works remain.

———

DEATH OF AN INFANT.

DEATH found strange beauty on that cherub brow,
And dash'd it out. There was a tint of rose
On cheek and lip ;——he touch'd the veins with ice,
And the rose faded.——Forth from those blue eyes
There spoke a wishful tenderness,——a doubt
Whether to grieve or sleep, which Innocence
Alone can wear. With ruthless haste he bound
The silken fringes of their curtaining lids
For ever. There had been a murmuring sound
With which the babe would claim its mother's ear,
Charming her even to tears. The spoiler set
His seal of silence. But there beam'd a smile
So fix'd and holy from that marble brow,——
Death gazed and left it there ;——he dared not steal
The signet-ring of heaven.

———

WITH WILD FLOWERS TO A SICK FRIEND.

RISE from the dells where ye first were born,
From the tangled beds of the weed and thorn,
Rise! for the dews of the morn are bright,
And haste away with your brows of light.—
—Should the green-house patricians with gathering frown,
On your plebeian vestures look haughtily down,
Shrink not,—for *His* finger your heads hath bow'd,
Who heeds the lowly and humbles the proud.—
—The tardy spring, and the frosty sky,
Have meted your robes with a miser's eye,
And check'd the blush of your blossoms free,—
With a gentler friend your home shall be;
To a kinder ear you may tell your tale
Of the zephyr's kiss and the scented vale;—
Ye are charm'd! ye are charm'd! and your fragrant sigh
Is health to the bosom on which ye die.

MISSOLONGHI.

FAMINE hath worn them pale, that noble band;—
  Yet round the long beleaguer'd wall,
  With wasted frame, and iron hand,
  Like watching skeletons they stand,
      To conquer or to fall.

Hark!—Hark! the war-cry. Swells the shout
  From wild Arabia's wandering rout,
  From turbid Nilus' swarthy brood,
  From Ibrahim's host who thirst for blood,
  'T is answer'd from the echoing skies,
      Sons of Miltiades, arise!—

Aged men, with temples gray!—
Why do *ye* haste to the battle fray?—
Home to the couch of ease, and pray.—
But ah! I read on those brows of gloom,
That your sons have found a gory tomb,
And ye with despair and grief opprest,
Would strike ere ye share their clay-cold rest.—

With features pale, yet sternly wrought
To all the agony of thought,
Yon widow'd mothers mount the tower,
To guard the wall in danger's hour :——
Fast by their side in mute distress,
Their little sons unwavering press,
Taught from their cradle-bed to know
The bitter tutelage of wo,
No idle fears in their bosoms glow,
But pride and wrath in their dark eyes glance,
As they lift their martyr'd father's lance.

Yet more !—Yet more !—At beat of drum
 With wildly flowing hair,
Helle's beauteous maidens come,
 The iron strife to dare.——
 Sadly sweet from those lips of rose,
 The death-song of Bozzaris flows,
 It is your dirge, ye turban'd foes !——
Rise, soul of Pindar ! strike the shadowy lyre,
Start from your sculptured tombs, ye sons of fire !
Snatch, snatch those gentle forms from war's alarms,
And throw your adamantine shield around their shrinking
 charms.

 Louder swells the battle-cry ;
 God of Christians ! from the sky
 Behold the Turk's accursed host
 Come rushing in.——'T is lost !— 'T is lost !——
  Ye bold defenders, die !——
O thou, who sang'st of Ilion's walls the fate,
Unseal thy blinded orbs, *thine own* are desolate.

 The stifled sob of mighty souls
  Rises on the glowing air,
 And the vow of vengeance rolls,
  Mingled with the dying prayer :
" Now, by the spirits of the brave,
Sires, who rode on glory's wave,
By red Scio's wrongs and groans,
By Ipsara's unburied bones,
Our foes beneath these reeking stones,
  Shall find a grave."

Earth heaves, as if she gorged again
Usurping Korah's rebel train,

She heaves, with blast more wild and loud,
Than when with trump of thunders proud,
The electric flame subdues the cloud,
Torn and dismember'd frames are thrown on high,
And then the oppressor and oppress'd in equal silence lie.

Come, jewell'd Sultan, from thine hall of state!
Exult o'er Missolonghi's fall,
With flashing eye, and step elate
The blood-pools count around her ruin'd wall.—
Seek'st thou thus with glances vain
The remnant of thy Moslem train?—
Hither they came, with haughty brow,
They conquer'd here,—where are they now?
Ask the hoarse vulture with her new-flesh'd beak,
Bid the gaunt watch-dog speak,
Who bay'd so long around his murder'd master's door,—
They, with shriek and ban can tell
The burial-place of the infidel,
Go! bind thy turban round thy brow of shame,
And hurl the mutter'd curse at thy false prophet's name.

Ancient and beautiful!—who stand'st alone
In the dire crusade, while with hearts of stone
Thy sister nations close the leaden eye
Regardless of thine agony.
Such friends had He, who once with bursting pore,
On sad Gethsemane a lost world's burden bore.—
Leave, leave the sacred steep
Where thy lone muses weep,
Forth from thy sculptured halls,
Thy pilgrim-haunted walls,
Thy classic fountains' crystal flood,
Go!—angel-strengthen'd to the field of blood.
Raise thy white arm,—unbind thy wreathed hair,
And God's dread name upon thy breastplate wear,
Stand in *His might*, till the pure cross arise
O'er the proud minaret, and woo propitious skies.

————

BURIAL OF THE YOUNG.

There was an open grave,—and many an eye
Look'd down upon it. Slow the sable hearse

Moved on, as if reluctantly it bare
The young, unwearied form to that cold couch,
Which age and sorrow render sweet to man.
—There seem'd a sadness in the humid air,
Lifting the long grass from those verdant mounds
Where slumber multitudes.—
    —There was a train
Of young, fair females, with their brows of bloom,
And shining tresses. Arm in arm they came,
And stood upon the brink of that dark pit,
In pensive beauty, waiting the approach
Of their companion. She was wont to fly,
And meet them, as the gay bird meets the spring,
Brushing the dew-drop from the morning flowers,
And breathing mirth and gladness. `Now` she came
With movements fashion'd to the deep-toned bell:—
She came with mourning sire, and sorrowing friend,
And tears of those who at her side were nursed
By the same mother.
    Ah! and one was there,
Who, ere the fading of the summer rose,
Had hoped to greet her as his bride. But death
Arose between them. The pale lover watch'd
So close her journey through the shadowy vale,
That almost to his heart, the ice of death
Enter'd from hers. There was a brilliant flush
Of youth about her,—and her kindling eye
Pour'd such unearthly light, that hope would hang
Even on the archer's arrow, while it dropp'd
Deep poison. Many a restless night she toil'd
For that slight breath which held her from the tomb,
Still wasting like a snow-wreath, which the sun
Marks for his own, on some cool mountain's breast,
Yet spares, and tinges long with rosy light.
——Oft o'er the musings of her silent couch,
Came visions of that matron form which bent
With nursing tenderness, to soothe and bless
Her cradle dream : and her emaciate hand
In trembling prayer she raised—that He who saved
The sainted mother, would redeem the child.
Was the orison lost ?—Whence then that peace
So dove-like, settling o'er a soul that loved
Earth and its pleasures ?—Whence that angel smile
With which the allurements of a world so dear
Were counted and resign'd ? that eloquence

So fondly urging those whose hearts were full
Of sublunary happiness to seek
A better portion?   Whence that voice of joy,
Which from the marble lip in life's last strife
Burst forth, to hail her everlasting home?
—Cold reasoners! be convinced.   And when ye stand
Where that fair brow, and those unfrosted locks
Return to dust,—where the young sleeper waits
The resurrection morn,—Oh! lift the heart
In praise to Him, who gave the victory.

TO THE MOON.

HAIL beauteous and inconstant!—Thou who roll'st
Thy silver car around the realm of night,
Queen of soft hours! how fanciful art thou
In equipage and vesture.—Now thou com'st
With slender horn piercing the western cloud,
As erst on Judah's hills, when joyous throngs
With trump and festival saluted thee;
Anon thy waxing crescent 'mid the host
Of constellations, like some fairy boat,
Glides o'er the waveless sea; then as a bride
Thou bow'st thy cheek behind a fleecy veil,
Timid and fair; or, bright in regal robes,
Dost bid thy full orb'd chariot proudly roll,
Sweeping with silent rein the starry path
Up to the highest node,—then plunging low
To seek dim Nadir in his misty cell.—
——Lov'st thou our earth, that thou dost hold thy lamp
To guide and cheer her, when the wearied sun
Forsakes her?—Sometimes, roving on, thou shedd'st
The eclipsing blot ungrateful, on that sire
Who feeds thy urn with light,—but sinking deep
'Neath the dark shadow of the earth dost mourn
And find thy retribution.
                    —Dost thou hold
Dalliance with ocean, that his mighty heart
Tosses at thine approach, and his mad tides,
Drinking thy favoring glance, more rudely lash
Their rocky bulwark?—Do thy children trace
Through crystal tube our coarser-featured orb
Even as we gaze on thee?—With Euclid's art

Perchance, from pole to pole, her sphere they span,
Her sun-loved tropics—and her spreading seas
Rich with their myriad isles.   Perchance they mark
Where India's cliffs the trembling cloud invade,
Or Andes with his fiery banner flouts
The empyrean,—where old Atlas towers,—
Or that rough chain whence he of Carthage pour'd
Terrors on Rome.—Thou, too, perchance, hast nursed
Some bold Copernicus, or fondly call'd
A Galileo forth, those sun-like souls
Which shone in darkness, though *our* darkness fail'd
To comprehend them.—Canst thou boast, like earth,
A Kepler, skilful pioneer and wise ?—
A sage to write his name among the stars
Like glorious Herschel ?—or a dynasty
Like great Cassini's, which from sire to son
Transmitted science as a birthright seal'd ?
—Rose there some lunar Horrox,—to whose glance
Resplendent Venus her adventurous course
Reveal'd, even in his boyhood ?—some La Place
Luminous as the skies he sought to read ?—
Thou deign'st no answer,—or I fain would ask
If since thy bright creation, thou hast seen
Ought like a Newton, whose admitted eye
The arcana of the universe explored ?
Light's subtle ray its mechanism disclosed,
The impetuous comet his mysterious lore
Unfolded,—system after system rose,
Eternal wheeling through the immense of space,
And taught him of their laws.—Even angels stood
Amazed, as when in ancient times they saw
On Sinai's top, a mortal walk with God.—
—But he to whom the secrets of the skies
Were whisper'd—in humility adored,
Breathing with childlike reverence the prayer,
—" When on yon heavens, with all their orbs, I gaze,
Jehovah !—what is man ? "

A VISION OF THE ALPS.

ITALIA's vales in verdure slept,
While spring her humid odors wept,

With wreaths the breathing statue bound,
The fallen dome with ivy crown'd,
And bade old Tiber's yellow wave
With fuller flow its margin lave.
   Low at the base of Alps sublime,
    Where the columbar cypress grows,
And falling streams with tuneful chime
To slumber lull the ear of time,
   His cell a hermit chose.
Once at his peaceful door reclined,
While lonely musings soothed his mind,
Soft mists involved his favorite tree,
In fainter murmurs humm'd the bee,
And in bright tints gay fancy drew
A vision o'er his cheated view.
   A lovely form, in robes of light,
Came gliding o'er his raptured sight ;
Fresh garlands 'mid her tresses glow'd,
Around her steps strange beauty flow'd,
Attendant birds pour'd forth their lays,
And prank'd their plumage in her praise,
The fawn came bounding o'er the earth,
The tufted violets sprang to birth,
The olive donn'd its vesture pale,
And fragrance floated on the gale.
Then, bold o'er Alpine cliffs she sped,
The snow-wreath vanish'd at her tread,
The singing rills went leaping down,
The forest caught its graceful crown,
And warblers cheer'd with carols loud,
The cottage cradled on the cloud.
   Still, by the hermit's anxious eye
Her form was traced ascending high,
Where the last tints of verdure die.
Even there, amid that dreary bound,
Some hardy, slumbering flowers she found,
Touch'd their chill lids, and kiss'd the tear
That dimm'd their eye of azure clear,
As leaning on their frosted bed,
Their petals to the storm they spread.
   With graceful step, yet half afraid,
Toil'd onward the celestial maid,
And long and vainly strove with fate,
The imprison'd streams to liberate ;

The blushing snows her wand confest,
Yet held the vassals to their breast,
And soften'd by her aspect sweet,
The ice threw diamonds at her feet.
Yet save the eagle-king, whose cry
Came hoarsely from the blacken'd sky,
Motion nor sound was lingering there,
Amid that realm of chill despair.
It seem'd throughout the drear domain
　　That Life, too fiercely tried,
Contending with the blast in vain,
　　Had like the taper died.
She paused—for towering bold and high,
A splendid fabric met her eye.
Of thick ribb'd ice, in arches pure,
With battlement and embrasure,
And cluster'd columns, tall and white:
And frost-work tracery, dazzling bright,
And turrets frowning at the cloud,
Gleam'd forth its architecture proud.
Here, age on age, with painful thought,
The troubled elements had wrought,
To stretch the rampart's massy line,
With wreaths the pillar'd halls to twine,
And 'neath the lash of tempests rude,
Had oft their bitter task pursued,
Arranging Winter's glittering spoil,
With slow and aggregated toil.
　　The admiring fair, with wonder fraught,
An entrance to the structure sought;
But a grim form her course withstood,
Whose frigid eye congeal'd her blood.
　　Aged, yet strong at heart he seem'd,
His reverend beard like silver stream'd,
Of polish'd ice, the sparkling gem
Adorn'd his kingly diadem,
And closer, as he spoke, he prest
His ermine mantle o'er his breast.
"Say! who art thou, intruder bold,
　　Who near this lofty throne,
Would with its monarch audience hold,
　　Unbidden and alone?
Why com'st thou thus with footstep free,
Unnamed, unheralded, to me?"

Recoiling from his brilliant cell,
Whose breath in freezing tide,
Congeal'd to sudden ice-drops fell,
The undaunted maid replied ;
" I come, on Nature's mission kind,
Oppression's victims to unbind,
To bid the sceptred tyrant bow,
And wake a smile on Misery's brow.
The realm of bliss my care extends,
Man, beast and insect are my friends.
Each nursling of the nested grove,
Each plant, and flower, and leaf, I love."
With kindling eye, and front of pride,
The scornful monarch stern replied ;
" Nature and thou, are wise to give
Wild Freedom's boon to all who live !
The maddening flame promiscuous hurl'd,
Would wrap in anarchy the world.
Go ! haste the hour when none shall view
The million meekly serve the few ;
O'erturn the thrones which, fix'd as fate,
By Time's strong oath are consecrate,
Then lift your wonder-working rod,
And Earth enfranchised, war with God!
Bold and puissant must ye be,
To rend this guarded dome from me !"
His hand he raised in gestures strong,
And angry blasts shriek'd wild and long.
Vindictive Hail, with frozen eye,
Pour'd forth his keen artillery,
And Snow unlock'd, with threatening mien,
A bleak and boundless magazine.
With blanching lip and bloodless cheek
The stricken stranger strove to speak.
Though from her brow the garland fell
Scentless and pale, yet, strange to tell,
Reviving courage warm'd her breast,
And firmer tones the might confest
That may with woman dwell.
" If from thy cold, unenvied state,
Thy palace proud as desolate,
Where fetters bind the free,
One glance thy kingly eye would deign
To mark the blessings of my reign,
Disarm'd thy rage might be.

The chainless rill, the new-born flower,
The carol from the leafy bower,
The strains that from creation roll,
When on my harp she breathes her soul,
Are emblems of the joy that springs,
  Deep, measureless, unspoken,
When the dark chain of despot kings
  Is from the spirit broken.
Hear'st thou such music in *thy* hall
When warring blasts hold festival?"
  "Thou, who t' annul the law dost seek
By which the strong control the weak,
Wouldst thou in frantic madness sweep
This glorious structure to the deep?
Whelm in the dust yon turrets proud
Which hurl their gauntlet 'gainst the cloud?
And make these gem-encrusted plains
A vulgar haunt for piping swains,
And brawling brooks, and baby bowers,
And nameless troops of vagrant flowers?
Usurper, hence!" he rudely said,
And trembling from his realm she fled;
For thundering o'er the rocky crown,
An avalanche rush'd fiercely down,
And in its wide and wrecking storm
Perchance had whelm'd her shrinking form.
But a bright cloud its tissued fold
Unclasp'd, of crimson blent with gold,
And soaring on its wing she rose
Homeward to heaven, to find repose
Upon her couch of fadeless rose.
  The waking hermit, o'er whose head
The lustre of this pageant fled,
Retraced its scenes with wonder new,
And musing thus the moral drew.
  "The genial gifts of Spring to earth,
Methinks, are types of Freedom's birth,
And the dark winter of my dream
Oppression's emblem well may seem;
For many a clime that meets our view,
Will prove these varying symbols true."

CONNECTICUT RIVER.

FAIR RIVER! not unknown to classic song;—
Which still in varying beauty roll'st along,
 Where first thy infant fount is faintly seen,
A line of silver 'mid a fringe of green;
Or where, near towering rocks, thy bolder tide,
To win the giant-guarded pass, doth glide;
Or where, in azure mantle, pure and free,
Thou giv'st thy cool hand to the waiting sea;—
Though broader streams our sister realms may boast,
Herculean cities, and a prouder coast,
Yet, from the bound where hoarse St Lawrence roars
To where La Plata rocks the sounding shores;
From where the urns of slimy Nilus shine,
To the blue waters of the rushing Rhine;
Or where Ilissus glows like diamond spark,
Or sacred Ganges whelms its votaries dark,
No brighter skies the eye of day may see,
No soil more verdant, nor a race more free.
—See, where, amid their cultured vales, they stand,
The generous offspring of a simple land;
Too rough for flattery, and all fear above,
King, priest, and prophet, in the homes they love.
On equal laws their anchor'd hopes are stay'd,
By all interpreted, and all obey'd.
Alike the despot and the slave they hate,
And rise firm columns of a happy state.
To them content is bliss; and labor, health;
And knowledge, power; and true religion, wealth.
 The farmer, here, with honest pleasure sees
His orchards blushing to the fervid breeze,
His bleating flocks, the shearer's care who need,
His waving woods, the winter fire that feed,
His hardy steers, that break the yielding soil,
His patient sons, who aid their father's toil,
The ripening fields, for joyous harvest drest,
And the white spire that points a world of rest.
—His thrifty mate, solicitous to bear
An equal burden in the yoke of care,
With vigorous arm the flying shuttle heaves,
Or from the press the golden cheese receives;
Her pastime, when the daily task is o'er,
With apron clean, to seek her neighbor's door,

Partake the friendly feast, with social glow,
Exchange the news, and make the stocking grow;
Then, hale and cheerful, to her home repair,
When Sol's slant ray renews her evening care,
Press the full udder for her children's meal,
Rock the tired babe, or wake the tuneful wheel.
  See, toward yon dome, where village science dwells,
What time the warning clock its summons swells,
What tiny feet the well known path explore,
And gaily gather from each sylvan door.
The new wean'd child, with murmur'd tone proceeds,
Whom her scarce taller baby-brother leads,
Transferr'd as burdens, that the house-wife's care
May tend the dairy, or the fleece prepare.
Light-hearted group! who gambol wild and high,
The daisy pluck, or chase the butterfly,
Till by some traveller's wheels aroused from play,
The stiff salute, with face demure, they pay,
Bare the curl'd brow, or stretch the ready hand,
The untutor'd homage of an artless land.
The stranger marks, amid the joyous line,
The *little baskets* whence they hope to dine;
And *larger books*, as if their dexterous art
Dealt most nutrition to the noblest part.
Long may it be, ere luxury teach the shame
To starve the mind, and bloat the unwieldy frame!
  Scorn not this lowly race, ye sons of pride!
Their joys disparage, nor their hopes deride;
From germs like these have mighty statesmen sprung,
Of prudent counsel, and persuasive tongue;
Bold patriot souls, who ruled the willing throng,
Their powerful nerves by early labor strong;
Inventive minds, a nation's wealth that wrought,
And white-hair'd sages, skill'd in studious thought
Chiefs, who the field of battle nobly trod,
And holy men, who fed the flock of God.
  Here, 'mid the graves by time so sacred made,
The poor, lost Indian slumbers in the shade;
He, whose canoe with arrowy swiftness clave,
In ancient days, yon pure, cerulean wave;
Son of that spirit, whom in storms he traced,
Through darkness follow'd, and in death embraced,—
He sleeps an outlaw, 'mid his forfeit land,
And grasps the arrow in his moulder'd hand.
Here too, those warrior sires with honor rest,

Who bared in freedom's cause the valiant breast,
Sprang from their half drawn furrow, as the cry
Of threaten'd liberty came thrilling by,
Look'd to their God, and rear'd in bulwark round
Breasts free from guile, and hands with toil embrown'd,
And bade a monarch's thousand banners yield—
Firm at the plough, and glorious in the field;
Lo! here they rest, who every danger braved,
Unmark'd, untrophied, 'mid the soil they saved.
—Round scenes like these, doth warm remembrance glide,
Where emigration rolls its ceaseless tide.
On western wilds, which thronging hordes explore,
Or ruder Erie's serpent-haunted shore,
Or far Huron, by unshorn forests crown'd,
Or red Missouri's unfrequented bound,
The exiled man, when midnight shades invade,
Couch'd in his hut, or camping on the glade,
Starts from his dream, to catch, in echoes clear,
The boatman's song that pleased his boyish ear;
While the sad mother, 'mid her children's mirth,
Paints with fond tears a parent's distant hearth,
Or charms her rustic babes, with tender tales
Of thee, blest River! and thy velvet vales;
Her native cot, where ripening berries swell,
The village school, and sabbath's holy bell;
And smiles to see the infant soul expand
With proud devotion for *that father land*.

FLORA'S PARTY.

LADY FLORA gave cards for a party at tea,
To flowers, buds, and blossoms of every degree;
So from town and from country they throng'd at the call,
And strove by their charms to embellish the hall.
First came the exotics, with ornaments rare,
The tall Miss Corcoris, and Cyclamen fair,
Auricula splendid, with jewels new-set,
And gay Polyanthus, the pretty coquette.
The Tulips came flaunting in gaudy array,
With the Hyacinths, bright as the eye of the day;
Dandy Coxcombs and Daffodils, rich and polite,
With their dazzling new vests, and their corsets laced light;

While the Soldiers in Green, cavalierly attired,
Were all by the ladies extremely admired.
But prudish Miss Lily, with bosom of snow,
Declared that "those gentlemen stared at her so,
It was horribly rude,"—so retired in a fright,
And scarce stay'd to bid lady Flora good night.
There were Myrtles and Roses from garden and plain,
And Venus's Fly-Trap they brought in their train,
So the beaux throng'd around them, they scarcely knew why,
At the smile of the lip, or the glance of the eye.
Madam Damask complain'd of her household and care,
That she seldom went out save to breathe the fresh air,
There were so many young ones and servants to stray,
And the thorns grew so fast, if her eye was away.
"Neighbor Moss-Rose," said she, "you who live like a queen,
And ne'er wet your fingers, don't know what I mean."
So the notable lady went on with her lay,
Till her auditors yawn'd, or stole softly away.
The sweet Misses Woodbine from country and town,
With their brother in law, the wild Trumpet, came down,
And Lupine, whose azure eye sparkled with dew,
On Amaranth lean'd, the unchanging and true ;
While modest Clematis appear'd as a bride,
And her husband, the Lilac, ne'er moved from her side,
Though the belles giggled loudly, and said, "'T was a shame
For a young married chit such attention to claim ;
They never attended a route in their life,
Where a city-bred man ever spoke to his wife."
Miss Piony came in quite late, in a heat,
With the Ice-Plant, new spangled from forehead to feet ;
Lobelia, attired like a queen in her pride,
And the Dalias, with trimmings new furnish'd and dyed,
And the Blue-bells and Hare-bells, in simple array,
With all their Scotch cousins from highland and brae.
Ragged Ladies and Marigolds cluster'd together,
And gossip'd of scandal, the news and the weather ;
What dresses were worn at the wedding so fine
Of sharp Mr Thistle, and sweet Columbine ;
Of the loves of Sweet-William and Lily the prude,
Till the clamors of Babel again seem'd renew'd.
In a snug little nook sate the Jessamine pale,
And that pure, fragrant Lily, the gem of the vale ;
The meek Mountain-Daisy, with delicate crest,
And the Violet, whose eye told the heaven in her breast ;
And allured to their group were the wise ones, who bow'd

To that virtue which seeks not the praise of the crowd.
But the proud Crown Imperial, who wept in her heart,
That their modesty gain'd of such homage a part,
Look'd haughtily down on their innocent mien,
And spread out her gown that they might not be seen.
The bright Lady-Slippers and Sweet-Briars agreed
With their slim cousin Aspens a measure to lead ;
And sweet 't was to see their bright footsteps advance,
Like the wing of the breeze through the maze of the dance.
But the Monk's-Hood scowl'd dark, and, in utterance low,
Declared " 't was high time for good christians to go ;
He 'd heard from his parson a sermon sublime,
Where he proved from the Vulgate, to dance was a crime."
So, folding the cowl round his cynical head,
He took from the sideboard a bumper, and fled.
A song was desired, but each musical flower
Had " taken a cold, and 't was out of her power ; "
Till sufficiently urged, they broke forth in a strain
Of quavers and trills that astonish'd the train.
Mimosa sat trembling, and said, with a sigh,
" 'T was so fine, she was ready with rapture to die."
And Cactus, the grammar-school tutor, declared
" It might be with the gamut of Orpheus compared ;
Then moved himself round in a comical way,
To show how the trees once had frisk'd at the lay.
Yet Night-Shade, the metaphysician, complain'd,
That the nerves of his ears were excessively pain'd ;
" 'T was but seldom he crept from the college," he said,
" And he wish'd himself safe in his study or bed."
There were pictures, whose splendor illumined the place
Which Flora had finish'd with exquisite grace ;
She had dipp'd her free pencil in Nature's pure dyes,
And Aurora retouch'd with fresh purple the skies.
So the grave connoisseurs hasted near them to draw,
Their knowledge to show, by detecting a flaw.
The Carnation took her eye-glass from her waist,
And pronounced they were "not in good keeping or taste ;
While prim Fleur de Lis, in her robe of French silk,
And magnificent Calla, with mantle like milk,
Of the Louvre recited a wonderful tale,
And said " Guido's rich tints made dame Nature turn pale."
The Snow-Ball assented, and ventured to add
His opinion, that " *all Nature's coloring was bad ;* "
He had thought so, e'er since a few days he had spent
To study the paintings of Rome, as he went

To visit his uncle Gentiana, who chose
His abode on the Alps, 'mid a palace of snows.
But he took on Mont Blanc such a terrible chill,
That ever since that he 'd been pallid and ill."
Half wither'd Miss Hackmatack bought a new glass,
And thought with her nieces, the Spruces, to pass;
But bachelor Holly, who spy'd her out late,
Destroy'd all her plans by a hint at her date.
So she pursed up her mouth, and said tartly, with scorn,
" *She could not remember before she was born.*"
Old Jonquil, the crooked-back'd beau, had been told
That a tax would be laid upon bachelor's gold;
So he bought a new coat, and determined to try
The long disused armor of Cupid so sly ;
Sought for half-open'd buds in their infantine years,
And ogled them all, till they blush'd to their ears.
Philosopher Sage on a sofa was prosing.
With dull Dr Chamomile quietly dozing ;
Though the Laurel descanted, with eloquent breath,
Of heroes and battles, of victory and death,
Of the conquests of Greece, and Bozzaris the brave,
" He had trod in his steps, and had sigh'd o'er his grave."
Farmer Sun-Flower was near, and decidedly spake
Of " the poultry he fed, and the oil he might make ;"
For the true hearted soul deem'd a weather-stain'd face,
And a toil-harden'd hand were no marks of disgrace.
Then he beckon'd his nieces to rise from their seat,
The plump Dandelion, and Cowslip so neat,
And bade them to " pack up their duds and away,
For the cocks crow'd so loud 't was the break o' the day."
——'T was indeed very late, and the coaches were brought,
For the grave matron flowers of their nurseries thought ;
The lu strewas dimm'd of each drapery rare,
And the lucid young brows look'd beclouded with care ;
All save the bright Cereus, that belle so divine,
Who joy'd through the curtains of midnight to shine.
Now they curtsey'd and bow'd as they moved to the door,
But the Poppy snored loud ere the parting was o'er,
For Night her last candle was snuffing away,
And Flora grew tired though she begg'd them to stay ;
Exclaim'd, " all the watches and clocks were too fast,
And old Time ran in spite, lest her pleasures should last."
But when the last guest went, with daughter and wife,
She vow'd she " was never so glad in her life ;"
Call'd out to her maids, who with weariness wept,

To "wash all the glasses and cups ere they slept ;"
For " Aurora," she said, " with her broad staring eye,
Would be pleased, in the house, some disorder to spy ;"
Then sipp'd some pure honey-dew, fresh from the lawn,
And with Zephyrus hasted to sleep until dawn.

MUSING THOUGHTS.

I DID not dream, and yet untiring thought
Rang such wild changes on the spirit's harp,
It seem'd that slumber ruled.
                    A structure rose
Deep founded and gigantic.   Strangely blent
Its orders seem'd.   The dusky Gothic tower
Ecclesiastical, the turret proud
In castellated pomp, the palace dome,
The grated dungeon, and the peasant's cot.
Were grouped within its walls.
                    A throne was there,
A king with all his gay and courtly train
In robes of splendor, and a vassal throng
Eager to do his will, and pleased with chains
Of gilded servitude.   The back-ground seem'd
Darken'd by Misery's pencil.   Famine cast
A tinge of paleness o'er the brow of toil,
While Poverty, to soothe her naked babes,
Shriek'd forth a broken song.
                    Then came a groan—
A rush, as if of thunder: and the earth
From yawning clefts breathed forth volcanic flames,
While the huge fabric, rocking to its base,
A ruin seem'd.   A miserable mass
Of tortured life roll'd through the burning gates,
And spread terrific o'er the parching soil,
Like blacken'd lava.   Then there was a pause,
As if the dire convulsion mourned its wreck.
To the rent walls the sad survivors clung,
And, even 'mid smouldering fires, the artificers
Wrought to uprear the pile.
                    But all at once
A bugle blast was heard—a courser's tramp—
While a stern warrior waved his sword, and cried,

"Away! away!" Like dreams the pageant fled,
Monarch, and royal dame, and nobles proud.
So there he stood alone, array'd in power
Supreme and self-derived.
         Where the rude Alps
Mock with their battlements the bowing cloud,
His eagle-banner stream'd. Pale Gallia pour'd
Incense as to an idol, mixed with blood
Of her young conscript hearts. Chain'd in wild wrath,
The Austrian lion couch'd; even Cæsar's realm
Cast down its crown pontifical, and bade
The Eternal city lay her lip in dust.
The Land of Pyramids bent darkly down,
And from the subject nations rose a voice
Of wretchedness that awed the trembling globe.
Earth, slowly rising from her thousand thrones,
Did homage to the Corsican, as he
The favor'd patriarch in his dream beheld
Heaven, with her sceptred blazonry of stars,
Bow to a reaper's sheaf. But fickle man,
Though like the sea he boast himself awhile,
Hath bounds to his supremacy. I saw
A listed field, where the embattled kings
Drew in deep wrath their armed legions on.
The self-crown'd warrior blench'd not, and his sword
Gleam'd like the flashing lightning, when it cleaves
The vaulted firmament. In vain, in vain!
The hour of fate had come. From a fair isle,
'Gainst whose bold rocks the foil'd Pacific roars,
I heard above the troubled surge, the moan
Of a chafed spirit warring with its lot;
And there, where every element conspired
To make Ambition's prison doubly sure,
The mighty warrior gnaw'd his chain, and died.

ROBERT C. SANDS,

OF New York, one of the present editors of the Commercial Advertiser, in that city, wrote in conjunction with James Wallis Eastburn, the poem of Yamoyden, a tale of the wars of King Philip. Mr Eastburn was a native of England, but received his education here. He had prepared himself for the ministry, and was on the point of assuming the charge of a congregation in Virginia, when his feeble health caused him to undertake a voyage to the West Indies. He died on the passage, December 2d, 1819, at the age of twentytwo.

Yamoyden was written while the authors resided in separate parts of the country,—the one in New York, and the other in Rhode Island,—the plan of the poem having been previously agreed upon, and the parts assigned : but it was not published during the lifetime of Mr Eastburn. After his death, Mr Sands revised the work, and gave it some additions, and it was published in 1820. This poem, although executed under great disadvantages, certainly displays poetical talent of a superior order, and we are inclined to award it the preference among all those of its kind which have been founded upon our aboriginal history. The striking peculiarities of the Indian character and superstition, are introduced with great felicity, and the descriptions are handled with a reach of thought and expression that we do not often see surpassed.

Mr Sands has not, since the publication of this work, occupied himself with verse, except, we believe, in the case of a single casual performance. Those parts of Yamoyden which can be identified as his, leave us no room to doubt that his powers are equal to an undertaking in the very highest walk of poetry. Should he be inclined to devote again to the muse, with any steady and well studied effort, a portion of that fine talent which he is daily throwing away upon the common concerns of life, we feel confident in assuring him a rank among the foremost of those who are enriching our native literature, and winning for themselves unfading wreaths of the sacred laurel.

YAMOYDEN.

PROEM.

Go FORTH, sad fragments of a broken strain,
The last that either bard shall e'er essay ;
The hand can ne'er attempt the chords again,
That first awoke them, in a happier day:
Where sweeps the ocean breeze its desert way,
His requiem murmurs o'er the moaning wave ;
And he who feebly now prolongs the lay,
Shall ne'er the minstrel's hallowed honors crave ;
His harp lies buried deep in that untimely grave!

Friend of my youth! with thee began the love
Of sacred song ; the wont, in golden dreams,
'Mid classic realms of splendors past to rove,
O'er haunted steep, and by immortal streams ;
Where the blue wave, with sparkling bosom gleams
Round shores, the mind's eternal heritage,
For ever lit by memory's twilight beams ;
Where the proud dead, that live in storied page,
Beckon, with awful port, to glory's earlier age.

There would we linger oft, entranced, to hear,
O'er battle fields, the epic thunders roll ;
Or list, where tragic wail upon the ear,
Through Argive palaces shrill echoing, stole ;
There would we mark, uncurb'd by all control,
In central heaven, the Theban eagle's flight ;
Or hold communion with the musing soul
Of sage or bard, who sought, 'mid Pagan night,
In loved Athenian groves, for truth's eternal light.

Homeward we turn'd to that fair land, but late
Redeem'd from the strong spell that bound it fast,
Where Mystery, brooding o'er the waters, sate
And kept the key, till three millenniums past ;
When, as creation's noblest work was last,

Latest, to man it was vouchsafed, to see
Nature's great wonder, long by clouds o'ercast,
And veil'd in sacred awe, that it might be
An empire and a home, most worthy for the free.

And here, forerunners strange and meet were found,
Of that blest freedom, only dream'd before;—
Dark were the morning mists, that linger'd round
Their birth and story, as the hue they bore.
"Earth was their mother;"—or they knew no more,
Or would not that their secret should be told;
For they were grave and silent; and such lore,
To stranger ears, they loved not to unfold,
The long-transmitted tales, their sires were taught of old.

Kind nature's commoners, from her they drew
Their needful wants, and learnt not how to hoard;
And him whom strength and wisdom crown'd, they knew,
But with no servile reverence, as their lord.
And on their mountain summits they adored
One great, good Spirit, in his high abode,
And thence their incense and orisons pour'd
To his pervading presence, that abroad
They felt through all his works,—their Father, King, and God.

And in the mountain mist, the torrent's spray,
The quivering forest, or the glassy flood,
Soft falling showers, or hues of orient day,
They imaged spirits beautiful and good;
But when the tempest roar'd, with voices rude,
Or fierce, red lightning fired the forest pine,
Or withering heats untimely sear'd the wood,
The angry forms they saw of powers malign;
These they besought to spare, those blest for aid divine.

As the fresh sense of life, through every vein,
With the pure air they drank, inspiring came,
Comely they grew, patient of toil and pain,
And, as the fleet deer's, agile was their frame;
Of meaner vices scarce they knew the name;
These simple truths went down from sire to son,—
To reverence age,—the sluggish hunter's shame,
And craven warrior's infamy, to shun,—
And still avenge each wrong, to friends or kindred done.

From forest shades they peer'd, with awful dread,
When, uttering flame and thunder from its side,
The ocean-monster, with broad wings outspread,
Came, ploughing gallantly the virgin tide.
Few years have past, and all their forests' pride
From shores and hills has vanish'd, with the race,
Their tenants erst, from memory who have died,
Like airy shapes, which eld was wont to trace,
In each green thicket's depths, and lone, sequester'd place.

And many a gloomy tale Tradition yet
Saves from oblivion, of their struggles vain,
Their prowess and their wrongs, for rhymer meet,
To people scenes, where still their names remain;
—And so began our young, delighted strain,
That would evoke the plumed chieftains brave,
And bid their martial hosts arise again,
Where Narragansett's tides roll by their grave,
And Haup's romantic steeps are piled above the wave.

Friend of my youth! with thee began my song,
And o'er thy bier its latest accents die;
Misled in phantom-peopled realms too long,—
Though not to me the muse averse deny,
Sometimes, perhaps, her visions to descry,—
Such thriftless pastime should with youth be o'er;
And he who loved with thee his notes to try,
But for thy sake such idlesse would deplore,—
And swears to meditate the thankless muse no more.

But no! the freshness of that past shall still
Sacred to memory's holiest musings be;
When through the ideal fields of song, at will,
He roved, and gather'd chaplets wild with thee;
When, reckless of the world, alone and free,
Like two proud barks, we kept our careless way,
That sail by moonlight o'er the tranquil sea;
Their white apparel and their streamers gay,
Bright gleaming o'er the main, beneath the ghostly ray;—

And downward, far, reflected in the clear
Blue depths, the eye their fairy tackling sees;
So, buoyant, they do seem to float in air,
And silently obey the noiseless breeze;—

Till, all too soon, as the rude winds may please,
They part for distant ports: The gales benign
Swift wafting, bore, by Heaven's all-wise decrees,
To its own harbor sure, where each divine
And joyous vision, seen before in dreams, is thine.

Muses of Helicon! melodious race
Of Jove and golden-hair'd Mnemosyne!
Whose art from memory blots each sadder trace,
And drives each scowling form of grief away!
Who, round the violet fount, your measures gay
Once trod, and round the altar of great Jove;
Whence, wrapt in silvery clouds, your nightly way
Ye held, and ravishing strains of music wove,
That soothed the Thunderer's soul, and fill'd his courts above.

Bright choir! with lips untempted, and with zone
Sparkling, and unapproach'd by touch profane;
Ye, to whose gladsome bosoms ne'er was known
The blight of sorrow, or the throb of pain;—
Rightly invoked,—if right the elected swain,
On your own mountain's side ye taught of yore,
Whose honor'd hand took not your gift in vain,
Worthy the budding laurel-bough it bore,—
Farewell! a long farewell! I worship you no more!

————

Know ye the Indian warrior race?
How their light form springs in strength and grace,
Like the pine on their native mountain side,
That will not bow in its deathless pride;
Whose rugged limbs of stubborn tone
No flexuous power of art will own,
But bend to Heaven's red bolt alone!
How their hue is deep as the western die
That fades in Autumn's evening sky;
That lives for ever upon their brow,
In the summer's heat, and the winter's snow;
How their raven locks of tameless strain,
Stream like the desert courser's mane:

How their glance is far as the eagle's flight,
And fierce and true as the panther's sight:
How their souls are like the crystal wave,
Where the spirit dwells in the northen cave ;
Unruffled in its cavern'd bed,
Calm lies its glimmering surface spread ;
Its springs, its outlet unconfess'd,
The pebble's weight upon its breast
Shall wake its echoing thunders deep,
And when their muttering accents sleep,
Its dark recesses hear them yet,
And tell of deathless love or hate !

———

SONG.

THEY say that afar in the land of the west,
Where the bright golden sun sinks in glory to rest,
'Mid fens where the hunter ne'er ventured to tread,
A fair lake unruffled and sparkling is spread ;
Where, lost in his course, the rapt Indian discovers,
In distance seen dimly, the green isle of lovers.

There verdure fades never ; immortal in bloom,
Soft waves the magnolia its groves of perfume ;
And low bends the branch with rich fruitage depress'd,
All glowing like gems in the crowns of the east ;
There the bright eye of nature, in mild glory hovers:
'T is the land of the sunbeam,—the green isle of lovers !

Sweet strains wildly float on the breezes that kiss
The calm-flowing lake round that region of bliss ;
Where, wreathing their garlands of amaranth, fair choirs
Glad measures still weave to the sound that inspires
The dance and the revel, 'mid forests that cover
On high with their shade the green isle of the lover.

But fierce as the snake with his eyeballs of fire,
When his scales are all brilliant and glowing with ire,
Are the warriors to all, save the maids of their isle,
Whose law is their will, and whose life is their smile ;
From beauty there valor and strength are not rovers,
And peace reigns supreme in the green isle of lovers.

And he who has sought to set foot on its shore,
In mazes perplex'd, has beheld it no more;
It fleets on the vision, deluding the view,
Its banks still retire as the hunters pursue;
O! who in this vain world of wo shall discover,
The home undisturb'd, the green isle of the lover!

ODE TO THE MANITTO OF DREAMS.

SPIRIT! thou spirit of subtlest air,
Whose power is upon the brain,
When wondrous shapes, and dread, and fair,
As the film from the eyes
At thy bidding flies,
To sight and sense are plain!

Thy whisper creeps where leaves are stirr'd;
Thou sighest in woodland gale;
Where waters are gushing thy voice is heard;
And when stars are bright,
At still midnight,
Thy symphonies prevail!

Where the forest ocean, in quick commotion,
Is waving to and fro,
Thy form is seen, in the masses green,
Dimly to come and go.
From thy covert peeping, where thou layest sleeping,
Beside the brawling brook,
Thou art seen to wake, and thy flight to take
Fleet from thy lonely nook.

Where the moonbeam has kiss'd
The sparkling tide,
In thy mantle of mist
Thou art seen to glide.
Far o'er the blue waters
Melting away,
On the distant billow,
As on a pillow,
Thy form to lay.

Where the small clouds of even
Are wreathing in heaven
Their garland of roses,
O'er the purple and gold,
Whose hangings enfold
The hall that encloses
The couch of the sun,
Whose empire is done,—
There thou art smiling,
For thy sway is begun;
Thy shadowy sway,
The senses beguiling,
When the light fades away,
And thy vapor of mystery o'er nature ascending,
The heaven and the earth,
The things that have birth,
And the embryos that float in the future is blending.

From the land, on whose shores the billows break
The sounding waves of the mighty lake;
From the land where boundless meadows be,
Where the buffalo ranges wild and free;
With silvery cot in his little isle,
Where the beaver plies his ceaseless toil;
The land where pigmy forms abide,
Thou leadest thy train at the even tide;
And the wings of the wind are left behind,
So swift through the pathless air they glide.

Then to the chief who has fasted long,
When the chains of his slumber are heavy and strong.
Spirit! thou comest; he lies as dead,
His wearied lids are with heaviness weigh'd;
But his soul is abroad on the hurricane's pinion,
Where foes are met in the rush of fight,
In the shadowy world of thy dominion
Conquering and slaying, till morning light!

Then shall the hunter who waits for thee,
The land of the game rejoicing see
Through the leafless wood,
O'er the frozen flood,
And the trackless snows
His spirit goes,

Along the sheeted plain,
Where the hermit bear, in his sullen lair,
Keeps his long fast, till the winter hath past,
And the boughs have budded again.
Spirit of dreams ! all thy visions are true,
Who the shadow hath seen, he the substance shall view :

Thine the riddle, strange and dark,
Woven in the dreamy brain ;—
Thine to yield the power to mark
Wandering by, the dusky train ;
Warrior ghosts for vengeance crying,
Scalp'd on the lost battle's plain,
Or who died their foes defying,
Slow by lingering tortures slain.

Thou the war-chief hovering near,
Breathest language on his ear ;
When his winged words depart,
Swift as arrows to the heart ;
When his eye the lightning leaves ;
When each valiant bosom heaves ;
Through the veins when hot and glowing
Rage like liquid fire is flowing ;
Round and round the war pole whirling,
Furious when the dancers grow ;
When the maces swift are hurling
Promised vengeance on the foe ;
Thine assurance, Spirit true !
Glorious victory gives to view !

When of thought and strength despoil'd,
Lies the brave man like a child ;
When discolor'd visions fly,
Painful, o'er his gazing eye,
And wishes wild through his darkness rove,
Like flitting wings through the tangled grove,—
Thine is the wish ; the vision thine,
And thy visits, Spirit! are all divine !

When the dizzy senses spin,
And the brain is madly reeling,
Like the Pow-wah, when first within
The present spirit feeling ;

When rays are flashing athwart the gloom,
Like the dancing lights of the northern heaven,
When voices strange of tumult come
On the ear, like the roar of battle driven,—
The Initiate then shall thy wonders see,
And thy priest, O Spirit! is full of thee!

Spirit of dreams! away! away!
It is thine hour of solemn sway;
And thou art holy; and our rite
Forbids thy presence here tonight.
Go light on lids that wake to pain;
Triumphant visions yield again!
If near the Christian's cot thou roam,
Tell him the fire has wrapt his home:
Where the mother lies in peaceful rest,
Her infant slumbering on her breast,
Tell her the red man hath seized its feet,
And against a tree its brains doth beat:
Fly to the bride who sleeps alone,
Her husband forth for battle gone;
Tell her, at morn,—and tell her true,—
His head on the bough her eyes shall view;
While his limbs shall be the raven's prey:—
Spirit of dreams! away! away!

———

SONG OF THE POW-WAHS.

Beyond the hills the Spirit sleeps,
His watch the power of evil keeps;
The Spirit of fire has sought his bed,
The Sun, the hateful Sun is dead.
Profound and clear is the sounding wave,
In the chambers of the Wakon-cave;
Darkness its ancient portal keeps;
And there the Spirit sleeps,—he sleeps.

Come round on raven pinions now,
Spirits of ill, to you we bow!
Whether ye sit on the topmost cliff,
   While the storm around is sweeping,
'Mid the thunder shock, from rock to rock

To view the lightning leaping;
As ye guide the bolt, where towers afar
    The knotted pine to heaven,
And where it falls, your serpent scar
    On the blasted trunk is graven:—
Whether your awful voices pour
Their tones in gales that nightly roar;—
Whether ye dwell beneath the lake,
In whose depths eternal thunders wake,—
Gigantic guard the glittering ore,
That lights Maurepas' haunted shore,—
On Manataulin's lonely isle,
The wanderer of the wave beguile,—
Or love the shore where the serpent-hiss
And angry rattle never cease,—
Come round on raven pinion's now!
Spirits of evil! to you we bow.

Come ye hither, who o'er the thatch
Of the coward murderer hold your watch;
Moping and chattering round who fly
Where the putrid members recking lie,
Piece-meal dropping, as they decay,
O'er the shuddering recreant day by day;
Till he loathes the food that is whelm'd amid
The relics, by foul corruption hid;
And the crawling worms about him bred
Mistake the living for the dead!

Come ye who give power
To the curse that is said,
And a charm that shall wither
To the drops that are shed
On the cheek of the maiden,
Who never shall hear
The kind name of Mother
Saluting her ear;
But sad as the turtle
On the bare branch reclining,
She shall sit in the desert,
Consuming and pining;
With a grief that is silent,
Her beauty shall fade,
Like a flower nipt untimely,
On its stem that is dead.

Come ye who as hawks hover o'er
The spot where the war-club is lying,
Defiled with the stain of their gore,
The foemen to battle defying;
On your dusky wings wheeling above,
Who for vengeance and slaughter come crying:
For the scent of the carnage ye love,
The groans of the wounded and dying.

Come ye, who at the sick man's bed,
Watch beside his burning head;
When the vaunting juggler tries in vain
Charm and fast to soothe his pain,
And his fever-balm and herbs applies,
Your death watch ye sound till your victim dies.

And ye who delight
The soul to affright,
When naked and lonely,
Her dwelling forsaken,
To the country of spirits
Her journey is taken;
When the wings of a dove
She has borrow'd to fly,
Ye swoop from above,
And around her ye cry;
She wanders and lingers
In terror and pain,
While the souls of her kindred
Expect her in vain.

By all the hopes that we forswear;
By the potent rite we here prepare;
By every shriek whose echo falls
Around the Spirit's golden walls;
By our eternal league made good;
By all our wrongs and all our blood;
By the red battle-axe uptorn;
By the deep vengeance we have sworn;
By the uprooted trunk of peace,
And by the wrath that shall not cease,
Where'er ye be, above, below,
Spirits of ill! we call ye now!

ROBERT DINSMOOR,

WAS Born at Londonderry, New Hampshire, October 7th, 1757. His education and early life were those of a common farmer's boy. He served as a soldier at the capture of Burgoyne. We believe he is still living at the place of his nativity. He has attracted much notice in his neighborhood, by his newspaper rhymes, and during the last year, the works of the "Rustic Bard," which title he has assumed, made their appearance in a volume. Mr Dinsmoor is of Scotch descent, and nearly all his verses are in the dialect of that country.

THE BRAES OF GLENNIFFER.

KEEN blaws the wind o'er the braes o' Glenniffer,
The auld castle turrets are cover'd wi' snaw!
How changed sin' the time that I met wi' my lover,
Amang the green bushes by Stantley green shaw!

The wild flowers o' simmer were springing sae bonny,
The mavis sang sweet frae the green birken tree!
But far to the camp they hae march'd my dear Jonnie,
An' now it is winter wi' nature an' me.

Then ilk thing around us was blithsome an' cheerie,
Then ilk thing around us was bonnie an' braw;
Now naething is heard but the wind whistling dreary,
Now naething is seen but the wide spreading snaw.

The trees are a' bare, an' the birds mute an' dowie,
They shake the cauld drift frae their wings as they flee;
They chirp out their plaints seeming wae for my Jonnie,
'T is winter wi' them, an' its winter wi' me.

Yon cauld sleety cloud as it skiffs the bleak mountain,
An' shakes the dark firs on its stey rocky brae,
While down the deep glen bawls the snaw-flooded fountain,
That murmur'd sae sweet to my laddie an' me.

'T is na the loud roar o' the wintry wind swallowin',
'T is na the cauld blast brings the tear i' my e'e ;
For O gin I saw but my bonnie Scot's callan,
The dark days o' winter were simmer to me !

SAMUEL WOODWORTH,

Is a native of Scituate, in Massachusetts, and was born January 13th, 1785. He was the son of a farmer, who was not furnished with the means of giving his children anything more than a very scanty tuition. At the age of fourteen, he attracted the attention of the minister of the parish, by some poetical attempts, and was taken by him under his own roof. The minister bestowed much pains upon his education, and made endeavors to collect a subscription to send him to college, but failing in this, the connexions of young Woodworth put him in mind of the necessity of betaking himself to some occupation for his maintenance. He chose that of a printer, and travelling to Boston, put himself as an apprentice in the office of the Columbian Centinel. He remained here till his indentures were out in 1806, and set off for New York, but his cash failing, he was compelled to stop at New Haven, where he procured employment in the office of a weekly publication called The Herald, for which he exercised both his composing stick and his pen. In less than a year, he resolved upon establishing a weekly miscellany of his own, and partly with the avails of his industry for that short period, and partly by obtaining credit, furnished himself with a printing apparatus, and issued a paper, to which he gave the name of The Belles Lettres Repository. Of this paper he was the editor, publisher, printer, and very often the carrier. His thrift and industry however, were not crowned with success. After a trial of two months, the paper was dropped, and he returned

to Boston, and thence to Scituate. Leaving his native place
after a short stay, he went to Baltimore, and from that city to
New York, where he married, settled, and still resides.

Mr Woodworth has been a writer in several of the public
journals, besides serving as editor to a number of literary
miscellanies, such as The War, The Casket, and The Halcyon
Luminary. In all these, he has written numerous poetical
articles. He is the author of The Champions of Freedom, a
novel, which appeared about the year 1816, and of several
dramatic pieces, namely, The Deed of Gift, Lafayette, or the
Castle of Olmutz, The Locket, The Widow's Son, and The
Rose of the Forest. A collection of his poems was published
in a volume in 1818, and another in 1827.

The short piece entitled The Bucket, is the most esteemed
of Mr Woodworth's writings. It is a very happy performance, natural in thought and expression, and distinguished for
the musical sweetness of its numbers. The engaging live-
liness and simplicity of this little strain have made it very
popular.

THE BUCKET.

How dear to this heart are the scenes of my childhood !
  When fond recollection presents them to view ;
The orchard, the meadow, the deep tangled wild wood,
  And every loved spot which my infancy knew ;
The wide spreading pond, and the mill which stood by it,
  The bridge, and the rock where the cataract fell ;
The cot of my father, the dairy house nigh it,
  And e'en the rude bucket which hung in the well.
The old oaken bucket, the iron-bound bucket,
The moss-cover'd bucket which hung in the well.

That moss-cover'd vessel I hail as a treasure,
  For often at noon, when return'd from the field,
I found it the source of an exquisite pleasure,
  The purest and sweetest that nature can yield.
How ardent I seized it with hands that were glowing,
  And quick to the white pebbled bottom it fell,
Then soon with the emblem of truth overflowing,

And dripping with coolness, it rose from the well.
The old oaken bucket, the iron-bound bucket,
The moss-cover'd bucket arose from the well.

How sweet from the green mossy brim to receive it,
   As poised on the curb it inclined to my lips!
Not a full blushing goblet could tempt me to leave it,
   Though fill'd with the nectar that Jupiter sips.
And now far removed from the loved situation,
   The tear of regret will intrusively swell,
As fancy reverts to my father's plantation,
   And sighs for the bucket which hangs in the well.
The old oaken bucket, the iron-bound bucket,
The moss-cover'd bucket which hangs in his well.

THE LANDSEND.

THE gale was propitious, all canvas was spread,
   As swift through the water we glided,
And the tear drop yet glisten'd which friendship had shed,
   Though the pang whence it sprang had subsided.
Fast faded in distance each object we knew,
   As the shores which we loved were retiring,
And the last grateful object which linger'd in view,
   Was the beacon on landsend aspiring.

Ah! here, I exclaim'd, is an emblem of life,
   For 't is but a turbulent ocean,
Where passion with reason is ever at strife,
   While our frail little barks are in motion.
The haven of infancy, calm and serene,
   We leave in the distance retiring,
While memory lingers to gaze on some scene,
   Like the beacon on landsend aspiring.

O may I be careful to steer by that chart,
   Which wisdom in mercy has given,
And true like the needle, this tremulous heart,
   Be constantly pointing to heaven.
Thus safely with tempests and billows I 'll cope,

And find, when at last they 're subsiding,
On the landsend of life there 's a beacon of hope,
To the harbor of happiness guiding.

LOVE'S EYES.

Love's eyes are so enchanting,
Bright, smiling, soft and granting,
Pulses play at every ray,
And hearts at every glance are panting.
Before the beamy eye of morn
We view the clouds of night receding;
So tender glances banish scorn,
For who can frown while Love is pleading?
Love's eyes are so enchanting, &c.

No bandage can those eyes conceal,
Though bards in fabled tales rehearse it;
For if we wore a mask of steel,
Affection's ardent gaze would pierce it.
Love's eyes are so enchanting, &c.

Beware, then, lest some artful elf
The infant's smiles and armor borrow,
To win a throb of joy for self,
And give his victims years of sorrow.
Love's eyes are so enchanting, &c.

THE PRIDE OF THE VALLEY.

The pride of the valley is lovely young Ellen,
Who dwells in a cottage enshrined by a thicket,
Sweet peace and content are the wealth of her dwelling,
And Truth is the porter that waits at the wicket.
The zephyr that lingers on violet-down pinion,
With Spring's blushing honors delighted to dally,
Ne'er breathed on a blossom in Flora's dominion,
So lovely as Ellen, the pride of the valley.

She 's true to her Willie, and kind to her mother,
  Nor riches nor honors can tempt her from duty ;
Content with her station, she sighs for no other,
  Though fortunes and titles have knelt to her beauty.
To me her affections and promise are plighted,
  Our ages are equal, our tempers will tally ;
O moment of rapture, that sees me united
  To lovely young Ellen, the pride of the valley.

WREATH OF LOVE.

Let Fame her wreath for others twine,
The fragrant Wreath of Love be mine,
  With balm-distilling blossoms wove ;
Let the shrill trumpet's hoarse alarms
Bid laurels grace the victor's arms,
  Where havoc's blood-stain'd banners move.
Be mine to wake the softer notes
Where Acidalia's banner floats,
  And wear the gentler Wreath of Love.

The balmy rose let stoics scorn,
Let squeamish mortals dread the thorn,
  And fear the pleasing pain to prove ;
I 'll fearless bind it to my heart,
While every pang its thorns impart,
  The floweret's balsam shall remove ;
For, sweeten'd by the nectar'd kiss,
'T is pain that gives a zest to bliss,
  And freshens still the Wreath of Love.

Give me contentment, peace, and health,
A moderate share of worldly wealth,
  And friends such blessings to improve ;
A heart to give when misery pleads,
To heal each rankling wound that bleeds,
  And every mental pain remove ;
But with these give—else all deny—
The fair for whom I breathe the sigh,
  And wedlock be a Wreath of Love.

Connubial bliss, unknown to strife,
A faithful friend—a virtuous wife,
  Be mine for many years to prove :
Our wishes one, within each breast
The dove of peace shall make her nest,
  Nor ever from the ark remove ;
Till call'd to heaven, through ages there
Be ours the blissful lot to wear
  A never fading Wreath of Love.

JOHN PIERPONT.

MR PIERPONT is a native of Litchfield in Connecticut, and was born on the 6th of April, 1785. He was educated at Yale College, and received his degree in 1804. He studied law and practised for a while at Newburyport. He then removed to Baltimore, where he was one of the contributors to the Portico during the most successful period of that work. About ten years since he became pastor of Hollis Street church in Boston, and continues in that station at the present time, enjoying in addition to his reputation as a poet, a degree of popularity as a preacher which very few among our native clergymen have gained.

The earliest occasion on which Mr Pierpont appeared to the public in his poetical capacity, was as the author of The Portrait, a poem delivered in public at Newburyport in 1812, and afterwards published. In 1816 appeared at Baltimore, The Airs of Palestine, a performance not at first designed for publication, but written in the cause of charity. It was intended, to use the author's own words, "that the recitation of it should form a part of the performances of an evening concert of Sacred Music for the benefit of the poor. It was indeed a volunteer in the cause ; but its aid was coldly received, or rather was coldly declined wherever it made its trembling advances ; and it was thus stung into the resolution of appearing before the public ; not indeed to solicit the succor of charity for others, but the rites of hospitality for itself."

Since this period he has not attempted any poetical work of magnitude, but has occasionally tuned his lyre at public solemnities, and on festive occasions. Besides these original performances he has compiled for the use of schools, The American First Class Book and The National Reader, two manuals, which for sound judgment and correct taste in the selection of matter, are superior to any works of the kind which have appeared in our language. They are now in very extensive use throughout the country, and are becoming daily more esteemed in our seminaries of education. The principal aim in making these compilations we cannot too warmly applaud, namely, that of cherishing a national spirit and taste, and inspiring a love for our native institutions, literature and manners.

The Airs of Palestine is the one among Mr Pierpont's poems to which he is chiefly indebted for his poetical reputation. It has passed several times through the press in this country and abroad, and has gained its author among foreign critics, the distinction, if not of the most highly gifted, at least of the most correct of the American poets. As regards the character of this work, which has been received from the first with a degree of interest equal if not superior to that attending any modern poem which has made its appearance among us; it may be remarked in general, that it possesses those sterling qualities which offer a permanent attraction, and will continue to win our regard, unaffected by the waverings of popular taste, or the influence of the new schools and doctrines which from time to time may spring up and give currency to novelties of style and matter in poetical composition. Its beauties require no minute and elaborate comment to unfold them to our comprehension; but are of a nature to be relished by the common reader, unpractised in the mysteries of criticism, who admires accordingly as he is affected,—as well as by him who judges them with a more delicate and philosophical perception of their niceties.

The main scope of the poem is to illustrate the influence of music upon the passions of mankind, and consequently, its moral nature and tendency, by themes taken from sacred history. The instances selected for this purpose evince a refined and happy taste, which singles out with unerring judgment from among the great mass of materials at hand, that which is best adapted to the object in view. The transitions, where it becomes necessary to vary the theme, in some degree, for the introduction of minor topics, are managed with consummate skill.

Mr Pierpont has not attempted to distinguish himself by those bold and daring flights which so many of our modern poets are accustomed to essay in putting their powers to the proof. His muse wings her way with a calm and graceful flight, luxuriating in the sunbeam and breasting the mountain breeze, but she does not plunge among the thunder clouds, or shake her pinions in the strife of the hurricane. The poetry of the present day is rife with those tumultuous elements which have their seat in the deep recesses of human thought and emotion, with storms of sweeping and destructive passion, and acute mental feeling,—subjects with which our stripling bards fearlessly venture to grapple, ignorant of the nature of what they have seized upon, and the powers which the control of such things demand. Hence the small proportion among the great amount of verse that is yearly given to the world, which is blessed with more than a temporary reputation. By attempting achievements to which its powers are not adapted, genius itself must experience a failure. Let it not be thought a disparagement in the case of the present writer to say that he has not aimed at so much as many others. He has undertaken a work which in its successful execution, shows the hand of a master, and leaves us to believe that he is capable of yet greater things.

Mr Pierpont has been spoken of as a faithful scholar of the school of Pope, in regard we suppose to the mechanical structure of his verse ; for in the essentials of poetry, we apprehend the qualities of these writers, have too little in common to warrant us in coupling them together. In the polish, and flow of his numbers, he may be classed, if it be necessary to point out a master, with that author ; but his lines are free from the monotony of cadence which prevails to such a degree in the versification of Pope ; while in vivid and beautiful imagery, and richness of language, he claims to be ranked in an order widely distinct from the bard of Twickenham.

The use of double rhymes in this poem has been censured. That they ever disagree with the solemnity of the subject, as has been objected, we find it difficult to perceive, while the reason assigned for their introduction under the circumstances in which the work was composed, seems to us satisfactory. "The poem," as the author remarks, "was begun and ended with the idea that it would be publicly rehearsed ; and I was aware how difficult even a good speaker finds it, to recite the best heroic poetry for any length of time without perceiving in his hearers the somniferous effects of a regular cadence. The double rhyme was therefore occasionally thrown in like a ledge of rocks in a smoothly gliding river, to break the current which without it, might appear sluggish, and to vary the melody, which otherwise might become monotonous."

Mr Pierpont's poetry is small in amount, but is destined to outlive the voluminous productions of many of his contemporaries. His patriotic and devotional songs written for public occasions, show a talent for lyrical composition which would raise him to eminent distinction without the aid of his descriptive poetry.

AIRS OF PALESTINE.

At the dun cloud that, slowly rising, holds
The Summer tempest in its gloomy folds,
Though, o'er the ridges of its thundering breast,
The King of Terrors rides, and shakes his lightning crest,
Fearless we gaze, when those dark folds we find
Fringed with the golden light, that glows behind.
So, when one language bound the human race,
On Shinar's plain, round Babel's mighty base,
Gloomily rose the minister of wrath;
Dark was his frown, destructive was his path;
That tower was blasted by the touch of heaven;
That bond was burst—that race asunder driven:
Yet, round the Avenger's brow, that frown'd above,
Play'd Mercy's beams—the lambent light of Love.
All was not lost, though busy Discord flung
Repulsive accents from each jarring tongue;
All was not lost; for Love one tie had twined,
And Mercy dropp'd it, to connect mankind:
One tie, whose airy filaments invest,
Like Beauty's zone, the calm or stormy breast;
Wake that to action, rule of this the strife,
And, through the mazy labyrinths of life,
Supply a faithful clue, to lead the lone
And weary wanderer to his Father's throne.
   That tie is Music. How supreme her sway!
How lovely is the Power that all obey!
Dumb matter trembles at her thrilling shock;
Her voice is echo'd by the desert rock;
For her, the asp withholds the sting of death,
And bares his fangs, but to inhale her breath;
The royal lion leaves his desert lair,
And, crouching, listens when she treads the air;
And man, by wilder impulse driven to ill,
Is tamed, and led by this enchantress still.
Who ne'er has felt her hand assuasive steal
Along his heart—That heart will never feel.
'T is hers to chain the passions, soothe the soul,
To snatch the dagger, and to dash the bowl
From Murder's hand; to smooth the couch of Care,
Extract the thorns, and scatter roses there;
Of pain's hot brow, to still the bounding throb,

Despair's long sigh, and Grief's convulsive sob.
How vast her empire! Turn through earth, through air,
Your aching eye, you find her subjects there;
Nor is the throne of heaven above her spell,
Nor yet beneath it is the host of hell.
    To her, Religion owes her holiest flame:
Her eye looks heaven-ward, for from heaven she came.
And when Religion's mild and genial ray,
Around the frozen heart begins to play,
Music's soft breath falls on the quivering light;
The fire is kindled, and the flame is bright;
And that cold mass, by either power assail'd,
Is warm'd—made liquid—and to heaven exhaled.
    Here let us pause :—the opening prospect view :—
How fresh this mountain air!—how soft the blue,
That throws its mantle o'er the length'ning scene!
Those waving groves—those vales of living green—
Those yellow fields—that lake's cerulean face,
That meets, with curling smiles, the cool embrace
Of roaring torrents, lull'd by her to rest;—
That white cloud, melting on the mountain's breast:
How the wide landscape laughs upon the sky!
How rich the light that gives it to the eye!
    Where lies our path ?—though many a vista call,
We may admire, but cannot tread them all.
Where lies our path ?—a poet, and inquire
What hills, what vales, what streams become the lyre?
See, there Parnassus lifts his head of snow;
See at his foot the cool Cephissus flow;
There Ossa rises; there Olympus towers;
Between them, Tempe breathes in beds of flowers,
For ever verdant : and there Peneus glides
Through laurels, whispering on his shady sides.
Your theme is music :—Yonder rolls the wave,
Where dolphins snatch'd Arion from his grave,
Enchanted by his lyre :—Cithæron's shade
Is yonder seen, where first Amphion play'd
Those potent airs, that, from the yielding earth,
Charm'd stones around him, and gave cities birth.
And fast by Hæmus, Thracian Hebrus creeps
O'er golden sands, and still for Orpheus weeps,
Whose gory head, borne by the stream along,
Was still melodious, and expired in song.
There Nereids sing, and Triton winds his shel ;

There be thy path—for there the muses dwell.
　No, no—a lonelier, lovelier path be mine:
Greece, and her charms, I leave, for Palestine.
There, purer streams through happier valleys flow,
And sweeter flowers on holier mountains blow.
I love to breathe where Gilead sheds her balm;
I love to walk on Jordan's banks of palm;
I love to wet my foot in Hermon's dews;
I love the promptings of Isaiah's muse:
In Carmel's holy grots I'll court repose,
And deck my mossy couch with Sharon's deathless rose.
　Here arching vines their leafy banner spread,
Shake their green shields, and purple odors shed;
At once repelling Syria's burning ray,
And breathing freshness on the sultry day,
Here the wild bee suspends her murmuring wing,
Pants on the rock, or sips the silver spring;
And here—as musing on my theme divine,
I gather flowers to bloom along my line,
And hang my garland in festoons around,
Enwreath'd with clusters, and with tendrils bound;
And fondly, warmly, humbly hope, the Power,
That gave perfumes and beauty to the flower,
Drew living water from this rocky shrine,
Purpled the clustering honors of the vine,
And led me, lost in devious mazes, hither,
To weave a garland, will not let it wither:—
Wond'ring, I listen to the strain sublime,
That flows, all freshly down the stream of time,
Wafted in grand simplicity along,
The undying breath, the very soul of song.
Down that long vale of years are sweetly roll'd
The mingled voices of the bards of old;
Melodious voices! bards of brightest fire!
Where each is warm, how melting is the quire!
Yet, though so blended is the concert blest,
Some master tones are heard above the rest.
　O'er the cleft sea, the storm in fury rides:
Israel is safe, and Egypt tempts the tides:
Her host, descending, meets a wat'ry grave,
And o'er her monarch rolls the refluent wave.
The storm is hush'd: the billows foam no more,
But sink in smiles: there's Music on the shore.
On the wide waste of waters, dies that air

Unheard ; for all is death and coldness there.
But see! the robe that brooding Silence throws
O'er Shur reclining in profound repose,
Is rent, and scatter'd, by the bursts of praise,
That swells the song th' astonish'd Hebrews raise.
The desert waked at that proud anthem, flung
From Miriam's timbrel and from Moses' tongue :
The first to Liberty that e'er was sung.
    But if, when joy and gratitude inspire,
Such high-toned triumph walks along the lyre,
What are its breathings, when pale sorrow flings
Her tearful touches o'er its trembling strings ?
    At Nebo's base, that mighty bard resigns
His life and empire in prophetic lines.——
Heaven, all attention, round the poet bends,
And conscious earth, as when the dew descends,
Or showers as gentle, feels her young buds swell,
Her herbs shoot greener, at that fond farewell.
Rich is the song, though mournfully it flows :
And as that harp, which God alone bestows,
Is swept in concert with that sinking breath,
Its cold chords shrink, as from the touch of death.
It *was* the touch of death!——Sweet be thy slumbers,
Harp of the prophet! but those holy numbers,
That death-denoting, monitory moan.
Shall live, till Nature heaves her dying groan,
From Pisgah's top his eye the prophet threw,
O'er Jordan's wave, where Canaan met his view.
His sunny mantle and his hoary locks
Shone, like the robe of Winter, on the rocks.
Where is that mantle ?——Melted into air.
Where is the prophet ?——God can tell thee where.
    So, on the brow of some romantic height,
A fleecy cloud hangs hovering in the light,
Fit couch for angels ; which while yet we view,
'T is lost to earth, and all around is blue.
    Who is that Chief, already taught to urge
The battle stream, and roll its darkest surge,
Whose army marches through retiring seas,
Whose gory banner spreading on the breeze,
Unfolds o'er Jericho's devoted towers,
And, like the storm o'er Sodom, redly lowers?
The moon can answer ; for she heard his tongue,
And cold and pale o'er Ajalon she hung.

The sun can tell :—O'er Gibeon's vale of blood,
Curving their beamy necks, his coursers stood,
Held by that hero's arm, to light his wrath,
And roll their glorious eyes upon his crimson path.
What mine, exploding, rends that smoking ground ?
What earthquake spreads those smouldering ruins round ?
The sons of Levi, round that city, bear
The ark of God, their consecrated care,
And, in rude concert, each returning morn,
Blow the long trump, and wind the curling horn.
No blackening thunder smoked along the wall :
No earthquake shook it :—Music wrought its fall.
 The reverend hermit, who from earth retires,
Freezes to love's, to melt in holier fires,
And builds on Libanus his humble shed,
Beneath the waving cedars of his head :—
Year after year, with brighter views revolving,
Doubt after doubt, in stronger hopes dissolving ;—
Though neither pipe, nor voice, nor organ's swell,
Disturb the silence of his lonely cell ;
Yet hears enough, had nought been heard before,
To wake a holy awe, and teach him to adore.
For, ere the day with orisons he closes,
Ere on his flinty couch his head reposes,
A couch more downy in the hermit's sight,
Than beds of roses to the Sybarite ;
As lone he muses on those naked rocks,
Heaven's last light blushing on his silver locks.
Amid the deepening shades of that wild mountain,
He hears the burst of many a mossy fountain,
Whose crystal rills in pure embraces mingle,
And dash, and sparkle down the leafy dingle,
There lose their liquid notes :—with grateful glow,
The hermit listens, as the waters flow,
And says there 's Music in that mountain stream,
The storm beneath him, and the eagle's scream.
 There lives around that solitary man,
The tameless music, that with time began ;
Airs of the Power, that bids the tempest roar,
The cedar bow, the royal eagle soar ;
The mighty Power, by whom those rocks were piled,
Who moves unseen, and murmurs through the wild.
What countless chords does that dread Being strike !
Various their tone, but all divine alike :

There, Mercy whispers in a balmy breath,
Here, Anger thunders, and the note is death ;
There, 't is a string that soothes with slow vibration,
And here, a burst that shakes the whole creation.
By heaven forewarn'd, his hunted life to save,
Behold Elijah stands by Horeb's cave ;
Grieved that the God, for whom he 'd warmly striven,
Should see his servants into exile driven,
His words neglected, by those servants spoken,
His prophets murder'd, and his altars broken.
His bleeding heart a soothing strain requires :
He hears it :——softer than Æolian lyres,
" A still, small voice," like Zephyr's dying sighs,
Steals on his ear :——he may not lift his eyes,
But o'er his face his flowing mantle flings,
And hears a whisper from the King of kings.
    Yet, from that very cave, from Horeb's side,
Where spreads a desert prospect, wild and wide,
The prophet sees, with reverential dread,
Dark Sinai rear his thunder-blasted head ;
Where erst was pour'd on trembling Israel's ear,
A stormier peal, that Moses quaked to hear.
In what tremendous pomp Jehovah shone,
When on that mount he fix'd his burning throne !
Thick, round its base, a shuddering gloom was flung ;
Black, on its breast, a thunder-cloud was hung :
Bright, through that blackness, arrowy lightnings came,
Shot from the glowing vail, that wrapp'd its head in flame.
And when that quaking mount the Eternal trod,
Scorch'd by the foot of the descending God,
Then blasts of unseen trumpets, long and loud,
Swell'd by the breath of whirlwinds, rent the cloud,
And Death and Terror stalk'd, beneath that smoky shroud.
    Seest thou that shepherd boy, of features fair,
Of eye serene, and brightly flowing hair,
That leans, in thoughtful posture, on his crook,
And, statue-like, pores o'er the pebbly brook ?
Yes : and why stands he there, in stupor cold ?
Why not pursue those wanderers from his fold ?
Or, 'mid the playful children of his flocks,
Toss his light limbs, and shake his amber locks,
Rather than idly gaze upon the stream ?——
That boy is lost in a poetic dream :
And, while his eye follows the wave along,
His soul expatiates in the realm of song.

For oft, where yonder grassy hills recede,
I 've heard that shepherd tune his rustic reed:
And then such sweetness from his fingers stole,
I knew that Music had possess'd his soul.
Oft, in her temple shall the votary bow,
Oft, at her altar breathe his ardent vow,
And oft suspend, along her coral walls,
The proudest trophies that adorn her halls.
Even now, the heralds of his monarch tear
The son of Jesse from his fleecy care,
And to the hall the ruddy minstrel bring,
Where sits a being, that was once a king.
Still, on his brow, the crown of Israel gleams,
And cringeing courtiers still adore its beams,
Though the bright circle throws no light divine,
But rays of hell, that melt it while they shine.
  As the young harper tries each quivering wire,
It leaps and sparkles with prophetic fire,
And, with the kindling song, the kindling rays
Around his fingers tremulously blaze,
Till the whole hall, like those bless'd fields above,
Glows with the light of melody and love.
  Soon as the foaming demon hears that psalm,
Heaven on his memory bursts, and Eden's balm;
He sees the dawning of too bright a sky;
Detects the angel in the poet's eye;
With grasp convulsive, rends his matted hair;
Through his strain'd eye-balls shoots a fiend-like glare:
And flies, with shrieks of agony, that hail,
The throne of Israel, and the breast of Saul;
Exiled to roam, or, in infernal pains,
To seek a refuge from that shepherd's strains.
  The night was moonless:—Judah's shepherds kept
Their starlight watch: their flocks around them slept.
To heaven's blue fields their wakeful eyes were turn'd,
And to the fires that there eternal burn'd.
Those azure regions had been peopled long,
With Fancy's children, by the sons of song:
And there, the simple shepherd, conning o'er
His humble pittance of Chaldean lore,
Saw, in the stillness of a starry night,
The Swan and Eagle wing their silent flight;
And, from their spangled pinions, as they flew,
On Israel's vales of verdure shower the dew:
Saw there, the brilliant gems, that nightly flare,
In the thin mist of Berenice's hair;

And there, Boötes roll his lucid wain,
On sparkling wheels, along the etherial plain ;
And there, the Pleiades, in tuneful gyre,
Pursue for ever the star-studded Lyre ;
And there, with bickering lash, heaven's Charioteer
Urge round the Cynosure his bright career.
   While thus the shepherds watch'd the host of night,
O'er heaven's blue concave flash'd a sudden light.
The unrolling glory spread its folds divine,
O'er the green hills and vales of Palestine ;
And lo ! descending angels, hovering there,
Stretch'd their loose wings, and in the purple air,
Hung o'er the sleepless guardians of the fold :—
When that high anthem, clear, and strong, and bold
On wavy paths of trembling ether ran :
"Glory to God ;—Benevolence to man ;—
Peace to the world :"—and in full concert came,
From silver tubes, and harps of golden frame,
The loud and sweet response, whose choral strains
Linger'd and languish'd on Judea's plains.
Yon living lamps, charm'd from their chambers blue,
By airs so heavenly, from the skies withdrew :
All ?—all, but one, that hung and burn'd alone,
And with mild lustre over Bethlehem shone.
Chaldea's sages saw that orb afar,
Glow unextinguish'd ;—'t was Salvation's Star.
   Hear'st thou that solemn symphony, that swells
And echoes through Philippi's gloomy cells ?
From vault to vault the heavy notes rebound,
And granite rocks reverberate the sound.
The wretch, who long, in dungeons cold and dank,
Had shook his fetters, that their iron clank
Might break the grave-like silence of that prison,
On which the Star of Hope had never risen ;
Then sunk in slumbers, by despair oppress'd,
And dream'd of freedom in his broken rest ;
Wakes at the music of those mellow strains,
Thinks it some spirit, and forgets his chains.
'T is Paul and Silas ; who, at midnight, pay
To him of Nazareth a grateful lay.
Soon is that anthem wafted to the skies :
An angel bears it, and a God replies.
At that reply, a pale, portentous light
Plays through the air,—then leaves a gloomier night.
The darkly tottering towers,—the trembling arch,—

The rocking walls confess an earthquake's march,—
The stars look dimly through the roof:—behold,
From saffron dews and melting clouds of gold,
Brightly uncurling on the dungeon's air,
Freedom walks forth serene :—from her loose hair,
And every glistening feather of her wings,
Perfumes that breathe of more than earth she flings,
And with a touch dissolves the prisoner's chains,
Whose song had charm'd her from celestial plains.
  'T is night again : for Music loves to steal
Abroad at night; when all her subjects kneel,
In more profound devotion, at her throne :
And, at that sober hour, she 'll sit alone,
Upon a bank, by her sequester'd cell,
And breathe her sorrows through her wreathed shell.
Again 't is night—the diamond lights on high,
Burn bright, and dance harmonious through the sky :
And Silence leads her downy-footed hours,
Round Sion's hill, and Salem's holy towers.
The Lord of Life, with his few faithful friends,
Drown'd in mute sorrow, down that hill descends.
They cross the stream that bathes its foot, and dashes
Around the tomb, where sleep a monarch's ashes ;
And climb the steep, where oft the midnight air
Received the Sufferer's solitary prayer.
There, in dark bowers imbosom'd, Jesus flings
His hand celestial o'er prophetic strings ;
Displays his purple robe, his bosom gory,
His crown of thorns, his cross, his future glory :—
And, while the group, each hallow'd accent gleaming,
On pilgrim's stuff, in pensive posture leaning—
Their reverend beards, that sweep their bosoms, wet
With the chill dews of shady Olivet—
Wonder and weep, they pour the song of sorrow,
With their loved Lord, whose death shall shroud the morrow.
Heavens ! what a strain was that ! those matchless tones,
That ravish " Princedoms, Dominations, Thrones ; "
That, heard on high, had hush'd those peals of praise,
That seraphs swell, and harping angels raise,
Soft, as the wave from Siloa's fount that flows,
Through the drear silence of the mountain rose.
How sad the Saviour's song ! how sweet ! how holy !
The last he sung on earth :—how melancholy !
Along the valley sweep the expiring notes :
On Kedron's wave the melting music floats :

From her blue arch, the lamp of evening flings
Her mellow lustre, as the Saviour sings:
The moon above, the wave beneath is still,
And light and music mingle on the hill.
   The glittering guard, whose viewless ranks invest
The brook's green margin, and the mountain's crest,
Catch that unearthly song, and soar away,
Leave this dark orb, for fields of endless day,
And round the Eternal's throne on buoyant pinions play.
   Ye glowing seraphs, that enchanted swim,
In seas of rapture, as ye tune the hymn
Ye bore from earth—O say, ye choral quires,
Why in such haste to wake your golden lyres?
Why, like a flattering, like a fleeting dream,
Leave that lone mountain, and that silent stream?
Say, could not then the "Man of Sorrows" claim
Your shield of adamant, your sword of flame?—
Hell forced a smile, at your retiring wing,
And man was left—to crucify your King.
   But must no other sweets perfume my wreath,
Than Carmel's hill and Sharon's valley breathe?
Are holy airs borne only through the skies,
Where Sinai thunders, and where Horeb sighs?
And move they only o'er Arabia's sea,
Bethesda's pool, the lake of Galilee?
And does the hand that bids Judea bloom,
Deny its blossoms to the desert's gloom?
No:—turn thine eye, in visionary glance,
To scene's beyond old ocean's blue expanse,
Where vast La Plata rolls his weight along,
Through worlds unknown to science and to song,
And, sweeping proudly o'er his boundless plain,
Repels the foaming billows of the main.
Let Fancy lap thee in Paraguay's bowers,
And scatter round thee Nature's wildest flowers:
For Nature there, since first her opening eye
Hail'd the bright orb her Father hung on high,
Still, on her bosom wears the enamel'd vest,
That bloom'd and budded on her infant breast;
Still, to the sportive breeze that round her blows,
Turns her warm cheek, her unshorn tresses throws;
With grateful hand her treasured balm bequeaths,
For every sigh the enamor'd rover breathes,
And even smiles to feel the flutterer sip
The virgin dew that cools her rosy lip.

There, through the clouds, stupendous mountains rise,
And lift their icy foreheads to the skies ;
There, blooming valleys and secure retreats
Bathe all thy senses in voluptuous sweets :
Reclining there, beneath a bending tree,
Fraught with the fragrant labors of the bee,
Admire, with me, the birds of varied hue,
That hang, like flowers of orange and of blue,
Among the broad magnolia's cups of snow,
Quaffing the perfumes, from those cups that flow.
    But, is all peace, beneath the mountain shade ?
Do Love and Mercy haunt that sunny glade,
And sweetly rest upon that lovely shore,
When light retires, and nature smiles no more ?
No :—there, at midnight, the hoarse tiger growls :
There, the gaunt wolf sits on his rock and howls :
And there, in painted pomp, the yelling Indian prowls.
    Round the bold front of yon projecting cliff,
Shoots, on white wings, the missionary's skiff,
And, walking steadily along the tide,
Seems, like a phantom, o'er the wave to glide,
Her light cymar unfolded to the breeze,
That breaks not, though it moves, the mirror of the seas.
    Lo, at the stern, the priest of Jesus rears
His reverend front, plough'd by the share of years.
He takes his harp :—the spirits of the air
Breathe on his brow, and interweave his hair,
In silky flexure, with the sounding strings :—
And hark !—the holy missionary sings.
'T is the Gregorian chant :—with him unites,
On either hand, his quire of neophytes,
While the boat cleaves its liquid path along,
And waters, woods, and winds protract the song.
    Those unknown strains the forest war-whoop hush :
Huntsmen and warriors from their cabins rush,
Heed not the foe, that yells defiance nigh,
See not the deer that dashes wildly by,
Drop from their hand the bow and rattling quiver,
Crowd to the shore, and plunge into the river,
Breast the green waves, the enchanted bark that toss,
Leap o'er her sides, and kneel before the cross.
    Hear yon poetic pilgrim of the west,
Chant Music's praise, and to her power attest.
Who now, in Florida's untrodden woods,
Bedecks, with vines of jessamine, her floods,

And flowery bridges o'er them loosely throws ;—
Who hangs the canvas where Atala glows,
On the live oak, in floating drapery shrouded,
That like a mountain rises, lightly clouded ;—
Who, for the son of Outalissa, twines,
Beneath the shade of ever whispering pines,
A funeral wreath, to bloom upon the moss,
That time already sprinkles on the cross,
Raised o'er the grave, where his young virgin sleeps,
And Superstition o'er her victim weeps ;—
Whom now, the silence of the dead surrounds,
Among Scioto's monumental mounds ;
Save that, at times, the musing pilgrim hears
A crumbling oak fall with the weight of years,
To swell the mass that Time and Ruin throw,
O'er chalky bones, that mouldering lie below,
By virtues unembalm'd, unstain'd by crimes,
Lost in those towering tombs of other times ;
For where no bard has cherish'd Virtue's flame,
No ashes sleep in the warm sun of Fame.—
With sacred lore this traveller beguiles
His weary way, while o'er him Fancy smiles.
Whether he kneels in venerable groves,
Or through the wide and green savanna roves,
His heart leaps lightly on each breeze, that bears
The faintest cadence of Idumea's airs.
  Now, he recalls the lamentable wail,
That pierced the shades of Rama's palmy vale
When Murder struck, throned on an infant's bier,
A note, for Satan's, and for Herod's ear.
Now, on a bank, o'erhung with waving wood,
Whose falling leaves flit o'er Ohio's flood,
The pilgrim stands ; and o'er his memory rushes
The mingled tide of tears, and blood, that gushes
Along the valleys, where his childhood stray'd,
And round the temples where his father pray'd.
How fondly then, from all but Hope exiled,
To Zion's wo recurs Religion's child !
He sees the tear of Judah's captive daughters
Mingle, in silent flow, with Babel's waters ;
While Salem's harp, by patriot pride unstrung,
Wrapp'd in the mist, that o'er the river hung,
Felt but the breeze, that wanton'd o'er the billow,
And the long, sweeping fingers of the willow.
  And could not Music soothe the captive's wo ?
But should that harp be strung for Judah's foe ?

While thus the enthusiast roams along the stream,
Balanced between a revery and a dream,
Backward he springs : and, through his bounding heart,
The cold and curdling poison seems to dart.
For, in the leaves, beneath a quivering brake,
Spinning his death-note, lies a coiling snake,
Just in the act, with greenly venom'd fangs,
To strike the foot, that heedless o'er him hangs.
Bloated with rage, on spiral folds he rides ;
His rough scales shiver on his spreading sides ;
Dusky and dim his glossy neck becomes,
And freezing poisons thicken on his gums ;
His parch'd and hissing throat breathes hot and dry ;
A spark of hell lies burning on his eye :
While, like a vapor, o'er his writhing rings,
Whirls his light tail, that threatens while it sings.
Soon as dumb Fear removes her icy fingers
From off his heart, where gazing wonder lingers,
The pilgrim, shrinking from a doubtful fight,
Aware of danger, too, in sudden flight,
From his soft flute throws Music's air around,
And meets his foe, upon enchanted ground.
See ! as the plaintive melody is flung,
The lightning flash fades on the serpent's tongue ;
The uncoiling reptile o'er each shining fold
Throws changeful clouds of azure, green and gold ;
A softer lustre twinkles in his eye ;
His neck is burnish'd with a glossier dye ;
His slippery scales grow smoother to the sight,
And his relaxing circles roll in light.
Slowly the charm retires :—with waving sides,
Along its tract the graceful listener glides ;
While Music throws her silver cloud around,
And bears her votary off, in magic folds of sound.
On Arno's bosom, as he calmly flows,
And his cool arms round Vallombrosa throws,
Rolling his crystal tide through classic vales,
Alone,—at night,—the Italian boatman sails.
High o'er Mont Alto walks, in maiden pride,
Night's queen :—he sees her image on that tide,
Now, ride the wave that curls its infant crest,
Around his brow, then rippling sinks to rest ;
Now, glittering dance around his eddying oar,
Whose every sweep is echoed from the shore ;

Now, far before him, on a liquid bed
Of waveless water, rests her radiant head.
How mild the empire of that virgin queen!
How dark the mountain's shade! how still the scene!
Hush'd by her silver sceptre, zephyrs sleep
On dewy leaves, that overhang the deep,
Nor dare to whisper through the boughs, nor stir
The valley's willow, nor the mountain's fir,
Nor make the pale and breathless aspen quiver,
Nor brush, with ruffling wing, that glassy river.
    Hark!—'t is a convent's bell :—its midnight chime.
For music measures even the march of Time :—
O'er bending trees, that fringe the distant shore,
Gray turrets rise :—the eye can catch no more.
The boatman, listening to the tolling bell,
Suspends his oar ;—a low and solemn swell,
From the deep shade, that round the cloister lies,
Rolls through the air, and on the water dies.
What melting song wakes the cold ear of night?
A funeral dirge, that pale nuns, robed in white,
Chant round a sister's dark and narrow bed,
To charm the parting spirit of the dead.
Triumphant is the spell! with raptured ear,
That uncaged spirit hovering lingers near ;—
Why should she mount? why pant for brighter bliss,
A lovelier scene, a sweeter song, than this?
    On Caledonia's hills, the ruddy morn
Breathes fresh :—the huntsman winds his clamorous horn.
The youthful minstrel from his pallet springs,
Seizes his harp, and tunes its slumbering strings.
Lark-like he mounts o'er gray rocks, thunder-riven,
Lark-like he cleaves the white mist, tempest-driven,
And lark-like carols, as the cliff he climbs,
Whose oaks were vocal with his earliest rhymes.
With airy foot he treads the giddy height ;
His heart all rapture, and his eye all light ;
His voice all melody, his yellow hair
Floating and dancing on the mountain air,
Shaking from its loose folds the liquid pearls,
That gather clustering on his golden curls ;—
And, for a moment, gazes on a scene,
Tinged with deep shade, dim gold, and brightening green ;
Then plays a mournful prelude, while the star
Of morning fades :—but when heaven's gates unbar,
And on the world a tide of glory rushes,

Burns on the hill, and down the valley blushes ;
The mountain bard in livelier numbers sings,
While sunbeams warm and gild the conscious strings,
And his young bosom feels the enchantment strong,
Of light, and joy, and minstrelsy, and song.
   From rising morn, the tuneful stripling roves,
Through smiling valleys and religious groves ;
Hears there, the flickering blackbird strain his throat,
Here, the lone turtle pour her mournful note,
Till night descends, and round the wanderer flings
The dew drops dripping from her dusky wings.
Far from his native vale, and humble shed,
By nature's smiles, and nature's music led,
This child of melody has thoughtless stray'd,
Till darkness wraps him in her deepening shade.
The scene he smiled on, when array'd in light,
Now lowers around him with the frown of night.
   With weary foot the nearest height he climbs,
Crown'd with huge oaks, giants of other times ;
Who feel, but fear not autumn's breath, and cast
Their summer robes upon the roaring blast,
And glorying in their majesty of form,
Toss their old arms, and challenge every storm.
Below him, ocean rolls :—deep in a wood,
Built on a rock, and frowning o'er the flood,
Like the dark Cyclops of Trinacria's isle,
Rises an old and venerable pile :
Gothic its structure ; once a cross it bore,
And pilgrims throng'd to hail it and adore.
Mitres and crosiers awed the trembling friar,
The solemn organ led the chanting quire,
When in those vaults the midnight dirge was sung,
And o'er the dead, a *requiescat* rung.—
Now, all is still :—the midnight anthem hush'd :—
The cross is crumbled, and the crosier crush'd.
And *is* all still ?—No : round those ruin'd altars,
With feeble foot as our musician falters,
Faint, weary, lost, benighted, and alone,
He sinks, all trembling, on the threshold stone.
Here nameless fears the young enthusiast chill :
They 're superstitious, but religious still,
He hears the sullen murmur of the seas,
That tumble round the stormy Orcades,
Or, deep beneath him, heave with boundless roar,
Their sparkling surges to that savage shore ;

And thinks a spirit rolls the weltering waves
Through rifted rocks, and hollow rumbling caves.
   Round the dark windows clasping ivy clings,
Twines round the porch, and in the sea-breeze swings;
Its green leaves rustle :—heavy winds arise :
The low cells echo, and the dark hall sighs.
Now Fancy sees th' ideal canvas stretch'd,
And o'er the lines that Truth has dimly sketch'd,
Dashes with hurried hand the shapes that fly
Hurtled along before her frenzied eye.
The scudding cloud that drives along the coast,
Becomes the drapery of a warrior's ghost,
Who sails serenely in his gloomy pall,
O'er Morven's woods and 'Tura's mouldering wall,
To join the feast of shells, in Odin's misty hall.
Is that some demon's shriek, so loud and shrill,
Whose flapping robes sweep o'er the stormy hill ?
No—'t is the mountain blast, that nightly rages,
Around those walls, gray with the moss of ages.
Is that a lamp sepulchral, whose pale light
Shines in yon vault, before a spectre white ?
No :—'t is a glow-worm, burning greenly there,
Or meteor, swimming slowly on the air.
What mighty organ swells its deepest tone,
And sighing heaves a low, funereal moan,
That murmurs through the cemetery's glooms,
And throws a deadlier horror round its tombs?
Sure, some dread spirit o'er the keys presides!
The same that lifts these darkly thundering tides ;
Or, homeless, shivers o'er an unclosed grave ;
Or shrieking, off at sea, bestrides the white-maned wave.
   Yes!—'t is some Spirit that those skies deforms,
And wraps in billowy clouds that hill of storms.
Yes :—'t is a Spirit in those vaults that dwells,
Illumes that hall, and murmurs in those cells.
Yes :—'t is *some* Spirit on the blast that rides,
And wakes the eternal tumults of the tides.
That Spirit broke the poet's morning dream,
Led him o'er woody hill and babbling stream,
Lured his young foot to every vale that rung,
And charm'd his ear in every bird that sung ;
With various concerts cheer'd his hours of light,
But kept the mightiest in reserve till night ;
Then, throned in darkness, peal'd that wildest air,
Froze his whole soul, and chain'd the listener there.

That mighty spirit once from **Teman** came :
Clouds were his chariot, and his coursers flame.
Bow'd the perpetual hills :—the rivers fled :—
Green ocean trembled to his deepest bed :—
Earth shrunk aghast,—eternal mountains burn'd,
And his red axle thunder'd as it turn'd.
  O ! thou dread Spirit! Being's End and Source !
O ! check thy chariot in its fervid course.
Bend from thy throne of darkness and of fire,
And with one smile immortalize our lyre.
Amid the cloudy lustre of thy throne,
Though wreathy tubes, unheard on earth, are blown,
Swelling one ceaseless song of praise to thee,
Eternal Author of Eternity !
Still *hast* thou stoop'd to hear a shepherd play,
To prompt his measures, and approve his lay.
Hast thou grown old, Thou, who for ever livest!
Hast thou forgotten, Thou, who memory givest !
How, on the day thine ark, with loud acclaim,
From Zion's hill to mount Moriah came,
Beneath the wings of cherubim to rest,
In a rich vail of Tyrian purple drest ;
When harps and cymbals join'd in echoing clang,
When psalteries tinkled, and when trumpets rang,
And white-robed Levites round thine altar sang !
Thou didst descend, and, rolling through the crowd,
Inshrine thine ark and altar in thy shroud,
And fill the temple with thy mantling cloud.
And now, Almighty Father, well we know,
When humble strains from grateful bosoms flow,
Those humble strains grow richer as they rise,
And shed a balmier freshness on the skies.
  What though no cherubim are here display'd,
No gilded walls, no cedar colonnade,
No crimson curtains hang around our quire,
Wrought by the ingenious artisan of Tyre ;
No doors of fir on golden hinges turn ;
No spicy gums in golden censers burn ;
No frankincense, in rising volumes, shrouds
The fretted roof in aromatic clouds ;
No royal minstrel, from his ivory throne,
Gives thee his father's numbers or his own ;—
If humble love, if gratitude inspire,
Our strain shall silence even the temple's quire,
And rival Michael's trump, nor yield to Gabriel's lyre

In what rich harmony, what polish'd lays,
Should man address thy throne, when nature pays
Her wild, her tuneful tribute to the sky!
Yes, Lord, she sings thee, but she knows not why.
The fountain's gush, the long resounding shore,
The zephyr's whisper, and the tempest's roar,
The rustling leaf, in autumn's fading woods,
The wintry storm, the rush of vernal floods,
The summer bower, by cooling breezes fann'd,
The torrent's fall, by dancing rainbows spann'd,
The streamlet, gurgling through its rocky glen,
The long grass, sighing o'er the graves of men,
The bird that crests yon dew-bespangled tree,
Shakes his bright plumes, and trills his descant free.
The scorching bolt, that from thine armory hurl'd,
Burns its red path, and cleaves a shrinking world ;
All these are music to Religion's ear :—
Music, thy hand awakes, for man to hear.
Thy hand invested in their azure robes,
Thy breath made buoyant yonder circling globes,
That bound and blaze along the elastic wires,
That viewless vibrate on celestial lyres,
And in that high and radiant concave tremble,
Beneath whose dome adoring hosts assemble,
To catch the notes, from those bright spheres that flow,
Which mortals dream of, but which angels know.
    Before thy throne, three sister Graces kneel ;
Their holy influence let our bosoms feel!
Faith, that with smiles light up our dying eyes ;
Hope, that directs them to the opening skies ;
And Charity, the loveliest of the three,
That can assimilate a worm to thee.
For her our organ breathes ; to her we pay
The heart-felt homage of an humble lay ;
And while to her symphonious chords we string,
And Silence listens while to her we sing,
While round thine altar swells our evening song,
And vaulted roofs the dying notes prolong,
The strain we pour to her, wilt thou approve,
For Love is Charity, and Thou art Love.

THE PILGRIM FATHERS.

THE pilgrim fathers—where are they?
　The waves that brought them o'er
Still roll in the bay, and throw their spray
　As they break along the shore :
Still roll in the bay, as they roll'd that day,
　When the May-Flower moor'd below,
When the sea around was black with storms,
　And white the shore with snow.

The mists, that wrapp'd the pilgrim's sleep,
　Still brood upon the tide ;
And his rocks yet keep their watch by the deep,
　To stay its waves of pride.
But the snow-white sail, that he gave to the gale,
　When the heavens look'd dark, is gone ;—
As an angel's wing, through an opening cloud,
　Is seen, and then withdrawn.

The pilgrim exile—sainted name !—
　The hill, whose icy brow
Rejoiced, when he came, in the morning's flame,
　In the morning's flame burns now.
And the moon's cold light, as it lay that night
　On the hill-side and the sea,
Still lies where he laid his houseless head ;—
　But the pilgrim—where is he ?

The pilgrim fathers are at rest :
　When Summer 's throned on high,
And the world's warm breast is in verdure dress'd,
　Go, stand on the hill where they lie.
The earliest ray of the golden day
　On that hallowed spot is cast ;
And the evening sun, as he leaves the world,
　Looks kindly on that spot last.

The pilgrim *spirit* has not fled :
　It walks in noon's broad light ;
And it watches the bed of the glorious dead,
　With the holy stars, by night.
It watches the bed of the brave who have bled,

And shall guard this ice-bound shore,
Till the waves of the bay, where the May-Flower lay,
Shall foam and freeze no more.

WARREN'S ADDRESS TO THE AMERICAN SOLDIERS, BEFORE THE BATTLE OF BUNKER HILL.

STAND! the ground's your own, my braves!
Will ye give it up to slaves?
Will ye look for greener graves?
  Hope ye mercy still?
What's the mercy despots feel!
Hear it in that battle peal!
Read it on yon bristling steel!
  Ask it—ye who will.

Fear ye foes who kill for hire!
Will ye to your *homes* retire?
Look behind you! they 're afire!
  And, before you, see
Who have done it!—From the vale
On they come!—and will ye quail?—
Leaden rain and iron hail
  Let their welcome be!

In the God of battles trust!
Die we may—and die we must:—
But, O, where can dust to dust
  Be consign'd so well,
As where heaven its dews shall shed
On the martyr'd patriot's bed,
And the rocks shall raise their head,
  Of his deeds to tell!

ON LAYING THE CORNER STONE OF THE BUNKER HILL MONUMENT.

O, is not this a holy spot?
  'T is the high place of freedom's birth!

VOL. II.   23*

God of our fathers! is it not
　　The holiest spot of all the earth?

Quench'd is thy flame on Horeb's side;
　　The robber roams o'er Sinai now;
And those old men, thy seers, abide
　　No more on Zion's mournful brow.

But on *this* hill thou, Lord, hast dwelt,
　　Since round its head the war-cloud curl'd,
And wrapp'd our fathers, where they knelt
　　In prayer and battle for a world.

Here sleeps their dust: 't is holy ground:
　　And we, the children of the brave,
From the four winds are gather'd round,
　　To lay our offering on their grave.

Free as the winds around us blow,
　　Free as the waves below us spread,
We rear a pile, that long shall throw
　　Its shadow on their sacred bed.

But on their deeds no shade shall fall,
　　While o'er their couch thy sun shall flame
Thine ear was bow'd to hear their call,
　　And thy right hand shall guard their fame.

INDEPENDENCE.

DAY of glory! welcome day!
Freedom's banners greet thy ray;
See! how cheerfully they play
　　With thy morning breeze,
On the rocks where pilgrims kneel'd,
On the heights where squadrons wheel'd,
When a tyrant's thunder peal'd,
　　O'er the trembling seas.

God of armies! did thy "stars
In their courses" smite his cars,
Blast his arm, and wrest his bars

From the heaving tide?
On our standard, lo! they burn,
And, when days like this return,
Sparkle o'er the soldier's urn,
    Who for freedom died.

God of peace!—whose spirit fills
All the echoes of our hills,
All the murmurs of our rills,
    Now the storm is o'er;—
O, let freemen be our sons;
And let future Washingtons
Rise, to lead their valiant ones,
    Till there's war no more.

By the patriot's hallow'd rest,
By the warrior's gory breast,
Never let our graves be press'd
    By a despot's throne:
By the pilgrim's toil and cares,
By their battles and their prayers,
By their ashes,—let our heirs
    Bow to thee alone.

FOR A LADY'S ALBUM.

Grace is deceitful, and beauty vain.—SOLOMON.

OH, say not, wisest of all the kings
    That have risen on Israel's throne to reign!
Say not, as one of your wisest things,
    That grace is false, and beauty vain.

Your *harem* beauties resign! resign
    Their lascivious dance, their voluptuous song!
To your *garden* come forth, among things divine,
    And own you do grace and beauty wrong.

Is beauty vain because it will fade?
    Then are earth's green robe and heaven's light vain;
For this shall be lost in evening's shade,
    And that in winter's sleety rain.

But earth's green mantle, prank'd with flowers,
  Is the couch where life with joy reposes;
And heaven gives down, with its light and showers,
  To regale them, fruits; to deck them, roses.

And while opening flowers in such beauty spread,
  And ripening fruits so gracefully swing,
Say not, O king, as you just now said,
  That beauty or grace is a worthless thing.

This willow's limbs, as they bend in the breeze,
  The dimpled face of the pool to kiss;
Who, that has eyes and a heart, but sees
  That there is beauty and grace in this!

And do not these boughs all whisper of Him,
  Whose smile is the light that in green arrays them;
Who sitteth, in peace, on the wave they skim,
  And whose breath is the gentle wind that sways them?

And are not the beauty and grace of youth,
  Like those of this willow, the work of love?
Do they not come, like the voice of truth,
  That is heard all around us here from above?

Then say not, wisest of all the kings
  That have risen on Israel's throne to reign!
Say not, as one of your wisest things,
  That grace is false, and beauty vain.

HENRY PICKERING,

Is a resident of Salem, Massachusetts, and son of the Hon.
Timothy Pickering. We have met with the name of this
gentleman but recently. His poetry is perhaps too much of
the old school, to suit the taste of the day. He is, however,
a poet, and his works will doubtless survive much that is
read and admired more, at the present moment.

One of the characteristics of a poet, we apprehend to be, an imagination which perceives the beauties of nature, but never perceives them alone ; as the moon has its halo, and the rainbow its imitation, so to him has every leaf, and flower, and wood, and waterfall, some associated counterpart. Such an imagination is a mirror, which catches the forms of nature, and reflects their moral resemblances as the lake gives to the eye a duplicate of the landscape, more beautiful than that which blooms along its border.

We think the specimens which follow, will show their author to be possessed of this master talent of a poet in a high degree of perfection. If the reader is disposed to be critical, he may perhaps observe an occasional want of music in the versification. The writer, also, is too partial to blank verse; a vehicle not generally suited to other than great subjects.—If Mr Pickering were to write under any very strong sense of responsibility to public opinion, he would easily remove the defects we have noticed.

TO A BEAUTIFUL LAKE.

RAPT in a vision of the barbarous past,
I saw upon thy marge a wild-eyed race,
    And, startled, heard the yell
    That echoed round thy shores!

And now, enchanted with the picture fair,
Which Fancy holds to view, I fain would blend
    The murmur of thy waves,
    And warblings of my lute.

Translucent flood! within thy ever pure
And stainless breast, the heavens with wonder view
    As beautiful a heaven,
    As tranquil and serene:

The while, a new creation spreads around—
Hills piled on hills, seem laughing in thy wave,
    And groves, inverted, nod
    To like majestic groves.

And what if o'er thy brink no frowning cliffs
Impend—no cloud-tipt mountains, as with wall
    Insuperable, fence
    Thee from the northern blast,—

Yet dost thou scornful mock its utmost force,
And ruffian winter's rudest breath defy ;
    Fiercely he sweeps along,
    But may not chain thy wave.*

And still exulting with the dancing spring,
Thou seest new beauties deck thy soft domain ;
    And when from summer's gaze
    The earth dejected shrinks,

Thou spread'st thy dazzling bosom to the sun :
While pleased, anon, with Autumn's rainbow hues
    And mournful shell, thou bidd'st
    Thy waves wild music make.

In that glad moment, when the star of morn
Leads up the effulgent day, and liquid pearls
    Are on the flowers, and thou
    In snowy mist art wrapp'd,—

How have I stood, delighted, to behold
The sun, like a young deity look forth,
    And, with a glance, thy face
    At once again unveil !

And when the golden curtains of the west
Are gathering round his couch, and his last ray
    Descending, seems to melt
    In thy unruffled flood,—

How have I rivetted my eye on thee,
And wish'd that on my breast a heavenly gleam

*Seneca Lake is not known to freeze.

Might fall, and thus within
My soul as softly sink!

Yet if there be a more propitious hour,
'T is when the moon from out the silvery east
    In chasten'd splendor beams,—
    And sheds o'er thee, and o'er

The tranquil earth, her mild and holy light:
A shadowy grandeur then invests the scene,
    While through the willing mind
    A pleasing sadness steals.

O fond remembrance!—but what boots it now
To sing of absent charms? Thou calmly sleep'st
    Beneath thy circling hills,
    While I am tempest-tost!

Yet brighter eyes, and innocent as bright,
Shall long upon thy varied beauties gaze,
    And young glad beings too
    Delight in thee to lave:

And science, haply, on thy banks shall rear
Her proudest domes; and. emulous of fame,
    Bards, yet unborn, shall chant
    In lofty verse thy praise.

DAPHNE.

> " Elle etoit de ce monde ou les plus belles choses
>   Ont le pire destin ;
> Et, rose, elle a vecu ce que vivent les roses,
>   L'espace d'un matin."
>
> *Malherbe.*

THE winds are hush'd ; but the chill air of night
Pervades my shivering frame. The crisped leaves
Which lately waved in undulations soft,
To every genial breeze, and look'd so green,—
But now were wafted from the neighboring wood,
And cumber all my solitary paths.
Softly I tread the mazy labyrinth, lest

The rustling noise should interrupt the deep
And fearful stillness round.   'T is thus amid
The forest wilds, when Autumn crowns, as now,
The plenteous year, and the gay antler'd herds
Look sleek, the unwearied hunter threads his way,
And with a step, cautious as Guilt, pursues
The timid chase.   But what shall I alarm
In these deserted haunts, where none of choice
Repair, save those whom wretchedness has taught,
After long toil, to seek for refuge *here?*
The mole has burrow'd deep, and heeds me not;
The bat has ta'en his headlong flight in search
Of gentler skies, or nestles in some lone
And cover'd nook; while at my feet sleep those,
Whom not the crash of worlds shall wake again!
Hah! is it so? and wilt not thou awake,
My dear, lamented Daphne?   Shall that form,
That form so heavenly fair, ne'er bloom again?
Thy dust, alas! is not commingled here
With kindred dust; but doth it aught avail?
Lo! where repose the long forgotten race,
The lengthen'd line of thy progenitors:
Whilst thou, o'ercanopied by balmier heavens,
Beneath the tamarind and the orange tree
Fit resting place hast found!   No winter there
Shivers the glories of the circling year,
Nor tarnishes the lustre of the groves:
Thy favorite myrtle there can never die—
There every gale wafts perfumes o'er thy grave!
Ah why, 'mid scenes thus fair, should man decay?
With lavish bounty nature there adorns
The wild, and bids the flowers perpetual bloom,
And yet to him a longer date denies,—
Nay, warns him thence before his custom'd time.
And such, my Daphne, was thy hapless lot!
And worse—for thou wast fated twice to die—
And twice in the full vernal bloom of youth—
The cup at *parting* bitterer than Death's!
How wast thou torn, all lovely as thou wast,
And beauteous too as Maia's self when flush'd
By genial beams of the young sun, from arms
Unwilling to be loosed from thine!   How flow'd
Thy tears, when every tenderer tie which bound
Thee here, was sunder'd!   And how throbb'd thy heart
When, in a last embrace, 't was press'd to mine!

But years since that sad parting have gone by,
And years have flown since thou wast rapt to heaven!
Yet how can I forget or thou forgive?
True thou didst oft invite me to thy home,
Didst beckon me amid thy fragrant groves
To taste of golden fruits, and blissful breathe
Thy incensed air,—and, dearer far, enjoy
Thy converse sweet:—but, such my wayward mood,
I spurn'd the call (though softer not than thine
An angel's voice) or thought, as worldlings do,
At fitting hour to come. Thus wisdom's fool'd,
And thus was I infatuated too.
My Daphne! art thou then for ever fled?
O once again appear as thou wast wont!
Thou smilest in my dreams; and when I wake,
I pay thee with my late repentant tears:
Tears are thy due—ah, doubly due from one
On whom thy infant eyes beam'd only love—
Whom thou remember'dst to thy latest breath!

FLOWERS.

" La vue d'une fleur caresse mon imagination et flatte mes sens a un point inexprimable : elle reveille avec volupte le sentiment de mon existence."

Mad. Roland.

THE impatient morn,
With gladness on his wings, calls forth " Arise!
To trace the hills, the vales, where thousand dyes
The ground adorn,
While the dew sparkles yet within the violet's eyes:"

And when the day
In golden slumber sinks, with accent sweet
Mild evening comes to lure the willing feet
With her to stray,
Where'er the bashful flowers the observant eye may greet.

Near the moist brink
Of music-loving streams they ever keep,
And often in the lucid fountains peep;

Oft, laughing, drink
Of the mad torrent's spray, perch'd near the thundering steep

And everywhere
Along the plashy marge, and shallow bed
Of the still waters, they innumerous spread;
Rock'd gently there
The beautiful Nymphæa* pillows its bright head.

Within the dell,
Within the rocky clefts they love to hide;
And hang adventurous on the steep hill-side;
Or rugged fell,
Where the young eagle waves his wings in youthful pride.

In the green sea
Of forest leaves, where nature wanton plays,
They modest bloom: though through the verdant maze
The tulip-tree
Its golden chalice oft triumphantly displays:

And, of pure white,
Embedded 'mid its glossy leaves on high,
There the superb Magnolia lures the eye;
While, waving light,
The locust's myriad tassels scent the ambient sky.

But O, ye bowers,—
Ye valleys where the spring perpetual reigns,
And flowers unnumber'd o'er the purple plains
Exuberant showers,—
How fancy revels in your lovelier domains!

All love the light;
And yet what numbers spring within the shade,
And blossom where no foot may e'er invade;
Till comes a blight,—
Comes unaware,—and then incontinent they fade!

And thus they bloom,
And thus their lives ambrosial breathe away;
Thus flourish too the lovely and the gay:

*The white-pond lily.

And the same doom
Youth, beauty, flower, alike consigns to swift decay.

———

I THOUGHT IT SLEPT.

[From Recollections of Childhood.]

I saw the infant cherub—soft it lay,
As it was wont, within its cradle, now
Deck'd with sweet smelling flowers.   A sight so strange
Fill'd my young breast with wonder, and I gazed
Upon the babe the more.   I thought it slept—
And yet its little bosom did not move!
I bent me down to look into its eyes,
But they were closed : then, softly clasp'd its hand,
But mine it would not clasp.   What should I do ?
" Wake, brother, wake ! " I then impatient cried,
" Open thine eyes, and look on me again ! "
He would not hear my voice.   All pale beside
My weeping mother sat, " and gazed and look'd
Unutterable things."   Will he not wake ?
I eager ask'd : She answer'd but with tears.
Her eyes on me, at length, with piteous look
Were cast—now on the babe once more were fix'd—
And now on me : then with convulsive sigh
And throbbing heart, she clasp'd me in her arms,
And in a tone of anguish faintly said—
" My dearest boy ! thy brother does not sleep ;
Alas ! he 's dead ; he never will awake."
He 's dead ! I knew not what it meant, but more
To know I sought not.   For the words so sad,
"He never will awake"—sunk in my soul :
I felt a pang unknown before, and tears
That angels might have shed, my heart dissolved.*

*From this little tale of unaffected childish sorrow, Mr Agate (an estimable
young artist of New York) has produced a very touching picture.   It was exhibited
during the last season, at the National Academy in that city.

———

TO THE FRINGILLA MELODIA.*

Joy fills the vale,
With joy ecstatic quivers every wing,
As floats thy note upon the genial gale,
          Sweet bird of spring!

The violet
Awakens at thy song, and peers from out
Its fragrant nook, as if the season yet
          Remain'd in doubt—

While from the rock
The columbine its crimson bell suspends,
That careless vibrates, as its slender stalk
          The zephyr bends.

Say! when the blast
Of winter swept our whiten'd plains,—what clime,
What sunnier realm thou charm'dst,—and how was past
          Thy joyous time?

Did the green isles
Detain thee long? or, 'mid the palmy groves
Of the bright south, where liberty now smiles,
          Did'st sing thy loves?

O, well I know
Why thou art here thus soon, and why the bowers
So near the sun have lesser charms than now
          Our land of flowers:

Thou art return'd
On a glad errand,—to rebuild thy nest,
And fan anew the gentle fire that burn'd
          Within thy breast.

And thy wild strain,
Pour'd on the gale, is love's transporting voice—
That, calling on the plumy choir again,
          Bids them rejoice:

*The song-sparrow.

Nor calls alone
T' enjoy, but bids improve the fleeting hour—
Bids all that ever heard love's witching tone,
Or felt his power.

The poet too
It soft invokes to touch the trembling wire;
Yet ah, how few its sounds shall list, how few
His song admire!

But thy sweet lay,
Thou darling of the spring! no ear disdains;
Thy sage instructress, nature, says "Be gay!"
And prompts thy strains.

O, if I knew
Like thee to sing, like thee the heart to fire,—
Youth should enchanted throng, and beauty sue
To hear my lyre.

Oft as the year
In gloom is wrapp'd, thy exile I shall mourn—
Oft as the spring returns, shall hail sincere
Thy glad return.

THE WATERFALL.

Impetuous Torrent! Nature piled
Thy rocks amid the sylvan wild;
With flower and shrub their crags she graced,
And through them thy dark pathway traced:
Then bade thee with resistless force
Pursue thy mad, tumultuous course,
Plunging from slippery steep to steep
Till lost in the profounder deep,—
While 'mid the rush of waters round,
Eternal thunders shake the ground!

Impetuous Torrent! Time, perhaps,
For centuries hath mark'd thy lapse;

Yet has that ruthless spoiler fear'd
To mar the work which nature rear'd.
Still in rude grandeur tower thy rocks,
Still all restraint thy current mocks,
In verdant pride still wave thy trees,
Sway'd ever by the varying breeze;
And the dark cliffs, where wild flowers cling,
And where the bee flies murmuring,
In matchless beauty robed still,
Aye sets at nought the painter's skill.
And here upon thy margent green,
The Indian hunter once was seen,
Gazing on thee in thoughtful mood,
Or bounding swift, as he pursued
Panther or deer across the glade,
Nor reck'd the coil thy waters made.
Child of the Forest! thou art fled,
Thy joys, thy pastimes, all are sped;
The antler'd herd are far away,
The panther is no more thy prey,
Nor more the timorous Echo wakes,
Startled as when thy war-whoop breaks:
And yet in Fancy's view still near,
Thou brightly art depicted here.
The rock that spurns the rush of waves,
Is thy stern soul, that danger braves;
Amid the flood's incessant roar
Thy dreaded voice I hear once more;
And as I mark its maddening strife,
I think o'er all thy stormy life:
While through the spray that falls in showers
Upon the trees, the shrubs, the flowers,
That wild, bright heaven, so dear to thee,
In yon ethereal brede I see.

Impetuous Torrent! other times
And other men from distant climes,
Have now arrived; and thou despoil'd
Of all thy charms, thy proud waves soil'd
By busy art, shalt be a theme
Fit only for a poet's dream.
Yet should the forest shade no more
The banks o'er which it waved before,
And all thy lovelier features too
Vanish for ages from the view,—

Still through the mournful waste shalt thou
Pursue thy raptnrous course as now:
And when the race that here bear sway
Are in oblivion swept away,
Thou shalt resume thy pristine reign—
And, deck'd in beauty, once again,
Shalt the brown hunter's heart rejoice,
And wake the forest with thy voice.

DESCRIPTIVE SONNETS.

SUNLIGHT ON THE WATER.

" THERE is nothing more beautiful than water. It has always the same pure
flow, and the same low music, and is always ready to bear away your thoughts
upon its bosom, like the Hindoo's barque of flowers, to an imaginative heaven."
Unwritten Poetry.

THERE is a balmy freshness in the air;
And as the sunbeams on its surface gleam
It seems as if upon the rippled stream
A shower of diamonds fell: or as if there,
Fantastic knit in frolic mood, some fair
Invisible Spirits in the instant wound
On airy tiptoe through the measured round,
And left their dazzling foot-prints everywhere.
'T is a glad sight! and many a time I 've stood
Upon the fringed banks the streamlets lave,
Or perch'd me where some rock o'erhangs the flood,
To see the light thus kiss each little wave:
Ay! gaze even yet almost with the same joy
As when I was a young gay-hearted boy.

AUTUMNAL PICTURE: A SKETCH.

SEE how the forest waves! The gnarled oak
Even bends—and as the unruly wind sweeps through
Its sturdy branches, showers of leaves bestrew
The ground, or diverse fly ; the crow, just broke
From out the warring wood, with ominous croak

Wheels heavily through air ; the glorious hue
Of the bright mantle summer lately threw
O'er earth, is gone ; and the sere leaves now choke
The turbid fountains and complaining brooks ;
The o'ershadowing pines, alone, through which I rove,
Their verdure keep, although it darker looks :
And hark ! as it comes sighing through the grove,
The exhausted gale a Spirit there awakes,
That wild and melancholy music wakes.

THE RAINBOW AFTER A SUMMER TEMPEST.

Symbol of peace ! lo, there the ethereal bow !
And see, on flagging wing, the storm retreats
Far 'mid the depths of space ; and with him fleets
His lurid train—the while in beauty glow
Vale, hill and sky once more.   How lustrous now
Earth's verdant mantle ! and the woods how bright !
Where grass, leaf, flower, are sparkling in the light—
Prompt ever with the slightest breeze to throw
The rain drops to the ground.   Within the grove
Music awakes ; and from each little throat,
Silent so long, bursts the wild note of love ;
The hurried babblings of the rill denote
Its infant joy ; and rushing swift along,
The torrent gives to air, its hoarse and louder song.

EVENING SUNLIGHT.

How beautifully soft it seems to sleep
Upon the lap of the unbreathing vale,
And where, unruffled by the gentlest gale,
The lake its bosom spreads, and in its deep
Clear wave, another world appears to keep,
To steal the heart from this ! for through the veil
Transparent we may see, tree, rock, hill, dale,
And sapphire sky, and golden mountain steep,
That real seem, though fairer than our own :—
Still, picture faint of that pure region drawn

By prophet's pen, but not to mortal shown,
Where flow rivers of bliss—and vale, and lawn
Are strewn with flowers immortal—where, alone,
Night never comes, and day is without dawn.

HENRY C. KNIGHT,

Is a native, we believe, of Rowley in Massachusetts. He
wrote the Cypriad and other poems, published in 1809, and a
further collection in two volumes, published in 1821.

THE COUNTRY OVEN.

I sing the oven—glowing, fruitful theme.
Happy for me, that mad Achilles found,
And weak Ulysses erst, a servile bard,
That deign'd their puny feats, else lost, to sing.
And happy that Æneas, feeble man!
Fell into hands of less emprise than mine;
Too mean the subject for a bard so high.
Not Dante, Ariosto, Tasso, dared
Sport their gross minds in such grand element.
Nor he, dame nature's master-journeyman,
Who nimbly wrought a comic tragedy,
As poet woos a muse, one Shakspeare called!
Nor Milton, who embattled Devils sung;
Nor bold Sir Blackmore, who an Epic built,
Quick as can mason rear a chimney stack;
Nor later these, Klopstock and Wieland famed,
Who sung, this King of Elves, that King of kings;
Dared the prolific Oven blaze in song.
Expect not now of Furnaces to hear,
Where Æolus dilates the liquid glass;
Nor where the Hollanders, in nests of tow,
With mimic nature, incubate their eggs;
For the Domestic Oven claims my powers.
Come then, from kilns of flame, and tropic suns,
Each salamander Muse, and warm my brain.

Need I describe?—Who hath a kitchen seen
And not an arched concavity call'd Oven?
Grand farinaceous nourisher of life!
See hungry gape its broad mouth for its food,
And hear the faggots crackling in its jaws,
Its palate glowing red with burning breath.
Do not approach too near; the ingulphing draught
Will drink your respiration ere you list.
    Glance now the fire-jambs round, and there observe
Utensils formed for culinary use.
Shovel and tongs, like ancient man and wife,
He, with his arms akimbo, she in hoops,
There, dangling sausages in chains hang down;
As Sciences and Arts, distinct, allied;
Or, as in Union bound our sister States.
Here, flayed eels, strung pendant by the waist;
So swing aloof victims in heathen climes;
O Algier hearts! to mock at writhing pain.
And, high in smoke-wreaths, ponderous ham to cure;
So may each traitor to his country hang!
And, thick on nails, the housewife's herbs to dry;
Coltsfoot for pipe, and spearmint for a tea.
Upon the hearth, the shrill-lunged cricket chirps
Her serenade, not waiting to be press'd.
And Sue, poking the cinders, smiles to point,
As fond associations cross the mind,
A gallant, ring, or ticket, fashion'd there.
And purring puss, her pied-coat licked sleek,
Sits mousing for the crumbs, beside black Jack.
He, curious drone, with eyes and teeth of white,
And natural curl, who twenty falls hath seen,
And cannot yet count four!—nor ever can,
Though tasked to learn, until his nose be sharp.
'T is marvel, if he thinks, but when he speaks;
Else, to himself, why mutter loud, and strange,
And scold, and laugh, as half a score were by?
In shape and parts, a seed of Caliban!
He now is roasting earth-nuts by the coals,
And hissing clams, like martyrs mocking pain;
And sizzing apples, air-lanced with a pin;
While in the embers hops the parching corn,
Crack! crack! disploding with the heat, like bombs.
Craunching, he squats, and grins, and gulps his mug,
And shows his pompion-shell, with eyes and mouth,

And candle fitted, for the tail of kite,
To scare the lasses in their evening walk—
For, next day, and Thanksgiving-Eve will come.
   Now turn we to the teeming Oven; while,
A skilful midwife, comes the aged dame;
Her apron clean, and nice white cap of lawn:
With long lean arm, she lifts the griding slice,
And inward slides it, drawing slowly out.
In semi-globes, and frustums of the cone,
Tann'd brown with heat, come, smoking, broad high
    loaves;
And drop-cakes, ranged like cocks round stack of hay:
Circles and segments, pies and turn-overs,
For children's children, who stand teasing round,
Scorching their mouths, and dance like juggler's apes,
Wishing the pie more cool, or they less keen.
Next, brown and wrinkled, like the good dame's brow,
Come russet-coated sweetings, pulp for milk;
A luscious dish—would one were brought me now!
And *kisses*, made by Sue for suitor's pun.
And when the morrow greets each smiling face,
And from the church, where grateful hearts have pour'd,
Led by the Man of God, their thanks and prayers,
To Him, who fills their granaries with good,
They hurry home, snuffing the spicy steams;
The pious matron, with full heart draws forth
The spare-rib crisp—more savory from the spit!
Tall pots of peas and beans—vile, flatulent;
And puddings, smoking to the rafter'd walls;
And sweet-cup custards, part of the dessert.
These all, concreted some, some subtilized,
And by the generative heat matured,
A goodly birth, the welcome time brings forth.
   Illustrious Oven! warmest, heartiest friend!
Destroy but thee, and where were festive smiles?
We, cannibals, might terrify and seethe;
Or dry blood-reeking flesh in the cold sun;
Or, like the Arab, on his racing horse,
Beneath the saddle swelter it for food.
   And yet, ere thou give us, we must give thee.
Thus many an Oven barren is for life.
O poverty! how oft thy wishful eye
Rests on thine Oven, hungry as thyself!
Would I might load each Oven of the poor,
With what each palate craves—a fruitless wish!

Yet seldom hear we Industry complain ;
And no one should complain, who hath two eyes,
Two hands, and mind and body, sound and free.
And such, their powers to worthy ends applied,
Be pleased, indulgent Patroness, to feed.

F. S. KEY,

OF Baltimore, is the author of the short lyrical piece entitled The Star-Spangled Banner, which has enjoyed a high
popularity. Of the occasion which led to the composition of
these lines, the following account is given.—A gentleman had
left Baltimore, with a flag of truce, for the purpose of getting
released from the British fleet, a friend of his who had been
captured at Marlboro'. He went as far as the mouth of the
Patuxent, and was not permitted to return, lest the intended
attack on Baltimore should be disclosed. He was, therefore,
brought up the Bay to the mouth of the Patapsco, where the
flag vessel was kept under the guns of a frigate, and he was
compelled to witness the bombardment of Fort M'Henry, which
the admiral had boasted that he would carry in a few hours.
He watched the flag at the Fort, through the whole day, with
an anxiety that can be more easily conceived than described,
until the night prevented him from seeing it. In the night,
he watched the bomb shells, and at early dawn, his eye was
again greeted by the proudly waving flag of his country.

STAR SPANGLED BANNER.

O! say, can you see, by the dawn's early light,
  What so proudly we hail'd at the twilight's last gleaming,
Whose broad stripes, and bright stars, through the perilous
    fight,
  O'er the ramparts we watch'd were so gallantly streaming?

And the rockets' red glare, the bombs bursting in air,
Gave proof through the night that our flag was still there;
  O! say, does that Star-spangled Banner yet wave,
  O'er the land of the free, and the home of the brave?

On the shore dimly seen through the mists of the deep,
  Where the foe's haughty host in dread silence reposes,
What is that which the breeze, o'er the towering steep,
  As it fitfully blows, half conceals, half discloses?
Now it catches the gleam of the morning's first beam;
In full glory reflected, now shines on the stream.
  'T is the Star-spangled Banner, O! long may it wave
  O'er the land of the free, and the home of the brave.

And where is that band who so vauntingly swore
  That the havoc of war, and the battle's confusion,
A home and a country, should leave us no more!
  Their blood has wash'd out their foul footsteps' pollution.
No refuge could save the hireling and slave,
From the terror of flight, or the gloom of the grave,
  And the Star-spangled Banner in triumph doth wave,
  O'er the land of the free, and the home of the brave.

O! thus be it ever when freemen shall stand,
  Between their loved home, and the war's desolation,
Blest with vict'ry and peace, may the Heaven-rescued land
  Praise the Power that hath made and preserved us a nation.
Then conquer we must, when our cause it is just,
And this be our motto—" *In God is our trust* ; "
  And the Star-spangled Banner in triumph shall wave
  O'er the land of the free, and the home of the brave.

KATHARINE A. WARE.

MRS WARE is the daughter of the late Dr Joseph W. Rhodes of Rhode Island. She was born at Quincy, Massachusetts. Her first attempts at verse attracted the notice of her kinsman Robert Treat Paine, and the praises which she received from him incited her to follow her inclination for poetry. The earliest production of her's, that attracted public notice, was a poem entitled "Columbia's Bard," written at the age of fifteen, and published on the death of Mr Paine. These lines were included in the volume of his works which appeared after his death. From this period, to the time of her marriage with Mr Charles A. Ware, of the United States Navy, we hear little of her poetry, except some trifling contributions to the corners of a newspaper. Shortly after this event, she was called upon by a committee for a national ode for the anniversary of the seventeenth of June. The favorable reception which this ode received, caused her to be constantly solicited for others, on public occasions, and in several instances she complied. Bostonians well remember the circumstance of a little girl of five years old, who presented a wreath and a copy of verses to Lafayette, at his arrival on Boston Common; this was Mrs Ware's eldest child.

During a year's residence in New York, Mrs Ware became favorably known as a writer for the American Atheneum, and received many liberal tokens of approbation from the editor of that paper, and others. She was complimented also with a gold chain, from the manager of the Chatham Theatre, for an ode which was recited in honor of Governor Clinton at the canal celebration.

In January, 1828, she commenced a periodical publication in Boston called The Bower of Taste. In this, and other similar works, her verses have been given to the public.

THERE IS A VOICE.

THERE is a voice in the western breeze,
  As it floats o'er spring's young roses !
Or sighs among the blossoming trees,
  Where the spirit of love reposes :
It tells of the joys of the pure and young,
Ere they wander life's wildering paths among.

There is a voice in the summer gale,
  Which breathes amid regions of bloom !
Or murmurs soft, through the dewy vale,
  In moonlight's tender gloom :
It tells of hope, unblighted yet—
And of hours, that the soul can *ne'er forget !*

There is a voice in the autumn blast,
  That wafts the falling leaf,
When the glowing scene is fading fast—
  For the hour of bloom is brief :
It tells of *Life*—its sure decay—
And of earthly splendors, that pass away !

There is a voice in the wintry storm,
  For the *blasting spirit* is there—
Breathing o'er every vernal charm,
  O'er all that was bright and fair ;
It tells of death, as it moans around,
And the lonely hall returns the sound.

And there 's a voice—a small, still voice,
  That comes, when the *storm is past*—
It bids the sufferer's heart rejoice !
  In the haven of peace at last ;
It tells of joys, beyond the grave,
And of Him who died a world to save !

GREECE.

WHERE Art's wide realm in mouldering ruin sleeps,
And Science o'er departed glory weeps—
Where wreathing ivy shrouds in dark array,
The desolating progress of decay—

Where time is ranging with remorseless tread,
Amid the trophies of the mighty dead,
There, Grecia's genius hovers o'er the scene
Of ruin'd grandeur—glories that *have been*—
Views the vast wreck of power with kindling eye,
And kneels beside the tomb of Poesy.
Where fame's proud relics strew her classic ground,
In gloomy majesty she glides around,
Pausing, with rapt devotion, to survey
The prostrate splendors of her early day.
Those ancient courts, where erst with wisdom fraught,
Her senate listen'd, and her sages taught;
Where that bold patriot, firm in virtue's cause,
The immortal Solon, thunder'd forth his laws!
The temple raised to Theseus' mighty name—
The storied arch of Hadrian's deathless fame!
Raises her eye to where, with beam divine,
Apollo blush'd upon the Delphic shrine—
As bow'd that chief, to learn a nation's fate,
Who gave his royal life, to save the state.
With pride, she seeks Dodona's sacred grove,
Where towers the temple of imperial Jove,
Frowning, in ruin'd majesty sublime,
The proudest wreck that braves the blast of time!
Shows the broad Stadium, where the gymnic art,
Nerved the young arm, and energized the heart—
Gave a bold race of warriors to her field,
Whose godlike courage was their only shield!
Surveys that grot, where still her olives twine
In wild luxuriance o'er its fallen shrine—
Where Dian's vestal daughters came to lave
Their snowy bosoms in Ionia's wave.
All dark and tuneless are those laurel shades,
Which once enshrined Castalia's classic maids—
For barbarous hands have raised their funeral pyre
And hush'd the breathings of their seraph lyre—
Save when the light of heaven around it plays,
And wakes the hallow'd chant of other days!
Oh! then, 'mid storied mounds, and mouldering urns,
Once more, the flame of inspiration burns!
Here, pilgrim Genius comes to muse around,
To wake one strain o'er consecrated ground!
From prostrate fanes, and altars of decay,
He learns the glory of their former day—
And, in the tender blush of twilight gloom,

He writes the story of some ruin'd tomb ;
From dark oblivion snatches many a gem,
To glisten in his own fair diadem.
Immortal Byron ! thou, whose courage plann'd
The rescue of that subjugated land—
Oh ! hadst thou lived to rear thy giant glaive,
Thou 'dst bid the Christian cross triumphant wave !
Mark'd the pale crescent wave 'mid seas of blood,
And stamp'd proud Grecia's freedom in the flood.
But, Oh ! 't was fate's decree thou should'st expire,
Swan-like, amid the breathings of thy lyre—
Even in the sacred light of thine own song—
As sinks the glorious sun amid the throng
Of bright robed clouds, the pageantry of Heaven—
Thy last retiring beam to earth was given.
Where Scio's isle blushes with Christian gore,
And recreant fiends still yell around her shore ;
Where Missolonghi's bloody plain extends,
'Mid war's red blots, Athena's Queen descends.
Mark, where she comes—in all the pomp of wo—
Darkling around her sable vestments flow—
With throbbing bosom in the tempest bare—
Wild, on the breeze, floats her unwreathed hair,
Though learning's classic diadem is there.
Where fate's dark clouds the face of heaven deform—
With steadfast brow—she meets the bursting storm,
Turns to Olympus with imploring eye,
And claims the ægis of her native sky.
Hark ! round its base th' eternal thunders roll,
And Jove's own lightnings flash from pole to pole—
His voice is *there !* he bids creation save
Minerva's "first born," from a barbarous wave.

———

THE PARTING.

SHE loved him e'en in childhood, with that pure
Devotion, which the bosom feels secure
In youthful innocence—when first the heart
Elects its idol, sacred and apart
From other beings :—oh ! there is a truth,
A beam, that wakes not when the glow of youth
Is past,—'t is like the ray that morning throws,
Upon the bosom of the blushing rose.

She was a creature—such as painters love
To draw,—like her who to imperial Jove
The nectar'd goblet bore ; just such an eye,
And such a cheek was hers—its roseate dye
Seem'd borrow'd from the morning—her bright hair
Like braided gold, wreath'd round a brow as fair
As Parian marble—all those curving lines
That mark perfection—and which taste defines
As beautiful, gave to her youthful form
A loveliness, a grace, so thrilling warm
That every motion seem'd to speak a soul
Whose inborn radiance illumed the whole.
He too, was in life's joyous spring ; the glow
Of sunny health was on his cheek—his brow
Was bold and fearless,—his keen eagle eye
Was looking forth to scenes of victory ;
For *War* had plumed his crest—and nerved his arm—
And there was breathing round him, all the charm
Of high devotion to his country's weal ;—
While the bright panoply of gold, and steel,
That mail'd his breast—and flash'd upon his brow—
Gave proud assurance of the soldier's vow.

　　　*　　　　　*　　　　　*　　　　　*

He dream'd not that he loved her—for in truth
He knew the child e'en from her earliest youth.
Oft had he look'd upon the young Eloise
As a sweet being whom he wish'd to please—
To gather roses for, and braid her hair,
To guard her with a brother's tender care—
But never dream'd of love, for haply he
Had fix'd his hopes on higher destiny.
With pride he heard his summon to the field :
Yet, had his heart its secret thoughts reveal'd,
Some shades of sadness had been lingering there,
On leaving home, and friends, and scenes so fair
He came to bid adieu—'t was a mild night
Of softest moonshine—and its dewy light
Was on the shrubs, and flowers that bloom'd around—
And there was music in the soothing sound
Of the bright rill that murmur'd through the glade,
And sparkled 'neath the willow's pensile shade,
The summer breeze was sighing through its boughs
In whispers, soft as youthful lovers' vows.
She was reclining in the latticed bower—
Musing, as 't were upon the stilly hour.

"Dear Eloise!" he said—(the sudden flush
Of new-born feeling call'd a crimson blush
On her young cheek, that made the life-blood start
In thrilling eddies round his conscious heart,)
"Dear Eloise—I come to bid adieu—
To these fair scenes, to happiness, and you.
Hast thou no wish—no blessing, for thy friend?
Who, far from thee, and all he loves, shall wend
His pilgrimage, through wilderness and toil,
Uncheer'd by friendship's voice—or Beauty's smile.
He laid his hand upon her seraph head,
Press'd a warm kiss upon her brow, and said—
"May heaven preserve thee, pure, as angels are—
The world is wicked—lovely one—beware!
Thou art an orphan—would that title might
Protect thy innocence from the fell blight
Of those who hover in fair virtue's way,
To tempt the steps of guileless youth astray.
Would I could guard thee—but my path of life
Lies through the ranks of war, 'mid battle's strife—
There duty calls me—should I ne'er return,
Say—wouldst thou sorrow o'er thy soldier's urn?
Yet if some future day I dare to claim
The dear bought honors of a hero's name—
May Eloisa's fond remembrance prove
Her youthful friendship ripen'd into love?"
Pure as a vestal's hymn that breathes to heaven!
That night, their vows of mutual faith were given.

* * * *

Years have roll'd on—but yet no warrior came
With laurell'd brow, his youthful bride to claim—
Years have roll'd on—the wintry frosts have shed
Their sparkling crystals o'er his lowly bed.
Where proud St Lawrence wreathes his crested wave,
That youthful hero found an early grave.
But though unwept by fond affection's tear—
A soldier's honors graced his funeral bier.
Years have roll'd on since Nature's loveliest child,
Within her garden bower in beauty smiled—
Years have roll'd on, and spring with annual bloom
Still twines her wreath o'er Eloisa's tomb,
While kindred spirits hymn her requiem there,
And freight with sweetest sounds the balmy air.

SARAH J. HALE.

MRS HALE was born at Newport, New Hampshire, October 24th, 1790. Her husband, David Hale, Esq. died in 1822. Her first work was published in 1823. It was a volume of poems selected mostly from articles written for amusement in years previous. The necessities of a fatherless family made her an author. The profits of her volume, however, were not such as to encourage her to pursue the vocation, and she contemplated no further enterprise of a literary character, but the failure of all her other attempts to support her family com pelled her once more to appear before the public. In 1827, she published "Northwood," a novel in two volumes, which was very favorably received. Since that period, she has cont buted to many of the periodicals of the day, souvenirs, &c. both prose and verse, the latter under the signature of "Cornelia." In January 1828, she undertook the editorship of the Ladies' Magazine, published in Boston, where she now resides. It gives us pleasure to state, that her talents have been so well appreciated, that her efforts to provide for her children have thus far been crowned with success.

THE FATHER'S CHOICE.*

Now fly, as flies the rushing wind—
Urge, urge thy lagging steed!
The savage yell is fierce behind,
And life is on thy speed.

* In the year 1697, a body of Indians attacked the town of Haverhill, Massachusetts, killed and carried into captivity forty inhabitants. A party of the Indians approached the house of an individual, who was abroad at his labor, but who, on their approach, hastened to the house, sent his children out, and ordered them to fly in a course opposite to that in which danger was approaching. He then mounted his horse, and determined to snatch up the child with which he was unwilling to part, when he should overtake the little flock. When he came up to

And from those dear ones make thy choice—
  The group he wildly eyed,
When "father!" burst from every voice,
  And "child!" his heart replied.

There 's one that now can share his toil,
  And one he meant for fame,
And one that wears her mother's smile,
  And one that bears her name.

And one will prattle on his knee,
  Or slumber on his breast ;
And one whose joys of infancy,
  Are still by smiles express'd.

They feel no fear while he is near;
  He 'll shield them from the foe :
But oh ! his ear must thrill to hear
  Their shriekings, should he go.

In vain his quivering lips would speak,
  No words his thoughts allow ;
There 's burning tears upon his cheek,
  Death's marble on his brow.

And twice he smote his clenched hand—
  Then bade his children fly !
And turn'd, and even that savage band
  Cower'd at his wrathful eye.

Swift as the lightning wing'd with death,
  Flash'd forth the quivering flame !
Their fiercest warrior bows beneath
  The father's deadly aim.

them, about two hundred yards from his house, he was unable to make a choice,
or to leave any one of the number. He therefore determined to take his lot with
them, and defend them from their murderers, or die by their side. A body of
the Indians pursued, and came up with him ; and when at a short distance, fired
on him and his little company. He returned the fire, and retreated alternately ;
still, however, keeping a resolute face to the enemy, and so effectually sheltered
his charge, that he finally lodged them all safe in a distant house.

Not the wild cries, that rend the skies,
  His heart or purpose move ;
He saves his children, or he dies
  The sacrifice of love.

Ambition goads the conqueror on,
  Hate points the murderer's brand—
But love and duty, these alone
  Can nerve the good man's hand.

The hero may resign the field,
  The coward murderer flee ;
He cannot fear, he will not yield,
  That strikes, sweet love, for thee.

They come, they come—he heeds no cry,
  Save the soft childlike wail,
"O father, save !" "My children, fly !"
  Were mingled on the gale.

And firmer still he drew his breath,
  And sterner flash'd his eye,
As fast he hurls the leaden death,
  Still shouting, "children fly !"

No shadow on his brow appear'd,
  Nor tremor shook his frame,
Save when at intervals he heard
  Some trembler lisp his name.

In vain the foe, those fiends unchain'd,
  Like famish'd tigers chafe,
The sheltering roof is near'd, is gain'd,
  All, all the dear ones safe !

THE VICTOR'S CROWN.

A crown for the victor—a crown of light !
From a land where the flowers ne'er feel a blight,

Was gathered the wreath that around it glows,
And he who o'ercometh his treacherous foes,
  That radiant crown shall gain : —
A king went forth on the rebel array
That arose where a beautiful hamlet lay—
He frown'd—and there 's nought save ashes and blood
And blacken'd bones where that hamlet stood,
  Yet his treacherous foes he hath not slain.

A crown for the victor—a crown of light!
Encircled with jewels so pure and bright,
Night never hath gloom'd where their lustre glows,
And he who can conquer his proudest foes,
  That glorious crown shall gain :—
A hero came from the crimson field,
And low at his feet the pale captives kneel'd—
In his might he had trodden a nation down,
But he may not challenge the glorious crown,
  For his proudest foe he hath not slain.

A crown for the victor—a crown of light!
Like the morning sun, to the raptured sight
From the night of a dungeon raised, it glows :
And he who can slay his deadliest foes,
  That shining crown shall gain :—
With searching eye and stealthy tread,
The man of wrath sought his enemy's bed—
Like festering wounds are the wrongs he hath borne,
And he takes the revenge his soul hath sworn,
  But his deadliest foe he hath not slain.

A crown for the victor—a crown of light!
To be worn with a robe whose spotless white
Makes darkness seem resting on Alpine snows—
And he who o'ercometh his mightiest foes
  That robe and crown shall gain :—
With eye upraised—and forehead bare,
A pilgrim knelt down in holy prayer—
He hath wrestled with self and with passion striven,
And to him hath the sword of the Spirit been given—
  O, crown him, for his foes—his sins are slain!

THE LIGHT OF HOME.

My boy, thou wilt dream the world is fair,
  And thy spirit will sigh to roam,
And thou must go ;—but never when there,
  Forget the light of home.

Though pleasure may smile with a ray more bright,
  It dazzles to lead astray :
Like the meteor's flash 't will deepen the night,
  When thou treadest the lonely way.

But the hearth of home has a constant flame,
  And pure as vestal fire :
'T will burn, 't will burn, for ever the same,
  For nature feeds the pyre.

The sea of ambition is tempest tost,
  And thy hopes may vanish like foam ;
But when sails are shiver'd and rudder lost,
  Then look to the light of home.

And there, like a star through the midnight cloud,
  Thou shalt see the beacon bright,
For never, till shining on thy shroud,
  Can be quench'd its holy light.

The sun of fame 't will gild the name,
  But the heart ne'er felt its ray ;
And fashion's smiles, that rich ones claim,
  Are but beams of a wintry day.

And how cold and dim those beams must be,
  Should life's wretched wanderer come !
But my boy, when the world is dark to thee,
  Then turn to the light of home.

————

THE GIFTS.

Lady, I 've climb'd the mountain side,
  And roam'd the flowery lea,

And gather'd the garden's glowing pride,
And the rose and lily in soft bands tied,
  A garland meet for thee.

O the wreath is fair—but fairest flowers
  They fade too easily!
And they fold their leaves at evening hours,
And they droop and die when the tempest lowers,
  Then offer not flowers to me.

Lady, earth's richest mines I 've sought,
  And search'd the deep blue sea,
Where coral caves are with gems inwrought,
And these diamonds pure, and pearls I 've brought,
  As fitting gifts for thee.

O, those are gifts the great demand,
  They are offer'd on bended knee,
With a grudging heart by the servile band,
A tribute or bribe to the tyrant's hand,
  Then offer not pearls to me.

Lady, this glittering star to gain,
  The price of victory,
I rush'd upon the battle plain,
And traced my path by the heaps of slain—
  This star I 'll pledge to thee.

O, titled fame! an airy word,
  A puff of vanity!
Ah, think what crimson streams are pour'd,
That man, weak man, may be hail'd a Lord!
  Then offer not rank to me.

Lady, I have a heart as pure
  As the birthright of the free:
And the faith I vow will for aye endure,
And my love as flowers to the spring is sure;—
  This heart I 'll give to thee.

O, 't is now thy words have power to move!
  My warm tears speak for me;
For on earth below, or in heaven above,
The richest gift is the heart of love—
  And here 's a heart for thee!

THE MOTHER TO HER CHILD.

ONE kiss, my boy upon thy cheek,
   That cheek so young and bright,
And once again I 'd hear thee speak
   Thy softly lisp'd " good night."
Then rest, and not a shade of earth
   Can cloud thy slumbers fair ;
Dark dreams from worldly cares have birth,
   And thou hast nought of care.
O why might not life's silver tide
With thee thus ever smoothly glide !

Who gazes on the bloom of May,
   Nor sighs that all will wither?
And yet the blossoms must decay
   Ere we the fruit may gather ;
And life's sweet morning buds of joy
   Like spring-flowers soon depart ;
And thou must change, yet wear, my boy,
   Life's freshness in thy heart.
Pure feelings, like the flower's perfume,
Embalm the memory of its bloom.

Man's lot, dominion o'er the earth,
   Maketh his sinews strong,
And that proud lot will lead thee forth
   All ardent 'mid the throng.
Life's onward path is wrapp'd in night,
   And dangers are its fame ;
Ambition holds an eagle flight,
   And spurns at quiet's name,
And pleasure's siren songs entice,
And flowers conceal the precipice.

O ! wilt thou wander then, my boy ?——
   Away ! ye idle fears,——
Why shroud our sun of present joy
   In clouds of future years?
There 's One will watch thee though I sleep
   Where morning never shone ;
There 's One thy faltering steps can keep,
   Wouldst thou His voice were known?
Then list amid the world's wide din
The still, small voice thy heart within.

ENOCH LINCOLN,

THE present governor of the State of Maine, is a native of Worcester, Massachusetts. He was educated for the law, and besides exercising that profession has been several times a representative in congress from the state over which he now presides. He is the author of The Village, a poem published in 1816, an unpretending performance, but one of merit and interest.

The Village is a picture of rural scenery and character, accompanied with such moral reflections as the matters touched upon are calculated to awaken. It has of course nothing imposing in the subject, nor is there anything brilliant or striking in the style, no straining after novelties of thought or fine expressions. As the author disdains the use of the common stock of embellishments which belong to verse, this production has perhaps little which were we to refine our criticism, would pass for downright poetry. But it has a fund of good sense and direct obvious meaning which compensates for the want of more showy qualities. Those who bend with interest over the sober and moral page of Cowper, or are delighted with the simplicity and pathos of Goldsmith, will find The Village a work which will afford high satisfaction in the perusal. The tone of sentiment which prevails throughout is noble and elevated, and the political and moral precepts highly commendable. The versification is perhaps a little heavy, and the language occasionally prosaic. There is, however, a strength of feeling, and at times an eloquence, displayed in the poem that render the reader in some degree insensible to their defects.

THE VILLAGE.

SHALLOW and deep, by turns, and swift and slow,
There I behold the winding Saco flow.

In early spring, when showers increase its tides,
And melted snows pour down the mountains' sides,
I've seen it raging, boisterous, and deep,
O'erflow its banks and through the upland sweep.
The farmer's hopes, the lumberer's hard earn'd thrift,
Logs, bridges, booms, and boats were all adrift ;
Trees, fences, fields, whate'er opposed its course,
Were torn and scatter'd by the o'erwhelming force.
  Loosed from the fold to crop the tender feed,
The hungry flock were grazing on the mead.
Their saving Ararat, a trifling mound,
Secured them from the deluge spreading round,
Till, taught no more to let the stragglers roam,
The careless shepherd bore them to their home.
And then, from spouting clouds no longer fed,
Our little Nile return'd within its bed.
  Along its borders, spreading far and wide,
The tall, straight pines appear on every side.
To these thick woods the hardy laborer goes,
And rears his sheltering tent amid the snows,
His couch the hemlock's twigs, his household ware,
A jug and basket fill'd with simplest fare.
Ye, who indulge in indolence and ease,
Whom spleen invades and moody vapors seize,
To whom each day an age of trouble seems,
Whose nights are wakeful or disturb'd by dreams,
Observe the happy quiet of his rest,
And learn, like him, by labor to be blest.
Ye bloated epicures, disease's prey,
Who waste in vile excess your lives away,
Observe his frugal board, be wise at length,
And gain like him, from temperance, health and **strength**.
The frosty boreal blast, the pelting storm,
Solstitial suns, or seasons mildly warm,
The western breezes, or the southern air,
Alike to him, wake not one passing care.
With nervous arm he wields the keen-edged axe,
And plies anew each day untired attacks,
Till by his strokes the forest level'd round,
With prostrate trunks and branches heaps the ground.
The oxen, faithful sharers of his toil,
Drag to the river's brink the heavy spoil,
Thence floated downward to the distant mart,
And changed from Nature's form to works of Art.
  But not alone the lofty pine trees fall,
The axe unsparing strikes alike on all.

Now a rich treasury of golden grain,
Few moons have wax'd and waned since yonder plain,
A shady solitude, a drear retreat,
Had scarcely known the print of human feet.
When, joining hand in hand, what charms imparts
The potent touch of Labor and the Arts.
Planted by them, the sweetly scented rose,
On dreary wilds, in blooming beauty grows;
The fields, where famine reign'd or wild beasts ranged,
By them to peopled villages are changed.
Their aid invoked, with no retarding fears,
His cumber'd land the sturdy yeoman clears.
Fell'd by his strokes, the forest prostrate lies ;
Its vital sap the glowing summer dries,
And last the bonfires burn, the boughs consume,
And spreading flames the hemisphere illume.
The fresh'ning breezes fan the growing blaze,
Bear the light sparks, and cloudy columns raise,
And whirl the storm of rushing fire along
O'er lighted hills, and crackling vales among.
Swift fly the birds, as spreads the ruin round,
The frighted reptiles hide within the ground,
And all the forest tribes grow wilder at the sound.
But see yon simple hut, of structure rude,
Of unplaned boards contrived and logs unhew'd :
The threat'ning fires pursue their blasting way,
And the low fabric falls their certain prey.
Alas! 'twas Poverty's last hope,—the place
Where dwelt Contentment with her sister, Peace.
Ah! Charity, thou comforter of wo,
Wipe now the tears from Misery's eye that flow :
Thou Angel Almoner of pitying heaven,
Now let thy treasures of relief be given,
Take to thy bosom the poor child of need,
The houseless shelter, and the hungry feed :
By blessings wing'd their prayer shall make its way
To heaven's high Chancery ; there will God repay.
  More sacred than the Thunderer's chosen oak,
Let not the maple feel the woodman's stroke.
Fair maple ! honors purer far are thine
Than Venus' myrtle yields, or Bacchus' vine ;
Minerva's olive, consecrated tree,
Deserves not half the homage due to thee.
The queen of trees, thou proudly tower'st on high,
Yet wave thy limbs in graceful pliancy.

On yonder river's bank, around thy root,
The closely interweaving fibres shoot,
And numerous branches spreading far and wide,
Swiftly the wind, strongly must rush the tide
To overthrow thy deep and stately strength,
And on the strand to measure out thy length.
From every twig of thee, as blows the breeze,
Fly the ripe germes, the little embryo trees,
And form'd with each a wing by Nature's care,
Float lightly, quivering in the passing air,
Or, dropping, fall upon the stream and flow
With rich alluvion, and to forests grow.
Fair maple! let thy leaves my brows surround,
And laurel wreaths I trample on the ground.
The suffering Negro in West Indian Isles,
Soothed at thy name, amid his sorrow smiles,
Hope's cheering rays dispel his gloomy care,
And tinge with dawning light his deep despair.
Do not our soil and frosty clime insure
Sweets as salubrious, exquisite and pure,
As those which burning suns, or humid air
With swarming insects fill'd, and slaves prepare?
They do! our blest New England's fruitful soil
Requires no culture by a servile toil;
No master's torturing lash offends the ear,
No slave is now nor ever shall be here.
Whene'er he steps upon our sacred fields,
Their guardian Genius an asylum yields,
His chains drop from him, and on Reason's plan,
He claims the gift of God, the rights of man.

    *   *   *   *   *   *

    Enough of mountains, rocks, and woods, and streams:
We turn our view to more instructive themes:
The varied landscape let us cease to scan,
And strive to sketch the qualities of man,
Whilst from the camera of the faithful brain,
We paint the little village of the plain.
Let others trace a more extensive view,
And different scenes with higher aim pursue:
Let them become familiar with the great,
And ope the hidden mysteries of state,
Or march with conquering armies and rehearse
The deeds of heroes in the epic verse:
My lowly subjects humbler strains invite,
And check the Fancy's more aspiring flight:

Yet, though the numerous hamlets rise around,
And many tempting charms in each abound,
She will not stray from this her little sphere ;
The brief epitome of all is here.
    With admiration fill'd, by beauty fired,
By virtue awed, by all her charms inspired,
With sacred tenderness and watchful care,
First should I pay my homage to the fair.
Satire avaunt ! throw down thy poison'd darts,
Forbear to fix thy wounds in female hearts,
Forbear to draw from Beauty's eye the tear,
A scornful jest to barb, or point a sneer.
True, some are mark'd by follies, subjects fit
For jeers and taunts, for laughter and for wit.
A jilt may cheat you, a coquette may vex,
A Messalina may disgrace her sex,
A Clytemnestra may her husband kill,
A father's blood a furious Tullia spill,
A cruel Mary light the Smithfield fire,
And numerous victims in the flames expire ;
But is the starry firmament less bright,
Or would you veil the blaze of solar light,
Because a transient cloud obscures the one,
Or now and then a spot comes o'er the sun ?
Exceptions to their sex those monsters call,
And for their faults and crimes condemn not all.
For one of those a thousand you may find
Of charming person and of cultured mind.
Behold the politic, the good Queen Bess
By virtuous rule a happy nation bless,
A Joan of Arc invading armies brave,
And fall herself a tottering realm to save.
See the Czarina, as her father great,
In all the arts and policy of State,
The heroine Roland tyrant power defy,
The patriot Corday for her country die,
With learning fraught, Dacier's scholastic page,
By female genius signalize an age,
And, in our native land, a Warren's name
Rank near a Gibbon's on the roll of Fame,
And Adams, rich in history's various lore,
The arduous path of literature explore ;
With Shakspeare, great blasphemer of the fair,
" Woman thy name is Frailty," then declare,
The " semper varium " of the bard relate

Who sang the lovely Dido's hapless fate,
And let the strains of satire all be sung,
From bitter Juvenal down to pungent Young;
Those female worthies still shall live in fame,
And honor's haloes circle every name;
Still shall the virtues of a countless crowd
Proclaim the bards malicious, false and proud.
The foul injustice of their pens to show,
Proofs, living proofs, full many here I know.
And now forgive, ye fair, if, bold and rude,
The muse unbidden on your homes intrude;
'T is not to drag you to the common gaze,
For modest merit shinks from public praise;
'T is not, with flattery's sycophantic guile,
To smooth a frowning brow or win a smile;
But 't is to pay the homage which is due,
To Truth, to Beauty, Innocence and you.
Some could I name, who never fail to please
By manners joining dignity and ease;
Strictly correct in everything they say,
In Virtue's balance every act they weigh,
And while to all the social duties true,
Good their delight and heaven their hopeful view.
Even watching envy not a fault can find,
But owns them pure of heart and rich in mind:
Censure is dumb, while families and friends
Revere those virtues, which the world commends.
    Thrice happy he, by Fortune highly bless'd,
By such, as husband loved, or child caress'd,
And whom the ties of marriage, or of blood,
Have made the guardian angels of his good.
Ye men of pleasure, roving, wild, and gay,
Can lawless riot these pure joys repay?
Say which, through life's great voyage, will **rather please,**
Love's furious whirlwind or its gentle breeze?
Say, when enjoyments have the senses pall'd,
And unimpassion'd Reason is recall'd
To hold again her abdicated throne,
Do you not feel abandon'd and alone?
When on your spirits moody sorrow weighs,
When on your health destructive sickness preys,
When on your rights invade malignant foes,
Assail your fame, and stab at your repose,
Surely no greater good by pitying heaven
Can, in its vast beneficence, be given,

Than one, the friend in all the scenes of life,
The kind companion, and the loving wife.
Yet truth must own such paragons are rare,
And few so good, so lovely, and so fair.
Though frequent quarries may the earth unfold,
Yet rare are diamonds or the mines of gold:
So we perceive the mass of human kind,
Though fair in spots, is rough and unrefined.
Those bless'd with beauty and by virtue loved,
Of manners polish'd and of taste improved,
Are precious gems, 'midst barren mountains found,
Where dreary wastes and frowning cliffs abound.
'T is happily contrived that man is made
With tastes and powers of every varying shade.
Hence every one the other's wants subserves,
And each her own peculiar praise deserves,
As well the housewife 'neath the humble roof,
Plying the wheel and laboring warp and woof,
As the gay charmer, mistress of the heart,
Who plays in higher life a brighter part.
But she above all competition towers
Who adds to other gifts high mental powers.
    *   *   *   *   *   *

   But man, wild, active, versatile, and bold,
What pen his various nature can unfold,
Depict his actions, character, and mien,
And dramatize the vast and changeful scene!
Behold him here, the Village for his stage,
The scenery Nature, and the plot the Age,
Life's tragi-comic subject for the Play,
And Actors of all stamps, from grave to gay,
From bustling, strutting, pompous, loud, and vain,
To simple merit's large and lowly train.
Think not the moment lost, as these we scan,
For the best " study of mankind is man."
   First comes the lawyer; 't is an honor'd name,
A title glorious on the roll of Fame,
Too dear for wealth, which birth cannot bestow,
Or flattery wreathe around a lordling's brow;
A title from the fane of Science borne,
By weary vigils earn'd, by wisdom worn,
Of import vast, in which the honors blend
Of honor's champion and of freedom's friend;
Yet Justice fails the sacred name to save
From profanation of the fool and knave,
Who, jackdaws still, the peacock's pomp assume,
And strut in pride with half a pilfer'd plume.

     *   *   *   *   *

    Prompt with demurrers, skilful in abatements,
To circumvention train'd, and bold in statements,
Each villain's hireling, used by every knave,
Of meanest wretches even a meaner slave,
To rob too cowardly, too proud to steal,
The pettifogger preys on public weal,
And makes some Justice, a commission'd fool,
For paltry aims a secret legal tool,
Or deeper cheats, to gain him larger fees,
Performs by quibbles, sophistry and pleas.
As princes, heedless whether wrong or right,
Their forces sell in foreign wars to fight;
So he, for fees or popular applause, ·
Fits out his arguments for any cause,
Like hireling Hessians still enlists for pay,
Nor cares who falls or conquers in the fray.
Does Law's plain letter stare him in the face ;
Its spirit then must take the letter's place ;
But if the spirit shall oppose his aim,
The letter then must perfect reverence claim.
His declaration do clear proofs deny,
Does Reason give his sophistry the lie ;
Then Reason 's false and not to be believed,
And every witness perjured or deceived.
If, notwithstanding his absurd harangues,
Neglect attends him or dark want o'erhangs,
Fictitious indorsees his costs may swell,
Or clients under par their notes may sell !
Or if by clients, whom his frauds have warn'd,
Avoided, fear'd, despised, abhorr'd, and scorn'd,
Yet may his malice rob some wealthy foe,
Whilst perjury aids to lay the victim low.
If vengeance urge or avarice allure,
No virtue 's safe and no estate secure.
O'er your whole life the never-sleeping spy,
Whilst memory notes, directs his piercing eye,
And if, perchance, with careless feet you stray
From law's oft doubtful and much winding way,
At once the villain, dead to honest shame,
Urges his bloodhounds on your wealth and fame,
Turns pimp to catchpolls, and would take with joy
From off a hangman's hands his vile employ.
    When bless'd with soul and gifted with a mind,
And such there are, we honest lawyers find,
Those whose high office is to guard the laws,
And vindicate from wrong the righteous cause,

We yield the meed of merited applause :
Yes more, even those whom headstrong passions urge,
To tempt of daring vice the utmost verge,
Who, great in crimes, in their eccentric course,
Superior art display or mightier force,
If Genius beam its animating fire,
We cannot help to pity and admire ;
But when thick skull'd, dispassionate, and mean,
A creeping villain or dull rogue is seen,
If not from sense of justice quite exempt,
We load the wretch with hatred and contempt.
A lawyer he ! O no ; he sinks the name
To lowest depths of infamy and shame.
Much more the humble appellation fits
Of petty scribe of low, vexatious writs,
Whom ne'er a single ray of fancy warms
To cheer the gloom of precedents and forms,
Extortion's drudge, a mere machine, which Jews,
In works too vile for them, may freely use.
    Provoked by insults or some trifling wrong,
To vengeance urged law's mazy path along,
The fretful litigant resolves to fit
Th' offending neighbor with a "*special writ.*"
Varus, a lawyer skill'd in legal arts,
Of high repute for management and parts,
Of boldest courage to maintain a lie,
In reasoning subtle, in evasion sly,
To feeling dead, in principle a knave,
Forever craving as the insatiate grave,
And now mayhap by hunger urged to seize
On any job which gives a chance for fees,
His client's burning fury feeds with oil,
Urges the suit and lights him to the spoil.
'Squire Quirk, the Justice, to dispense the laws
Sits in the pride of power to judge the cause,
Grave as an owl in solemn state presides,
And as sly Varus bids, the cause decides :
Vain all authorities, and justice vain,
Not Dexter's self a single point could gain :
Cold as the snows which freeze around the pole,
No eloquence could warm his frigid soul ;
Dark as the shades of Milton's Stygian night,
His mind admits no glimmering ray of light ;
Too dull for reasoning and too proud for shame,
No power can move him from his steadfast aim.
    Resolved, in folly's and in knavery's spite,

In other courts to vindicate his right,
The aggrieved defendant, now on fortune's wheel,
Still by reviews, new trial, and appeal,
Through every change of law is whirl'd around,
And whirls and changes still, but gains no ground.
At last his wealth, by fritters worn away,
By lawyers' fees and witnesses in pay,
Through long delays although he wins his cause,
He falls beneath the bulwark of the laws ;
Yet blame not them, themselves most wise and pure,
But those who use them to oppress the poor :
They 're speculators, usurers, and knaves,
And those who condescend to be their slaves,
On whom should rest th' accumulated weight
Of private anger and of public hate.

    *   *   *   *   *   *   *

  Yet O ! beware of Party Spirit's rage,
The course of direst ills to every age,
The lowering cloud o'er freedom's brilliant star,
Heavy with ruin, black with civil war.
As where in deserts of Arabian lands
Some gushing spring spouts up amidst the sands,
Its dewy freshness feeds the towering palms,
And clothes the spot with all of Nature's charms :
But when the hot Sirocco rushes by,
The withering beauties catch the blast and die :
So, 'midst a world of tyranny and dread,
Where blooming Freedom droops its flowery head,
In this blest land, its blushing honors blow,
And ripening fruits in rich luxuriance grow ;
But Party Spirit's pestilential power
Wilts the fair growth and blights the charming flower,
While factious feuds and unforgiving hate
Waste half the civil honors of our state.
The Ins and Outs a constant warfare wage,
With all the malice of vindictive rage,
With all the ardor avarice inspires,
And all ambition's stimulating fires.
To either side unnumber'd followers throng,
Some right in motive, most in action wrong,
Assailants fierce, accoutred cap a pie,
In pride's and prejudice's panoply.
With loud declaiming demagogues at head,
Or now and then, perchance, by statesmen led,
Resolved, though conquer'd, still to scorn to yield,
They take with clash of arguments the field :

Truth tilts with Error and she hurls amain
Her forceful weapons, but she hurls in vain ;
On Folly's mail they fall with thundering sound,
And blunted fall unhonor'd by a wound.

*   *   *   *   *   *

Some meanly selfish, a more venal crew,
With nought but power or riches in their view,
While frowning virtue interdicts in vain,
Use basest means the favorite end to gain.
At patriot merit slander's shafts they aim,
With vacant heads and noisy tongues declaim,
Decry the statesman, puff the stupid knave,
Support the traitor, stigmatize the brave,
Call wisdom folly, honor's self defame,
Discolor truth and everything misname.
And why ? Forsooth a rival to disgrace,
To win a salary or to steal a place.

*   *   *   *   *   *

Aloof, the Patriot eyes the scene below,
With calm contempt or with indignant glow.
His wide philanthropy spreads unconfined,
Beyond a Party's bounds to all mankind ;
His liberal mind a general system frames,
And in that system knows no private aims,
No views to self, no patronage of friends,
No mean contrivances for paltry ends.
No factious tumults move his steadfast soul,
No lures entice him, and no threats control ;
Through changing times, 'midst all the scenes of State,
As stern as Justice, and as fix'd as Fate,
He stands sublime and nobly stems the storm
Of Folly's rage and popular alarm,
Till, all his greatness by the world confess'd,
Fear'd by the vicious, by the good caress'd,
He meets at last the meed he spurn'd to claim,
The unsought prize of office and of fame ;
Yet office adds to him no higher grace,
'T is he reflects his brightness on his place.
Diffusive blessings widely swell around,
And public weal with party spoils is crown'd.
Ye virtuous yeomen, guardians of the land,
Be yours the heart, the ever ready hand,
Such worth to aid, such wisdom to select,
Such truth to shield, such honor to protect.
What though no gay armorials declare

Of titled knaves that he 's the legal heir?
His rank is first by Heraldry of heaven,
To whom the powers of intellect are given.
What though no pomp his humble state allows?
He 's truly rich whom virtue's wealth endows:
Placed on the level where your fortunes rest,
He knows your wants, he feels when you 're oppress'd,
Enjoys your good, participates your pains,
Sinks as you fall, and as you prosper gains.
Such, your wise choice, in happy union blend
The servant, statesman, patriot, and friend.
Your forms of government, by Wisdom given,
Have met the approving smile of favoring heaven.
Your rightful heir, posterity demands
Your sainted sires' entailment at your hands.
O guard it with the Vestal's sleepless care,
And leave it even more perfect and more fair.

JOHN C. M'CALL,

Is a native of Philadelphia, and received an education for the bar, but we understand is not at present engaged in practice. He is known as the author of The Troubadour, The Condottier, Fleurette, and other small poems. The first named of these is the only one we have had an opportunity of seeing. It has many passages of rich and graceful description, which dispose us to think highly of the author's poetical talent. We must add, that this poem is marked by some of the strangest metrical anomalies that have ever come in our way. Mr M'Call we are informed, writes only for amusement, and does not seem to bestow the necessary attention upon the more mechanical department of poetry. We should be gratified to see him put forth his strength upon a work of higher character, with a studied and persevering effort.

THE TROUBADOUR.

THE mists lay dreaming on the mountain's breast,
The lazy winds were sinking into rest,
And softly breathing as they died away,
Sigh'd o'er the splendors of departing day.
In awful grandeur 'mid a blaze of light
That threw its countless hues, of colors bright,
O'er clouds and hills, o'er dells and babbling streams,
The sun of even shed his crimson beams.
The hollow murmurs of the rushing rill,
The mellow horn that sounded 'cross the hill,
The nightly anthem of the feather'd host,
All golden sounds and sober evening's boast,
Mix'd their sweet discords with seraphic skill,
And held the wanderer listening at their will.
The lowing herds crept slowly 'long the vale,
And distant echoes bore the hunter's hail.
The curling smoke above the foliage flew,
Fantastic wreathing as the zephyrs blew.
The merry tabor, and the pipe's shrill sound
Made buoyant light the village-maidens' bound,
As in the mazy grass they beat the ground.
The evening breeze bore fragrance on its wing,
O'er all the richest odors scattering.
In frowning grandeur, on the distant height,
An antique castle lower'd in its might;
Its lofty turrets blushing with the hue
That now o'er all the scene the red sun threw.
Its lord the bold Sir Brian de Valance,
The pride and boast of all chivalric France,
Here held his court amid Provençal peers,
Stranger alike to pity and to fears.
'T was evening's hour, when down the mountain's road,
A stranger Minstrel solitary strode.
Fatigued he seem'd, and faint—his gait was slow,
And oft he stopp'd to listen to the flow
Of streams precipitate, that fell with sound
Of soothing music on the ear, and found
Their devious paths o'er all the rugged ground.
Or else he gazed on all the fairy scene
Of rocks and hills, and laughing plains between;
The towering mounts that in succession grew
Up to the clouds, and all their shadows threw
On richest vineyards, where the bursting grape
Blush'd 'mid the tendrils that its clusters drape;

Which, intertwined in light and meshy rings,
Like feathers on the bird of Eden's wings.
Onward he came, and o'er his back was slung
A harp—and from his graceful shoulders hung
The garb that poets of the time then wore,
While nature's richest, noblest stamp he bore
Of light etherous on his open brow,
Though something sad was on his features now.
His port was such as ladies love to view,
Haught and chivalric—yet besides there grew
A poet's sadness o'er his speaking face,
That paled his front, but stole no single grace.

    *   *   *   *

In Bryan's hall the revels were begun,
Many a heart had now been lost and won.
Blazing with light the rich and festive room,
With scorn shut out the coming night's dull gloom.
The pride of France and chivalry had met,
And winsome pleasure wanton'd without let:
The joyous laugh from lip to lip went round,
And sense enchanted drank the thrilling sound.

    *   *   *   *

The moon held pale dominion o'er the scene,
While light and fleecy clouds were oft between
Her and the earth in all their beauty seen,
Alt'ring their vaporous forms and sailing on,
Their magic changes hardly seen ere gone,
Veiling the silver graces of that orb,
Whose modest charms all other charms absorb.
A bugle's call then sounded from the gate.
The warder enter'd, and with feudal state,
Whisper'd his lord, who cries " throw ope the door,
And let us welcome greet the 'Troubadour,
He comes with skilful harp, and soft'ning lay:
Ne'er to such guests can courtly knights say nay."
The doors flew open, and with graceful mien,
The Minstrel enter'd in his garb of green.
In wild luxuriance o'er his front there play'd,
Thick, clustering locks that even blacker made
The swarthy hue that darken'd in his face,
And lent his flashing eye a gloomier grace;
While in the lowly bow he made around,
More of the knight than peasant there was found.
Now ceased the lively dance, and dames drew near
The harp's full tone and melody to hear.
Then lowly bending o'er the strings he rung
A wild and mournful prelude ere he sung.

*   *   *   *

With wilder'd eye the lady Ella stood,
Watching the Troubadour as though she would
Recall some well-known air, or former tone,
Shadow or light that o'er his face had flown.
"It is—and yet it cannot be—that air!
And yet his brow was wont to be so fair.
That voice and I should sure be well acquaint."

*   *   *   *

The Minstrel watch'd the changes of her thought,
And when the warm and well-known glance he caught,
Like Egypt's statue kiss'd by golden beams
Of mantling morn new-waking from her dreams,
A full, harmonious peal of music threw
From chords melodious—soft as summer dew.
He ceased—and bowing lowly once again,
The melting echoes of his wondrous strain,
Borne on the bosom of the evening breeze
Died 'mid the shadows of the distant trees.
Then came a burst of rich and noble praise,
The poet's choicest meed for all his lays,
From pleasure-beaming eyes and lips where smiles,
With wildest sporting, flung around their wiles.
O'er one fair face the hue of joy was thrown;
With lustrous gladness every feature shone.
She look'd her thanks, but trusted not her voice,
Content in blissful silence to rejoice.
With courteous grace his thanks the Baron made,
And turning to his glittering menials, bade
Them bear the gold-embossed beaker near,
Then pledged his guest and every high-born peer
But as he quaff'd the sparkling liquour down,
His searching eye was lower'd with a frown;
A sudden thought seem'd crossing o'er his mind,
And with his falcon-glance he seem'd to find,
As every lineament he sternly scann'd,
With look so long accustom'd to command,
Some well-known feature in the Minstrel's face,
Whose dusky forehead gave of change no trace.

*   *   *   *

While through the hall loud peals of rapture rung
And pleasure's accents dwelt on every tongue,
A happy moment then the Minstrel caught,
Whispering, to tell the tidings that he brought.
"Oft, my loved Ella, since that hated morn,

When fierce—and more—when unrequited scorn,
Fell withering from thy father's lip, to blast
My fair and knightly fame—but that is past,
I will not strike upon a chord that rings
No mellow music—but that wildly flings
Its piercing discord on the shuddering air.
Oft with various guise and subtle care
I watched thy casement—under which I sung
Some air of kinder days past by, and hung
On quivering lights, and gliding forms that past
With breathless hope, still praying that at last,
Thy form would glad my sight, and once again
Thy melting accents chase acutest pain.
Alas! you came not—then with desperate hand,
I caught the harp of Minstrels of our land ;
Threw o'er my face the nut-brown olive hue,
And from the knight a wandering poet grew,
Hoping amid the revels of the time,
An entrance for the Trouvere and his rhyme ;
Then won with melody, like him of old,
A prize denied to conquering love of gold."
Here glancing on a stern and martial form
Whose features bore the impress of the storm ;
Like some fierce figure by Salvator drawn,
Darkling and towering in his strength of brawn ;
'Mid rocks and gloomy woods and savage men
Waiting at th' entrance of some banditt's den ;
The fire's dull embers pouring their red light
On stern, wild features, and on armor bright :
The brow of Guiscard darken'd, and his eye
Threw out a light, as though he would defy,
In th' hour of gasping death, the warrior dark,
Who took of song and dance but slender mark.

    *   *   *   *

While old age lives on mem'ry of the past,
Youth feeds on hope delusive to the last;
A cheating phantom follows as it flies,
Deck'd with gay promise though embalm'd in lies.
In rapt and burning syllables he told
His lover's tale—while smooth and swiftly roll'd
In course untired and same the heedless hour.
The morning-moon, half hid amid the bower,
In streams of silver light descending, shed
Her rays soft melting on the flow'ring bed,
That seem'd with dewy fragrance to repay
The wand'ring kisses of each smiling ray.

The fleeting wind too bore upon its breast
The grateful essence—and with odors dress'd,
Lavish'd its perfumed riches all around,
On dames—knights—marble—and the verdant ground.
And now not mark'd, the lovers stood beside
A lofty, narrow casement—opening wide
Its painted leaves (whose glowing colors told
Some tale chivalric, where a Baron bold
For love had died—struck by a rival's hand,
Who smiled and waved aloft his bloody brand.)
Ella look'd up into her lover's face—
And round her mouth with melancholy grace,
A faint smile languish'd, as she earnest pray'd
No fate of theirs should be like that portray'd
With cunning skill, upon the polish'd glass.
Laughing, her lover bade the boding pass.
Yet still the gentle girl in silence sigh'd,
O'er her wild fancies brooding, strove to hide
Even from her timid self her chilling fear,
Her soft eye glistening with the heavy tear.

  *   *   *   *

The lady listen'd to his ardent theme
Like one entranced in a rapturous dream.
"My arms and horse," then said the youthful knight,
Those that must serve me in the morrow's fight,
Conceal'd, I left amid the forest's gloom,
Hard by the rough-wrought cross and ruin'd tomb.
Thou must remember, love, 't was there I first,
In fond, but low and broken accents durst
Tell thee I loved—amid the awful scene
Of towering trees—wild streams and rude rocks green
With antique moss—and 'neath that sacred sign,
All holy men have ever deem'd divine,
Our faith we mutual pledged. Now I retread
That path, and at the dwelling of the dead
The coming morn must bide.—If in the just
Yon haughty Julian and thy Guiscard thrust,
Thy lovely image still will brace my arm,
Still lend new vigor, and preserve from harm.
Then should he fail, thy father may relent
And pitying yield his oft withheld consent.

  *   *   *   *

At once to shun remark or curious glance,
Aside each turn'd, to watch the entangling dance,
Where floating lightly through its endless maze

Young beauties sought and won th' admiring gaze.
From rich-gemm'd ringlets spicy odors flew,
From streaming curls of every sunny hue.
In Grecian folds the snowy draperies hung,
While wreaths of velvet flowers were o'er them strung.
Love-darting eyes in melting softness shone,
And vermeil lips dropt words of mellowest tone.
Their white, impearled arms, thrown light in air,
Strew'd rose, and hyacinths, and blossoms rare.
The dewy freshness of the leafy showers
Rain'd essence o'er the hall, now strewn with flowers.
Soft voices sang with air and tone as sweet
As those of sea-maids when they haply meet
Some blooming boy, who rides the foamy wave,
Drinks the rich music, and forgets the grave
That yawns—and gazes on the syren's hairs
That stream unearthly beautiful, and dares,
Of billows' wrath unmindful, still to feed
Enrapt upon their smiles—and seems, indeed,
To deem it bliss t' obey th' enticing sign,
And plunge in awful depths for love divine.
His billowy tomb then quickly rears
Its foam-topp'd pyramid—and disappears.

     *   *   *   *

With fragrant breath the morning now arose,
On joy gay smiling, and on keenest woes :
The stars, sown o'er the jetty head of night,
In brilliance paled before the orb of light ;
Dark seas of mist roll'd back their murky wave
Before the bright, young beams that richly lave,
In tints prismatic all his vaporous throne,
In glittering splendor, awful and—alone.
The cool breeze, rambling, woke the sleeping leaves,
With that soft breathing that alternate heaves
The yellow harvest and the quiet lake,
And balmy freshness showers o'er the brake.
Ella arose, and from the casement hung
Enchanted, on the quiet scene that flung
Its still and fragrant spell on all around.
Far up the sloping hills the merry sound
Was heard of early shepherd's pipe, and bell
Of grazing flocks, re-echoed from the dell.

     *   *   *   *

The hours flew onward, and in crowds the dames
And low-born serfs and knights of haughty names,

Gay in the rich array of gaudy dress,
In expectation, to the lists now press.
A lovely mead, romantically wild,
Stretch'd at the feet of rocks and cliffs uppiled
In forms grotesque—inclined its verdant breast,
Just swelling from the hills, in quiet rest.
The hoary forest cast its sombre shade,
In darkling masses thrown athwart the glade;
While, here and there, an aged, branching oak
The lengthen'd sameness of the green plain brake.
De Valance' lofty towers on the left,
Of beauty now and chivalry bereft,
With splendor glowing of the morning beam,
With richest tints of brightest purple gleam.
'T was here the lists enclosed with palisade,
Ran far across the smooth and grassy glade.
At each extremity was placed a gate,
Where heralds—pursuivants—and trumpets wait,
And men at arms to guard the portal's way,
Watch o'er the order of the gay tournay,
Decide the quality of knight, and fame
Of those who peril'd in the warlike game.
Pavilions, rich with gold and every dye,
At measured distance regularly lie;
Squires beside them, in grotesque array,
Guard the bright war-worn shields that near them lay,
Caress the foaming steed that rears from joy,
His gold bit champs or bites some martial toy.
To rich and lofty seats with velvet spread,
The lady guests, with Ella, now were led,
Soft eyes shone brightly, and some hearts beat high.
From one there came a deep, though smother'd sigh.
As queen of love and beauty on that day,
Peerless in rank young Ella led the way.
She passed like Luna on her azure sea,
In beauty sailing—yet reluctantly;
Like visions seen by Castaly's pure stream,
In the rapt poet's airy, radiant dream.
For her the acclaim of rapture bore no charm;
To one so gentle it echoed alarm;
And on her snowy lid and long eye-lash
Black care with laughing pleasure seem'd to clash.
Up to her sparkling throne she trembling pass'd,
Gazing on knights and plunging steeds—aghast.
Pallid she sat, and on the entrance-gate
Her deep gaze planted—as if fix'd by fate.

As yet, through all the waving plumes in sight,
Her anxious eye still sought the nodding white.
It came—and trumpets sounding, wildly threw
Their warlike clamors all the barriers through.
Clarions and cymbals cast their echoes round,
Fair women smiled, and chargers paw'd the ground.
The Heralds "Largess" cried, while golden showers
Fell plenteous o'er their heads, like falling flowers,
From bands of gallant peers and lovely dames,
Of martial line and far-famed, ancient names.
The Marshals too, arm'd cap-a-pie now stand,
Prepared at once to judge and to command.
With shouts and wild huzzas the lists resound,
To this knight first—and then to that redound.
Full twenty knights now ranged on either side,
Sternly impatient, for the signal bide.
Firm in the stirrup—and the spear in rest,
Each pants to put his armor to the test,
O'er one fierce party dark-brow'd Julian sways,
His polish'd armor glistening in the rays.
While through the steel-clad ranks he quickly glides,
And keenly eyes each warrior as he rides;
With careful glance he views each barbed steed,
And knight impatient for the warlike deed.
In firm array the adverse squadron stands,
With rich-dyed streamers, and with well-tried bran
And from the martial column Guiscard brooks
With burning ardor all his rival's looks.
Unknown, he asks a knightly rank and post,
Claims a front station in the armed host.

     *   *   *   *

Now blew the loud shrill trump its warrior cry:
The breathless audience waited silently;
While, circled in a cloud of blacken'd dust,
Each party clash'd and mingled in the just.
The sounds of clarions and of clanging arms
Falling with horrid jar—the wild alarms
Of martial outcries and the trampling steed,
Fled howling to the mountain from the mead.
A mist of darkling dust enwrap the field;
The lance now shatter'd, fell before the shield;
Horses and men now roll'd along the plain,
Bleeding—struck down—and writhing in their pain.
Cries of fierce agony with shouts were heard,
Dreadful commingling—as the coursers spurr'd,
With hoofs ensanguined tore the fallen knight,

Who helpless, shriek'd amidst the furious fight.
Gay, streaming plumage drifted on the gale,
As leaves autumnal with the loud breeze sail.
The piteous cries and groans of those who fell
Stole tremulously fearful o'er the dell.
Still o'er the scene spectators shouted loud,
And kerchiefs waved from out the beauteous crowd.
With skill and gallant guise young Guiscard fought,
Sternly impatient for his rival sought.
Willing they met, and 'mid the horrid din,
With fury strove the mastery to win.
    How fared that maid who madly gazed intent,
With eye distended and her fair neck bent?
With throbbing heart she gazed and madden'd brain,
On bright swords gleaming—and the bloody stain.
The pale and panting girl beheld the steel
On high bright beam and then beneath it reel,
Her lover prostrate—and she saw no more
Than that he fell, ensanguined with his gore;
A cry in deep, but still half-stifled wo,
(Like moan of loud winds baffled as they go.
Through dreary caverns speeding or some vault,
Angry or frighted at th' unlook'd-for halt,)
In plaintive agony she gave, and sunk,
A pale and lovely—yet a breathless trunk.
Sir Brian saw his beauteous daughter fall,
And sternly motion'd for the trumpet-call,
That rolls its peaceful clamors all around,
And drowns of mimic war the harsher sound.
With wildest uproar teem'd the tournay scene,
As borne off, lifeless, disappear'd its queen.
Whilst squires attending on each suffering Knight,
The deep wound stanch'd—unclasp'd the helmet bright;
Thirsting and faint the hapless Guiscard lay,
Wailing the fortune of th' unhappy day,
Till o'er the lists the Baron's rambling eye
With anger lighten'd—then fix'd instantly.
The fallen Knight he knows, and unquench'd hate
With rapid vehemence decides his fate;
That wakeful hate that burning, never dies
Till in the silent tomb its victim lies;
That canc'rous rots the heart where it has sway,
And night's dull hue spreads o'er each smiling day.
He turn'd with quick decision and command,
And scornful pointing with his unsheath'd brand,
Bade his arm'd menials to a dungeon bear,
And guard with fetters and their studied care,

The stubborn fool whose obstinacy led
Where meet reward should shower on his head.

*   *   *   *

Full oft the sun had bathed his glorious ray,
Crimsoning the waters of the distant bay ;
Dyed golden masses of the evening's cloud
With streaks of blushes, and with purple proud ;
Dropt on the leaning bark's white-swelling sail
Those tints that brighten e'en the canvas pale :
And lapt the glowing landscape in rich hues,
Whose dazzling 's mellow'd by the falling dews.
Long months had pass'd since Guiscard hapless lay,
Shut from the genial smiling of the day :
But now flew on the happy hour, when
Young Hope and Love might shed their joys again.
With passion's eloquence and conquering gold,
Rich in the latter—with the former bold ;
With tears and melting words, the lady brought
That tearful meeting she so fondly sought,
Entranced she sunk upon her lover's breast,
Content t' enjoy that happy—breathless rest,
Till by the trembling jailor roused in fear,
Th' escape she plans and dries the fruitful tear.
Long-told adieus—and frequent, then were past,
More mournful each and tenderer than the last,
Till pale with dread, the trembling soldier bore
His lingering mistress from the dungeon's door.
Noiseless as one of Autumn's stilly days,
When sluggish winds ne'er rouse the veiling haze
Which wraps in deep'ning mist the distant height,
Soft'ning the radiance of too brilliant light,
With stealthy pace they trod the vaulted way,
(Ne'er seen nor brighten'd by the cheering day,)
Nor dream't suspicion's glance, with subtle art,
Divined the secret of the maiden's heart.

*   *   *   *

Turn we to that fierce father once again,
The storm of passion raging in his brain.
With hurried pace he treads the princely hall,
While two dark menials summon'd at his call,
Their stern lord's mandate in the distance wait.
Sudden he turns and checks his rapid gait,
Beckons the ruffians to a nearer stand,
With haughty air delivers his command.
"Ye know the prisoner in the western tower ?

'T is well—then ere the coming morning's hour,
See that he dies ; and when the deed is done,
Pluck out his heart—I 've use for such a one."
Turning he marshals them their murderous way :
Wildly impatient chides the tardy day.
The breezy morn sped o'er its orient path,
Nor frown'd indignant on th' assassin's wrath :
Too well and swiftly done, the bloody deed
Nor darks its rising, nor controls its speed ;
Heaven's pure rays with equal bounty shed
Their balmy kiss on Crime and Virtue's head.
With smile malignant and with fiendish sneers,
The villains' full recital Brian hears ;
Lists the whole history of his victim's death,
The last deep sighing of his fleeting breath :
His wild hate gluts with long and gloomy gaze
On the dread relic that before him lays :
Now bids a servant, with ferocious air,
A deep gold goblet to his presence bear.
Throws in the bleeding object of his ire ;
Then as a gift from fond and doting sire,
Commands they bear it to his darling child,
" Fair as obedient—as sincere as mild."—
    O'er that sad daughter's brow the night-breeze flew,
Her fever's heat unbated by the dew.
The fresh'ning moisture of the morning air
Threw no soft coolness on that forehead fair :
Each snowy eye-lid swoln and drooping hung,
Told of a heart with speechless misery wrung.
Her tearless, mournful glance, towards heaven now led,
Spoke the dead calm of soul when hope is dead :
That cold, undying agony of mind,
Too keenly poignant e'er to be defined ;
That sinks but rarely to its short-lived rest,
And waking burns still fiercer in the breast.
A young and weeping page now slowly bore
That gorgeous beaker, chased with clotted gore,
Laid the dread offering at the lady's feet,
Trembling essay'd his message to repeat.
With sobs and faltering then he told his tale,
Deeply intent upon his mistress pale.
" My noble lord has sent," 't was thus it ran,
" That which he says will pleasure ye to scan,
'T was kind, he says, such precious gift to send,
'T was what ye prized e'en more than sire or friend.
I cannot tell, dear lady, what is meant,

But his eye burnt fiercely and his brow was bent,
And round his mouth there lurk'd a laughing scorn,
That seem'd of fiercest Hatred to be born."
With mien unchanging and with steadfast look,
The blood-stain'd goblet hapless Ella took.
The page's words now made its meaning plain,
All prayer or piteous plaint were now but vain:
Despair too, lent a calmness to her tone,
Nor fell one tear—nor solitary groan.
" My father hath done wisely," then she said,
" In such rich sepulchre should ~'   a laid
A heart whose feeblest pulse to honor beat,
The home of Courage—sacred Virtue's seat!
The richest tribute of my thanks then bear
That doting parent for his fostering care :
This precious gift is all I ever sought,
'T is far too costly e'er to have been bought."
The heavy, scalding tear o'erflowing then,
Her slumb'ring maiden-softness woke again.
With deep, unsated look of love intense,
That fix'd, unwandering gazing of the sense,
Her glance now fasten'd on the blood-stain'd urn,
While her pale cheek still paler 'gan to turn.
From the wild gipsy's casket then she took,
With mild and pensive but determined look,
A dark thick liquid, and with upturn'd eye,
She faintly smiled--and drank it instantly.
The deadly poison coursed its lightning way ;
Death's hue now wandered o'er her, as she lay.
The young and faithful page had gazed with air
Of love respectful—tender brother's care :
But when he saw that ghastly shadow creep
O'er his fair mistress' face, he ceased to weep :
Swift flew to summon to her couch's side
Her weeping maidens ere the lady died.
And when they came, they found that goblet prest
Closely and tightly on her panting breast.

          *   *   *   *

Now all grew silent—and pale Ella's eye,
Languid and glassy, sought the azure sky :
A gentle motion o'er her lips then ran,
As if she pray'd for that dark-hearted man ;
And then they closed—and with convulsive throe,
The spirit fled this scene of earthly wo.
On her fair face a holy calm was spread,
As if she slept—but not among the dead :

Her fallen lid, with blue, meandering ve:
Seem'd Parian marble with its wandering stain.

* * * *

 Sad wore that day in Brian's gilded halls,
And long its memory in those stately walls.
The silver tones of revelry had fled,
While grief's dull notes were wandering in their stead.
The piercing trumpet and the martial drum
Slept silent, 'mid the low and deepen'd hum
Of sorrowing vassals, on vain grief intent,
On mournful duties silently now bent.
The hour had con.._   that sad requiem said
By weeping friendship o'er the festering dead:
That harrowing—tearful moment, when the grave
Sullenly closes o'er the young and brave;
When the dread sound of fast descending mould
Strikes on the wounded heart so fearful cold.
Many that requiem heard, and told the tale
To those who listen'd, e'en when it was stale.

* * * *

 'T was a dark, chilly morn in bleak November,
Such as old, gray-bearded men remember:
The clouds were heavy—dull—and scattering,
Large drops of rain, at times, fell pattering
On red and purple leaves that strow'd the ground,
While the bl. blew with melancholy sound:
And falling foliage darken'd all the air,
Rich in autumnal dyes, of tints most fair.

* * * *

 And ever and anon a lulling note
Of sadful music, air-borne, seem'd to float
Through all the windings of the brown hued grove,
And with the harsher sounds rich sweetness wove.
Then the full, solemn hymning for the dead
Fell, sullen on the listening ear and spread,
While bursting on the sight a moving train
Crept slowly onward down the shelving plain.
Knights and fair women—holy priests—were seen,
In robes—fair flowing plumes—and costliest sheen.
Then the sad bier, with dim and black array,
In awful slowness pass'd upon its way.
Within its dark funereal bosom laid
The brave young knight beside the beauteous maid.
From those who gazed (a crowd of young and old,)
In unaffected grief, the big tears roll'd.

Of their sad passion many a tale went round,
Told with the low and fearful, smother'd sound.
Some said lord Brian, when his daughter died,
Wept madly, even in his hour of pride :
Raved o'er the lovely relics of that child,
In all the tempest of his passions wild.
'T was even lightly whisper'd he had sworn,
That the bright helm and glaive should ne'er be borne,
But that the pilgrim's staff or monkish beads
Best fitted one of such foul, bloody deeds.
Onward the long procession sadly pass'd,
Till to a lonely dell it came at last,
Where moody cypress and the clambering vine,
In close and loving meshes intertwine.
There in one grave lie maid and cavalier,
Their cold tomb bathed with many a sad tear :
And on its sculpture village damsels hung
Fresh flowers, and frequent in the evening sung.
Among the rustics too a lay went round,
That notes aerial wander'd o'er that ground,
On moonless nights, and when the wind was high,
And black clouds sailed heavily in the sky.
In that lone spot—beside a quiet stream
And mouldering ruin, those two lovers dream.

EDWIN C. HOLLAND

WAS a lawyer of Charleston, S. C., and died a few years
since. He published a volume of poetry which we have not
seen. The two following naval odes appeared in the Port
Folio in 1813.

THE PILLAR OF GLORY.

HAIL to the heroes whose triumphs have brighten'd
　The darkness which shrouded America's name ;
Long shall their valor in battle that lighten'd,
　Live in the brilliant escutcheons of fame :

Dark where the torrents flow,
And the rude tempests blow,
The storm clad spirit of Albion raves ;
Long shall she mourn the day,
When, in the vengeful fray,
Liberty walk'd like a god on the waves.

The ocean, ye chiefs, (the region of glory,
  Where fortune has destined Columbia to reign,)
Gleams with the halo and lustre of story,
  That curl round the wave as the scene of her fame :
    There, on its raging tide,
    Shall her proud navy ride,
The bulwark of freedom, protected by heaven ;
    There shall her haughty foe,
    Bow to her prowess low,
There shall renown to her heroes be given.

The Pillar of Glory, the sea that enlightens,
  Shall last till eternity rocks on its base,
The splendor of fame its waters that brightens,
  Shall light the footsteps of time in his race :
    Wide o'er the stormy deep,
    Where the rude surges sweep,
Its lustre shall circle the brows of the brave ;
    Honor shall give it light,
    Triumph shall keep it bright,
Long as in battle we meet on the wave.

Already the storm of contention has hurl'd
  From the grasp of Old England the trident of war,
The beams of our stars have illumined the world,
  Unfurl'd our standard beats proud in the air :
    Wild glares the eagle's eye,
    Swift as he cuts the sky,
Marking the wake where our heroes advance ;
    Compass'd with rays of light,
    Hovers he o'er the fight ;
Albion is heartless—and stoops to his glance.

RISE COLUMBIA.

WHEN Freedom first the triumph sung
  That crush'd the pomp of Freedom's foes,
The harps of heaven responsive rung,
  As thus the choral numbers rose,—
Rise Columbia! brave and free!
  Thy thunder when in battle hurl'd,
Shall rule the billows of the sea,
  And bid defiance to the world.

Supremely blest by fate's decree,
  Thy hardy tars in battle brave,
Shall plume thy wings and keep thee free
  As is the motion of thy wave.
    Rise Columbia, &c.

The stars that in thy banner shine,
  Shall rain destruction on thy foes,
Yet light the brave of every clime,
  To kindred friendship and repose.
    Rise Columbia, &c.

The storms that on thy surges rock,
  Around thy flag shall idly sweep:
Proof to the tempest's fiercest shock,
  Its stripes shall awe the vassal deep.
    Rise Columbia, &c.

Encircled with a flood of light,
  Thy eagle shall supremely rise,
Lead thee to victory in fight,
  And bear thy glory to the skies.
    Rise Columbia, &c.

DANIEL BRYAN

Is a native of Virginia, and has been a senator in the legislature of that state.   He is, we understand, at present Post Master at Georgetown, D. C.   He wrote The Mountain Muse, published some years since, and has been more recently known as the author of The Lay of Gratitude, a volume of verses on the reception of Lafayette, and The Appeal for suffering Genius, written to obtain charity for the " Boston Bard."

LAFAYETTE.

'AND this," he exclaims, " is the country whose charms
   A tyrant's rude fetter would mangle and mar!
Where the war-demon howls forth his chilling alarms,
   And the death-vulture hangs o'er his slaughtering car !
Columbia ! a pilgrim approaches thy shrine,
   The offerings he brings are his sword and his blood !
O ! make him thy champion—his life shall be thine !
   He seeks this high honor o'er ocean's dark flood."

Lo ! the beautiful wood-nymph of freedom appears !
   Wreaths of blooming magnolia her forehead entwine,
Around her an evergreen mantle she wears,
   And her eyes with effusions of tenderness shine :
Majestic and mild, the young Hero she meets,
   And accepts his devotion with smiles of delight ;
His heart to her wishes responsively beats,
   And she points where her votaries sustain the dread fight.

Entranced by her blessing and holy embrace,
   His soul is uplifted on pinions of flame,
And, as flies the swift steed in the emulous race,
   He rushes to battle, to conquest, and fame.—
Where danger and carnage bestride the red plain,
   And death's giant arm, through the dark thundering clouds,
Drives his broad lance and piles up his mountains of slain,
   The whirlwind of conflict our hero enshrouds !

    *   *   *   *

Descending through ether on pinions of snow,
  The angel of peace to our country returns,
Stripes the concave of blue with the dyes of her bow,
  And enshrines here in separate and beautiful urns,
The dust of the warriors who fell on our plains—
  Each nation's apart—yet in nearness arranged—
And her olive tree planting to shade the remains—
  Bids it flourish and bloom there through ages unchanged.

She waves her white flag, and two figures advance—
  The elder's a matron commanding and proud in her port—
But she meets with confusion the maiden's sweet glance,
  And her cheek seems of varied passions the sport:—
Her head wears a crown—but its splendor is dim—
  For its richest and loveliest jewel is gone!
On her arm hangs a banner whose emblem, so grim,
  And so couchant, was lately the pride of a throne.—

But now her bold lion is humbled and lorn—
  And where laurel and sea-weed once form'd his proud lair,
He is stretch'd on a bed that's dismantled and torn,
  And his eye is despoil'd of its conquering glare.
The younger—though stately—is modest of mien,
  And we know by her costume and aspect benign,
That in her loved presence before we have been,
  And that she is liberty's guardian divine!

ALONZO LEWIS.

Mr Lewis is a native of Lynn, Massachusetts, where he is
now employed as an instructer. A volume of his poems was
published in 1823, and he has since contributed others for the
newspapers.

DEATH SONG.

Great Sassacus fled from the eastern shores,
Where the sun first shines, and the great sea roars,
For the white men came from the world afar,
And their fury burnt like the bison star.

His sannaps were slain by their thunder's power,
And his children fell like the star-eyed flower ;
His wigwams are burnt by the white man's flame,
And the home of his youth has a stranger's name—

His ancestor once was our countryman's foe,
And the arrow was placed in the new-strung bow,
The wild deer ranged through the forest free,
While we fought with his tribe by the distant sea.

But the foe never came to the Mohawk's tent,
With his hair untied, and his bow unbent,
And found not the blood of the wild deer shed,
And the calumet lit, and the bear-skin bed.

But sing ye the Death Song, and kindle the pine,
And bid its broad light like his valor to shine ;
Then raise high his pile by our warriors' heaps,
And tell to his tribe that his murderer sleeps.

THE MINSTREL'S LOVE.

My love is a lady slender and fair,
Whose mantle is light as the thin blue air,
And falls from her neck as floatingly,
As the vapor that rolls o'er a moonlight sea

The clustering wreaths of her long thick hair,
Curl over her forehead, as dark and fair,
As the nightly clouds that heavily flow
Over star-loving Sunapee's mount of snow.

Like the moon which looks out from a cloudy sky,
Is the soul which beams from her large blue eye,
Where utterless thoughts appear and flee,
Like shadows of clouds o'er a sunny sea.

In the sleepless night, and the ceaseless stir
Of the busy day, my thought is with her,
And memory and love are with sighing repaid,
Because of the form of that slender maid.

THE WANDERER OF AFRICA.

He launch'd his boat where the dark waves flow,
Through the desert that never was white with snow
When the wind was still, and the sun shone bright,
And the stream glow'd red with the morning light.

He had sat in the cool of the palm's broad shade
And drank of the fountain of Kafnah's glade,
When the herb was scorch'd by the sun's hot ray,
And the camel failed on his thirsty way.

And the dark maids of Sego their mats had spread,
And sung all night by the stranger's bed;
And his sleep was sweet on that desert sand,
For his visions were far in his own loved land.

He was weary and faint in a stranger clime,
But his soul was at home as in youth's sweet time,
And he lay in the shade, by his cot's clear pool,
And the breeze which came by was refreshing and cool.

And the look of his mother was gentle and sweet,
And he heard the loved steps of his sister's light feet,
And their voices were soft and expressive and low,
Like the distant rain, or the brook's calm flow.

And this was the song which the dark maids sung,
In the beautiful strains of their own wild tongue;
"The stranger came far, and sat under our tree,
We will bring him sweet food, for no sister has he."

And the stranger went forth when the night-breeze had died,
And launch'd his light bark on the Joliba's tide;
And he waved his white kerchief to those dark maids,
As he silently enter'd the palmy shades.

And the maidens of Sego were sad and lone,
And sung their rude song, like the death spirit's moan:
"The stranger has gone where the simoom will burn,
Alas! for the white man will never return!"

NATHANIEL APPLETON HAVEN

WAS born in Portsmouth, New Hampshire, January 14th, 1790. He studied at Harvard College, and after receiving his degree, applied himself to theology, but soon relinquished the pursuit from ill health, and other causes. He then turned his attention to the law, and entered upon his practice in Portsmouth, where he passed the remainder of his life, excepting a short visit to Europe in 1815. He died June 3d, 1826, at the age of 36.

Mr Haven was for several years the editor of the Portsmouth Journal, and his writings in that paper may rank with the best newspaper effusions of our country. He wrote also a variety of other articles highly creditable to his talents and character, among them a few pieces of poetry. After his death, a selection from his works was published, with a biographical memoir by Professor Ticknor of Harvard University.

LINES ON FREDERIC THE GREAT.

—" Apres ma mort, quand toutes mes parties
Par la corruption sont aneanties,
Par un meme destin il ne pensora plus ! "
Frederic le Grand.

ARE these the dictates of eternal truth ?
  These the glad news your boasted reason brings ?
Can these control the restless fire of youth,
  The craft of statesmen, or the pride of kings ?

Whence is the throb that swells my rising breast,
  What lofty hopes my beating heart inspire ?
Why do I proudly spurn inglorious rest,
  The pomp of wealth, the tumult of desire ?

Is it to swell the brazen trump of fame,
  To bind the laurel round an aching head,
To hear for once a people's loud acclaim,
  Then lie for ever with the nameless dead ?

Oh no! far nobler hopes my life control,
   Presenting scenes of splendor, yet to be ;—
Great God, thy word directs the lofty soul
   To live for glory, not from man, but thee.

THE PURSE OF CHARITY.

THIS little purse, of silver thread
   And silken cords entwined,
Was given, to ease the painful bed,
   And soothe the anxious mind.

The maker's secret bounty flows,
   To bid the poor rejoice,
And many a child of sorrow knows
   The music of *her* voice.

The little purse her hands have wrought,
   Should bear her image still ;
And with her generous feelings fraught,
   Her liberal plans fulfil.

Its glittering thread should never daunt
   The humble child of wo ;
But well the asking eye of want
   Its silver spring should know.

While age or youth with misery dwell,
   To cold neglect consign'd,
No useless treasures e'er should swell
   The purse with silver twined.

AUTUMN.

I LOVE the dews of night,
   I love the howling wind ;
I love to hear the tempest sweep
O'er the billows of the deep !
   For nature's saddest scenes delight
   The melancholy mind.

Autumn ! I love thy bower
   With faded garlands drest :

How sweet, alone to linger there,
When tempests ride the midnight air !
   To snatch from mirth a fleeting hour,
   The sabbath of the breast !

Autumn! I love thee well ;
   Though bleak thy breezes blow,
I love to see the vapors rise,
And clouds roll wildly round the skies,
   Where from the plain, the mountains swell,
   And foaming torrents flow.

Autumn! thy fading flowers
   Droop but to bloom again ;
So man, though doom'd to grief awhile,
To hang on fortune's fickle smile,
   Shall glow in heaven with nobler powers,
   Nor sigh for peace in vain.

JAMES N. BARKER

WAS born at Philadelphia; he was a captain in the artillery, and served on the frontiers during the late war with Great Britain. When the war was over, he returned to his native city, where he continues to live at present. He has been an Alderman, and was for one year Mayor of the city of Philadelphia. Mr Barker is better known by his dramatic than by his other productions. As early as 1807, he produced a comedy at the Philadelphia Theatre, entitled " Tears and Smiles," and a melo drama founded on the story of Pocahontas, which he called " The Indian Princess, or La Belle Sauvage." These were represented with success. He dramatised Scott's Marmion, which was a very popular play, and still keeps possession of the stage. In 1817, he published a remarkably neat and sprightly comedy, entitled " How to try a Lover," which was never performed, and in 1823, he produced a tragedy, entitled " Superstition," the scene of which is laid in New England, and one of the principal characters is Goff, the regicide. This is the last of Mr Barker's dramatic efforts, and possesses considerable merit. It was performed but twice at the Chesnut Street Theatre, Philadelphia. Mr

Barker is also the author of several occasional pamphlets, the most interesting of which is entitled " Sketches of the Primitive Settlements on the River Delaware." He has written also in the Atlantic Souvenir. His writings are characterised by good taste, simplicity of language, and adherence to nature. His fancy is playful, and his images are such as are calculated rather to delight than startle.

LITTLE RED RIDING HOOD.

SHE was, indeed, a pretty little creature,
So meek, so modest : what a pity, madam,
That one so young and innocent, should fall
A prey to the ravenous wolf.
————— The wolf, indeed !
You 've left the nursery to but little purpose,
If you believe a wolf could ever speak,
Though, in the time of Æsop, or before.
—Was 't not a wolf, then ? I have read the story
A hundred times ; and heard it told : nay, told it
Myself, to my younger sisters, when we 've shrank
Together in the sheets, from very terror,
And, with protecting arms, each round the other,
E'en sobb'd ourselves to sleep.   But I remember,
I saw the story acted on the stage,
Last winter in the city, I and my school-mates,
With our most kind preceptress Mrs Bazely,
And so it was a robber, not a wolf
That met poor little Riding Hood i' the wood ?
—Nor wolf nor robber, child : this nursery tale
Contains a hidden moral.
————— Hidden : nay,
I 'm not so young, but I can spell it out,
And thus it is : children, when sent on errands,
Must never stop by the way to talk with wolves.
—Tut ! wolves again : wilt listen to me, child ?
—Say on, dear grandma.
————— Thus then, dear my daughter :
In this young person, culling idle flowers,
You see the peril that attends the maiden
Who, in her walk through life, yields to temptation,
And quits the onward path to stray aside,
Allured by gaudy weeds.
————— Nay, none but children,

Could gather butter-cups and May-weed, mother.
But violets, dear violets—methinks
I could live ever on a bank of violets,
Or die most happy there.
———— You die, indeed,
At your years die!
———— Then sleep, ma'am, if you please,
As you did yesterday in that sweet spot
Down by the fountain; where you seated you
To read the last new novel—what d'ye call 't—
The Prairie, was it not?
———— It was, my love,
And there, as I remember, your kind arm
Pillow'd my aged head: 't was irksome sure,
To your young limbs and spirit.
———— No, believe me,
To keep the insects from disturbing you
Was sweet employment, or to fan your cheek
When the breeze lull'd.
———— You 're a dear child!
———— And then,
To gaze on such a scene! the grassy bank,
So gently sloping to the rivulet,
All purple with my own dear violet,
And sprinkled o'er with spring flowers of each tint.
There was that pale and humble little blossom,
Looking so like its namesake Innocence;
The fairy-form'd, flesh-hued anemone,
With its fair sisters, call'd by country people
Fair maids o' the spring. The lowly cinquefoil too,
And statelier marigold. The violet sorrel
Blushing so rosy red in bashfulness,
And her companion of the season, dress'd
In varied pink. The partridge ever-green,
Hanging its fragrant wax-work on each stem,
And studding the green sod with scarlet berries—
—Did you see all those flowers? I mark'd them not.
—O many more, whose names I have not learn'd.
And then to see the light blue butterfly
Roaming about, like an enchanted thing,
From flower to flower, and the bright honey-bee—
And there too was the fountain, overhung
With bush and tree, draped by the graceful vine,
Where the white blossoms of the dogwood, met
The crimson red-bud, and the sweet birds sang
Their madrigals; while the fresh springing waters,
Just stirring the green fern that bathed within them,

Leapt joyful o'er their fairy mound of rock,
And fell in music—then pass'd prattling on,
Between the flowery banks that bent to kiss them.
—————— I dream'd not of these sights or sounds.
—————— Then just
Beyond the brook there lay a narrow strip,
Like a rich riband, of enamel'd meadow,
Girt by a pretty precipice, whose top
Was crown'd with rose-bay.   Half-way down there stood
Sylph-like, the light fantastic columbine
As ready to leap down unto her lover
Harlequin Bartsia, in his painted vest
Of green and crimson.
—————— Tut! enough, enough,
Your madcap fancy runs too riot, girl.
We must shut up your books of Botany,
And give you graver studies.
—————— Will you shut
The book of nature, too?—for it is that
I love and study.   Do not take me back
To the cold, heartless city, with its forms
And dull routine; its artificial manners
And arbitrary rules; its cheerless pleasures
And mirthless masquing.   Yet a little longer
O let me hold communion here with nature.
—Well, well, we 'll see.   But we neglect our lecture
Upon this picture—
—————— Poor Red Riding Hood!
We had forgotten her; yet mark, dear madam,
How patiently the poor thing waits our leisure.
And now the hidden moral.
—————— Thus it is :
Mere children read such stories literally,
But the more elderly and wise, deduce
A moral from the fiction.   In a word,
The wolf that you must guard against is—LOVE.
—I thought love was an infant; "toujours enfant."
—The world and love were young together, child,
And innocent—alas! time changes all things.
—'True, I remember, love is now a man.
And, the song says, "a very saucy one"—
But how a wolf?
—————— In ravenous appetite,
Unpitying and unsparing, passion is oft
A beast of prey.   As the wolf to the lamb,
Is he to innocence.
—————— I shall remember,

For now I see the moral.   Trust me, madam,
Should I e'er meet this wolf-love in my way,
Be he a boy or man, I 'll take good heed,
And hold no converse with him.
———— You 'll do wisely.
—Nor e'er in field or forest, plain or pathway,
Shall he from me know whither I am going,
Or whisper that he 'll meet me.
———— That 's my child.
—Nor, in my grandam's cottage, nor elsewhere,
Will I e'er lift the latch for him myself,
Or bid him pull the bobbin.
———— Well, my dear,
You 've learn'd your lesson.
———— Yet one thing, my mother,
Somewhat perplexes me.
———— Say what, my love,
I will explain.
———— This wolf, the story goes,
Deceived poor grandam first, and ate her up :
What is the moral here ?   Have all our grandmas
Been first devour'd by love ?
———— Let us go in ;
The air grows cool—you are a forward chit.

GEORGE WASHINGTON DOANE

WAS born in 1799.   In 1818, he received the degree of
Bachelor of Arts at Union College, Schenectady ; and in 1821
was admitted Master of Arts at the same college.   On the
19th of April, 1821, he received deacon's orders, from the Rt.
Rev. John Henry Hobart, Bishop of the Protestant Epis-
copal Church, in the Diocese of New York ; and was or-
dained Priest in 1823, by the same Prelate.   For three years
and a half, he officiated as a temporary assistant minister, in
Trinity Church, New York.   In 1824 he was elected to the
Professorship of Belles Lettres and Oratory, in Washington
College, Hartford, Connecticut, which place he filled, in conjunction with the rectorship of a neighboring parish, till the
last year (1828,) when he was settled as collegiate minister
in Trinity Church, Boston, in which situation he now remains.

As an author, Professor Doane has but once appeared, in his own name, before the public.   In 1824, he published, principally for circulation among his friends, "SONGS BY THE WAY, chiefly devotional, with translations and imitations."   He has also occasionally contributed to the Atlantic Magazine, the New York Review, and other literary journals.   His poetry is spirited and finished, and is evidently the offspring of a vigorous mind, enriched by study, and elevated by religious sentiments.

THAT SILENT MOON.

THAT silent moon, that silent moon,
　　Careering now through cloudless sky,
Oh! who shall tell what varied scenes
　　Have pass'd beneath her placid eye,
Since first, to light this wayward earth,
　　She walk'd in tranquil beauty forth.

How oft has guilt's unhallow'd hand,
　　And superstition's senseless rite,
And loud, licentious revelry,
　　Profaned her pure and holy light:
Small sympathy is hers, I ween,
　　With sights like these, that virgin queen.

But dear to her, in summer eve,
　　By rippling wave, or tufted grove,
When hand in hand is purely clasp'd,
　　And heart meets heart in holy love,
To smile, in quiet loneliness,
　　And hear each whisper'd vow and bless.

Dispersed along the world's wide way,
　　When friends are far, and fond ones rove,
How powerful she to wake the thought,
　　And start the tear for those we love!
Who watch, with us, at night's pale noon,
　　And gaze upon that silent moon.

How powerful, too, to hearts that mourn.
　　The magic of that moonlight sky,
To bring again the vanish'd scenes,
　　The happy eves of days gone by;
Again to bring, 'mid bursting tears,
The loved, the lost of other years.

And oft she looks, that silent moon,
　　On lonely eyes that wake to weep,
In dungeon dark, or sacred cell,
　　Or couch, whence pain has banish'd sleep:
Oh! softly beams that gentle eye,
On those who mourn, and those who die.

But beam on whomsoe'er she will,
　　And fall where'er her splendor may,
There's pureness in her chasten'd light,
　　There's comfort in her tranquil ray:
What power is hers to soothe the heart—
What power, the trembling tear to start!

The dewy morn let others love,
　　Or bask them in the noontide ray;
There's not an hour but has its charm,
　　From dawning light to dying day:—
But oh! be mine a fairer boon—
That silent moon, that silent moon!

OH! THAT I HAD WINGS LIKE A DOVE.

Who that has mingled in the fray,
　　Or borne the storms of life,
Has not desired to flee away
　　From all its sin and strife—
Has not desired, to flee away,
　　Like yonder startled dove,
And seek, in some far wilderness,
　　A nestling place of love—
Where the tumult, if heard, should excite no alarm,
And the storm and the tempest sweep by, without harm.

Who that has felt the rankling wound
　　Of disappointment's sting,
Or proved the worse than vanity
　　Of every earthly thing,
Has not desired, like yon sweet dove,
　　To wander far away,
And find some desert lodging place,
　　And there for ever stray—
Where the vain show of earth should no longer delude,
Where the fiend disappointment should never intrude.

Who that has felt the crumbling touch
　　Of premature decay,
Or, sorer far, has mourn'd o'er friends,
　　Torn from his heart away,

Has not desired, like yonder dove,
To seek some lonely nest,
And, far from earth's vain fellowship,
To dwell and be at rest——
Till the summons be heard, that shall bid him depart
And for ever rejoin the beloved of his heart.

And it shall be——that summons of joy shall be given,
To the converse of saints, to the mansions of heaven,
Where the cross of the sufferer shall no more be borne,
But the crown of the conqueror for ever be worn.

Thou, who seek'st this glorious prize,
Ask no more for wings of dove ;
Angel-pinion'd, thou shalt rise,
To the realms of peace and love.

Realms, where Christ has gone before,
Blissful mansions to prepare ;
Realms, where they who serve Him here,
Shall his power and glory share.

There, no battle-fray is heard ;
There, no tempest need be fear'd ;
Disappointment cannot sting,
Banish'd thence each hurtful thing,
Sickness comes not there, nor pain,
Death hath there no dark domain ;
Gather'd there, no foot shall rove
Of the happy friends we love ;
Gather'd there, no soul shall roam ;
'T is our own——our Father's home.

———

LINES, SUGGESTED BY A VERY BRILLIANT SUN-SETTING.

Oh ! see yon glowing occident,
With crimson, gold, and purple blent——
How high and wide the pageant's spread,
How far its gorgeous glories shed ;
Not all that the earth has of brightest and best,
Can vie with the splendors of yonder west.

Oh ! could we but mount to that golden clime,
And traverse those pathways of purple light,
To the perishing things of earth and time,
We 'd bid a long, and a glad " good night ! "
There, 'mid the glow of parting day,
Through amaranthine fields we 'd stray,

Drinking in, with ravish'd ears,
The music of the circling spheres;
Gazing on glories of brighter shine,
Than the richest gems of Golconda's mine;
Resting in bowers of sweeter perfume,
Than the "gardens of Gul," in their fairest bloom.

Fond enthusiast! see—it fades,
Even upon thy charmed sight;
Lost 'mid evening's gather'd shades,
Dying with the dying light;
Thus ever fades earth's loveliest,
Thus dies the brightest and the best.

I 've seen, in blooming loveliness,
The youthful maiden's angel form;
I 've seen, in towering stateliness,
The hero, breasting battle's storm;
The canker-worm of hopelessness
Has blighted all her bloom;
War's iron bolt, in ruthlessness,
Has sped him to the tomb:
Thus ever fades earth's loveliest,
Thus dies the brighest and the best.
Then count not maiden's loveliness,
Nor hero's towering stateliness,
   Mortal, dare be wise:
Let not thy soul's aspiring rest
On gilded east, or glowing west—
   Look beyond the skies!
There, far above that line of light,
Which bounds thy dim and shorten'd sight,
In never-dying glories, shine
The splendors of the world divine.
The new Jerusalem, the holy,
Whose foundations are of gold;
Garnish'd with the radiant glory,
Of thousand precious stones untold;
And the rainbow-circled throne,
   On its fiery axles wheeling;
And Jehovah's own Zion, the holy mount;
And the water of life, in its crystal fount;
   And the tree, with its leaves for the nations' healing:
Such as these, but numberless,
The glories of that heavenly place,
Where sorrow is never known, nor night,
For GOD and the LAMB are its joy and light.

SPIRIT OF SPRING.

SPIRIT, that from the breathing south,
    Art wafted hither on dewy wing,
        By the soften'd light of that sunny eye,
        And that voice of wild-wood melody,
    And those golden tresses wantoning,
And the perfumed breath of that balmy mouth.
        We know thee, Spirit of Spring—
Spirit of beauty, these thy charms, Spirit of Spring!

Spirit of Spring! thou com'st to wake
    The slumbering energies of earth;
        The zephyr's breath, to thee we owe,
        Thine is the streamlet's silver flow,
    And thine, the gentle flowerets' birth,
And their silence, hark! the wild birds break,
        For thy welcome, Spirit of Spring!—
Spirit of life, thy triumphs these, Spirit of Spring!

Spirit of Spring! when the cheek is pale,
    There is health in thy balmy air,
        And peace in that brow of beaming bright,
        And joy in that eye of sunny light,
    And golden hope in that flowing hair:
Oh: that such influence e'er should fail,
        For a moment, Spirit of Spring—
Spirit of health, peace, joy and hope, Spirit of Spring

Yet fail it must—for it comes of earth,
And it may not shame its place of birth,
Where the best can bloom but a single day,
And the fairest is first to fade away.

But oh! there's a changeless world above,
A world of peace, and joy, and love,
    Where, gather'd from the tomb,
The holy hopes that earth has cross'd,
And the pious friends that we loved and lost
    Immortally shall bloom.

Who will not watch, and strive, and pray,
That his longing soul may soar away,
    On faith's untiring wing,
To join the throng of the saints in light,
In that world, for ever fair and bright,
    Of endless, cloudless SPRING!

ON A VERY OLD WEDDING RING.

The device—two hearts united.
The motto—"*Dear love of mine, my heart is thine.*"

I LIKE that ring, that ancient ring
  Of massive form, and virgin gold
As firm, as free from base alloy,
  As were the sterling hearts of old.
I like it—for it wafts me back,
  Far, far along the stream of time,
To other men, and other days,
  The men and days of deeds sublime.
But most I like it as it tells
  The tale of well-requited love ;
How youthful fondness persevered
  And youthful faith disdain'd to rove ;—
How warmly *he* his suit preferr'd,
  Though *she*, unpitying, long denied,
Till, softened and subdued, at last,
  He won his fair and blooming bride ;—
How, till the appointed day arrived,
  They blamed the lazy-footed hours ;—
How then the white-robed maiden train
  Strew'd their glad way with freshest flowers ;—
And how, before the holy man,
  They stood in all their youthful pride,
And spoke those words, and vow'd those vows
  Which bind the husband to his bride ;
All this it tells ;—the plighted troth,
  The gift of every earthly thing,
The hand in hand, the heart in heart—
  For this I like that ancient ring.
I like its old and quaint device ;
  Two blended hearts—though time may wear them,
No mortal change, no mortal chance,
  "Till death," shall e'er in sunder tear them.
Year after year, 'neath sun and storm,
  Their hopes in heaven, their trust in God,
In changeless, heartfelt, holy love,
  These two, the world's rough pathways trod.
Age might impair their youthful fires,
  Their strength might fail, 'mid life's bleak weather,
Still, hand in hand, they travell'd on,—
  Kind souls ! they slumber now together.
I like its simple posy too ;
  "Mine own dear love, this heart is thine !"
Thine, when the dark storm howls along,
  As when the cloudless sunbeams shine.
"This heart is thine, mine own dear love !"

Thine, and thine only, and for ever;
Thine, till the springs of life shall fail—
  Thine, till the chords of life shall sever
Remnant of days departed long,
  Emblem of plighted troth unbroken,
Pledge of devoted faithfulness,
  Of heartfelt, holy love, the token—
What varied feelings round it cling!
For these, I like that ancient ring.

THE CLOUD BRIDGE: A REMEMBERED VISION.

Saw ye that cloud, which arose in the west,
As the burning sun sank down to his rest,
How it spread so wide, and tower'd so high,
O'er the molten gold of that glowing sky,
That it seem'd—Oh! it seem'd like some arched way,
As it beam'd and gleam'd, in that glorious ray,
    Where the spirit, freed
    From its earthly weed,
  - And robed in the white
    Of the saints in light,
Might pass from the waves of sin and wo,
To that world where ceaseless pleasures flow!

Ye saw that cloud, how it tower'd alone,
Like an arched path o'er the billows thrown,
How its pillars of azure and purple stood,
And mock'd at the dash of the angry flood,
While it beam'd—oh! it beam'd from its battlements high,
As it gleam'd, and stream'd, in that western sky,
    Such a flood of mellow and golden light,
    As chain'd and fix'd the ravish'd sight,
And pour'd, along our dark'ning way,
The peace and joy of celestial day.

Such, as we haste to our heavenly home,
Saviour! such be the sights that come—
Thus, while the visions of time flit by,
And the fashion of earth grows dim to our eye,
Thus, let the light—oh! the light of thy love,
Beam bright on our sight from the mansions above—
    Rending the gloom
    Which enwraps the tomb,
    And guiding our eye
    To that world on high,
Where the people who love thee, for ever shall share
The rest thou hast purchased, and gone to prepare.

NATHANIEL H. WRIGHT

WAS born at Concord, Massachusetts, in 1787. He was brought up to the occupation of a printer, in Boston. In 1809 or 1810, he established a newspaper in Newburyport, called The Independent Whig. He afterwards removed to Boston, and was the editor of another paper, entitled The Kaleidoscope. He died in Boston, May 13, 1824, aged 37. He wrote The Fall of Palmyra, a poem, and Boston, or a Touch at the Times. Besides these publications, he was the author of a multitude of fugitive pieces in the newspapers. He was a poet of considerable talent, and, with proper study and application, might have made a distinguished figure among the writers of the day. The Fall of Palmyra, we have not been able to procure. We are told that the author designed a second edition of it, a year or two after it appeared, but could not find a copy. Boston or a Touch at the Times, is a small pamphlet, and contains the two following pieces, which he selected as specimens of his style and ability.

THE ISLE OF FLOWERS.

In Huron's wave a lovely isle
   Gems the blue water's vast expanse.
There nature wears her sweetest smile,
   And sunbeams o'er her beauties dance.

In vain the angry billows beat
   Against its rock-encircled snore ;
The spray but makes its blossoms sweet,
   Expanding 'mid the tempest's roar.

But when the winds and waves are hush'd,
   And evening's shade is stealing on,
When the last beams of day have blush'd,
   And Hesper mounts his cloudless throne

How gently weep the dews of night,
   Which bow the tender harebell's head
And, falling noiseless, sweetly light
   Upon the spotless lily's bed.

Oh! were but man like that fair isle,
   In vain should trouble's tempests gloom;
Hope's fairest flowers around should smile,
   And faith and resignation bloom.

When life's last lingering beam should fade,
   The radiant star of peace would rise,
And dews of grace, at evening's shade,
   His spirit nurture for the skies.

THE STAR OF BETHLEHEM.

WHEN night her lonely shade has spread
Around the wayworn wanderer's head,
How welcome is the distant gleam
Of cottage taper's twinkling beam,
To guide and cheer his devious tread,
By marshy fen or mountain stream.
Thus in the wilderness of life,
When o'er us gloom the shades of strife,
When adverse fortune's tempests roll,
And beat upon the troubled soul,
There beams athwart affliction's night,
With rays of peace, a holy light:
Oh! 't is that bright and lovely star,
Which guides the wanderer from afar;
Which smiles upon the brow of even,
And holds its course in midway heaven.
   Mark'st thou the rainbow's beauteous hue
In yonder eastern sky of blue?
A moment, and the tints shall fade,
And all its glories sink in shade.
Or dost thou mark yon opening flower?
'T is but the blossom of an hour;
Its leaves shall by the winds be strown,
And where it bloom'd no more be known.
The solid globe shall pass away,
The fleeting atom of a day.

The sun, and every lesser light,
Shall all be quenched in endless night.
Yet shall the Star of Bethlehem shine,
A light of origin divine :
And when the flood of ruin streams,
That star shall brighter shed its beams.
It shone upon a Saviour's birth,
And chased the gathering gloom of earth.
No cloud obscures its holy ray,
Its torch was lit in realms above,
And from the shrine of boundless love
It flames with heaven's own lucid day.
When is fulfilled Jehovah's grace,
When other orbs no more have place,
'T will light th' immensity of space.

SOLYMAN BROWN

WAS born in Litchfield, Connecticut, and was graduated at
Yale College in 1812. He was designed, we believe, for the
ministry, but is at present a teacher in New York. He published in 1818 a volume of verse entitled, An Essay on American Poetry, &c.

LADY BYRON TO HER HUSBAND.

FARE thee well, inconstant lover !
 If thy fickle flame was love ;—
Though our transient joys are over,
 I can ne'er inconstant prove.

Man may boast a deathless passion,
 Swear his love shall ne'er decline ;
Yet, unfix'd as changing fashion,
 Woman's fate may change like mine !

Once I thought I might believe thee ;
 Might on Byron's oath rely ;

But my arms do scarce receive thee
  Ere thy oaths, unheeded, die.

From paternal arms you took me,
  Stole me from a mother's care ;
Then in wantonness forsook me
  For a less admiring fair.

Prayers and tears were unavailing,
  Nought thy purpose could beguile
Not a wife, her woes bewailing,
  Nor a lovely infant's smile.

Heaven had form'd thee for unkindness,
  Steel'd thy soul to all that 's mild
Dimm'd thy moral sight with blindness,
  Left thee Nature's wayward child.

Stay ! I must not—cannot chide thee ;
  What thou hast not, who can blame ?
Virtue is what heaven denied thee,
  And the world has done the same.

Think not I can e'er forget thee ;
  No, thy griefs will all be mine ;
I shall weep when foes beset thee,
  Smile when fortune's sun shall shine.

Must I—can I—shall a mother
  Hate the father of her child ?
Gracious Heaven ! my anguish smother,-
  At that name, my infant smiled !

Smiled to think she had a father
  To protect her growing years ;—
Unsuspecting orphan, rather
  Drown thine eye in floods of tears !

Father, now, sweet babe, thou hast not ;
  All his care you must forego ;
Other woes thy peace may blast not,
  Yet thou hast this keenest wo !

Orphan babe ! my care shall ever
  Guard thee from the ills of life ;

Death alone hath power to sever
Byron's babe and constant wife !

THE EMIGRANT'S FAREWELL.

FAREWELL to the land that my fathers defended ;
   Farewell to the field which their ashes inurn ;
The holiest flame on their altars descended,
   Which, fed by their sons, shall eternally burn :
Ah ! soft be the bed where the hero reposes ;
And light be the green turf that over him closes—
Gay Flora shall deck, with her earliest roses,
   The graves of my sires, and the land of my birth.
Adieu to the scenes which my heart's young emotions
   Have drest in attire so alluringly gay ;
Ah ! never, no never, can billowing oceans,
   Nor time, drive the fond recollections away !
From days that are past, present comfort I borrow ;
The scenes of to-day shall be brighter to-morrow ;
In age I 'll recall, as a balm for my sorrow,
   The graves of my sires, and the land of my birth.

I go to the West, where the forest, receding,
   Invites the adventurous axe-man along ;
I go to the groves where the wild deer are feeding,
   And mountain-birds carol their loveliest song :
Adieu to the land that my fathers defended,
Adieu to the soil on which freemen contended,
Adieu to the sons who from heroes descended,
   The graves of my sires and the land of my birth.
When far from my home and surrounded by strangers,
   My thoughts shall recall the gay pleasures of youth :
Though life's stormy ocean shall threaten with dangers,
   My soul shall repose in the sunshine of truth :
While streams to their own native ocean are tending,
And forest oaks, swept by the tempest, are bending,
My soul shall exult, as she 's proudly defending
   The graves of my sires, and the land of my birth.

JOSEPH RODMAN DRAKE.

Of New York, known as an associate of Halleck in writing the Croakers. He died in September 1820. He left behind him a poem in manuscript, entitled the Culprit Fay, which has been spoken of in favorable terms. The spirited National Ode, which follows, shows him to have been a poet of promising talent.

THE AMERICAN FLAG.

When Freedom from her mountain height,
Unfurl'd her standard to the air,
She tore the azure robe of night,
And set the stars of glory there!
She mingled with its gorgeous dyes
The milky baldric of the skies,
And striped its pure, celestial white
With streakings of the morning light;
Then from his mansion in the sun,
She call'd her eagle bearer down,
And gave into his mighty hand
The symbol of her chosen land.

Majestic monarch of the cloud!
Who rear'st aloft thy regal form,
To hear the tempest trumping loud,
And see the lightning-lances driven,
When stride the warriors of the storm,
And rolls the thunder-drum of heaven!
Child of the sun! to thee 't is given
To guard the banner of the free,
To hover in the sulphur smoke,
To ward away the battle-stroke,
And bid its blendings shine afar,
Like rainbows on the cloud of war,
The harbingers of victory.

Flag of the brave! Thy folds shall fly,
The sign of hope and triumph high!

When speaks the signal trumpet tone,
And the long line comes gleaming on,
(Ere yet the life-blood, warm and wet,
Has dimm'd the glistening bayonet,)
Each soldier's eye shall brightly turn,
To where thy meteor glories burn,
And, as his springing steps advance,
Catch war and vengeance from the glance !
And when the cannon-mouthings loud,
Heave in wild wreaths the battle-shroud,
And gory sabres rise and fall,
Like shoots of flame on midnight pall,—
There shall thy victor glances glow,
And cowering foes shall sink beneath
Each gallant arm that strikes below
That lovely messenger of death !

Flag of the seas ! on ocean's wave,
Thy stars shall glitter o'er the brave,
When death, careering on the gale,
Sleeps darkly round the bellied sail,
And frighted waves rush wildly back
Before the broadside's reeling rack,—
The dying wanderer of the sea
Shall look, at once, to heaven and thee,
And smile to see thy splendors fly,
In triumph o'er his closing eye.

Flag of the free heart's only home !
By angel hands to valor given,—
Thy stars have lit the welkin dome,
And all thy hues were born in heaven !
For ever float that standard sheet !
Where breathes the foe that stands before us
With Freedom's soil beneath our feet,
And Freedom's banner streaming o'er us !

JAMES ABRAHAM HILLHOUSE,

Is the son of the Hon. James Hillhouse of New Haven. He
received a degree at Yale College in 1808.   After this he engaged in business as a merchant in New York ; but latterly,
we believe, has attended to no occupation but that of letters.
His first publication was Percy's Masque, a dramatic poem,
which came out first in London, and was reprinted here in 1820.
In 1821 appeared at New York, Judgment, a Vision, a descriptive poem in blank verse, and in 1825, Hadad, a dramatic
poem.

Mr Hillhouse, as a poet, has rare qualities, and such as
would gain him high commendation at the hands of the most
rigid criticism.   He has a refined and mature taste, and his
writings are remarkable for correct sentiment and a clearness
and masculine vigor of language that form a striking contrast to
the vapid wordiness which infects so much of the poetry of his
cotemporaries.   He makes no lavish and unseasonable display
of ornament.   Everything is natural, appropriate, and happily
adjusted.   With a few trifling exceptions, he may be quoted
as a model of chaste and finished versification.   His writings
are not disfigured by any of those crudities of language which
result from a hasty execution in the mechanical department of
composition.   His diction is polished, and regulated with the
nicest care.   He has an animation of style, and a fulness and
condensation of thought, that never suffer his pages to grow
languid.   Hadad, his last performance, is the chief in merit.
It is a master-piece of its kind, and for just and skilful
arrangement of parts, dignity of sentiment, and propriety of
character, is, we think, exceeded by no poem founded on a scriptural theme.   We are not certain that any one among the great
masters of English verse of the present day, would have come
off with equal success from the bold attempt upon which he
has ventured in this work.   Scriptural poems are undertakings
peculiarly hazardous.   They do not in general appear to have
been treated very happily.   They venture into a region which

abounds with every requisite material for the most exalted poetical contemplation; but a study and wariness more than common are to be exercised in dealing with them. We are scrupulous to the last degree in exacting all the proprieties of character and niceties of circumstance, in matters which concern the objects of our religious reverence. We are struck here with failings which pass unregarded when they stand connected with other topics; for they occur to us in a double disadvantage, as offences against the common standard of taste, and as debasing the dignity of sacred writ. Hence the greater portion of scriptural poems have been unfortunate. They have either been managed with such a degree of diffidence and caution, inspired by the fear of committing trespass upon holy ground, as to cramp the powers of the writer, and debar him the proper use of his subject, or they have been marred by some anomaly of character or sentiment, or the commission of some violence upon the notions we are accustomed to entertain upon the matters in question, which is sufficient, in a subject of such peculiar delicacy, to produce an unfavorable effect.

But the work of Mr Hillhouse is an evidence of his ability to strive against all these disadvantages with success. He has escaped the faults which are attendant upon most performances of the same species, and seized with a bold hand upon the rich materials which the nature of his theme laid open before him.

We have enumerated what we conceive to be the distinguishing qualities of Mr Hillhouse's poetry, and given an opinion as to the just rank to be assigned him. Should the question be asked, why, possessing so many excellences, he is not more read among us, (for he has much less popularity than many others,) we answer, that the form and substance of his productions are sufficiently dissonant from the general taste of the moment, to account for this; nay, his very freedom from the reigning faults of our modern poetry has not been without its influence to this effect. We are grown fond of light reading. Fugitive verses have more charm for us than long productions elaborately planned and finished with study and toil.

Then the topic most in vogue with the great majority of our poets, and most acceptable, it would appear, to the readers of poetry now, is not one to which the present author has mainly trusted for the interest of his compositions. Amatory and sentimental strains are now predominant. The favorite poetry of the day is of this character. It has in general a cast of effeminacy, as before remarked. Mr Hillhouse's verse is of a different order. It is not designed for ‾ ‾ ‾nediate popularity by according with the momentary whim and fashion in literature, but for an endurance more lasting than the qualities which recommend the greater part of our most popular compositions would secure to it.

His two chief productions, though cast in the dramatic form, were not designed for representation on the stage. Though, in accordance with our plan in the outset, we have not entered so far into the province of the drama as to give any passages from works of that description, we shall not, for the reason just stated, be considered as departing from our limits by presenting the reader with a scene from Hadad. It would be unjust to resort to any other pages for an extract designed to represent this author fairly.

HADAD. SCENE III.

The garden of ABSALOM's *house on Mount Zion, near the palace, overlooking the city.* TAMAR *sitting by a fountain.*

Tam. How aromatic evening grows! The flowers,
And spicy shrubs exhale like onycha;
Spikenard and henna emulate in sweets.
Blest hour! which He, who fashioned it so fair,
So softly glowing, so contemplative,
Hath set, and sanctified to look on man.
And lo! the smoke of evening sacrifice
Ascends from out the tabernacle. Heaven
Accept the expiation, and forgive
This day's offences!—Ha! the wonted strain,
Precursor of his coming!—Whence can this—
It seems to flow from some unearthly hand—

Enter HADAD.

Had.   Does beauteous Tamar view, in this clear fount,
Herself, or heaven?
Tam.   Nay, Hadad, tell me whence
Those sad, mysterious sounds.
Had.   What sounds, dear Princess?
Tam.   Surely, thou know'st; and now I almost think
Some spiritual creature waits on thee.
Had.   I heard no sounds, but such as evening sends
Up from the city to these quiet shades;
A blended murmur sweetly harmonizing
With flowing fountains, feather'd minstrelsy,
And voices from the hills.
Tam.   The sounds I mean,
Floated like mournful music round my head,
From unseen fingers.
Had.   When?
Tam.   Now, as thou camest.
Had.   'T is but thy fancy, wrought
To ecstasy; or else thy grandsire's harp
Resounding from its tower at eventide.
I've lingered to enjoy its solemn tones,
Till the broad moon, that rose o'er Olivet,
Stood listening in the zenith; yea, have deem'd
Viols and heavenly voices answer'd him.
Tam.   But these—
Had.   Were we in Syria, I might say
The Naiad of the fount, or some sweet Nymph,
The goddess of these shades, rejoiced in thee,
And gave thee salutations; but I fear
Judah would call me infidel to Moses.
Tam.   How like my fancy! When these strains precede
Thy steps, as oft they do, I love to think
Some gentle being who delights in us
Is hovering near, and warns me of thy coming;
But they are dirge-like.
Had.   Youthful fantasy,
Attuned to sadness, makes them seem so, lady.
So evening's charming voices, welcomed ever,
As signs of rest and peace;—the watchman's call,
The closing gates, the Levite's mellow trump
Announcing the returning moon, the pipe
Of swains, the bleat, the bark, the housing-bell,
Send melancholy to a drooping soul.
Tam.   But how delicious are the pensive dreams
That steal upon the fancy at their call!

Had.   Delicious to behold the world at rest.
Meek labor wipes his brow, and intermits
The curse, to clasp the younglings of his cot ;
Herdsmen, and shepherds, fold their flocks—and hark !
What merry strains they send from Olivet !
The jar of life is still ; the city speaks
In gentle murmurs ; voices chime with lutes
Waked in the streets and gardens ; loving pairs
Eye the red west in one another's arms ;
And nature, breathing dew and fragrance, yields
A glimpse of happiness, which He, who form'd
Earth and the stars, had power to make eternal.
    Tam.   Ah ! Hadad, mean'st thou to reproach the Friend
Who gave so much, because he gave not all ?
    Had.   Perfect benevolence, methinks, had will'd
Unceasing happiness, and peace, and joy ;
Fill'd the whole universe of human hearts
With pleasure, like a flowing spring of life.
    Tam.   Our Prophet teaches so, till man rebell'd.
    Had.   Mighty rebellion ! Had he 'leaguer'd Heaven
With beings powerful, numberless, and dreadful,
Strong as the enginery that rocks the world
When all its pillars tremble ; mix'd the fires
Of onset with annihilating bolts
Defensive volleyed from the throne ; this, this
Had been rebellion worthy of the name,
Worthy of punishment.   But what did man ?
Tasted an apple ! and the fragile scene,
Eden, and innocence, and human bliss,
The nectar-flowing streams, life-giving fruits,
Celestial shades, and amaranthine flowers,
Vanish ; and sorrow, toil, and pain, and death,
Cleave to him by an everlasting curse.
    Tam.   Ah ! talk not thus.
    Had.   Is this benevolence ?—
Nay, loveliest, these things sometimes trouble me ;
For I was tutor'd in a brighter faith.
Our Syrians deem each lucid fount, and stream,
Forest, and mountain, glade, and bosky dell,
Peopled with kind divinities, the friends
Of man, a spiritual race allied
To him by many sympathies, who seek
His happiness, inspire him with gay thoughts,
Cool with their waves, and fan him with their airs
O'er them, the Spirit of the Universe,
Or Soul of Nature, circumfuses all

Far other once was Rosalie;
  Her smile was glad; her voice,
Like music o'er a summer sea,
  Said to the heart—rejoice.

O'er her pure thoughts did sorrow fling
  Perchance a shade, 't would pass,
Lightly as glides the breath of Spring
  Along the bending grass.

A sailor's bride 't was hers to be :—
  Wo to the faithless main!
Nine summers since he went to sea,
  And ne'er returned again.

But long, where all is wrecked beside,
  And every joy is chased,
Long, long will lingering Hope abide
  Amid the dreary waste!

Nine years—though all have given him o'er,
  Her spirit doth not fail;
And still she waits along the shore
  The never coming sail.

On that high rock, abrupt and bare,
  Ever she sits, as now;
The dews have damped her flowing hair,
  The sun has scorched her brow.

And every far-off sail she sees,
  And every passing cloud,
Or white-winged sea-bird, on the breeze,
  She calls to it aloud.

The sea-bird answers to her cry;
  The cloud, the sail float on.—
The hoarse wave mocks her misery,
  Yet is her hope not gone :—

It cannot go :—with that to part,
  So long, so fondly nursed,
So mingled with her faithful heart,
  That heart itself would burst.

When falling dews the clover steep,
  And birds are in their nest,
And flower-buds folded up to sleep,
  And ploughmen gone to rest,

Down the rude track her feet have worn,
  —There scarce the goat may go ;—
Poor Rosalie, with look forlorn,
  Is seen descending slow.

But when the gray morn tints the sky,
  And lights that lofty peak,—
With a strange lustre in her eye,
  A fever in her cheek,

Again she goes, untired, to sit
  And watch, the live-long day ;
Nor till the star of eve is lit,
  E'er turns her steps away.

Hidden, and deep, and never dry,—
  Or flowing, or at rest,
A living spring of hope doth lie
  In every human breast.

All else may fail, that soothes the heart,—
  All, save that fount alone ;
With that and life at once we part,
  For life and hope are one.

THE TAMED EAGLE.

He sat upon his humble perch, nor flew
    At my approach ;
    But as I nearer drew,
Looked on me, as I fancied, with reproach,
    And sadness too :

And something still his native pride proclaim'd,
    Despite his wo ;
    Which, when I marked,—ashamed
To see a noble creature brought so low,
    My heart exclaim'd,

Where is the fire that lit thy fearless eye,
  Child of the storm,
  When from thy home on high,
Yon craggy-breasted rock, I saw thy form
  Cleaving the sky ?

It grieveth me to see thy spirit tamed ;
  Gone out the light
  That in thine eye-ball flamed,
When to the midday sun thy steady flight
  Was proudly aimed!

Like the young dove forsaken, is the look
  Of thy sad eye,
  Who in some lonely nook,
Mourneth upon the willow bough her destiny,
  Beside the brook.

While somewhat sterner in thy downward gaze
  Doth seem to lower,
  And deep disdain betrays,
As if thou cursed man's poorly acted power,
  And scorned his praise.

Oh, let not me insult thy fallen dignity,
  Poor injured bird,
  Gazing with vulgar eye
Upon thy ruin ;—for my heart is stirr'd
  To hear thy cry ;

And answereth to thee, as I turn to go,
  It is a stain
  On man !—Thus, even thus low
Be brought the wretch, who could for sordid gain,
  Work thee such wo !

R. H. WILDE,

Or Georgia. We are not acquainted with the writer, except by a few articles in verse, which have appeared in the newspapers.

A FRAGMENT.

" 'T is many moons ago—a long—long time
Since first upon this shore a white man trod ;
From the great water to the mountain clime
This was our home ;—'t was given us by the God
That gave ye yours.—Love ye your native sod ?
So did our fathers too—for they were men !
They fought to guard it, for their hearts were brave,
And long they fought—we were a people then ;
This was our country—it is now our grave—
Would I had never lived, or died the land to save.

When first ye came, your numbers were but few,
Our nation many as the leaves or sand :
Hungry and tired ye were—we pitied you—
We called you brothers—took you by the hand—
But soon we found ye came to rob the land :
We quarrell'd—and your countrymen we slew,
Till one alone of all, remain'd behind,
Among the false he only had been true,
And much we loved this man of single mind,
And ever while he lived, to him were kind.

He loved us too, and taught us many things,
And much we strove the stranger's heart to glad ;
But to its kindred still the spirit clings,
And therefore was his soul for ever sad ;
Nor other wish or joy the lone one had,
Save on the solitary shore to roam,
Or sit and gaze for hours upon the deep,
That roll'd between him and his native home ;
And when he thought none mark'd him, he would weep,
Or sing this song of wo which still our maidens keep.

" My life is like the summer rose
That opens to the morning sky,
And ere the shades of evening close,
Is scatter'd on the ground—to die !
Yet on that rose's humble bed
The softest dews of night are shed,
As though she wept such waste to see,—
But none shall drop a tear for me !

My life is like the autumn leaf
That trembles in the moon's pale ray,
Its hold is frail—its date is brief,
Restless—and soon to pass away !
Yet, when that leaf shall fall and fade,
The parent tree will mourn its shade,
The wind bewail the leafless tree,
But none shall breathe one sigh for me !

My life is like the track of feet
Left upon Tampa's desert strand ;
Soon as the rising tide shall beat,
Their marks shall vanish from the sand ;
Yet, as if grieving to efface
All vestige of the human race,
On that lone shore loud moans the sea,
But none shall thus lament for me ! "

SAMUEL BARTLETT PARRIS

Was the son of the Rev. Martin Parris of Mansfield, and
was born at Kingston, Massachusetts, January 30th, 1806.
He received his early education from his father, and exhibited
a most extraordinary and precocious aptitude for learning. He
began the study of languages at the age of six. At ten years
of age he was examined for admission to college, and the
professors held him in their arms while he construed Virgil,
Cicero, and the Greek Testament. He was pronounced fit
for admission, but on account of his youth he returned home
and did not enter the university for two years. He was graduated at the age of fifteen, and entered upon the study of
medicine the year after. He received a medical degree in
1825, and began his practice at Attleborough in Massachusetts. He died September 21st, 1827, at the age of 21. A
collection of his writings in verse and prose was published
a few months since.

ON A SPRIG OF JUNIPER,

FROM THE TOMB OF WASHINGTON, PRESENTED TO THE AUTHOR.

THE meadow may boast of its thousand dyes,
For their varied splendors are far before thee ;
   But still more fair in the patriot's eyes
Is the humblest branch from the trunk that bore thee ;
For the place where it grows is a sacred spot,
With remembrance of high achievements fraught.

   Thou didst not thrive on the blood of the slave,
Whom the reeking sword of oppression slaughter'd ;
   But the grateful tears of the good and brave,
With a purer stream thy roots have water'd—
And green didst thou grow o'er the hero's bed,
When the tears of his *patriot son**** were shed.

   Say, where wert thou half an age ago,
When terrors were thronging around our nation—
   Where our land, by the word of its haughty foe,
Was mark'd with the sentence of desolation—
When the banner of freedom was wide unfurl'd
On the natal day of this western world—

   When our fathers spared no pain nor toil,
To purchase the blessing for their descendants,
   And seal'd with their blood on their native soil
Their claim to the glory of Independence—
When *Life, Wealth, Honor*, were all at stake
That the holy cause they would not forsake.

   Perhaps thou wast by the side of thy sire,
Whose branch to the breeze had for ages trembled,
   Where gather'd around the council-fire
The chiefs of the tawny tribes assembled,—
Or it might have shaded the hunter's track
On the lonely banks of the Potomac.

   And long on the place of the hero's sleep
May flourish the trunk, whence thou wert taken,
   But a grateful nation his name shall keep,

---

*This was written soon after La Fayette visited the tomb of Washington.

When lifeless and bare, of its leaves forsaken,
The trunk and the branch to the earth are cast
Before the might of the rushing blast.

For in distant ages the day shall come,
When the vengeance of time its pride shall humble—
And the arch of the proud mausoleum
O'er the mouldering urn of the dead shall crumble—
But till the last moment of time hath run
Shall live the remembrance of Washington.

Ah! soon must branches like thine be spread
O'er another's tomb—and o'er yet another's—
For now from the sorrows of earth have fled,
As with one accord, two patriot brothers,*
Whom heaven in mercy hath given to see
The day of their nation's Jubilee.

O! sadly, in tears sunk down, that day,
The sun, in the distant west declining—
But still in a holier splendor they
With their latest beams on earth were shining,
When they were call'd from earth to remove,
And shine in the realms of the blest above.

WILLIAM CUTTER,

Of Portland. The following piece is from the Legendary.

THE VALLEY OF SILENCE.

Has thy foot ever trod that silent dell ?—
'T is a place for the voiceless thought to swell,
And the eloquent song to go up unspoken,
Like the incense of flowers whose urns are broken;
And the unveil'd heart may look in and see,
In that deep, strange silence, its motions free,
And learn how the pure in spirit feel
That unseen Presence to which they kneel.

*Adams and Jefferson.

No sound goes up from the quivering trees,
When they spread their arms to the welcome breeze,
They wave in the zephyr, they bow to the blast,
But they breathe not a word of the power that pass'd ;
And their leaves come down on the turf and the stream,
With as noiseless a fall as the step of a dream ;
And the breath that is bending the grass and the flowers
Moves o'er them as lightly as evening hours.

The merry bird lights down on that dell,
And hushing his breath, lest the song should swell,
Sits with folded wing, in the balmy shade,
Like a musical thought in the soul unsaid ;
And they of strong pinion and loftier flight
Pass over that valley, like clouds in the night—
They move not a wing in that solemn sky,
But sail in a reverent silence by.

The deer in his flight has pass'd that way,
And felt the deep spell's mysterious sway—
He hears not the rush of the path he cleaves,
Nor his bounding step on the trampled leaves.
The hare goes up on that sunny hill—
And the footsteps of morning are not more still.
And the wild, and the fierce, and the mighty are there—
Unheard in the hush of that slumbering air.

The stream rolls down in that valley serene,
Content in its beautiful flow to be seen ;
And its fresh, flowery banks, and its pebbly bed
Were never yet told of its fountain-head.
And it still rushes on—but they ask not why ;
With its smile of light it is hurrying by ;
Still gliding or leaping, unwhisper'd, unsung,
Like the flow of bright fancies it flashes along.

The wind sweeps by, and the leaves are stirr'd,
But never a whisper or sigh is heard ;
And when its strong rush laid low the oak,
Not a murmur the eloquent stillness broke ;
And the gay young echoes, those mockers that lie
In the dark mountain sides, make no reply ;
But hush'd in their caves, they are listening still
For the songs of that valley to burst o'er the hill.

CHARLES C. BEAMAN.

I love society; I am o'erblest to hear
The mingling voices of a world; mine ear
Drinks in their music with a spiritual taste;
I love companionship on life's gray waste,
And might not live unheard;—yet that still vale—
It had no fearful mystery in its tale—
Its hush was grand, not awful—as if there
The voice of nature were a breathing prayer.
'T was like a holy temple, where the pure
Might join in their hush'd worship, and be sure
No sound of earth could come—a soul kept still,
In faith's unanswering meekness, for Heaven's will—
Its eloquent thoughts sent upward and abroad,
But all its deep, hush'd voices kept for God!

CHARLES C. BEAMAN,

OF Boston.

THE WATER EXCURSION.

A VISION.

THE earth it was gay,
And the air was bland
With the summer ray
Of a sunny land;
And the evening hour
Of soul-witching power,
With her radiant train,
Lit the earth and main;
When a beautiful barque was seen to glide,
Like a fairy sylph on the silver tide;
Not a zephyr breathed in her snow-white sails,
What cared she for the prospering gales?
Full many a rower was plying the oar,
And she was flying away from the shore,
To wander alone on the trackless deep,
While the world was hush'd in a breathless sleep.

All that the hand of taste could do,
Banners floating of every hue,
Flowery wreath and sparkling gem,
Girdled her round from stern to stem;
The fairest of the land was there,
With snowy robe and raven hair,
Bright eyes that beam'd expression's fire,
Beauty, all that hearts desire;
The flower of youthful chivalry,
With the young love's idolatry,
Offer'd homage at the shrine
Of woman's loveliness divine;
While the sweet and blithesome song,
Uprose from the joyous throng;
And the barque moved on in light,
Graceful as the queen of night,
Beautiful isles sprinkled the bay,
Silver'd o'er with the moonbeam's ray;
Verdure-clad isles, where shrubs and flowers,
The foliage of trees and bowers,
With fanciful dwellings woven between,
An air of enchantment breathed o'er the scene;
The beauties of nature blended with art,
Delight the most soothing gave to the heart;
The air around them was freighted with balm;
The harp's soft notes added grace to the charm;
As it broke from the covert of a flowery grove,
With woman's sweet voice—the tones that we love

They passed the island—alone on the sea
Broke the sound of their mirth and minstrelsy;
The barque glided on to the music's swell,
The silvery foam from the oar-blade fell,
When suddenly broke on the ravish'd ear,
Sounds that seem'd borne from a happier sphere;
The oarsmen plied no more their task,
Hush'd was the jest and jocund song;
And one more bold was heard to ask,
To whom do all these notes belong?
No answer came—they look'd and saw
What made them wonder and adore;
Seraphic forms in radiant white,
Sparkling in the moonbeam's light;
Circling round in the ocean's breast,
They lull'd every care to rest;
With golden harps they woke a strain,

No mortal hand can e'er attain,
Then mingling voices thrill'd the frame,
With rapture's most ecstatic flame—
The vision fled—I woke to see
Thy duller scenes—reality !

EVENING THOUGHTS.

How fades the world before me now !
  As lonely here I stand ;
The dews of evening on my brow,
  And silver on the land !

It seems to me a floating speck,
  The fragment of a cloud ;—
Are all my hopes upon that wreck,
  Oblivion soon will shroud ?

Oh no ! I have a hope afar,
  Among those orbs of light ;
It twinkleth yet, the Bethlehem star,
  As on its natal night.

Spring up, my soul ! and catch the ray,
  And nurse it to a flame ;
'T will burn in life's expiring day,
  For ever—and the same.

LOUISA P. SMITH,

Of Providence, (formerly Miss Hickman.)   Her volume of poems was published the present year.

THE HUMA.*

FLY on ! nor touch thy wing, bright bird,
  Too near our shaded earth,

* " A bird peculiar to the east. It is supposed to fly constantly in the air, and never touch the ground "

Or the warbling, now so sweetly heard
    May lose its note of mirth.
Fly on—nor seek a place of rest,
    In the home of " care-worn things,"
'T would dim the light of thy shining crest,
    And thy brightly burnish'd wings,
To dip them where the waters glide
That flow from a troubled earthly tide.

The fields of upper air are thine,
    Thy place where stars shine free,
I would *thy* home, bright one, were mine,
    Above life's stormy sea.
I would never wander—bird, like thee,
    So near this place again,
With wing and spirit once light and free—
    They should wear no more, the chain
With which they are bound and fetter'd here,
For ever struggling for skies more clear.

There are many things like thee, bright bird,
    Hopes as thy plumage gay,
Our air is with them for ever stirr'd,
    But still in air they stay.
And happiness, like thee, fair one!
    Is ever hovering o'er,
But *rests* in a land of brighter sun,
    On a waveless, peaceful shore,
And stoops to lave her weary wings,
Where the fount of " living waters" springs.

RECOLLECTIONS.

I 'VE pleasant thoughts that memory brings, in moments free
    from care,
Of a fairy-like and laughing girl, with roses in her hair;
Her smile was like the star-light of summer's softest skies,
And worlds of joyousness there shone, from out her witching
    eyes.

Her looks were looks of melody, her voice was like the swell
Of sudden music, notes of mirth, that of wild gladness tell;

SONNET.

YE clouds, that in your breasts the tempest bear,
  From whose dark folds the nimble lightnings leap ;
  Tell us, as through the vault of blue ye sweep,
Whence came ye, rolling in your strength, and where
Shadowing the heavens, do you now bend your course ?
  Shipwreck attends, dread messengers, your path—
  The giant forests stoop before your wrath,
And Ocean bends his trident to your force :
Already now your winged bolts of fire
  The skies inflame—your pealing thunders roll,
  And seem the earth to shake, from pole to pole,
Whilst hail and whirlwind mingle with your ire ?
Mortal !—seek not the Eternal to explore,—
We come his errands to fulfil—be silent and adore.

WILLIAM B. TAPPAN,

A NATIVE of Portsmouth, N. H. and now a resident of Philadelphia.   He has published two or three volumes of poetry.

RETROSPECTION.

'T is sweet, in seclusion, to look on the past,
  In life's sober twilight recall the day-dream ;
To mark the smooth sunshine, and skies overcast,
  That chequer'd our course as we moved down the stream.

For O there 's a charm in retracing the morn,
  When the star of our pleasure beam'd brightly awhile,
And the tear that in infancy water'd the thorn,
  By the magic of memory is changed to a smile.

How faint is the touch, no perspective bestowing,
  Nor scenery in nature's true colors array'd ;
How chaste is the landscape, how vividly glowing,
  Where the warm tint of fancy is mellowed by shade!

With cheerfulness then, Retrospection, I 'll greet thee,
   Though the nightshade be twined in thy bouquet of sweets,
In the eve of reflection this bosom will meet thee,
   While to the dear vision of childhood it beats.

And the heart that in confidence seeks its review,
   And finds the calm impress of innocence there,
With rapture anticipates happiness new,
   In hope yet to come, it possesses a share.

If in worlds beatific, affections unite,
   And those once dissever'd are blended in love;
If dreams of the past quicken present delight,
   Retrospection adds bliss to the spotless above.

WHY SHOULD WE SIGH?

WHY should we sigh when Fancy's dream,
   The ray that shone 'mid youthful tears,
Departing, leaves no kindly gleam,
   To cheer the lonely waste of years?
Why should we sigh?—The fairy charm
   That bound each sense in folly's chain
Is broke, and Reason, clear and calm,
   Resumes her holy rights again.

Why should we sigh that earth no more
   Claims the devotion once approved?
That joys endear'd, with us are o'er,
   And gone are those these hearts have loved?
Why should we sigh?—Unfading bliss
   Survives the narrow grasp of time;
And those that asked our tears in this,
   Shall render smiles in yonder clime.

WHEN DEATH SHALL LAY.

WHEN death shall lay this bosom low,
   And every murmur hush to sleep,
When those that give affection now,
   Shall o'er affection's memory weep,

I would not, when life's spark has flown,
  That strangers should receive the sigh ;
I would not, that a hand unknown,
  Should, reckless, close the slumbering eye :

But, on some throbbing breast reclined,
  That beat alone to love and me,
Each parting pang subdued, how kind,
  How peaceful, would my exit be.

I would not, that this lowly head
  Should pillow, cold, on foreign clay ;
I would not, that my grassy bed
  Should be from home and love away :

But, in my native village ground,
  Near kindred dust, these relics laid :
How calm my slumbers, how profound,
  Beneath the old tree's sombre shade.

O COME FROM A WORLD.

O COME from a world, where sorrow and gloom,
    Chastise the allurements of joy ;
A pathway bedimm'd, with no rays to illume,
    Save the meteor that shines to destroy ;
Where the thoughtless have revell'd, when mirth had no charm,
Where the wounded have wept, but still needed the balm.

O come from a world, where the landscape is chill,
    Or deceitfully blossoming fair,
The garden gives promise of bright flowers, still,
    The nightshade luxuriates there ;
That sky, now serene, blushing lovely and clear,
O heed not its beauty, the storm-cloud is near.

O come from a world, where the cup of delight
    Now sparkles and foams at the brim ;
For the laurels that wreath it, reflection shall blight,
    Its lustre, repentance shall dim ;
The lips, that convivial, have pledged thee the bowl,
Shall blanch with confusion when fear rives the soul.

O come from a world, where they that beguile
    Will lead thee to peril and fears;
For the heart that, confiding, hath welcomed its smile,
    Hath found it the prelude to tears:
Come then, there's a path by the reckless untrod;
O come, weary wanderer, it leads to thy GOD.

TO THE NORTH STAR.

BRIGHT Star, while thou thy lonely way
    Pursu'st in yon expanse of blue,
Thy gem-like form and steady ray
    Attract the heedless peasant's view,
And his, whose thoughts to unknown regions stray.

Full oft the wanderer, fortune's child,
    Benighted, sad, and doom'd to roam,
Beholds with joy thy aspect mild,
    That tells of happiness and home,
And guides him onward 'mid the trackless wild.

Oft, too, the sea-boy marks thy beam,
    When ocean sleeps in peaceful calm;
While o'er its breast thy gentle gleam
    Plays wanton, and with sacred charm
Lulls the wrapt soul in fancy's pleasing dream.

And oft, sweet Star, at even-tide,
    When all around is hush'd to rest,
My thoughts ascend, and pensive glide
    To distant climes and regions blest,
Where wo-worn care and grief would gladly hide.

And fancy whispers in mine ear,
    That those who once were here beloved,
To friendship and affection dear,
    Now from this fleeting scene removed,
Repose, bright Star, in thy ethereal sphere.

SAMUEL H. JENKS

WAS born in Boston in 1789. He was engaged in the mercantile profession for some years, but in 1821 he became editor and proprietor of the Nantucket Inquirer. During part of the year 1824, he conducted a paper in New York, called The National Union, and supporting the claims of Mr Crawford for the Presidency. He relinquished the Nantucket Inquirer in 1827, and has since been the editor of the Boston Evening Bulletin. He is known as a correct and intelligent writer. His lighter prose compositions have obtained him a well deserved reputation as a humorist.

O! MAY WE NOT WEEP?

" Weep not for those whom the veil of the tomb."—MOORE.

O! MAY we not weep for the loved who have fled
    From our presence on earth, though their home be in heaven;
And may not our tears at the grave of the dead,
    When flowing in silence and hope, be forgiven?
Shall death seize unheeded the friends of our bosom,
    The fairest and mildest in life's lovely bloom;
And throw them, unmourn'd, like the funeral blossom,
    To fade and corrode in the damps of the tomb?
O! may we not sorrow for those who have fled
    From our presence on earth, though their home be in heaven;
And may not our tears at the grave of the dead,
    When flowing in silence and hope, be forgiven?

Unmoved shall we wake from the dreams we enjoy'd,
    And find all our visions by death rudely torn?
Our peace by the sweeping blast rent and destroy'd—
    Like brutes shall we brook, or like man shall we mourn?
For, though quietly seal'd in the sepulchre's slumber,
    The forms of our valued companions repose;
E'en though with the spirits of bliss THEY may number,
    Yet may we not weep for OUR wasteness and woes?

Then say not, ye piously stern, that our grief
   Should be quench'd in oblivion, or frigidly borne :—
When the mildews of fate blight the young tender leaf,
   'T is NATURE'S COMMAND, and MAN'S DUTY, to mourn.

THE PATRIOT'S GRAVE.

On the spot where my war-couch stood,
   Where my spring-time of fame was pass'd,
Where the patriot's prayer, and the hero's blood
   Pour'd fervently and fast—

Where the spirit of glory stole
   O'er my earliest and brightest dream,
With the trumpet's blast and the drum's rude roll,
   And the falchion's dazzling gleam—

Lay me down on that hallow'd spot—
   Long in peace I may there remain ;
For the foeman's standard now waveth not
   On yonder battle-plain.

When this weary and struggling soul
   From its bondage of clay hath fled,
Make my humble grave on yon grassy knoll,
   'T is a meet and quiet bed !

On its brow there 's a blasted oak,
   Like its withering branch am I ;
Yet though ravens there may be heard to croak,
   Heaven's softest breeze shall sigh :—

And, my children, a stream glides there,
   Gently laving its verdant base ;—
Of perennial bliss 't is an emblem fair—
   It shall mark my resting place !

Once the proud and the gallant tread
   Of the warrior press'd that mound ;
But his comrades soon o'er the prostrate dead
   May pour the farewell round.

And when cometh my final strife,
    Let me be with my comforter,
That the last fond gaze of expiring life
    Be consecrate to her.

Then if far, far beyond the grave,
    Be the memory's employment free,
It shall cherish the look that affection gave,
    In all eternity!

O! 'tis sweet, when my task is done,
    Thus to witness my banner furl'd :—
When the storm is spent, so the setting sun
    Smiles on a parting world!

POWERS OF RHYME.

PEOPLE do n't commonly discern
The difference 'twixt POETRY and RHYME:
The former can be made to *thrill* and *burn,*
By master geniuses—and yet
No two words shall together *chime.*
E'en *Prose,* so called, may be po-et-
I-cal, and ring upon the ear
Harmoniously, without a grain of *jingle ;*
While *Rhyme,* all sound, with oftentimes
No symptom of idea,
Clinking, like handfuls of new dimes,
Causes one's very brain to tingle.

Some folks, *new words* will manufacture,
That have no sense nor meaning :—
They would denominate a crack *a cracture,*
Or, to make rhyme, call obloquy *obscening!*

The name of my French friend, *Piemont,*
(A name that 's smooth enough in song,)
Has often been distorted into *Pie*-mont—
A *hill of pies!*—just to make rhyme on 't!

This brings me to the tale that I was going
To tell, of Toby Grizzle, a rough clown
Who grew up *in the country*—for in *town*
The folks are polish'd, and extremely *knowing.*

Toby had never seen great towns and cities,
Where houses grow together by the acre;
To die then, and see only what his Maker
Had done in lands, and woods, and cattle—
Thought Toby, "'t were a thousand pities;
So, down to Boston, in my cart I'll rattle."

So *down* he went,
And turn'd *up* at the *Indian Queen;*
Amazement and astonishment—
At what he saw,
And what was *to be* seen,
Hung heavily upon his under-jaw.
This made him hungry, and he bought
A yard of gingerbread to stay his yearnings,
And after various crooks and turnings
He got into the *parlor*, as he thought;
But, reader, 't was the *kitchen*—
So *droll* was everything—and so *bewitching.*

The cook, of his *poetic powers* was boasting;
Betwixt whom and the scullion there arose
A disputation, whether rhyme or prose
Most clear ideas convey'd—

———Beef was there roasting
By dint of a huge *jack*—custom *antique!*
"Now," quoth the cook, "I'll speak
In *verse* to this fat lout, and ascertain
Whether my rhymes be not, *to all* men, *plain.*"

Says he to Toby, "May I be so bold
As to inquire how many hours have roll'd
Since you into these regions stroll'd?"
Quoth Toby, casting up his eager looks
To where the giddy jack-wheel whirl'd—
"Odsbludikins, and snaggers! rat it, and adzooks
Your *clock* goes faster than aunt Katy's;
And I'll be skinn'd and darn'd, for all the world,
If I can see to tell what time o' day 't is."

ANTHONY BLEECKER.

ANTHONY BLEECKER was descended from an old New York family, and was born in that state not long after the Declaration of Independence. He was educated after the peace in the city of New York, and completed his studies at Columbia College, where he studied about the same time with the late Governor De Witt Clinton, Vice President Tompkins, the Rev. Dr Mason, and other distinguished men, whose friendship he preserved throughout life. His tastes and habits were purely literary, but the state of society in the country at that time, afforded no encouragement for authorship, and the circumstances of his family compelled him to embrace some profession. He therefore devoted himself, though reluctantly, to the study and practice of the Law. He never succeeded as an advocate, for he was deficient in the talent of popular speaking, and an unconquerable diffidence hindered him from overcoming or overlooking this defect. He, however, became highly respected in his profession, for practical good sense, accurate and useful learning, and stainless honor and integrity. He settled in the City of New York, where his life flowed on equably in the quiet "chamber business" of the law, and particularly the equity practice, interspersed with various literary pursuits, until his fiftieth year, when, after a short illness, he died in the spring of 1827. Few men have led a more blameless and honorable life. Though a private citizen, without fortune, or political distinction, his death was widely felt as a public loss. His literary career corresponded to the general character of his mind. He never formally appeared before the public as an author, yet for thirty years, the newspapers and periodical literature of New York and Philadelphia, were constantly indebted to his lively fancy and good taste. Some of the most esteemed publications of the day owed much of their attraction to his aid, suggestion, or correction—the extent of which was known only to his immediate circle of friends. His poetry is all occasional, and may be found scattered through various literary journals, from 1800 to 1825.

ON REVISITING THE COTTAGE OF ROSA IN EARLY SPRING, AFTER A LONG ABSENCE.

SEVEN summers have flown, and once more do I see
  The fields and the groves I deserted so long:
Scarce a bud yet appears on the winter-beat tree,
  Nor a bird yet enlivens the sky with a song.

For though spring has returned, yet the chilly wind blows,
  And the violets and daisies still hide in the ground;
But one dear little flower, one beautiful Rose,
  Here blooms and here blushes the seasons all round.

Thou pride of the plain, little queen of the grove,
  Still fresh is thy foliage and sweet thy perfume,
And still the bright object of Paridel's love,
  As when thy first buds were beginning to bloom.

And though fate has decreed that he must not aspire
  This blossom divine on his bosom to wear,
Yet still must he cherish the tender desire,
  And make thee forever the theme of his prayer.

Blow gently, ye zephyrs, be genial, ye showers,
  Bright and warm be the sky o'er thy dear native vale,
And may no bitter blast ever ravage the bowers
  That guard thy fair frame from the merciless gale.

And when the short season of blooming shall end,
  Which fate to the children of nature hath given,
May some cherub of beauty, to snatch thee, descend,
  And bear thee to bloom in the gardens of heaven.

TRENTON FALLS, NEAR UTICA.

Ye hills, who have for ages stood
Sublimely in your solitude,

ANTHONY BLEECKER.

Listening the wild water's roar,
As thundering down, from steep to steep,
Along your wave-worn sides they sweep,
  Dashing their foam from shore to shore.

Wild birds, that loved the deep recess,
Fell beast that roved the wilderness,
  And savage men once hover'd round :
But startled at your bellowing waves,
Your frowning cliffs, and echoing caves,
  Affrighted fled the enchanted ground.

How changed the scene !—your lofty trees,
Which bent but to the mountain breeze,
  Have sunk beneath the woodman's blade ;
New sun-light through your forest pours,
Paths wind along your sides and shores,
  And footsteps all your haunts invade.

Now boor, and beau, and lady fair,
In gay costume each day repair,
  Where thy proud rocks exposed stand,
While echo, from her old retreats,
With babbling tongue strange words repeats,
  From babblers on your stony strand.

And see—the torrent's rocky floor,
With names and dates all scribbled o'er,
  Vile blurs on nature's heraldry ;
O bid your river in its race,
These mean memorials soon efface,
  And keep your own proud album free.

Languid thy tides, and quell'd thy powers,
But soon Autumnus with his showers,
  Shall all thy wasted strength restore ;
Then will these ramblers down thy steep,
With terror pale their distance keep,
  Nor dare to touch thy trembling shore.

But spare, Oh ! river, in thy rage,
One name upon thy stony page ;
  'Tis hers—the fairest of the fair ;
And when she comes these scenes to scan,
Then tell her, Echo, if you can,
  His humble name who wrote it there.

JUNGFRAU SPAIGER'S APOSTROPHE TO HER CAT.

A late London paper mentions that the celebrated Manheim Telescope, the master-piece of the famous Spaiger, a Hungarian optician, was recently destroyed in a singular manner. A servant of the Observatory having taken out the glasses to clean them, put them in again, without observing that a cat had crept into the tube. At night, the animal being alarmed at the strong powers of the Lunar rays, endeavored to escape; but the effort threw down the instrument, which, falling to the ground from the top of a tower, was broken to pieces. The writer, presuming that the cat was killed by the fall, imagines the daughter of the astronomer as breaking forth in the following Lament.

What whisker'd ghost, at this mild moonlight hour,
Invites my steps, and points to yonder tower?
'Tis Puss, my darling Puss; all bleeding! pale!
Gash'd are her ears, and scotch'd her lengthy tail.
Oh, tell thy tale, and I will lend an ear—
Then sweep to my revenge, Grimalkin, dear.
Oh say, did boys, or other cruel hounds,
Conspire thy death, and give those ghastly wounds?

Or, tell me Puss, 'tis what I dread the most,
Did some Kilkenny cat make thee a ghost?
Canst thou not speak? Ah then I'll seek the cause;
What see I here? the bloody prints of paws;
And oh, chaste stars! what broken limbs appear,
Here lie thy legs; the Telescope's lie here.
The Telescope o'erturn'd;—too plain I see
The cause, the cause of thy cat-astrophe.

Was it for this, my sire on topmost tower,
Gazed at the stars till midnight's dewy hour,
Outwatch'd the Bear, and saw Orion rise,
While Hesper lent her light to other skies?
Was it for this, he gave such strict command,
To clean the glasses with a careful hand,
And then to search the tube with nicest care,
To see nor cat, nor kit, were nestling there;
Lest, like old Sidrophel, star-gazing wight,
Who wisely made a comet of a kite,
My cat, perhaps, 'twixt Mercury and Mars,
Had help'd to swell the cat-alogue of stars.

O! say what led thee to that giddy height,
Thou Queen of cats! that witching time of night;

Was it cat-optrics fired thy feline heart,
And didst thou dare to act the sage's part,
And peeping at the moon, while stretch'd at ease,
Discover with delight 'twas all green cheese ?
Or didst thou wish to take a near survey,
Of that delicious stream, the milky-way,
And while the dog-star in the welkin raves,
To take a leap, and lap its cream-clad waves ?

Ah me ! what terrors through thy frame were spread,
When Luna's rays refracted on thy head,
And fill'd thy gooseberry eyes with beams so thick,
No wonder thou becam'st a lunatic ;
Lost all reflection ; scarce retain'd a hope,
Immured in a reflecting telescope.
The concave mirror first thy fury bore,
The convex lens but vexed thee the more :
Then all thy rage was to a focus brought ;
To tilt the tube was now thy only thought ;

Flounce—bounce :—it tumbles from the turret wall,
Breaking itself, but breaking not thy fall !
Oh direful fall !—But why indulge this wo ?
Can cat-aracts of tears avail thee now ?
No ; thou art bound to Hecate's wizzard shore,
Where Whittington's famed cat has gone before ;
And to appease thy ghost my task shall be,
To consecrate a cat-acomb to thee.

Embalm'd, dear shade, with true Egyptian care,
Across the Atlantic wave thy corpse I'll bear,
And where old Catskill props the western sky,
The fur-clad relics of my cat shall lie.
There shall thy favorite herbs and plants be found,
The cat-mint there shall shed its sweets around ;
The savory mushroom from the sod shall start,
And to the breeze its catsup sweets impart.
While the tall cat-tail, on the reedy shore,
Shall hang his head, and thy sad fate deplore.

One warbler of the grove will ne'er forget
To pay to thee his grateful, tuneful debt ;
The cat-bird, perch'd on the catalpa tree,
Shall squall that note he learnt, poor puss, from thee,

While from the mount, the valley, and the plain,
The weeping pole-cat shall repeat the strain.

EPITAPH OF MORNAI DU PLESSIS,
IMITATED FROM THE LATIN OF GROTIUS.

Nobility of soul, by nature given,
  Nobler than blood of proud ancestral line ;
Skill in the laws of men, and truths of Heaven,
  Maturest counsel ; eloquence divine,
With Mornai here repose ;—his tomb their hallow'd shrine.

G. A. GAMAGE,

A NATIVE of Massachusetts. He has been the editor of
several papers in this state, and New York. His poetry has
appeared under the signature of Montgarnier.

MY EARLY DAY.

" My early day, what joys were thine ! "
  And yet thou hadst some sorrows too ;
A varied wreath they join'd to twine,
  And 'midst it hope her blossoms threw—
Borne on the breeze, her rosy kiss
  Bade pleasure sojourn there,
Love came to tune her lute of bliss,
  And requiems sung to care.

Dear days of peace ! ah, whither fled ?
  O'er my young bower ye did but hover,
Then, like the dove, your pinions spread,
  And sought your home—the skies, forever !
Your morning gales my path beguiled,
  Nor whisper'd they should die so soon ;
Nor each bright bud that round it smiled,
  Dream of departing ere 't was noon.

But those are hush'd, and these are gone,
  And sadness rules the blighted scene;
I wander downcast and alone,
  Scarce mindful they have ever been!
So chill, time's marble foot hath pass'd
  Through childhood's dimpled vale,
No herb can bloom, no verdure last,
  To cheer life's evening pale.

Sweet hours! with golden pastimes fraught,
  On you I turn my streaming eye
And think—and in that racking thought,
  My heart—my gushing heart would die.
Ye conjure up each once-loved form,
  Each well-remember'd voice awaken—
Then show me how they met the storm,
  And sunk, on joy's bright shore forsaken.

Ne'er shall they mount with me again,
  I loved so well—yon sunny steep;
One stroke hath dash'd our hands in twain,
  And 'neath its broomwood hedge they sleep.
His pang descends not to their bed,
  Who sickens round the scene,
To know life's infant flowers are dead,
  Its riper thorns yet green.

On wing more swift than morning lark,
  My faded years unloved are borne;—
Where wilt thou land me, oh my bark,
  If not to youth's dear port we turn?
Must man o'erpass the beckoning vale,
  And all its winning sweets renounce?—
Alas! he spreads no second sail,
  He freights his bark but once!

Oh tell me, "step-dame nature," tell,
  Where shall thy wayward child abide,
On what far strand his spirit dwell,
  When life has spent its struggling tide?
Shall hope no more her taper mourn,
  Quench'd in the tear that sorrow sends;
Nor from the feast misfortune spurn
  The wishful wretch that o'er it bends?

No more shall folly's yellow wing
    O'er pleasure's path shed sickly dews?
Nor youth's delightful day of spring
    'Mid grief's dim cloud its lustre lose?
Say—ne'er shall wealth's gay-spangled plume
    Deceive, as when it erst was mine?
Nor love turn shuddering from the tomb;
    Nor joy at her short reign repine?

And when the grave its grassy veil
    Between these eyes and life shall spread,
Shall memory blight the primrose pale,
    That kindly strives to shade my bed?
Or shall the form that slumbers there,
    No more of pain nor death endure?
Oh, pour thine answer on my ear—
    "I've told thee—told thee, child—NO MORE!"

ALBERT G. GREENE,

OF Providence, the editor of the Rhode Island American.
He has lately published a poem delivered before the Philer-
menian Society, at Providence, from which we extract the
following.

LINES.

My object was to describe in some slight degree, the effects of that propensity of
the mind to be discontent with the real allotment of its situation, which is contin-
ually prompting it to dream of, and to seek for, more perfect fruition of the real
joys of life, or of the imaginary ones of its waking dreams; and to show, that
this feeling has been the cause of many proud and noble achievements; the spring
of many of the highest and most daring efforts of the imagination; and what is
of far more importance, the source of religious hope and faith, so far as these
are not founded on Revelation itself.   *Preface of the Author.*

How many wearied spirits have forgot
The pain and sorrow of their earthly lot,
Through Fancy's bright creations, tracing o'er
Some path of light, by Genius trod before;
While o'er the lyre, some gifted minstrel flings
A master's hand to wake its living strings,
Whose notes a bright and cheering spell can throw
Around the spirit in its hour of wo;
Can bid long vanish'd hope to life return,

And teach e'en rankling hate less deep to burn;
Until the latent virtue wakes, within
The heart long burden'd with accusing sin;
O'er its crush'd pride a healing influence pour,
And call up feelings never known before;
And come, with power assuasive of its pain;
Like Jubal's music o'er the soul of Cain.
   Though mazed in error, and defiled by sin,
The human soul still bears a light within,
Unquench'd, unquenchable, of heavenly birth,
Which, when refined from all the dross of earth,
Will not less brightly shine, than that, which now
Sheds glory round the burning seraph's brow.
And was this spark, from heaven's own altar caught,
Shrined in the human spirit then, for nought?
It is not so:—far be the thought profane;—
God never gave so rich a gift in vain.
'Tis this which yields all true poetic fire;
Which gives its soul of music to the lyre:
And, when from raptured thought, its numbers swell,
Makes its deep tones a mystery and a spell.
The gifted bard, to faith's extatic gaze,
Her shadowy worlds with brighter forms arrays;
Prompts each fond hope, for happier scenes, to rise
Beyond this earth and all its transient ties,
In scenes of more enduring joy to live,
Than all its transient wealth and pomp can give.
For this, how rich the bright returns, which pour
On the rapt bard from faith's unbounded store;
She throws a deeper spell around his dreams,
And gives his thrilling song its noblest themes.
Though oft the Bard's high gift may be misused;
And faith deceived, insulted and abused;
That light within the soul, though misemploy'd,
May long be dimm'd, but cannot be destroy'd;
For higher good, it still will prompt desire;
Fix'd in its laws, as earth's material fire;
Which, though on every side extends its rays,
Still *upward* ever points the unchanging blaze.
   Proud are the treasures of enduring worth
The sons of Genius have bequeathed to earth;
Rich are the themes which many a teeming mind,
Freed from its earthly cares, hath left behind.
But still of deeper power, and brighter far
Than all these trophies, glorious as they are,
Than all the proudest offerings, ever placed
By art and genius on the shrine of taste;

Have been those high conceptions, deep and vast,
Which, unembodied, from the soul have past;
Have left below no memory and no trace,
And found on earth, no fix'd abiding place ;
Untold, unwritten, unimpress'd on aught
Which can transmit or hold embodied thought,
Have lighted up some gifted spirit's way,
And with that spirit's hour, have pass'd away ;
The fleeting glories of whose vanish'd dream
Have gone, like sunlight o'er a shadow'd stream.
    Thus will the soul for ever seek relief,
In fancy's visions, from the pangs of grief ;
When worn with pain, with wasting sorrow tried,
And wounded hope and lacerated pride.—
This fix'd, unconquer'd impulse still is found
In every spot to earth's remotest bound.
No earthly good its deep desires can fill,
No earthly power its high aspirings still.
It seeks communion with some higher power,
On which to call in sorrow's boding hour.—
For this, the famed, the noble and the brave
Have, trembling, sought the Hermit's lonely cave :
For this, hath guilt unholy aid implored ;
Her charms awoke, her incantations pour'd ;—
The strong have quail'd, the mighty thrill'd with fear
At the dim visions of the aged Seer :—
For this, the blood of sacrifice hath flow'd,
The incense burn'd, the votive altar glow'd :
From this, arose the spirit-stirring deeds,
The deep-toned song, the strange, unearthly creeds,
The wild, the dark, the fearful and sublime,
That fill the annals of the olden time.
    When mild refinement first begins to pour
Her faintest rays o'er some benighted shore,
E'en then, within the rude untutor'd breast,
Will thoughts arise which cannot be repress'd.
Impatient, then, it strives to rend away
The shadowy veil which shrouds its future way ;
And at each step, its aspirations rise
For brighter scenes and higher destinies ;
And hopes are felt, unwearied and intense,
For scenes of joy beyond the bounds of sense ;
Till led by these, the long excited mind
Is wrapt in visions, dim and undefined ;
Till from the scenes of many a cherish'd dream,
It rears some wild and visionary scheme ;

To which, at length, the wearied mind adheres,
To calm its doubts and soothe its varied fears.
Then promised joys will haunt the mental view;
And fancy dream, till faith believes them true;
Whose power, in bright perspective, then reveals
Her blissful bowers and fair elysian fields;
Some gorgeous paradise of future rest,
Some verdant, cloudless island of the blest;
Where the freed soul will find its destined meed
For high endurance, or for dauntless deed;
For which the heart, in full confiding trust,
Will smile at fate, and calmly dare its worst;
The full fruition of those joys to gain,
For which, on earth, it pines and strives in vain;
Can spurn at savage torture, and can brave
The shafts of death, the darkness of the grave.
   Such was the faith, whose all absorbing sway
Was deeply felt in Europe's early day;
When by the watchfires of the battle plain,
The Runic bard pour'd forth his thrilling strain;
And roused the bosoms of the warrior throng,
With the wild themes of Scandinavian song:—
Told, that whene'er their closing battle cry
O'er the red field rose pealing to the sky,
From the dark regions of the stormy North,
The spirits of their sires were issuing forth;
The stern bold warriors of the olden time,
Whose names still lived in many a martial rhyme;
All, whose proud deeds were consecrate to fame,
Like eagles o'er the field of slaughter came,
In legions hovering in the viewless air,
The parting spirits of the slain to bear
To the vast hall of Odin; there to see
The joyous banquet spread eternally;
To hear the war-songs of their fathers, pour'd
From unseen harps, around the festive board;
While crown'd with joy, the sateless wassail cup,
With its bright mead for ever sparkling up,
Still, round the throng, should pass, with ceaseless flow,
To drown remembrance of all earthly wo.
   Thus, when amid our western forests' gloom,
The captive warrior hears the words of doom;
His daring heart, to high endurance wrought,
Is fill'd with all his fathers' faith have taught;
And all his own long cherish'd dreams, once more
O'er his rapt soul, their strengthening influence pour;

'Till nature sinks exhausted with her strife,
Beneath the glowing fire, the torturing knife.
E'en when the throe of mortal agony
Thrills through his heart and flashes from his eye,
One word of pride upon his foes is càst,
One glance of scorn the fiercest and the last.
Have not his fathers taught, that death like this
Is but the herald to a world of bliss ;—
That 't is but pain's last trial ; whence, the soul
Shall pass, no more to feel its stern control:
A dreamless sleep, from which it soon will wake,
By the blue waters of the sunny lake ;
To range for ever round its peaceful shore,
Where pain and torture can be felt no more.
   'T is faith thus wrought, whose fearful mysteries
Yield e'en weak woman strength for deeds like these ;
And bid, by Ganges' sacred stream, arise
The fires of self-devoting sacrifice :
While comes, for death array'd, without a tear,
The Indian widow, with her husband's bier.
Whate'er the gifts, rank, beauty, wealth, confer,
She feels, this world hath nothing more for her.
Through life, through death, indissolubly wed,
They must not part:—her place is by the dead.
And by that bier, with music and with song,
Behind the bright-robed priests, she moves along,
Amid the scenes of this terrific hour,
To seal the pledges of her bridal bower.
And there is shrined within that troubled breast,
By all its boding terrors unrepress'd,
Power to defy the fire's consuming pain ;
And feel that it doth not defy in vain.
Why stands she now, amid the circling dance,
Nor gives to aught around, one heeding glance ?
Why doth she gaze upon the viewless air,
As if some guardian spirit hover'd there ?
'T is not the priest's slow death-chaunt that she hears ;—
A holier music strikes her listening ears.
'T is not his thrilling exhortation now
That gives its life to her uplifted brow.
Hands, voices, urge her to the fatal spot ;
And chide her lingering : but she heeds them not.
No ; there are strains of more etherial tone,
Unearthly music, heard by her alone.
Her country's deities are circling nigh ;
She hears ten thousand voices in the sky.

" We have prepared for her the bridal wreath,
Who keeps her faith triumphant over death.
Oh, haste to meet, once more, the approving smile
Of him thou mournest, lost to thee awhile.
There are fair isles beyond the dark blue sea,
For those who keep their plighted faith like thee ;
Where the blest spirits of the faithful rove
In one unchanging round of joy and love ;
By sunny waters and unfading bowers,
And golden fruits, and ever blooming flowers.
Oh, what is there, that world of wo within,
Like those high joys which thou so soon may'st win ?"
With step elate, she gains her destined seat ;
And sees the red torch waving at her feet.
By him the loved one, hand in hand the while,
She proudly sits amid the blazing pile ;
And as the flames enwrap each quivering limb,
Raises aloft her wild funereal hymn :—
Swan-like, pours forth her last departing breath,
Amidst the anguish of the fires of death.

———

LUCIFER.

Son of the Morning : where art thou ?
Where is thy heaven-born glory now ?
Borne down by the Eternal Will,
O'erpower'd, but retaining still
Some traces of thy noble part,
Sublime in ruin still thou art.

Son of the Morning ; once, thy form
Was with celestial beauty warm.
The matchless grace which then it show'd,
In the third heaven's refulgence glow'd.
What peerless notes were on thy tongue,
When loud the blest Hosanna rung.

Thou wert the brightest in the zone
Of seraphs round the eternal throne :
That sight was open unto thee,
Which mortal eye can never see :
Thy feet, with Heaven's own radiance bright,
Once trod the paths of living light :

None but the arm of Might divine
Could hurl thee from a seat like thine !

Son of the Morning : where art thou;
Where is thy heaven-born glory now ?—
Thy form : there is a grandeur there,
But 't is the grandeur of despair :
There is a radiance in thine eyes,
But 't is the fire that never dies.—
Still in thy degradation, great,
Despising time, and scorning fate.

Redeeming love is not for thee :
Immutable is Heaven's decree :
Ages shall pass to ages gone ;
Eternity will circle on ;
All mortal joy and wo will cease ;
All nature's motion be at peace ;
But thou must stand, from all apart,
And be, for ever, what thou art.
Immutable thy fate must be ;
Redeeming love is not for thee.

WILLIAM H. BRADLEY

Was born we believe in Providence, Rhode Island, where he was educated as a physician. He died in the island of Cuba in 1825. He wrote Giuseppino, an Occidental Story, published in 1822, besides many fugitive pieces.

GIUSEPPINO.

To tell good stories is extremely pleasant ;
    To hear or read them, too, is quite agreeable ;
And, from the courtier downward to the peasant,
    Tales are retail'd by all.—You 'll even see a belle
Or dandy thus employ'd : so I, at present,
    If Dan Apollo will but render me able,
Am much inclined to give you a short specimen
Of what occurr'd to one of the most dressy men.

Authorship now is an improving business ;
  If one can strike out matters that are novel.
Though authors' brains will often get a dizziness,
  From too much labor, or be forced to grovel
In plagiarisms, undoubtedly it is an ease
  To knock out rhyme or prose, whether a hovel
Or palace be the scene of the disturbance
Which we describe, among hats, caps, or turbans.

Yet wonderful it is, I sing and say,
  Most marvellous, what ever-varied changes
Of narrative are dealt out, every day,
  As fancy, in her drunken frolics, ranges
Throughout invention's heaven and hell!—Delay
  Is dangerous, however wild and strange is
What I 'm about to write, so I must write it
For fear some other person should indite it.

I sate me down, good folk, to tell a story,
  Of which, I own, the truth might be suspected,
Even by credulous people ; and, what 's more, I
  Freely confess, I cannot recollect it :
But yet it was a vision of such glory
  I scarcely can suppose ye would reject it.
'T was all about a lady and a knight,
Who said and did—what I 've forgotten quite

In search of scenes and incidents I read
  Near half the old romances, through and through,
Which Southey has brought forward from the dead,
  With most Galvanic labor, and anew,
With steel clad wights, in peril was I led,
  Till weary of their toils and mine I grew :
So the chief knowledge gather'd from my reading
Is what I 'll mention as we are proceeding.

I found that many a literary chieftain,
  Had cull'd the gems from out this antique treasure ;
That what they left was by each humbler thief ta'en,
  To put in some new fiction at his leisure ;
I found—but guess!—no, you can 't guess my grief ta'en,
  At finding—Oh, presumption beyond measure !—
That collar-makers—I can scarce get farther
Had actually collar'd poor king Arthur.

I next discover'd, that the folk of quality
    Had not, of yore, such numerous expedients
To kill time and themselves, as the plurality
    Of modern genteel people.   The ingredients
With which they sweeten'd up the cold reality
    Were tourneys and such savage kind of pageants,
Wherein legs, arms, and necks oft got a fracture,
Although of the most giant manufacture.

Sad was the situation of the fair,
    Long, while a Bolingbroke, or a Plantagenet
Was king in London, (a great lord elsewhere)
    When one short week had stupor for an age in it,
To "ladies gay," who spent the livelong year,
    Remote from town, and truly would imagine it
Extravagant to give, in their own halls,
During that livelong year, one dozen balls.

Then was the ton, indeed a weighty matter,
    Which fancy moved but every hundred years
To a new pressure! Then a lady, at her
    First *coming out*, wore the same woman's gears
Which she wore on, (unless she grew much fatter)
    Till she was *going out ;* when lo, appears
Her daughter, deck'd in the same antique millinery,
With much manslaughter and intent to kill in her eye.

'Twas better with them, as historians tell us,
    In bluff King Hal's reign, and some time before him,
Though wives dared seldom flirt with civil fellows,
    In presence of their husbands, just to bore 'em.
They fear'd to make the horrid creatures jealous,
    And females were taught notions of decorum,
Stiff as their stomacher's tight elongation,
Or neck cloths of this stiff-neck'd generation.

Oh, could they have made books like lady M——n,
    What patchwork had we seen of feudal foolery !
Each lady's head, like that of lady Gorgon,
    Had left us hard examples of their drollery,
And we had known the centuries afore-gone,
    From banquet-hall quite downward to the scullery !
Would that our dear ancestresses had been crazy,
With some diverting kind of *idiosyncrasy*.

I bit my nails and pens, and then besprent all
   My paper o'er with ink, in thought oppress'd ;
Next, I resolved to write an Oriental
   Tale, and set out in ' Travels to the East,'
Driving away all notions Occidental.—
   I form'd a plot, and laid the scene, at last,
Somewhere between Calcutta and Aleppo,
When I bethought me of my old friend Beppo.

Then,—as I opened wide the window-shutter,—
   A light broke in on me, as bright as sudden.
Invention's wings began, at once, to flutter,
   (They had been once a goose's,) so, by Woden,
I sate down, to soar far from dust or gutter,
   While my good Genius said : " Pray where 's the good in
Your knack at rhyming, if its versatility
Can't afford matter for our risibility ?

The Beppo has outdone the Epic style.—
   Most modern Epics really are provoking
To sleep—and therefore, in a little while,
   The pack hight *servum pecus* shall have broken
Into full cry ;—leave your heroic toil,
   And start before them, till you have your book in
The gripe of printer's demon's !"—on this hint,
I wrote,—and having written, came to print.

But how to make a story ?—There 's the puzzle !
   Foregad, we have such multitudes to tell us
Stories on stories, both of those that guzzle
   At Helicon, and plain prosaic fellows,
That no one soon shall find a nook to nuzzle
   In fiction's storehouse :—Fate will yet compel us
To be mere readers. O ye geese and ganders,
Your wings shall cease to soar where Fancy wanders.

And here I humbly hint to Dr Brewster,
   That if he'd make us a kaleidoscope
To strike new subjects out, at every new stir,
   'T would give poor authors a consoling hope ;
For though the muses, when we call them, do stir,
   They 're monstrous indolent, and apt to mope.
The three times three, of late, are growing slatterns,
As I suppose, for want of good new patterns.

I 'll try to coax one of them now a little
    For something queer, good people to revive you.
Some tale of luckless love will not befit ill
    Your present taste, and this which now I give you
Will, without question, suit you to a tittle,
    If ye are young men and intend to wive you.
Hear then the history, both sad and funny,
Of one who fell to much in love—with money.

This is the love which first inflames the bosom,
    When for a penny some dear infant screeches.
This is the love which constantly pursues 'em,
    When fellows have got into coat and breeches,
And sigh for guineas,—then sigh for a new sum.—
    This lasting passion to all bosoms reaches,
Strengthen'd by age's weakness :—all love sham is,
Compared with this same ' auri sacra fames.'

But hold :—I feel myself too serious now,
    And must betake me once more to my bantering,
Telling a tale, according to my vow,
    In brisk *ottava rima*, freely sauntering
After sweet speculations, high and low ;
    Or, if I may, in a fine frenzy cantering
On reinless Pegasus, athwart whose saddle,
So many Gilpins have now got a straddle.

SAMUEL DEANE.

THE Rev. Samuel Deane of Scituate, Massachusetts, graduated at Brown University. His poem of the Populous Village was published in 1826.

THE POPULOUS VILLAGE.

THERE was a time, and that within the span
Of the brief memory of short-lived man,

When, close confined along the Atlantic seas,
The timid settler heard the western breeze,
And shrunk, expectant of the savage dart,
Or whizzing arrow, at his beating heart.
The western Mountains stood in awful forms,
Like clouds surcharged with tempest, fire and storms,
Whence the red bolt of rapid death might fly,
And whirlwinds rend the ocean and the sky;
For there did lurk the white-man's deadliest foe,
Gathering to burst upon the vales below.
A solemn race—a dark relentless clan,
That own'd no ties of blood with civil man;
A fearful foe—combining human art,
The wiles of serpents, and the tiger's heart:
Their sternest joy to daunt and scourge a race,
Soften'd by love—refined by Christian grace;
In tangled dells, where not heaven's light had shined,
They held their home—apt emblem of their mind.
Here many a beauteous stream majestic pours,
From distant mountains, to the ocean shores,
And in their course, enrich the earth in vain—
All unexplored, or hill, or vale, or plain,
And he was passing bold, who dared advance
Up toward their source, or e'en a thought to glance.
The soil was held by unresisted might,
The tiger's and the wolf's prescriptive right;
Nay e'en more awful images might wake—
Thick swarming skiffs along the stream and lake,
With desp'rate skill against the rapids glide,
Or down the cataract's tumultuous tide;
And hark! the warwhoop o'er the valley floats;—
The wolf's wild howls are music's softest notes.
But light at length prevails; darkness retreats,
To fix, in distant dens, her gloomy seats:
Improving nature, at this long delay
Indignant, from her barriers bursts away,
Shakes off the savage forms, by which oppress'd
She languish'd long, and with new charms is dress'd.
The dark, cold tribes, less boldly urge the strife,
And melt before the light of civil life:
And gathering courage now, the heroic swain
Pursues them far toward the western main;
Nor yet the flight, nor the pursuit gives o'er,
Until their strength and terrors are no more:
Then turns to peaceful homes, and brightning plains,
Where life to long-protracted age remains.

The yeomen still survive, whose eye can trace
Successive changes on our country's face :
Where forests frown'd, are shining cities seen,
And fields with Eden's bounty smile serene :
And many a soldier lives to tell the tales
Of deadly strife, 'mid yonder hills and vales ;
Can point the spot where raging battle stood,
The very turf that drank his father's blood ;
Can show the lake or stream where brothers bled,
Whose bones, scarce whiten'd, pave their lowly bed.
Perhaps some hero lives, who led the brave,
To freedom's boon, or honor's hallow'd grave ;
His locks scarce changed—scarce lost their raven hue
Still firm in strength—in thought and memory true ;
Come fancy ! come ! the image fair portray
Of some firm vet'ran, bending back his way
To yonder fields, the arena of his strife,
For home and country, liberty and life.
Bright in his memory is the open glade,
Remotest trace that industry had made ;
And fresh the image of the forest fierce,
Deep tangled, not meridian suns could pierce,
Where the grim savage, turning from his prey,
Slunk, like the wolf, and shunn'd the face of day.
Onward the veteran moves ; but where 's that lawn,
Once the last line that civil man had drawn ?
And where that wild wood rising dark and high,
Like strong embattled fortress to the sky ?
Lo ! other fields in endless prospect rise,
And like the horizon, still the forest flies.
Yet sure 't was here opposing armies stood ;
That is the stream that redden'd with his blood ;
It was from thence the wild man's warwhoop rose,
And here he stemm'd the onset of the foes ;
But lo ! the plain, hill, valley, all around,
With the bright Populous Village now are crown'd.
There, where the Indian often earth'd the wolf,
Along the brink of yonder tumbling gulph,
The rocks have yielded to the workman's hand,
And there in splendid palaces they stand.
Where the brisk waterfall, whose music found
No ear but echo once, to catch the sound,
Now, all its aid to human arts applied,
Prepares our food, and dress, and wealth beside :
See wheels on wheels, in mystic motion there !
The rattling engines of Minerva's care.

On yonder well-remember'd rising ground,
Where tallest firs with deepest shadows frown'd,
There now the noble Church sends up her spire,
To catch day's latest, and his earliest fire.
There, where the solitary wigwam stood,
Uncouthly form'd of stakes and leaves and mud,
Whose door stood wide, because it could not close,
To welcome weary wild men to repose ;
Or 'mid the clouds of smoke and filth, to share
The half-seeth'd members of the savage bear ;
There now the stately Inn, a spacious seat,
Invites the weary to refined retreat.
Around where ignorance had taken her stand,
With reign primeval, o'er the darken'd land,
See learning's nurseries at every turn,
Where every urchin finds the means to learn ;
And onward, see the high school's spacious halls,
And onward still, the prouder college walls.
Here bustling trade is laden with his bales ;
There commerce spreads her wings, unfolds her sails ;
Here on canals, deep freighted barges toil ;
There groaning wains with products of the soil ;
The thronging streets what busy numbers fill !
What tides of passengers roll onward still !
Not fled from want, but drawn by interest's bond,
To visit peopled regions far beyond.
There, where the guard-house frown'd upon yon height,
And weary sentinels wore out the night
With painful vigils, on their loaded arms,
To save the sleeping hamlet from alarms ;
There now the green-house, shaded with the vine,
And summer flowers, with evergreens entwine.
The terrors of the wilderness are fled,
And Niagara's thunders lose their dread ;
Down its deep chasm, no hazard of his life,
Goes the soft cit, and e'en his softer wife.
And Huron's shadowy shore lights up its brow,
And wild Oswego does but tinkle now,
Whose very name but sounded, once would dart
A nervous terror through a foreign heart.
All these are fled, and peace and plenty reign
O'er rising town and cultivated plain.

  *   *   *   *

Now to the decent church our thoughts return,
Whither our willing feet have often borne,

When solemn themes moved our vibrating strings,
And hope was pregnant with immortal things.
'Tis not alone, that village prospects round,
Are fill'd and finish'd by that spire—and crown'd.
'T is not alone the evidence that prayer,
And meek devotion, do not languish there;
A thousand prouder monuments may stand
Of wrested tithes from patient labor's hand;
Yet, with abated pleasure, freemen see
The loftiest piles, where not the heart is free;
'T is this that clothes thy fabric with its charms—
The free-will offering—shed from bounty's arms.
In gilded domes proud prelates may be found,
To cheat the hungry soul, with unknown sound;
But nought can win us, or delights impart,
Save truth's free breast, and language of the heart.
In native dignity, thy preacher stands,
More than the dignity of robes and bands;
Nor needs a surplice to convince your mind
His head can teach, his life can lead mankind:
Nor seeks a sacred office he, to hide
An infidel's false heart, or worldling's pride;
Nor shows the crackling flames of fiery zeal,
The bigot's selfish feelings to conceal.
On superstition's aid he rests no claim,
To wake devotion, or increase its flame;
One word of wisdom awes with truer grace
Than Endor's dame, with all her sickly race.
No prude, to rail at fashions of the times,
And pick at peccadilloes—while the crimes
That strike within, and deepest stains impart,
And damn the soul, scarce shock his tender heart;
No tyrant he, to rule the church with fear,
Nor lean upon her strength, to domineer:
When meek persuasion's force is fruitless seen,
His duty is discharged, his hands are clean.
His form and mien no sensualist betray,
Whose body o'er his soul usurps the sway;
Whose fair, smooth brow, and florid cheek declare,
No cure of souls, no love of learning there;
But comely paleness, decent leanness, shew
The scholar's patience, and the pastor's too—
To him philosophy's best light has shined,
Not to bewilder and mislead his mind,
Not his warm love to chill, or to recall
From that High King "who ruleth over all,"

Nor plunge in Nature's causes, and refine,
To miss the traces of the hand Divine ;
To push him on to doubt, and dark despair,
To feed his lambs with nature's stinted fare ;
Though wise in nature, he on grace relies,
To lead his flock, and win them to the skies.

  *   *   *   *

 But see ! above, and onward, and around,
What scenes of village pleasure still abound !
The open hill, the wood beyond the glade,
The broken chasm the trickling brook has made ;
There youth and age, and friends and lovers stray,
When o'er the scene the earliest zephyrs play.
The seats of living rock, the shady bower,
For summer's noon, or evening's balmy hour ;
The boughs of Autumn, with their fruits o'erborne ;
The golden promise of the ripening corn ;
The thousand pleasures that relieve the night,
When winter suns too soon withdraw their light ;
The youthful bands, with rural relish still,
Glide like the arrow down the ice-clad hill ;
Their graver sires, who deeper interests feel,
In councils sitting, on the public weal ;
The assembly's hall, where polish'd wit beguiles,
Or festive innocence presides and smiles ;
The long processions o'er the frozen lakes,
And the light joy that winter's music wakes.
How have we seen the purest of delight
Kindle and spread on many a bridal night !
Amidst the gay-dress'd group, the happy pair,
Smiled on by eager swain, and blushing fair ;
The bridegroom, joyful that this day has come—
The bride still press'd with lingering thoughts of home—
Parental cares, so oft foreboding ill—
Parental hope, that bids those fears be still ;
E'en wrinkled brows with smiles unwonted shine,
As in the sports of youth the grandsires join ;
The reverend pastor, fondly bent to call
Heaven's choicest blessings on his children all ;
His hand not much conversant with the gold,
That children of this world intensely hold ;
Pardon'd the more, if now his heart might be
Some trifle lighter for the marriage fee.

SAMUEL GILMAN.

MR. GILMAN is a native of Gloucester, Massachusetts, and was graduated at Harvard University in 1811. He has been for several years, settled as a clergyman in Charleston, S. C. He is understood to be the author of Memoirs of a New-England Village Choir, a prose work of great merit.

HISTORY OF A RAY OF LIGHT.

"LET there be light!" creation's Author spoke,
And quick from chaos floods of splendor broke—
On that magnificent, primeval morn,
Myself, an humble ray of light was born.
   Vain were the task to guess my native place ;
Rushing, careering, furiously through space,
Plunged amid kindred rays and mingling beams,
These are my first of recollection's gleams.
Oh ! with what joy we rioted along !
Darting afar, in young existence strong,
Onward we poured the unaccustomed day
Through tracts, the length of many a milky way.
(For know, we rays of light are living things,
Each with ten thousand pair of brilliant wings ;
No wonder then, when all those wings are stirr'd,
We flit it so much faster than a bird.)
At last, when youthful years and sports were done,
Choice, chance, or duty brought me to your sun ;
And, while my brother pencils fled afar,
To swell the glories of some viewless star,
'T was mine to fly about this work of heav'n,
Where one huge orb gave light and heat to seven,
Although short visits now and then I make,
To distant spheres, for recreation's sake.
   Ah ! ne'er shall I forget th' eventful day
When to this planet first I sped my way :
To many a twinkling throb my heart gave birth,
As near and nearer I approach'd the earth.
What was to be my fate ? for ever lost
In some dark bog ? or was I to be tost
In wild reflection, round some narrow spot,
Then sink absorb'd, inglorious and forgot ?
No, reader, no—far different the career

Which fate designed me to accomplish here :
Millions of splendid scenes 't was mine to grace,
Though my first act brought ruin to your race.
Trembling, I reach'd the serpent's glistening eye,
Then glanced, and struck the apple, hanging by,
Then, to your mother Eve reflected, flew,
And thus, at one exploit, a world o'erthrew !
Oh scene of wo ! the mischief I had wrought,
Those quick successive shocks, that stunn'd my thought,
The poisonous magic from that sire of lies,
The worse contagion in that woman's eyes,
All were too much for one poor ray of light,
New to his task, and meaning only right.
Distrest in heart, at once myself I hurl'd
Far to the outside of this injured world,
Wishing to wear my wretched life away,
'Mid scenes, where solitude and chaos lay.
At length, while wandering o'er these realms of wo,
I heard a small, sweet voice that whisper'd low
In tones of soothing—'t was a brother ray
Sent from the hand that first created day—
" No longer mourn," the darting angel said,
" The hopes of man are not for ever fled
From his own race a Saviour shall arise,
To lead him back to his forbidden skies ;
And hark ! when Bethl'em's beauteous star shall shine,
Its first and freshest radiance shall be thine ! "
    Cheer'd by these words, I long'd to gain once more
This lovely world, and try my fortune o'er.
Just then a globe, new struck from chaos out,
Met me, and turn'd my headlong path about;
Back to the sun with breathless speed I flew,
And thence rush'd down, where bright to Noah's view
The glorious rainbow shone—a lingering stop
I made within a small pellucid drop,
Touch'd its internal surface, and outright
Darted through air to glad the patriarch's sight.
Glancing from thence away, I sported on
Where'er by pleasure or by duty drawn ;—
Now tipping so . : bright drop of pearly dew,
Now plunging into heaven through tracks of blue,
Now aiding to light up the glorious morn,
Or twilight's softer mantle to adorn,
Now darting through the depths of ocean clear,
To paint a pearl—then to the atmosphere
Again reflected, shooting to the skies
Away, away, where thought can never rise ;

Then trav'ling down to tinge some valley flower,
Or point some beauty's eye with mightier power,
Or to some monarch's gem new lustre bring,
Or light with fire some prouder insect's wing,
Or lend to health's red cheek a brighter dye,
Or flash delusive from consumption's eye,
Or sparkle round a vessel's form by night,
Or give the glow-worm its phosphoric light,
Or clothe with terror threatening anger's glance,
Or from beneath the lids of love to dance,
Or place those little silver points on tears,
Or light devotion's eye, while mercy hears;
In short, to aid with my poor transient flings,
All scenes, all passions, all created things.
    Few rays of light have been where I have been,
Honor'd like me, or seen what I have seen:
I glow'd amid the bush, which Moses saw,
I lit the mount, when he proclaim'd his law:
I to that blazing pillar brought my mite,
Which glared along old Israel's path by night.
I lent a glory to Elijah's car,
And took my promised flight from Bethl'em's star.
    But not to holy ground was I confined,
In classic haunts my duties were assign'd.
I primed the bolts Olympian Jove would throw,
And Pluto sought me for his fires below:
Over and over gallant Phœbus swore,
I was the finest dart his quiver bore:
Oft was I sent a peeping, anxious ray
From Dian, hastening where Endymion lay:
When Iris shot from heaven, all swift and bright,
Thither I rush'd, companion of her flight:
From Vulcan's anvil I was made to glare,
I lent a horror to the Gorgon's stare,
I too have beam'd upon Achilles' shield,
And dropp'd from Helen's eye when Paris kneel'd;
Faithful Achates, every school-boy knows,
Struck from a flint my whole long year's repose:
Ten wretched days I pass'd in sobs and sighs,
Because I could not dance on Homer's eyes:
I once was decomposed from that pure oil,
Which cheer'd the Athenian sage's midnight toil:
I from the brazen focus led the van,
When Archimedes tried his frightful plan;
'T was I, from Cleopatra's orb that hurl'd
The fatal glance, which lost her slave the world:

I struck the sweetest notes on Memnon's lyre,
And quiver'd on the phœnix' funeral pyre.
   Nor ancient scenes alone engross'd my pranks,
The moderns likewise owe me many thanks.
Straight in at Raphael's skylight once I broke,
And led his pencil to its happiest stroke ;
I sparkled on the cross Belinda wore,
And tipp'd the Peri's wing of Thomas Moore ;
To Fontenelle I glided from above,
When whispering soft astronomy and love ;
And know, where'er the finest bards have sung
The moon's sweet praises with bewitching tongue,
Or that blue evening star of mellow light,
'T was always after I had touch'd their sight.
   Nor yet have poetry and painting shared
My sole regards—for science I have cared.
When Galileo raised his glass on high,
Me first it brought to his astonish'd eye ;
When Newton's prism loosed the solar beams,
I help'd to realize his heaven-taught dreams ;
When Herschel his dim namesake first descried,
I was just shooting from that planet's side.
At all eclipses and conjunctions nigh,
Of sun, or satellite, or primary,
Oft have I serv'd the longitude to fix—
And heavens ! in June of eighteen hundred six,
How all New England smiled to see me burst,
Out from behind her darken'd sun the first!
I form'd a spangle on the modest robes
Of Doctor Olbers' new-discover'd globes ;
I from the comet's path was downward sent,
When Bowditch seized me for an element :
Once trav'ling from a fourth-rate star to earth,
I gave the hint of abberration birth.
I led th' electric flash to Priestley's sight,
And play'd my sports round Franklin's daring kite ;
Absorb'd in copper once I long had lain,
When lo! Galvani gave me life again.
I taught the Swede that after sunny days,
Lilies and marigolds will dart forth rays ;
And when polarity made Savans stare
For the first time, be sure that I was there.
When iron first in oxygen was burnt,
When Davy his metallic basis learnt,
When Brewster shaped his toy for peeping eyes,
And Humboldt counted stars in southern skies,

'T was I that moved, while bursting on their sigh
The flush of wonder, triumph, and delight.
  Nor scarce does history boast one splendid scene
Or deep-mark'd era, where I have not been.
The sky-hung cross of Constantine, which turn'd
All Rome to truth, by my assistance burn'd ;
When the great charter England's rights restored,
I scared her monarch from a baron's sword ;
When pious Europe led the far crusade,
Did I not flash from Godfrey's wielded blade ?
Did chivalry one tournament display
Of dazzling pomp, from which I kept away ?
Was I not present at that gorgeous scene,
Where Leicester entertained old England's queen ?
Did I not sparkle on the iron crown
Which the triumphant Corsican took down ?
Did I not revel where those splendors shone,
When the fourth George assumed Britannia's throne ?
And last, not least, could I refuse to hear,
The summons of th' Atlantic Souvenir ?
No, gentlest reader, trust your humble ray,
'T is here at length I would for ever stay,
If to and fro I could descend and rise
'Twixt these bright pages and your brighter eyes ;
Absorb'd, reflected, radiated, bent,
With force emitted, or for ages pent,
Through the wide world so long and often toss'd ;
Th' excursive passion of my youth I 've lost.
I wish no more in my six thousandth year,
Than just to take my peaceful mansion here,
To deck these limnings with my happiest art,
And 'mid these leaves to play my brightest part.

CPSIA information can be obtained
at www.ICGtesting.com
Printed in the USA
BVHW081810220819
556561BV00019B/4173/P